Management of the Industrial Firm in the USSR

STUDIES OF THE

RUSSIAN INSTITUTE

COLUMBIA UNIVERSITY

MANAGEMENT OF THE INDUSTRIAL FIRM IN THE USSR

A STUDY IN SOVIET ECONOMIC PLANNING

By David Granick

COLUMBIA UNIVERSITY PRESS *New York* **1954**

THE TRANSLITERATION SYSTEM USED IN THIS SERIES IS BASED ON
THE LIBRARY OF CONGRESS SYSTEM WITH SOME MODIFICATIONS

LIBRARY OF CONGRESS CATALOG CARD NUMBER: 53-11451

COPYRIGHT 1954 COLUMBIA UNIVERSITY PRESS, NEW YORK

PUBLISHED IN GREAT BRITAIN, CANADA, INDIA, AND PAKISTAN

BY GEOFFREY CUMBERLEGE, OXFORD UNIVERSITY PRESS

LONDON, TORONTO, BOMBAY, AND KARACHI

MANUFACTURED IN THE UNITED STATES OF AMERICA

The Russian Institute

OF COLUMBIA UNIVERSITY

The Russian Institute was established by Columbia University in 1946 to serve two major objectives: the training of a limited number of well qualified Americans for scholarly and professional careers in the field of Russian studies, and the development of research in the social sciences and the humanities as they relate to Russia and the Soviet Union. The research program of the Russian Institute is conducted through the efforts of its faculty members, of scholars invited to participate as Senior Fellows in its program, and of candidates for the Certificate of the Institute and for the degree of Doctor of Philosophy. Some of the results of the research program are presented in the Studies of the Russian Institute of Columbia University. The faculty of the Institute, without necessarily agreeing with the conclusions reached in the Studies, believe that their publication advances the difficult task of promoting systematic research on Russia and the Soviet Union and public understanding of the problems involved.

The faculty of the Russian Institute are grateful to the Rockefeller Foundation for the financial assistance which it has given to the program of research and publication.

TO THE TEACHERS AT COLUMBIA UNIVERSITY

WHO HAVE TRAINED ME IN ECONOMICS

AND RUSSIAN STUDIES

Acknowledgments

FOR HIS GUIDANCE in formulating the problems of this dissertation, and for his most helpful criticism of it, I am particularly indebted to Professor Abram Bergson. My father has given valuable editorial assistance. Finally, my wife has helped to make this book possible through her assistance and her patience during my preoccupation with it.

Others who have especially helped me with their criticism at various stages of this work are Professors Arthur R. Burns, Robert K. Merton, John N. Hazard and John Maurice Clark of Columbia University, and Dr. Henry Ware, John Attlee, Warren Eason, Ernest V. Hollis, Jr., and Frank Riessman.

I also wish to express my appreciation to Professor Merle Fainsod and Professor Alexander Gerschenkron of the Russian Research Center at Harvard University for their valuable comments.

The Library of Congress, and in particular John T. Dorosh and Vladimir Gsovski of the Slavic Room and Foreign Law Section, have afforded me every opportunity for fruitful research. The Social Science Research Council has made this book possible through a fellowship which covered the entire period of research and much of the time required for writing. Both the Russian Institute of Columbia University and Fisk University have also been most generous with their aid.

The Soviet field is a controversial one. The writer is aware of a number of points at which those who have aided him might disagree with his conclusions. In any event, the responsibility for the views expressed is my own throughout.

D. G.

Contents

Management of the Industrial Firm in the USSR

I: Introduction

PURPOSE AND SCOPE

THIS IS A STUDY in Soviet economic planning with particular reference to the management of the individual firm in heavy industry. In the plant itself, the center of attention is on the plant director—the Soviet counterpart of the capitalist manufacturer. The main purpose of the study is to explore those aspects of Soviet economic planning in which plant executives play a direct role or in which their actions are immediately affected by other groups and organs.

We shall be concerned with how the thousands of individual industrial plants are integrated into a national administrative system and are guided by the top Government and Communist Party authorities. We shall want to know what methods are used to fight stultification of industry through administrative red tape; how much and what sorts of initiative are demanded from lower management and from the masses of workers; what criteria of "success" in exercising initiative have been established, and what efforts are made to reconcile conflicting criteria; and what methods are used to prevent the enterprise of junior officials and of the masses from running into channels which the nation's leaders prefer to keep closed.

Firm management has been singled out as the subject of this study because it is felt that it offers a fruitful vantage point from which to survey the field of Soviet industrial planning. The reasons for this are the following:

In studying a system of integration, there seems to be particular value in concentrating on the lowest bodies with which higher organs consistently deal. The firms are the basic units of Soviet industry. Essentially it is they rather than their component shops and departments which are planned for and supervised by higher organizations.

Secondly, Soviet leaders at all levels lay heavy stress upon the participation of nonadministrative personnel in the organization and supervision of planning and plan fulfillment. The extent and nature of such participation is naturally strongest and most readily seen in the lower units. Firm managements' decisions and activities are not only affected by outside industrial executives and by organizations such as the Communist Party, but also by those firm employees whose main jobs are quite outside the areas of planning, supervising and inspecting.

Thirdly, the firm is the Soviet unit most comparable to the capitalist enterprise in size, structure, and function. Since most present day non-Marxist theories of capitalist economics take as their starting point the individual business, there is an obvious advantage for purposes of comparison in using a similar unit as a fulcrum for an analysis of the Soviet economy.

Heavy industry has been chosen as the area of concentration. The scope of the study must be limited, and much more information is available about this section than about any other. Also, while one cannot automatically extend to all industry conclusions drawn from an analysis of this portion of it, it is precisely this segment with which we should be most concerned. For one thing, it has been more centrally organized than is customary in Soviet industry. Thus one of our main conclusions from this study, that considerable independence of decision making has been left to the individual firm management, can in all likelihood be properly extended to the rest of Soviet industry. Secondly, heavy industry is the basic part of any advanced economy, and most particularly of that of the Soviet Union which has been especially oriented towards the development of the means of production. Finally, it has employed over half the workers of all nationally directed industry[1] and has produced a considerably higher percentage of value of product.

[1] Heavy industry is defined for my purposes as including all manufacturing which was part of the Commissariat of Heavy Industry prior to its first division in 1936. Mining, oil drilling, and the operation of electric power stations are excluded from the study as nonmanufactures, although they were under this Commissariat. The

This study should provide strong evidence that the businessman or entrepreneur has survived, although in considerably altered form, in the highly centralized socialist economy of the Soviet Union. It should help to explain how much and what type of economic planning exists in Soviet industry. But its implications extend beyond the fields of economics and business. For it may also be considered as a study in Soviet principles and practices of administration as applied throughout Soviet society, although with specific reference to heavy industry.

Now for a word as to the study's limitations of scope. The entire question of forced labor in Soviet industry will be omitted on the ground that it requires separate study and treatment. Secondly, there will be no independent investigation of the role of the political police in supervision over the operations of industry. Such a study will be omitted in view of the scarcity of materials on this subject and the difficulties in using those available. In justification, it should be noted that the political police do not play any direct administrative role in the predominant part of the economy which is worked by free labor. Moreover, they do not have any formal powers of supervision over industry itself, being restricted to investigations of personnel for political reliability and for political offenses, possible sabotage or other actions considered criminal. Nevertheless, a brief discussion of the possible importance of the political police in the management of industry will be presented in Appendix D.

THE PERIOD COVERED: 1934-41

This investigation focuses on the limited prewar period of 1934-41. It is primarily intended to cast light on the methods cur-

main branches included are construction of machines and vehicles, metal fabrication, armaments, ferrous metallurgy, nonferrous metallurgy, chemicals, the rubber industry, and cement.

On April 1, 1935, the Commissariat of Heavy Industry contained roughly 68 percent of the industrial personnel of all the industrial commissariats of the country, excluding local industry. See TsUNKhU Gosplana SSSR (Central Administration of National Economic Accounting of the State Planning Commission of the USSR), *Trud v SSR* (Labor in the USSR), edited by A. S. Popov (Moscow: 1936), p. 49. On January 1, 1936, the manufacturing branches employed about 74 percent of the Commissariat's industrial workers. *(Ibid.,* p. 71.) Thus, even including the extractive industries and electric power stations in the total for all industry, roughly 50 percent of the total workers of Soviet industry are brought under our study.

rently used in operating Soviet industry, on the problems involved
and the solutions developed. However, due to the fact that information on Soviet industry has been relatively meager since the war,
this earlier period will be studied.

The cut-off date of 1941 has been chosen for the obvious reason
that this was the year when the Soviet Union entered the war, an
event which brought its own special economic problems and methods of solution. 1934 has been selected as the starting date for the
study because it was just about then that the pattern of economic
organization which now prevails in the Soviet Union had been
firmly established. The country had passed through the transition
periods of the New Economic Policy and of the First Five-Year
Plan, and had found the forms of economic administration which
have since been maintained.

All industry, except for minor handicrafts, had already been na-
tionalized. The day of the peasant working his own land was over;
collective farms and State farms dominated the agricultural scene.
Cooperatives and State stores handled most of the nation's com-
merce. Thus, with State-owned enterprises and State-guided cooperatives turning out the country's production, a basis had been
laid for the detailed integration of the economy through a national
plan. The problem no longer existed of having to persuade individual businessmen or peasants to carry out their allotted planned
tasks. Those types of special interests which are embodied in private ownership had ceased to stand in the way of plan fulfillment.

The planning system itself had gone through its initial develop-
mental period. Starting in the twenties as a collection of "Control
Figures" which were essentially only prognostications, Soviet planning had emerged in 1928 with the First Five-Year Plan. By 1934,
Soviet planning methods had developed considerably further. The
first bootstrap-construction effort over, a material base for more
stable planning methods had been established. The industrial
work force was also far more dependable and skilled; the proportion of new arrivals from the farms to the total number of employees had markedly receded. Soviet national planning was emerg-
ing from its infancy.

The first years of the thirties had seen the unfolding of a new
system of industrial organization. Firms were coordinated into the

centralized administrative structure by a complex system of direct orders from above combined with semi-independence of firms and the central guidance of their managements through the means of indirect financial controls and incentives. It was only in 1934 that "functional" organization both within and above firms was officially abandoned, and that a "line" system of undivided responsibility to a single higher authority replaced it.[2] Long before this, group management had been replaced with direction of each organization by only one individual.

The first years of our period saw the continuation of consumer rationing, but this ended during 1935. Abolishment of rationing caused a rise in the importance to workers of monetary incentives. The opportunity presented by the prevailing piece-rate system for higher earnings through greater productivity was of significance in the birth and rapid development of the Stakhanovite movement. The "business accounting" system could be and was employed as a major spur to both management and employees.

Of major note was the fact that important industrial posts were by 1934 mainly held by Communist Party members, and that these had had sufficient technical training to be able to carry out managerial duties themselves. In earlier years, Party members had often been managers in name only, and mistrusted prerevolutionary engineers had carried on the actual work. But by the mid-thirties a close interlocking of industrial management and Communist Party ranks had been achieved; the carrying out of managerial duties was normally treated as a full-time task for a capable Party man.

With this taking over of management by Party personnel and by those holding the Party's confidence, the Communist Party was in a position to carry out its policies through non-Party organizations and without its own direct administration. Industrial managers could be trusted equally with Party functionaries to implement the Party line. The program of giving great powers to management personnel could be followed without fear that these powers would be used to fight Communist Party policies.

All these fundamentals of present day Soviet industrial organization had been achieved in varying degrees before the beginning of the 1934-41 period which we are to study. Changes during these

---

[2] Cf. pages 30-31 for a definition of these two methods of organization.

prewar years were of a relatively minor nature, and the entire period can for our purposes be considered as homogeneous. Moreover, although details have unquestionably changed, a superficial study of the war and postwar years does not indicate that they have brought with them fundamentally new patterns.[3] Nevertheless, while the basic tenets of this study appear to me on the basis of such superficial reading in the postwar literature to apply to the present almost as well as to the period studied, specific analyses and conclusions should of course be taken as applying only to the years 1934-41.

MATERIALS USED

The problem of finding sufficient and trustworthy material is always a major difficulty for studies about the Soviet economy. Credit should be given to the pioneer study by G. Bienstock, S. M. Schwarz, and A. Yugow, *Management in Russian Industry and Agriculture*. But in general, there has been very little treatment by non-Soviet writers of the problems with which we shall deal. Thus it has been necessary to lean almost entirely on Soviet sources. However, I have tried to refer the reader to those books in English in which my conclusions are either supported or disputed.

My main reading has been in Soviet newspapers and magazines. Books and legal material have also been used, but they present more of a generalized and theoretic picture of Soviet industry than an account of its actual operation. Newspapers, on the other hand, give countless concrete descriptions of individual plants and their problems. My confidence in the accuracy of such material has been greatly enhanced by the fact that the firms and their officials are usually referred to by name. In actual practice, moreover, difficulties are not glossed over in the Soviet press. Newspaper and magazine articles, for example, are often highly critical of the work of firms and even of higher organs.

Where I quote from Soviet authorities as to official policy, care has been taken to see that the statements were made during the period covered in this study. References to statements made after

---

[3] Dr. Solomon Schwarz has, in conversation with me, suggested that there has been a major strengthening of the position of Communist Party functionaries in industry. I have no independent information on this subject.

the end of the period have only been given when it was felt that they reflected the same policy which existed earlier. Statements issued before the beginning of the period are used solely when they have been considered by Soviet writers as still applying to the years studied. Thus the danger is avoided, so far as is possible, of considering quotations in reference to different time-periods than those for which they have been held applicable by Soviet authorities.[4]

OUTLINE OF THE STUDY

Subsequent chapters treat the management of heavy industry's firms during 1934-41 in the following fashion:

Chapters II and III supply the background necessary for an understanding of the plant management's role in industry. There is a description of the hierarchical structure of industry from the level of the shop to that of the Council of Commissars, and a statement of the basic concept underlying Soviet administration-through-channels. A detailed presentation is offered of the personal characteristics of industrial executives on the plant level, of their degree of security and rate of advancement. These chapters are intended to describe the organizational milieu in which management has functioned and the personal traits of the managers which have conditioned their reactions to the Soviet industrial environment.

The next two chapters (IV and V) describe how the national plans have been formed and what role the firm personnel have played in this formulation. They also show the limitations of the plan as a guide to industrial operations.

Chapters VI and VII explain the nature of the different types of commands, supplementary to the plan, which have been given to firm managements by higher bodies. They point out the conditions under which the various forms of leadership have been employed. Within this framework, the degree and types of autonomy left to the firm managements are discussed.

An example of the fusion of centralized guidance and of plant independence is given in the following chapter (VIII) through a

---

[4] Cf. I. Stalin, Letter of July 28, 1950, to A. Kholopov, *Soviet Literature* 1950, No. 9, pp. 28-31, for an authoritative Soviet attack on such a use of quotations.

treatment of the very important field of procurement and marketing.

Chapters IX and X consider the criteria by which the success of plant directors has been evaluated. The significance of financial criteria and the ways in which they have been enforced are given particular attention.

Chapter XI presents a note on enforcement of controls over management, on the incentives offered them for proper behavior, and on the organizations concerned with enforcement.

Chapters XII and XIII deal with the role of the Communist Party and of mass worker participation in the administration of industrial firms and in the supervision over their managements. Both Soviet theory and its practice will be analyzed.

In the final chapter (XIV), an analysis of the administration of Soviet firms is made by comparing Soviet industrial organization with Max Weber's model of bureaucratic structure, and some conclusions are offered as to the success of the system in carrying out the ends of Soviet top leadership.

II: The Organizational Structure of Heavy Industry

THE PURPOSE of this chapter is to examine the administrative setting within which firm management functions. Before we can intelligently discuss the problems of managerial personnel and the methods used to direct their actions, we must know something about the organizational structure of industry, the lines of authority reaching from the shop upwards, the Soviet concepts of the proper degree and forms of centralization of authority, and the place of the firm in the entire picture. It is the task of this chapter to present both this material and data on the internal organization of the Soviet firm. Detail will be presented only to the extent that it is helpful for an understanding of managerial problems and actions.

SOVIET THEORIZING AS TO CENTRALIZATION

The Soviet attitude toward administration in general is most broadly covered by the concept that there must be centralized planning and leadership in all main questions, but that this should be accompanied by decentralization of operational functions.[1] While basic guidance is to be given from the center, it is the people on the spot who must make the concrete local decisions and guide the specific implementation of all plans.

[1] *Vsesoiuznaia Kommunisticheskaia Partiia (b) v rezoliutsiiakh i resheniiakh s"ezdov, konferentsii i plenumov TsK*, Chast' II: 1925-1935 (The All-Union Communist Party (Bolshevik) in Resolutions and Decisions of Congresses, Conferences and Plenums of the Central Committee, Part II), 5th edition (Moscow: 1936), p. 351. Hereafter cited as *VKP (b) v rez*. This reference was quoted as still in force by A. Arakelian in *Upravlenie sotsialisticheskoi promyshlennost'iu* (Administration of Socialist Industry), (Moscow: 1947), p. 189.

This statement of Soviet doctrine is, however, too vague to be illuminating. Almost all centrally administered bodies in the world could accept this as a formulation of their own policy. What we require is to know the content which Soviet theorists give to this form. A first approximation to this can be found in the concept of "democratic centralism." Developed originally in application to the Bolshevik party organization, it has been applied to the whole Soviet State administration.[2]

The elements of this concept relevant to the organization of industry are the following:

1. The structure of administration of industry is built on the basis of strict subordination of lower to higher organs. Officials are commonly appointed by their immediate superiors or by those not very far above. Directives of higher organs are obligatory for all bodies under them. Each organ supervises the activities of those below it, and checks on their execution of its orders.

2. Individual industrial units have obligatory planned tasks, the sum of which comprises the plan of the organ immediately in charge of these units.

3. In general, the method is followed of one-man-authority-and-responsibility for each economic unit. However, in higher organs which combine the work of many branches of the economy, group decision and responsibility—through collegia—is the governing system.[3]

Basic policies and political lines for industry are to be determined centrally. (Examples of such fundamental programs are the determination of the year's rate of investment, the selection of industries in which there must be an immediate concentration on

---

[2] Cf. I. I. Evtikhiev and V. A. Vlasov, *Administrativnoe pravo SSSR* (Administrative Law of the USSR), text for law institutes and faculties (Moscow: 1946), pp. 16-17, for a presentation in an approved legal text of the principle of democratic centralism in State administration.

[3] *Ibid.* The "democratic" elements of this principle of Soviet administration are not relevant to the organizational features to be discussed in this chapter and so have not been mentioned in the text. They are, however, twofold: 1. Personnel of leading organs of industry are appointed by elected bodies. 2. The centralized apparatus for administering industry stands on the base of the widest possible mass participation in its operational activities. While the system of one-man-authority-and-responsibility governs the carrying out of decisions, projected measures are often subjected to general discussion at meetings of employees of the economic unit involved.

high production, and the choosing of the forms of labor discipline and recruitment to be used.)

However, Soviet leaders have recognized that a single program may take many shapes in different areas and sectors of the economy. No one model should be established, wrote Lenin; rather unity in essence must be maintained through the medium of varied forms.[4]

In the direction of industrial operations, the emphasis of Soviet theory is entirely on concreteness. Industrial firms should not be guided in a "general" fashion, with orders which may or may not apply to a specific plant. The higher organs should approach each question in a thoroughgoing fashion, basing their decisions on analysis of the problems and possibilities of the individual firm.[5]

But, it is stated, no organization can direct one or two hundred firms and still take into account their individual problems and potentials.[6] By delegating to intermediary bodies the direct control over plant managements, the higher economic organs are freed for the more fundamental decisions. At the same time, it is the intermediary bodies which are in a position to give realistic decisions to plant managements.

Although the essence of proper leadership is viewed by Soviet leaders as residing in concrete instructions and guidance based on knowledge of real conditions, it must not be thought that this is "the" Soviet solution to problems of administration. For let it be pushed to an extreme, and it is denounced as the worst sort of "bureaucratic centralism." It is vigorously asserted that leadership by higher organs does not mean giving instructions as to petty details.[7] A happy medium must be found, leaving sufficient authority to the economic unit directly responsible for carrying out the assigned tasks.

In short, Soviet thinking on the key problem of centralization in industry is dominated by the twin desires to assure centralization of policy making and to minimize bureaucratic abuses. The strict

---

[4] V. Lenin, *Sochineniia* (Collected Works), 2d edition (Moscow-Leningrad: 1929), Tom XXII, p. 166, as quoted by L. Maizenberg in "O khoziaistvennom plane" (On the Economic Plan), *Planovoe Khoziaistvo* (Planned Economy), 1940, No. 10, p. 22.

[5] Cf. I. Stalin, *Voprosy Leninizma* (Problems of Leninism), 10th edition (Moscow: 1938), pp. 464-65.

[6] *Ibid.*

[7] Lenin as quoted by L. Maizenberg, *op. cit.*, p. 22.

subordination of lower to higher bodies is fundamental doctrine. Yet stultification in red tape is feared. Attempts by higher organs to control all details of plants' work are considered as deadly to change and flexibility. It is recognized that there is danger that officials will hide their inability to achieve results behind the strict observance of commands and the issuance of corresponding orders to those below them. While firm managements must follow policy made above, and while this policy should be as specific as possible, management's own initiative and resolute action are felt to be essential for industrial success.

THE HIERARCHICAL STRUCTURE OF INDUSTRY

The structure of Soviet heavy industry is hierarchical. All of it is ultimately under the direct control of the Council of Commissars of the Soviet Union which approves plans, makes changes in them, and can issue direct orders to units at any level. But between the Council of Commissars and the industrial shop, there are many intermediate units. One of these is the firm.

In Soviet industrial literature, the words "firm"[8] and "plant"[9] are used interchangeably and will be so used throughout this study. But "combinats" are also firms,[10] and commonly combine several plants.

For example, the Magnitogorsk firm at the end of 1938 dug iron ore, operated coking plants, open-hearth and blast furnaces, and rolling mills, and still had 63 percent of its personnel left for employment in auxiliary and secondary departments.[11] Thus while a single plant may be thought of as consisting of one factory building or several closely contiguous ones, a firm may have a far wider scope of operations.

Beginning at its lowest level, the industrial hierarchy has the

[8] Predpriiatie.

[9] Zavod.

[10] The distinction between a combinat and an ordinary firm seems to be mainly one of prestige. Cf. Postanovlenie (Decree) No. 184 of the Economic Council of February 5, 1940, in *Sobranie postanovlenii i rasporiazhenii pravitel'stva SSSR* (Collection of Decrees and Orders of the Government of the USSR), 1940, article 116. (Hereafter this source will be cited as *SPR*.) By this decree, a "plant" was raised to the status of a "combinat," and three of its "departments" to the status of "plants."

[11] *Industriia* (Industry), November 29, 1938, p. 1. (Hereafter cited as *Ind*.)

CHART OF THE ORGANS ABOVE THE TYPICAL

HEAVY INDUSTRY FIRM

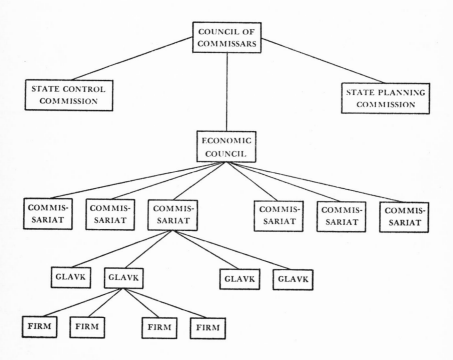

following elements: shops,[12] departments[13] (these are composed of several shops), firms, trusts, chief subdivisions (glavki) of the commissariats, the commissariats,[14] the Economic Council attached to the Council of Commissars of the Soviet Union, and finally the Council of Commissars itself.

Since heavy industry, like other sectors of Soviet society, is administered along the lines of "democratic centralism," each higher unit is empowered to exercise direct supervision over all lower bodies and to issue direct orders to them. Normally work is carried on through intermediate organs, but they can be and frequently are by-passed. The Commission of Soviet Control (an organ of the Council of Commissars) sometimes ignores commissariats and gives warnings directly to individual firm directors.[15] Glavki[16] may issue such detailed commands as one relating to the date for beginning repair work in an individual department of a combinat, a decision which would usually be left to the combinat or department management.[17] While directors of firms are in general granted the right to choose their subordinates, the Commissariat of Ferrous Metallurgy in 1940 directly appointed the superintendents of all of its firms' metallurgical departments.[18] Not only higher bodies but also those below may skip over the intermediate organs. Directors of plants frequently appeal to commissariats over the head of the glavk personnel. For the entire economy is considered as one unit, and the prime task is envisioned as that of operating it most efficiently. Any intermediate level of the industrial hierarchy—even that of firm management—may on occasion be ignored in relations between higher and lower bodies. Direct and "concrete" leadership by higher organs is constantly stressed by Soviet thinkers, and the skipping of links in the chain of command has a strong base in Soviet theory as well as in practice, although it is sometimes sharply condemned when it leads to confusion.

[12] Uchastki.

[13] Tsekhi.

[14] Since March, 1946, the commissariats have been called ministries.

[15] Cf. *Mashinostroenie* (Machine Construction), July 2, 1939, p. 1. (Hereafter, it will be cited as *Mash.*)

[16] The chief subdivisions of the commissariats.

[17] Cf. *Ind.*, September 5, 1938, p. 2.

[18] Letter of S. Reznikov, Head of the Glavk of the Metallurgical Industry of the South and Center, *Pravda* (Truth), October 4, 1940, p. 3.

When the production of heavy industry increased rapidly during the thirties, and the number of workers in each branch expanded, the existing glavki and commissariats faced an increasingly heavy burden. It was demanded that ever-closer links be forged between commissariat and glavki personnel and the units under them, so that "concrete" leadership could be exercised. Yet without a re-modeling of the system, the reverse process would have been inevitable.

The resulting reorganizations occurred entirely among the organizations above the firm level. Here incessant change was the rule. At the same time, existing shops, departments and firms remained fairly stable in structure.

Reorganization took the form of breaking up the Commissariat of Heavy Industry into a number of separate commissariats,[19] and of likewise splitting up the glavki. This still left glavki and commissariats which were immense when measured in terms of the number of workers under them.[20] Yet the number of firms under a single commissariat, and within it under a glavk, was held down.[21] In April, 1939, the Commissariat of General Machine Construction had only 139 firms;[22] in 1938, the Glavk of Light Machine Construction had 27.[23]

[19] The Commissariat of Defense Industry was formed from it in December, 1936, the Commissariat of Machine Construction in August, 1937. In 1939, the three commissariats were split into thirteen. An additional two were formed in 1941.

[20] When the Glavk of the Metallurgical Industry was split into five glavki in 1937, 300,000 workers were still left in the plants of the largest one while the other four had 250,000 together. (Report of a statement by I. P. Bardin, chief engineer of the Glavk of the Metallurgical Industry. *Ind.*, September 9, 1937, p. 1.) To direct these 300,000 men, the remaining large glavk had a central staff of 265. (*Ind*, May 23, 1938, p. 2.) The 1940 personnel plan for the Commissariat of Heavy Machine Construction included 1,993 posts in the central apparatus of the Commissariat and of its glavki. (Post. No. 463 of the Council of Commissars of the USSR—hereafter referred to as the SNK SSSR—April 5, 1940, *SPR*, 1940, article 287.) The 1940 plan for the Commissariat of Ferrous Metallurgy had 3,750 such posts. (Post. No. 1363 of the SNK SSSR of July 27, 1940, *SPR*, 1940, article 514.)

[21] In 1934 and 1935, many minor plants had been transferred out of the Commissariat of Heavy Industry and into the Republic Commissariats of Local Industry. In this fashion, the plants left under the various national commissariats in heavy industry were mostly large and so their number could be kept small.

[22] *Mash.*, May 15, 1939, p. 2.

[23] *Mash.*, April 23, 1939, p. 2. Similarly, in 1938 the Glavk of Heavy Machine Construction had ten firms, and the Glavk of the Machinery Industry had thirty-three. (*Ibid.*)

In principle, both commissariats and glavki are organized along the lines of each containing certain industries. But in practice, this principle is not pushed too far,

Prior to and simultaneously with the policy of creating new glavki and commissariats, trusts were rapidly being eliminated in heavy industry.[24] These trusts were bodies intermediate between glavki and firms, and their elimination meant the abolition of one rung of the hierarchical ladder. By early 1938, they were virtually restricted in heavy industry to the extractive branches.[25]

Just as trusts were eliminated in order to bring the glavki into direct contact with their firms,[26] so too there was a tendency toward by-passing the glavki and placing large firms directly under the commissariats.[27] In early 1935, nine firms were thus situated.[28]

mainly because commissariats and glavki set up units to produce materials and equipment that their firms require, and secondarily because the Council of Commissars often finds that particular commissariats have facilities for producing goods other than those of their branches or that they have by-products or wastes which can be used for such purposes. Thus on January 1, 1936, there was included in the Commissariat of Heavy Industry only 29 percent of the number of firms and 69 percent of the personnel working in machine construction and in metal fabrication. (*Trud v SSSR*, p. 154.) In 1937, the 29 plants of the Glavk of Medium Machine Construction produced the most varied types of products with no general common feature. See Brigada TsIO (Brigade of the Central Scientific-Research Institute for the Organization of Production), "Spetsializatsiia i kooperirovanie v glavsredmashe" (Specialization and Cooperation in the Glavk of Medium Machine Construction). *Organizatsiia Upravleniia* (Organization of Administration), 1937, No. 6, pp. 79-80. Hereafter, *Organizatsiia Upravleniia* will be cited as *Org. Uprav.*

In late 1938, 148 firms of the Commissariat of Machine Construction were engaged in producing consumers' goods. (T. Oparyshev, head of the production and technical group of the Central Sector of Consumers' Goods of the Commissariat of Machine Construction, writing in *Mash.*, September 26, 1938, p. 3.)

[24] While on January 1, 1934, only 182 firms of the Commissariat of Heavy Industry were not under trusts or ob"edineniia (another intermediary form), there were 355 such by January 1, 1936. See A. V. Venediktov, *Gosudarstvennaia sotsialisticheskaia sobstvennost'* (State Socialist Property), (Moscow-Leningrad: 1948), p. 725. Although these 355 were less than 13 percent of the total number of firms in the Commissariat (cf. *Trud v SSSR*, p. 71), they were responsible for 70-75 percent of the Commissariat's production. (Venediktov, *op. cit.*, p. 725.)

[25] "Khronika: Otchetnost' po sebestoimosti v 1938 godu" (Chronicle: The Accounts Regarding Costs in 1938), *Planovoe Khoziaistvo*, 1938, No. 2, p. 138.

[26] Venediktov, *op. cit.*, p. 725.

[27] Considerations other than size also seem to have guided such elimination of glavki. Regional factors were clearly involved when, of the seven machine-construction and metal-fabrication plants directly under the Commissariat of Heavy Industry on January 1, 1934, five were in a single oblast of the Ukraine. *Mashinostroitel'naia promyshlennost' SSSR: spravochnik zavodov, stroitel'stv, trestov i glavnykh upravlenii soiuznoi, respublikanskoi i mestnoi mashinostroitel'noi i metalloobrabotyvaiushchei promyshlennosti. Tom pervyi.* (The Machine-Construction Industry of the USSR: Reference Book on Plants, Constructions, Trusts and Chief Administrations of All-Union, Republic and Local Machine-Construction and Metal-Fabricating Industry. Volume I (Moscow: 1933), pp. 1-2.

[28] Venediktov, *op. cit.*, p. 726.

By July, 1940, 42 firms had been placed directly under one commissariat, and there were at least eight others with no glavki above them in two other commissariats of heavy industry.[29]

But with the reduction in the size of the glavki, there simultaneously took place a considerable strengthening of their powers over those firms which remained under their authority. This played a leading role in binding together the total productive capacity under their control, irrespective of how it was distributed among the firms.

In 1936, glavki were given much greater powers over the supply of materials and fuel for their firms,[30] and over the redistribution of their firms' finances.[31]

In November, 1937, the Council of Commissars recommended a reorganization of the internal apparatus of the glavki in all industrial commissariats. The apparatus was to be made up primarily of command sectors, each in charge of a number of firms in their entirety.[32] A system of engineer-dispatchers was to be organized within each glavk to control the work of the firms.[33] It was held that when this reorganization had been carried out, the glavk dispatcher should be "the *central figure* of the apparatus of the glavk."[34] A dispatcher was to cover one or more firms, and his main role was to be that of "a living link" between the firms and the glavk. As a representative of the glavk, and one spending at least half his time at its headquarters, his function was to exercise daily

[29] Post. No. 463 of the SNK SSSR of April 5, 1940, *SPR*, 1940, article 287. Statute of Narkomsredmash SSSR (Commissariat of General Machine Construction), approved by Post. No. 976 of the SNK SSSR of July 2, 1939, *SPR*, 1939, article 310. Post. No. 1363 of the SNK SSSR of July 27, 1940, *SPR*, 1940, article 514.

For a further explanation of this entire process of reorganization, see Appendix A.

[30] Post. of the TsIK (Central Executive Committee) and SNK SSSR of July 15, 1936, *Biulleten' finansovogo i khoziaistvennogo zakonodatel'stva* (Bulletin of Financial and Economic Laws and Regulations), 1936, No. 21. (Hereafter, this Bulletin will be cited as *BFKhZ*.) Also see B. N. Iakobson, "O zadachakh snabzhenchesko-sbytovykh sistem v sviazi s reorganizatsiei otraslevykh snabov i sbytov" (On the Tasks of the Procurement-Marketing Systems in Connection with the Reorganization of the Branch Procurement and Marketing Organs), *Snabzhenie i Skladskoe Khoziaistvo Prompredpriiatii* (The Procurement and Warehouse Economy of the Industrial Firms)—hereafter cited as *Snab. i Sklad.*—1937, No. 2, p. 19.

[31] Post. of the TsIK and SNK SSSR of July 15, 1936, *BFKhZ*, 1936, No. 21.

[32] *Ind.*, November 12, 1937, p. 2 and *Mash.*, November 12, 1938, p. 1.

[33] *Mash.*, November 12, 1938, p. 1.

[34] Lead editorial in *Mash.*, November 12, 1938, p. 1. Italics in original.

supervision over all aspects of the work of his firms. He was to ferret out their weak points and suggest corrective measures, while at the same time getting aid for the firms from the glavk. Through these glavk dispatchers, the glavk was to be able to muster all the resources of its firms. One firm would not have idle lathes while another found work piling up for lack of cutting facilities.

Although it appears that the glavk dispatchers ran afoul of the plant directors and did not reach the stature originally intended for them, yet glavk coordination of production facilities greatly increased in the late thirties.[35]

The budding-forth of new commissariats and glavki created a pressing problem: How were they to be coordinated? When all of heavy industry had been included in one commissariat, about 68 percent of the industrial working force of all the industrial commissariats—excluding local industry—was under one head.[36] Firms of this one commissariat had provided for almost all of each other's needs for materials, fuels, and equipment, and had received most of each other's products. The greatest part of the planning and coordination required could be done by the commissariat itself. But when the original Commissariat of Heavy Industry was broken up, interorganizational links had to be vastly extended to handle interbranch coordination. This necessitated a far stronger State Planning Commission as well as a powerful committee composed of top Government leaders to guide all the commissariats.[37]

Thus the Economic Council of the Council of Commissars was formed as the Government's working committee in continuous session, and was charged with the direction of the economy and with supervision and coordination of all economic commissariats.[38] It was composed of the chairman and all vice-chairmen of the Council of Commissars as well as of a representative of the trade unions.[39] In 1940, it was decided that the Council could not success-

[35] For material about glavk dispatchers, see *Mash.*, November 12, 1938, pp. 1 and 3, and *Mash.*, July 29, 1939, p. 3.

[36] Cf. footnote 1 on page 5.

[37] Concluding remarks of V. Molotov at the XVIIIth Congress of the All-Union Communist Party (Bolshevik) on March 17, 1939, published in *Problemy Ekonomiki*, 1939, No. 3, p. 78. Hereafter, the All-Union Communist Party (Bolshevik) will be referred to as the VKP(b).

[38] Post. No. 273 of the SNK SSSR of November 23, 1937, *BFKhZ*, 1937, No. 32/33.

[39] *Ibid.*

fully function so long as its members each directed an individual branch of the economy, and thus it was divided into six councils, each headed by a full-time chairman, and with each council guiding several commissariats.[40] The State Planning Commission was likewise strengthened and expanded.

THE FIRM AS THE "BASIC UNIT" OF INDUSTRY

Since December, 1939, Soviet theory has picked out the firm as "the basic link in the administration of industry."[41] If we ask what is more "basic" about it than about units above or below, it is difficult to find a clear-cut theoretic answer. The best that can be said is that it possesses a different sort of financial independence and responsibility from that of any other unit, but even this distinction cannot be pushed too far. In practice, however, the answer is clear: Ordinarily and in essence, higher organs treat the firm as the lowest unit of industry to be dealt with in plans and in checks on the execution of these plans. The firm is considered as "independent" in a fashion different from any of its components. One of the indications of the bedrock character of the firm is that while trusts, glavki, and commissariats have been formed, split, and recomposed, their firms have remained extremely stable in structure. A firm is not considered as just another link in administration to be changed at administrative convenience.

The reason for this special treatment is that the firm is structured in such a fashion as to make it an integrated production unit. In 1936, firms with a complete cycle of metallurgical production turned out 79 percent of the country's pig iron, 61 percent of its ingot steel, and 69 percent of its rolled metal.[42] In 1940, armament firms produced 70 to 75 percent of their own requirements of machine tools.[43]

Thus there are normally sound engineering reasons for the

[40] *Ind.*, April 18, 1940, p. 1.

[41] Post. of the Central Committee (hereafter referred to as TsK) VKP(b) of December 5, 1929, *Pravda*, December 14, 1929, p. 2.

[42] L. Eventov, "K itogam bor'by dvukh sistem za 20 let" (On the Results of the Fight between the Two Systems over 20 years), *Planovoe Khoziaistvo*, 1937, No. 8, p. 153.

[43] Sh. Ia. Turetskii, *Vnutripromyshlennoe nakoplenie v SSSR* (Intra-Industry Accumulation in the USSR), (Moscow: 1948), p. 110.

bounds set for a firm, although, like capitalist enterprises, Soviet firms sometimes expand in every direction with no technological rhyme or logic behind such growth. While strong efforts have continually been made to unite the facilities of different firms so that one could sublet excess work to another with idle capacity, such "cooperation" between them did not seem to take hold during the prewar period. Many firm directors even made statements minimizing the capacity of their plants in order to avoid such orders, and higher authorities were not able to overcome "the psychology of an 'isolated' economy."[44] A considerable degree of self-sufficiency was thus necessary for a firm if it was to produce successfully.

The desire for integration has led to the building of giant firms which are relatively self-contained, a procedure which was only officially criticized in the Soviet Union in 1938.[45] While heavy industry had over 3,000 firms by 1938,[46] 180 of them produced more than half of its production.[47] On January 1, 1936, the percentages of personnel of firms of heavy industry (irrespective of whether they were under national industrial commissariats) who worked in firms with over 1,000 employees were: for ferrous metallurgy— 98.4 percent; for machine and vehicle construction and metal fabrication—76.4 percent; for the chemical industry—71.3 percent; and for the cement industry—47.9 percent.[48]

In discussing the place of the "firm" in Soviet heavy industry, we must make the implicit assumption of an essential homogeneity among the different organizations coming under this title. For if there is no such homogeneity as to rights and functions, the concept of the "firm" becomes one of purely administrative use in the Soviet Union and serves no analytic function. To what extent is the assumption of homogeneity justified?

Since there are both giant and small firms, it is to be expected that there will be a difference in the attention which they can com-

---

[44] Cf. *Za Industrializatsiiu* (For Industrialization)— hereafter cited as *Z.I.*—February 27, 1937, p. 1, and *Mash.*, October 6, 1937, p. 2.

[45] Post. of the SNK SSSR of February 26, 1938, discussed in *Mash.*, June 4, 1938, p. 2.

[46] Cf. *Trud v SSSR*, p. 71.

[47] *Ind.*, May 17, 1938, p. 1.

[48] *Trud v SSSR*, pp. 144, 152, 129, and 136. For firms with over 3,000 employees, the figures were respectively: 87.0 percent, 54.7 percent, 32.2 percent, and 18.2 percent. If we were to consider the Commissariat of Heavy Industry alone, the percentages would be far higher.

mand for their needs. Glavki are more likely to know the concrete problems existing in major firms, and to offer them real aid and guidance.[49] Smaller firms, whose requirements of many types of goods are too small to warrant shipment directly from producing plants and who thus receive their supplies from warehouses, are much less likely to get their allotments of materials than are firms large enough to take direct shipments.[50] Likewise, firms producing priority goods get much more attention and aid (e.g., in receiving supplies and labor force) than do others. There have been frequent announcements of large State grants of premiums to be distributed among outstanding personnel of firms in defense industry,[51] while such funds do not seem to have been allocated to equally successful plants in other sectors.[52]

But such differences as these among firms seem the only important ones that exist. While legally there is a difference between the firms within a trust and those directly under glavki and commissariats, in practice the difference is virtually nil and they can be considered as a single class.[53] Firms in the Soviet Union's heavy industry seem to differ among themselves much in the same respect as do companies in American heavy industry. Despite the multitude of variations in position, there is a basic homogeneity in organization, function, and control.

What, then, are the rights of a State-owned firm? Of what does its "independence" consist?

The fundamental statement of the Soviet firm's position, which

[49] Cf. *Ind.*, May 17, 1938, p. 1.

[50] Cf. Korostin and Cherniakhovskii, "Zadachi skladskogo metallosnabzheniia i rabota skladov Stal'sbyta i snabsbytov" (Tasks of Warehousing in Metal Procurement and the Work of the Warehouses of the Steel Marketing Organ and of the Procurement-Marketing Agencies), *Snab. i Sklad.*, 1935, No. 2, p. 29. See also, B. N. Iakobson, *op. cit.*, p. 20.

[51] Cf. Post. No. 577 of the SNK SSSR of April 28, 1939, *SPR*, 1939, article 200.

[52] This statement is an evaluation made from a reading of the daily industrial press.

[53] Cf. *Grazhdanskoe pravo*, Tom I (Civil Law, Volume I), edited by Professors M. M. Agarkov and D. M. Genkin (Moscow: 1944), pp. 166-68. See also, Venediktov, *op. cit.*, pp. 730-31. Although Soviet legislation, courts, and arbitration practice have long treated firms existing within a trust as independent legal entities, this treatment has not been ratified in Soviet law. While firms directly under glavki and commissariats are legal entities and bear sole property responsibility for their own affairs, firms operating under a trust share legal responsibilitiy for their financial obligations with the trust. But this legal distinction has found no reflection in Soviet practice, even in the courts.

still holds today, was set forth in the proclamation of December 5, 1929, by the Central Committee of the Communist Party USSR.[54] The firm is to observe strictly all production and financial plans approved for it by higher organs, but is independent within the limits set. Its management bears complete responsibility for fulfilling the allotted program, and it has the right and duty to establish tasks for its component units. The firm is given tasks as to quantity, quality, and assortment of production; use of materials; size of labor force; etc. These are all stated in natural terms.

But in addition, the firm is placed on a "business accounting"[55] basis. It pays for its materials, fuel, labor force, etc., and receives a money return for its products. Virtually all of these purchases and sales are covered by contracts—mainly annual—with other firms and organizations. If the contracts are violated, the firm may sue the other party or may itself be sued. A sum of money fixed by its annual plan is placed at its disposal in the State Bank to serve as a revolving working-capital fund. It has an independent balance at the Bank, against which its expenditures and receipts are debited and credited. One major index of a firm's success is financial—whether actual costs per unit are lower than planned expenses.

While it had been emphasized even earlier, business accounting throughout industry received great impetus from a speech by Stalin in 1931.[56] Stalin insisted that firms and higher industrial organs must lay great stress on business accounting—that is, on reducing money costs to a minimum and, wherever possible, on earning a profit from the sale of their production.[57] He clearly implied that each firm and higher organ of industry should be judged independently by its success in this field.[58]

Under the business accounting system, the firm management is given the right to maneuver its financial resources in such a way as to best cover its needs. True, this maneuverability is limited by all sorts of restrictions written into the firm's annual plan, but it is

[54] *Pravda*, December 14, 1929, p. 2.
[55] Khozraschët.
[56] Speech of June 23, 1931, to a Conference of Business Executives, *Voprosy Leninizma*, 10th edition, pp. 440-66.
[57] This, theoretically, could not be done by price raising, as price policy is set centrally. Thus Stalin was referring solely to cost reductions.
[58] *Voprosy Leninizma*, 10th edition, pp. 461-63.

still present and is very real.[59] In addition, premiums are attached to financial results.[60]

Particularly since 1937, great emphasis has been placed upon firms of heavy industry being profitable (having receipts greater than expenditures) rather than solely on the reduction of their costs below the planned level. Price changes in 1936 as well as cost reductions over many years were expected to make it feasible for firms to be profitable and to exist and operate without subsidies from the State Budget. Beginning with 1937, all special premiums were intended normally to come out of the firm's profits. Thus, increasingly through the thirties, business accounting for heavy industry's firms came to mean the requirement of living within their income and even of showing a profit.[61]

In order to permit it to operate according to business accounting rules, the firm is granted two types of owned capital and a major legal source of credit.

[59] For a model charter drawn up for firms of the Commissariat of Heavy Industry, cf. *Istochniki sovetskogo grazhdanskogo prava*, Tom I (Sources of Soviet Civil Law, Volume I), a study-aid for colleges (Moscow: 1938), pp. 87-90.

[60] Subdivisions of firms such as departments are also considered independent and usually operate on a business accounting basis. (Cf. *ibid.*, p. 89.) The differences between business accounting for the firm and that for the departments are these. (1) The firm alone is responsible for all its financial obligations, neither its Commissariat nor the Commissariat of Finance bearing any responsibility for unpaid bills. (Venediktov, *op. cit.*, pp. 734-35.) The firm's units do not have such financial responsibility, the firm itself being liable for all obligations incurred by them. (2) The firm has a separate sum of working capital and an individual Bank balance. The plant departments do not have these, and so cannot have financial relations directly with units outside their firm. See V. Kontorovich, *Tekhpromfinplan promyshlennogo predpriiatiia* (The Technical-Industrial-Financial Plan of the Industrial Firm), (Moscow: 1948), p. 221. Business acounting for the plant departments means only the making of a financial plan for the department in which is set forth its planned costs of production and planned value of product, the keeping of accounts as to its actual costs and money value of production, and the giving of premiums for achieving financial results better than those planned. *(Ibid.)*

[61] It would be easy to exaggerate the significance of 1936 as a turning point for heavy industry in the fight for profitability. Only in 1938 and 1939 did extractive industries such as coal and oil become profitable even "in a general way." (Turetskii, *op. cit.*, p. 297.) Ferrous metallurgical plants as a whole suffered losses in the first quarter of 1939 (*Ind.*, June 24, 1939, p. 1), and many of the major plants still had to be subsidized in late 1940 (*Ind.*, August 25, 1940, p. 3). While machine construction was the most profitable sector of heavy industry (M. Bogolepov, "K peresmotru tsen na oborudovanie" [Toward a Revision of Prices for Equipment], *Plan*, 1937, No. 7, p. 51), important glavki were still being subsidized in late 1938. (Cf. the speech of P. N. Pichugina at the Second Session of the Supreme Soviet of the Soviet Union, printed in *Mash.*, August 14, 1938, p. 2.)

Every firm has an allocated supply of "fixed capital" which consists of the buildings and equipment at its disposal. The value of
this "fixed capital" is shown on the firm's books, and one of the
firm's costs is its amortization. But as equipment is replaced by
allocations from higher bodies, the firm passes on a large part of
its depreciation account to its glavk, keeping only an allotted percentage for capital repair work.

The firm also possesses "owned working capital," a sum of
money granted to it and placed to its account in the State Bank.
This is used as a revolving fund for the running expenses of the firm,
and is replenished from the sale of the firm's products.[62]

Finally, the State Bank issues credits to firms for additional working-capital needs.[63] Book credit by other firms or organizations has
been forbidden in order to maintain financial control by the State
Bank, yet such credits appear to have existed in sizable quantities.[64]

While the firm is granted "ownership" over funds in order to
give it "independence," the concept of ownership is as relative as
that of independence. For while the firm is the "basic unit" of
heavy industry, it is still only a link in a chain of command. A
firm's "fixed capital" of buildings and equipment can be taken
away from it, sometimes with and sometimes without monetary
compensation.[65] The amount of a firm's "owned working capital"

[62] On October 1, 1935, the total working capital funds of the Commissariat of
Heavy Industry were distributed in this fashion: 53 percent in stocks needed for
production, 7 percent in semifabricates purchased by the firms, 38 percent in unfinished production, and 1 percent in goods waiting to be marketed. Data of the
Central Statistical Agency—TsUNKhU—presented by P. Khromov in "K voprosu ob
oborotnykh fondakh promyshlennosti" (On the Question of the Working Capital of
Industry), *Problemy Ekonomiki*, 1937, No. 1, p. 72.

[63] Heavy industry has mainly been financed out of "owned working capital" rather
than by Bank loans. Bank loans as a percentage of the total working capital of the
industrial firms of heavy industry were only 8 percent on January 1, 1936 and 1937,
and 6 percent on January 1, 1938. See V. Sitnin and Z. Simkin, "Usilit' kontrol' rublem
v tiazhëloi promyshlennosti" (In Order to Strengthen the Control by the Ruble in
Heavy Industry), *Planovoe Khoziaistvo*, 1940, No. 2, p. 23. Despite an experiment
with increasing the importance of Bank loans in heavy industry, the proportion was
still at most only 9 percent on January 1, 1940, and seemed to decline from this
level between January and October, 1940. See E. Kasimovskii, "O kreditovanii gotovykh izdelii" (On the Crediting of Finished Goods), *Den'gi i Kredit* (Money and
Credit), 1940, No. 6-7, p. 18. "Za reshitel'nuiu perestroiku bankovskoi raboty" (For
the Determined Reconstruction of Bank Work), *Den'gi i Kredit*, 1940, No. 6-7, pp. 1-2.

[64] Cf. I. Aberbakh, "Oborotnye sredstva i kreditovanie promyshlennosti" (Working
Capital and Crediting of Industry), *Den'gi i Kredit*, 1940, No. 4-5, p. 46.

[65] Venediktov, *op. cit.*, pp. 627-28.

may be set anew each year in line with its production plan, and its commissariat and glavk can take away any "surplus" even during the year.[66] Yet even such an "ownership" gives the firm a stability possessed by no lower unit.

THE SYSTEM OF MANAGEMENT IN INDUSTRY

Up to this point, we have been considering the role of the firm as an organization in the total structure of Soviet heavy industry. Now let us turn to the system of management of the firm and of the bodies which control it.

Soviet writers argue that if industry is to work for results rather than solely according to rules, responsibility must be allotted. If criticism by the masses and by superiors is to be effective, all must know who is to be held accountable for given sectors of work; otherwise, buck-passing will prevail. But no one can seriously be asked to shoulder responsibility without also being given the necessary authority. Thus Soviet leaders have laid great stress on the system of one-man-authority-and-responsibility.[67]

This principle has held a place in Soviet theory from the first days of the Revolution. Paraphrasing Lenin, the stormy democracy of the working masses expressed in meetings must be combined with iron discipline during the period of work—incontestable obedience to the will of a single individual during these hours.[68]

Long before the beginning of the period of this study—1934—the concept of one-man-authority-and-responsibility was spelled out for industrial firms.[69] The director of the firm is to be held personally responsible for the fulfillment of the firm's annual plan and of all its production tasks. He appoints all administrative and technical personnel of the firm, although the head of a department should be given considerable voice in choosing his own aids.[70] The

[66] *Ibid.*, p. 734.
[67] Edinonachalie.
[68] Lenin, *Sochineniia*, 2d edition, Volume XXII, p. 464, quoted by F. Koshelev in "O bol'shevistskikh metodakh upravleniia sotsialisticheskim khoziaistvom" (On the Bolshevik Methods of Administering the Socialist Economy), *Den'gi i Kredit*, 1940, No. 6-7, p. 50.
[69] Post. of the TsK VKP(b) of September 5, 1929, published in *Pravda*, September 7, 1929, p. 1.
[70] Actually, some management personnel have always been appointed by the same organ which appoints the director.

director's operational orders are unconditionally obligatory for all plant personnel, irrespective of what their role may be in Communist Party or trade union organizations.[71]

Thus, in Soviet theory, the director is considered as the absolute "master" in his firm. But he must beware of abusing this position. He is expected to maintain close ties with the masses and to accept their "useful" suggestions.[72] It has been frequently pointed out by Soviet speakers that any director who interprets one-man-authority-and-responsibility as meaning that he is free from supervision by the masses and active workers ("actives") should be quickly awakened to the facts of Soviet life.[73]

What this means in practice can be seen in the area of hiring and firing. While the director is personally responsible for appointing and removing plant personnel, he is obliged to consider the opinions of the Communist Party and trade-union organizations in his plant. An appointment or removal is his own decision—and he will be held accountable for it—but if the Party or trade-union organization disagrees with the move, they have the right to appeal to higher organs.[74] The director cannot dodge his duty of deciding whether their recommendations are "correct," for once he follows them he assumes responsibility for them. Should he, on any aspect of the firm's operations, ignore Party or union recommendations later approved by higher authorities as correct, he will generally be considered to have acted "bureaucratically."[75]

The pattern of one-man-authority-and-responsibility applies not only to the firm, but also to all industrial bodies above the firm and to departments and shops within it. The essence of the system lies in giving one individual sufficient authority to manage a production unit, and then in holding him strictly answerable for its functioning.

In this fashion, the Soviet leaders hope to eradicate the safe and conservative approach of those officials who simply desire to follow commands from above by issuing implementing orders. At the

---

[71] Post. of the TsK VKP(b) of September 5, 1929, *Pravda*, September 7, 1929, p. 1.
[72] *Ibid.*
[73] Cf. V. M. Molotov's report of March 28, 1937, to the Plenum of the TsK VKP(b), *Z.I.*, April 20, 1937, p. 4.
[74] Post. of the TsK VKP(b) of September 5, 1929, *Pravda*, September 7, 1929, p. 1.
[75] The Soviet use of the term "bureaucrat," has a purely derogatory meaning.

1941 All-Union Communist Party Conference, Central Committee member Malenkov stated succinctly: "A situation should not be tolerated where a director, wishing to excuse himself for the poor work of his firm, continually refers to the fact that his orders were not fulfilled although they were correct and were given in time."[76] Every firm director is to be forced to show initiative and to act creatively. Since he must answer for results, his mere following of the beaten and approved track cannot be the way to security.

Although the concept of one-man-authority-and-responsibility is dominant in Soviet theorizing regarding economic administration, a contradictory element is also present. This element is the stress on the group or collegium system for making decisions.

At the end of 1931, Stalin strongly condemned the making of decisions by one man.[77] "Decisions by individuals are always or almost always one-sided. . . ." In each collegium, he said, there are people with opinions which must be considered. They are capable of correcting one-sided views and suggestions and of bringing their own experience to bear on the question under discussion. Decision making by collegia, said Stalin, makes possible the avoidance of serious mistakes.[78]

Clearly, here was an implied criticism of one-man-authority-and-responsibility. Yet that implied criticism has never been developed into a direct attack upon it. Soviet administrators have followed a practice of using the one-man and collegium systems of decision making as alternatives in different situations.

In 1934, collegia were ordered liquidated in all bodies handling economic work except for organs with an elected membership.[79] (These latter were the All-Union and Republic Councils of Commissars, and local councils in charge of local industry.) Previously,

---

[76] Report to the Conference, *Chërnaia Metallurgiia* (Ferrous Metallurgy), February 16, 1941, p. 3. (Hereafter cited as *Ch.M.*)

[77] In his interview of December 13, 1931, with Emil Ludwig. *Lenin i Stalin: sbornik proizvedenii k izucheniiu istorii VKP(b)*, Tom III (Lenin and Stalin: Collection of Works for the Study of the History of the All-Union Communist Party [Bolshevik], Volume III), (Moscow: 1936), pp. 524-25. This quotation was later referred to by S. Zodionchenko in "Rabota chlenov raikoma partii" (Work of the Members of the District Committee of the Party), *Partiinoe Stroitel'stvo* (Party Organization), 1937, No. 17, p. 27. (Hereafter, *Partiinoe Stroitel'stvo* will be cited as *Part. Stroit.*)

[78] *Lenin i Stalin*, pp. 524-25.

[79] Post. of the TsIK and SNK SSSR of March 15, 1934, *BFKhZ*, 1934, No. 9.

collegia had existed at the heads of commissariats as advisory and semiauthoritative bodies. Although commissariats were thus made subject solely to one-man authority, advisory councils, with numerous representatives from the firms, were created for each commissariat and were ordered to meet every two months.[80] By 1938, the advisory collegia of at least some commissariats had been reconstituted and were composed of the top leaders of the commissariat and of its main subdivisions.[81]

In higher Party and State organs, the collegium system of decision making is supreme. While the demarcation line between those bodies to be ruled by one man and those to be governed by group leadership is uncertain and ever-changing, the guiding principle seems to be to favor one-man-authority-and-responsibility in all administrative units of industry concerned with the operation of a single given sector. Certainly this administrative method is never questioned in its application to the management of firms. The supposed better quality of collegium decisions appears to be considered a luxury which on the operational level is expendable.

A major facet of the concept of one-man-authority-and-responsibility has been the strong condemnation of functionalism in industry. This has been the case since 1934.

Both firms and commissariats were earlier organized on a functional basis. Within the firm, for example, the head of a department would not be operationally responsible to any single man but rather to a number of sector heads. He would receive uncoordinated orders from the plant administration sectors of production planning, economic planning, procurement, repair of equipment, wages and personnel, etc. While theoretically the director was his superior, actually orders would come from these different sectors, and his complaints and requests would be directed to them. Similarly, each plant would be under the many functionally organized glavki of its commissariat.

The Soviet leaders consider that this system has resulted in con-

<hr/>

[80] *XVII s"ezd vsesoiuznoi kommunisticheskoi partii (b), 26 ianvaria—10 fevralia 1934 g.,* stenograficheskii otchët *(XVII Congress of the All-Union Communist Party [Bolshevik], January 26—February 10, 1934,* stenographic report), (Moscow: 1934), p. 673.

[81] Cf. *Mash.,* August 22 and 27, 1938, p. 2. Post. No. 354 of the SNK SSSR of March 19, 1938, *SPR,* 1938, article 78.

fusion and irresponsibility. Within the firm, no sector head knew the general conditions and needs of any of the departments he was directing. He was acquainted only with his own aspect of each department's work. Thus, said Soviet critics, the functional sectors were inevitably divorced from the realities of production—which can only be grasped by someone in a position to consider all the tasks and potentialities of the production unit. They could direct the organizations under them only in a formalistic fashion through the issuing of unintegrated orders. In the eyes of the XVIIth Party Congress, they offered no concrete leadership to industry.[82]

In 1934, the abolition of the functional system was ordered for all production units from departments up to the commissariats.[83] In its place was set up a "line" organization in which each production unit was to have only one body directly above it, charged with supervising all of its work. The old system lingered on in the commissariats, but was again ordered completely rooted out in 1937.[84]

The abolition of functional organization in industry appears to have been a successful step in the struggle to overcome irresponsibility and formalism of leadership. But the price of this achievement was a loss in division of labor within management. Experts in one aspect of work were no longer able to concentrate on making decisions in their own specialities. True, advisory sectors were maintained within which such specialization continued; but decision making was to be done by people who required a broad knowledge of all elements of the operations of their industry. It is perhaps because of this loss in division of labor and because of the need for more broadly trained executives under the new policy that the 1934 command of a Party Congress to end functionalism in industry was not enforced within the apparatus of the glavki until at least 1937.

Inside the firm, "line" organization of management has meant a system in which there is a straight line of authority running upward from the brigadier and foreman to the director. Specialized sectors of the plant administration have an advisory function but they cannot give orders to heads of production units.

[82] Report of Politbureau member L. M. Kaganovich, *XVII s"ezd VKP(b)*, pp. 534-35.
[83] Resolution of the Party Congress, *ibid.*, p. 672.
[84] *Ind.*, November 12, 1937, p. 2

While the system of managerial organization differs from industry to industry and even somewhat from plant to plant, its main outlines have been extremely stable since 1934 when the functional pattern was abandoned.[85]

The lowest production unit is the brigade. Several brigades work in each shop during each shift, and several shops comprise a department. All departments are under the technical director or chief engineer, who is in turn responsible to the director of the firm. Various advisory organs of management, as well as the several units carrying on the firm's auxiliary work, are under the chief engineer or the director.

The brigadier stands as the lowest-ranking administrator. He works in production along with the other members of his brigade, but is in charge and gives training on the job to those who require it. Like all other executives, he is appointed from above, in this case, by the department superintendent.

Above the brigadier is the shift foreman of the shop. The senior shift foreman, or in larger shops a separate foreman, is in charge of the shop and all of its shifts. Particularly since 1940, the shop foreman has been raised to a figure of major importance.[86]

While in practice he seems to have spent most of his time arranging for supply for his shop and filling out reports, the foreman's main official functions are those of control and supervision over the production processes and use of equipment, the prevention of spoilage, and the placing of workers at specific tasks with proper instructions. All orders of management are to be transmitted to the workers through him; he has the right to hire and fire (with the approval of the department superintendent), on his own authority to impose sanctions on workers and to give them premiums within designated limits, and to rate workers' efficiency and qualifications

[85] Cf. the statutes adopted unanimously by the 1934 conference of the Commissariat of Heavy Industry for the organization of departments and firms of ferrous metallurgy, the machine construction industry, and the chemical industry, presented in *Soveshchanie khoziaistvennikov, inzhenerov, tekhnikov, partiinykh i profsoiuznykh rabotnikov tiazhëloi promyshlennosti 20-22 sentiabria 1934 g.*, stenograficheskii otchët (Conference of Executives, Engineers, Technicians, Party and Trade-Union Workers of Heavy Industry of September 20-22, 1934, stenographic report), (Moscow-Leningrad: 1935), pp. 341-95. See also, Arakelian, *op. cit.*, pp. 169-75.

[86] Cf. Post. No. 900 of the SNK SSSR and the TsK VKP (b) of May 27, 1940, *SPR*, 1940, article 361.

for determination of appropriate wage scales.[87] Where the Soviet foreman actually has possessed such powers, he would seem to have had a type of authority which has generally been taken away from foremen in large-scale American industry and transferred to higher management. More normally, in the prewar period, however, Soviet foremen did not exercise such major rights to reward and punish. In fact, the poor pay of foremen compared to that of highly skilled production workers under them often made it difficult to recruit the best workers for these managerial jobs.

The department superintendent is directly subordinate to either the chief engineer or director. He works out the detailed annual plan of his department, sets piece rates and work norms within the over-all limits given to him, and is responsible for the work of the department as a whole. The departments are considered as independent units on a business accounting basis, and the superintendent of a major department is indeed an important man—sometimes even warranting appointment and dismissal by the commissariat itself.

The first assistant to the director is the technical director or chief engineer. He is in charge of production, of the planning of flow between departments, of working out norms and standards and of making improvements, and of distributing materials, equipment, and the firm's labor force.

In over-all charge of the firm's work is the director. Obedience to his orders is obligatory for all personnel of the firm, and generally speaking he has complete hiring and firing rights.

Within the plant administration are a number of staff sectors. Chief among these are the planning-production and technical sectors. These compose the concrete plans for the firm and for its components, determine supply needs, and both work out new technological processes and improve old ones. In addition there are other sectors such as those of labor and wages; finances and bookkeeping; technical and quality control; chief mechanic; and procurement and marketing.

Finally, there are auxiliary units which are part of the firm and are subordinate to the director. These include transport, housing, subsidiary plants, children's nurseries, etc.

[87] *Ibid.*

From this description of management it can be seen that, if we make an exception for the planning work which is related to plan "limits" sent down by higher organs, the formal organization of firm management in the Soviet Union is not vastly different from that in the United States. It is true that much greater attention is given to instruction of workers, as is natural in a less technically advanced country. Also, as we shall see later, more stress is placed upon the enlistment of worker participation in the life of the firm. But as most of the day-to-day problems of management in actually operating a plant are much the same in both economies, it is not too surprising that the organization of this work is also similar. The significant area of difference between the production work of managements in the Soviet Union and in the United States lies in the basis upon which decisions are made and in the relations of management to the workers of the plant and to other nonmanagerial organizations.

III: The Composition of Firm Management

NO ADMINISTRATIVE SYSTEM can be properly understood without knowledge about the sort of people who are operating it. Officials do not act as automatons in carrying out a policy and applying regulations; their interpretations depend upon their personal backgrounds. A complex and inconsistent set of regulations for firm management might lead to continuous attempts to observe them and so result in stultification of operations if directors and their aids were of a particular type; on the other hand, if they were people with other sorts of backgrounds, it could lead to frequent and open violation of the rules.

Thus a description of the traits of Soviet plant executives is very important for a proper understanding of the role of plant management. Besides, of course, the subject should hold considerable interest in its own right.

PROTOTYPES OF DIRECTORS

While this chapter will lean mainly on statistical material for all heavy industry, it is perhaps advisable to begin with a few sparse biographies of firm directors. These may help to illustrate the typical combinations of features found in a single man. In presenting brief biographies of the men who, during the period under study, were directors of three leading metallurgical firms, including the largest in the country—Magnitogorsk—I believe that I have chosen prototypes of the directors of heavy industry during the years 1934-41.

There were four directors of Magnitogorsk in our seven and one half years. The first, A. P. Zaveniagin, was born in 1901—the son of a railroad machinist. In 1917, he joined the Communist

Party, and by 1918 was the secretary of a District Party Committee. He continued in numerous local leadership posts within the Party until 1923, and then entered an engineering college which he left only in 1930. One to two years after graduation, he was made chief of the metallurgical section of the Supreme Council of the National Economy and soon after became assistant head of the Glavk of Ferrous Metallurgy. As part of the campaign to strengthen the leadership of firms, he was appointed director of a major metallurgical plant in early 1933. In the fall of 1933, he was switched to the post of director of Magnitogorsk. Here he continued until early 1937, by which time he had also become a candidate (substitute member) of the Central Committee of the Communist Party and a member of the Central Executive Committee of the Soviet Union. In March, 1937, he was promoted to First Assistant Commissar of Heavy Industry—a post he held at least through February, 1938.[1] But from this position he plummeted downward to the directorship of an Arctic Circle construction job.[2]

P. I. Korobov, Zaveniagin's successor at Magnitogorsk, has an entirely different history. He was born in 1902, the son and grandson of skilled metallurgical workers, and he himself began work in a metallurgical plant as an apprentice at the age of 14. Six years later he left to attend the engineering college from which he graduated in 1926. Thereupon he returned to his old plant as a shift engineer, and advanced to assistant to a department chief and then to chief of the blast furnace department. In 1933, he was appointed department superintendent of a second firm, and in 1935 was switched to blast furnace head at Magnitogorsk. In the same year, he was enrolled as a member of the Communist Party.[3] In 1936, he became chief engineer of Magnitogorsk, and in March, 1937, its director. This post was only a steppingstone upward, as in January, 1939, he was appointed First Assistant Commissar of Ferrous Metallurgy.[4]

K. N. Ivanov succeeded him at Magnitogorsk in early 1939. Ivanov also had worked his way up within industry, having been

[1] Data is mainly from Z.I., March 15, 1937, p. 1.
[2] John Scott, Behind the Urals (Cambridge, Mass.: 1942), p. 204.
[3] As membership books of the Party were closed during this period, it required a special decision of the Central Committee to make him a member.
[4] Data is mainly from Z.I., March 16, 1937, p. 1.

superintendent of a rolling mill department in 1937 and then chief engineer of Magnitogorsk. Between February and July, 1939, he in turn was replaced by G. I. Nosov, who remained director through June, 1941.

Nosov was the son of a metallurgical worker and had attended an engineering college. After graduation, he began as a skilled workman at an open-hearth furnace. He worked at one job for six months, and then at others until he knew almost all the trades employed in an open-hearth department. With this practical experience added to his engineering training, he was appointed at the end of 1937 assistant to the chief engineer of the firm. Within two and a half years, he was directing Magnitogorsk.[5]

Our second firm, Hammer and Sickle of Moscow, had two directors in the period of this study. P. F. Stepanov, director from 1925 to June, 1938, represents a third type of director. In contrast to both Zaveniagin and Korobov, he received no formal education. He had entered industry as a young boy in 1905, and was director of a small machine-building firm in the early twenties. In 1925 he was made director of the Hammer and Sickle firm despite the fact that at the time he knew nothing about metallurgy. Here he worked as a successful manager for thirteen years. His next post—which would seem to have been a demotion—was head of the Moscow office of the Glavk of Steel Pipe. He continued downward when he was dismissed from this job in January, 1939, as a disciplinary example for not having enforced the recent Work Discipline Law.

G. M. Il'in succeeded Stepanov as director and still headed the firm in June, 1941. The son of a skilled metallurgical worker, he came to the open-hearth department of Hammer and Sickle in 1921 as an unskilled worker. Here he learned his father's trade, and was a foreman by 1937 at least. He had joined the Communist Party in 1930, and in 1937 was elected to the Party Committee of his department of the plant. While he was still working as a foreman, the plant elected him Chairman of the Regional Commission on Elections to the Supreme Soviet of the Soviet Union. Shortly afterwards, he became a member of the Central Commission on Elections to the Supreme Soviet of the Russian Republic and then

[5] Data on Nosov is mainly from *Ind.,* January 26, 1938, p. 3.

was elected a member of this Soviet. Following these honors, he was promoted from foreman to director of the same firm.[6]

The Stalingrad Stalin Metallurgical Plant has had four directors, of whom I know the histories of only the first two. I. G. Makarov, director from 1932 to 1937, was an "old Bolshevik." He came from a poor peasant family, lost his father early, and was working in a steel plant by the age of 15. He joined the Social Democratic Party (which included the Bolsheviks) in 1905. During the Tsarist regime, he lived underground, underwent several years' banishment, and once escaped from prison. In 1916, the large plant in which he was a lathe worker went on strike under his leadership. In 1917, he conducted Bolshevik propagandizing among the soldiers of the garrison of his town and led in the supplying of arms to the workers. With the success of the Bolshevik Revolution, Makarov became the first "Red Director" of the plant whose strike movement he had led. From then until 1929, he was transferred to the leadership of plant after plant—most of them metallurgical—with the task of bringing them into production. In 1929, he was finally sent to an industrial academy for a brief engineering education, and then was moved into the apparatus of the Commissariat of Heavy Industry. With the recognition of the need for bolstering plant leadership, he was sent in 1932 to the Stalin Metallurgical Plant as its director. In January, 1937, he was promoted to head of the Glavk of Specialized Metals, and in May, 1938, to Assistant Commissar of Heavy Industry. But he did not make good at this last job, and within a year had been demoted to director of a medium-sized machine-building firm.[7]

His successor replaced him for only six months as a step in his climb up the industrial ladder. Born in 1900, F. F. Riazanov had become an apprentice in a metallurgical plant at the age of 15. One year later, he joined the Communist Party. After taking part for two years in the Civil War, he worked in trade-union organizations for several more years. By 1927, he had been chosen Chairman of the City Council of the city of Dnepropetrovsk. At this

[6] Data is mainly from *Ind.*, June 9, 1938, p. 3; P. Fedulov's article "Partiinyi komitet odnogo tsekha" (The Party Committee of One Department), *Part. Stroit.*, 1938, No. 14, p. 45; and *Mash.*, March 27, 1939, p. 2.

[7] Data is mainly from *Ind.*, December 4, 1937, p. 2.

point he was removed from activity, and was sent to an industrial academy and to an engineering college until 1932. Upon graduation, he took up important posts immediately. For two years he worked as assistant director of one metallurgical firm, as shift engineer and then assistant department-superintendent of a second, and at the end of 1933 he was appointed director of a third. In January, 1937, he was switched to the leadership of the more important Stalin Plant. But after only half a year he was again promoted, this time to head the Glavk of Metallurgical Production. In little less than a year he proved a failure in this post of greater responsibility, and was removed. But within about two years, he was once again director of a major metallurgical firm.[8]

In these directors' biographies, we can observe the roads typically followed to the post of director. Zaveniagin and Riazanov are representative of those young men who did good and even important work in nonindustrial posts, were sent to engineering schools, and quickly moved up to directors' positions. Makarov is the old revolutionary and strike leader who became a director in the earliest days of the Revolution, and received a formal education only after holding major industrial posts and acquiring great practical experience. Stepanov is the director without schooling who learned on the job, and who—contrary to the usual practice—remained at a single plant for many years. Il'in worked in the same plant for seventeen years without getting above the rank of foreman, and then suddenly jumped to that of director. Korobov and Nosov early received an engineering education, and then made their way through many industrial jobs to the post of director.

CHARACTERISTICS OF MANAGERIAL PERSONNEL AS SHOWN STATISTICALLY

Let us now leave the field of examples and follow a statistical picture of the characteristics of men in plant management. Data on heads of glavki will also be given to serve as a basis of com-

[8] Data is mainly from Z.I., June 2, 1937, p. 1. Riazanov was succeeded in mid-1937 by Ia. T. Marmazov, who remained director until the fourth quarter of 1939. S. Liadov then took over through June, 1941. Unfortunately, I have no information about either of these two.

parison. Figures presented below are for the 1934-36 period only, unless specifically stated to the contrary.[9]

PARTY MEMBERSHIP: Membership in the Communist Party is almost universal among directors of firms of heavy industry. Soviet studies indicate that at least 97 percent of the directors are Party members. While in 1938 the Central Committee of the Communist Party condemned the widespread tendency of keeping non-Party people from leadership roles, and although it specifically mentioned the post of plant director as one to which they should be promoted,[10] there is no evidence indicating that the proportion of Party members among directors declined significantly if at all thereafter.

The percentage of Party members among the heads of glavki has been as overwhelming as among directors. Such guidance of major economic units by Party people is not surprising. With political reliability the first criterion for leadership personnel, a man would normally have been accepted into the Party before he had reached the stage in his career where his previous service would justify his consideration for a top management post.

The same predominance of Party members has not, however, been characteristic of the lower management of firms. Only one third of the chief engineers (or technical directors) have been Party members; this seems due to their post being considered more narrowly technical than that of director.[11] Likewise, only one third of all foremen have been Party members, and this appears to be a result of their having only minor responsibility as well as their often being younger men who have not yet proved themselves sufficiently to justify Party membership. The percentage of Party membership among department superintendents has fallen be-

---

[9] Sources, unless given in the footnotes, are indicated in Appendix B.

[10] Post. of the TsK VKP(b) of March 4, 1938, *Part. Stroit.*, 1938, No. 6, p. 62.

[11] A 1935 study conducted by the Labor Sector of the Central Statistical Administration and the newspaper *Z.I.* of the Commissariat of Heavy Industry indicates that there was no greater percentage of Party membership among the chief engineers under 37 years of age than among those older. This study covered 240 chief engineers. See Tsentral'noe Upravlenie Narodno-Khoziaistvennogo Uchëta Gosplana SSSR, Otdel uchëta truda, *Sostav rukovodiashchikh rabotnikov i spetsialistov Soiuza SSSR* (The Composition of Administrative Personnel and of Specialists of the USSR), (Moscow: 1936), pp. 15-17.

tween that of directors and that of the other executives, one half of them being Party members; the same reasons seem to hold for them as for foremen. Material for 1938 and 1939 shows a picture similar to that of 1934-36, with almost half of that part of the plant leadership from foreman up which had newly risen from the ranks being made up of non-Party people.[12]

PERIOD OF JOINING THE PARTY: By categorizing Party members according to the period in which they entered the Party, we can attain further insight into the political background of management. Sixty to 65 percent of all directors joined the Party in the 1917-21 period of prelude to Revolution, the Revolution itself, and the Civil War. Only 10 percent of their memberships dated before 1917, and 25 percent from the years 1922-28. Thus directors were mostly men who had joined the Party in its first period of great growth—during the struggle to create and defend the Soviet Government.

Heads of glavki—the directors' superiors—were men of a different group. Thirty-five to 45 percent of them were Old Bolsheviks, whose Party cards dated from 1916 or earlier. Virtually all the rest were of the 1917-21 vintage.

The corps of Party members among chief engineers of firms was composed of men who had joined much later than did most directors. As of 1936, roughly one third came from each of the three periods of 1917-21, 1922-28, and post-1928.[13] Party members among the chief engineers would seem to have been of quite a different stamp than the directors. They joined the Party after attaining important industrial posts and after the Party was firmly established in power. They were not political Party men turned economic administrators, but rather engineers who were secondarily Party people.

This division between heads of glavki, directors, and chief engineers is also shown by the age at which members entered the Party. While glavki heads averaged roughly 18 years of age at the

[12] Cf. *Mash.* for the fourth quarter of 1938 and the first quarter of 1939.

[13] As with directors, the percentage of those entering the Party after 1928 grew greatly between 1934 and 1936. But while it was still tiny among directors in 1936, this was far from the case among chief engineers.

time of joining, directors were 22 and chief engineers 26 years old.[14]

AGE: The age of managerial personnel is significant not only as one indication of their experience, but also as a guide to their initiative and willingness to take risks. The folk traditions of all peoples testify to the greater enterprise and daring of youth in general, and Stalin has added his own testimony with specific regard to Soviet industrial management.[15]

Almost all directors were between 30 and 50 years old, with the 30 to 40 age category having a slight edge. Only 1 to 3 percent were 24 to 30, and 3 to 5 percent over 50. The heads of glavki, as is consistent with our other data, were somewhat older. None were under 30, the 40 to 50 age group was one and one-half times as large as the 30 to 40, and 10 to 12 percent of these chiefs were over 50.

Chief engineers, interestingly enough, had much the same age breakdown as did directors, the only difference being in the group over 50 which made up 10 to 12 percent of the total. Thus at least half of them were men whose experience in industry began after the Revolution, and they were of the same generation as their superiors, the directors. Department superintendents were, as we would expect, a somewhat younger group: 10 percent were 24 to 30, and 50 to 60 percent between 31 and 40.

EDUCATION: Education is a characteristic in which composition changed rapidly even during so short a period as 1934-36.

Back in 1931, Stalin had pointed out a fundamental precondition for genuine one-man-authority-and-responsibility. "Until there are among us Bolsheviks," he said, "enough people with a good grasp of technique, business management and finance, we will not have real one-man-authority-and-responsibility."[16] No

---

[14] These figures were derived from a comparison of the arithmetic means of age and length of time in the Party for the different groups. The only significantly controversial open-end category is that of Party membership before 1917; the midpoint has here arbitrarily been taken as 1908.

[15] I. Stalin, Report of March 10, 1939, on the Work of the Central Committee of the Communist Party to the XVIIIth Congress of the VKP(b), *Voprosy Leninizma*, 11th edition (Moscow: 1947), p. 596.

[16] *Voprosy Leninizma*, 10th edition, p. 444.

industrial head can really exercise authority, according to Stalin, if he does not combine a knowledge of technical details and business management with his fundamental political qualifications. Without this combination, he can only allocate responsibility and can have no genuine control over how it is exercised. The realization of this Soviet concept of administration was seen in 1931 as being held back by the limited education and experience of managerial personnel, and its greater effectiveness was considered to be dependent on prior improvement in training.

The Soviet leaders placed great stress upon improving the educational background of managerial personnel. It should be noted, however, that during the 1934-36 period each management group retained its distinguishing educational characteristics; for while the training of the groups improved, it was not in such a fashion as to make the education of any group skip out of its original ranking.

Of management above the foreman level, directors had by far the least education. Those with only primary schooling made up 50 percent of the total in 1934, and still comprised 40 percent in 1936. Those with higher education rose from 26 percent to 46 percent; but of this latter figure, one third had received the brief and inferior education provided by the industrial academies.[17] The proportion with higher education has, however, continued to grow, and by 1939 it included 82 to 87 percent of the directors of defense industry and of ferrous metallurgy.[18]

The heads of glavki had a much higher educational level. In 1934-36, 60 to 65 percent of them had had regular engineering training, and only 20 percent had stopped with primary education.[19] Chief engineers of firms had a still higher educational level, 87 to 90 percent of them being graduate engineers. The younger

[17] Cf. Post. No. 2349 of the TsK VKP(b) of November 19, 1940, *SPR,* 1940, article 765, for an official Soviet categorization of this course as inferior to the regular engineering one.

[18] Commissar of the Aviation Industry, M. M. Kaganovich, Speech at the XVIIIth Party Congress, *Ind.,* March 23, 1939, p. 2. Commissar of Ferrous Metallurgy, F. A. Merkulov, Speech at the XVIIIth Party Congress, *Ind.,* March 22, 1939, p. 4. It is most probable, however, that this proportion was higher than that existing in heavy industry as a whole in 1939.

[19] Glavki heads and chief engineers were the only groups showing no educational rise between 1934 and 1936.

body of department superintendents was intermediate between directors and chief engineers, and it is this group which showed the most rapid growth in education. From 1934 to 1936, the proportion with an engineering education rose from 55 percent to 80 percent and almost none were graduates of the poorer industrial academies; those with only lower education declined from 20 percent to 8 percent.

When we descend to the lowest managerial level—the foremen —we find at the end of 1933 only 2 percent with higher education and 7 percent with a technical secondary education. Here we are dealing with men who learned their trade solely through experience. Yet by 1940 they had reached a level of education in heavy machine-construction firms where the Government found it feasible to forbid the appointment of foremen in this industry who did not have at least a secondary technical education, unless they were first given an examination by a certifying commission of the firm as a whole.[20]

PERIOD IN THE INDUSTRIAL BRANCH:[21] Just as education is an indication of ability to administer industrial units, so too is the length of time which personnel have spent in their particular branch of industry.[22] In 1934, 25 percent of all directors had worked in their branch for over ten years, and another 40 percent had worked there for five to ten years. But 17 percent were new arrivals with under three years' service. The heads of glavki had far more seniority in their branch. Sixty percent had been in it for over ten years, 19 percent for five to ten years, and only 6 percent for less than three.

But while such longer service by the heads of glavki is to be ex-

[20] Post. No. 900 of the SNK SSSR and the TsK VKP(b) of May 27, 1940, SPR, 1940, article 361.
[21] While "branch" is not defined in the presentation of the following statistics, normal Soviet usage takes it as a very broad category. "Branches," as defined in a 1936 study by the Central Statistical Administration, are such large groupings as ferrous metallurgy, machine construction and metal fabrication, the coke-chemical industry, principal chemicals, cement, and the rubber industry. See A. Vinnikov, "K peresmotru norm vyrabotki v promyshlennosti" (Toward the Revision of the Work Norms in Industry), Plan, 1937, No. 8, p. 38.
[22] The period that management personnel have worked in their given branch includes only the years during which they have held white-collar jobs. Any time spent in the branch as manual workers is not included.

pected due to their higher age level and the greater responsibility of their posts, chief engineers also had far longer service than had directors. Forty-eight percent of them had been in the branch for over ten years, 27 percent for five to ten, and only 5 percent for less than three.[23] As they were of roughly the same age distribution as the directors, their considerably longer service is an indication of the fact that technical ability and experience were far more important requirements for the post of chief engineer than for that of director. Directors were far more prone to have been in highly varied fields of work—even nonindustrial ones—and to have been appointed to their posts on the basis both of proven administrative ability and of skill in political analysis of the events with which they dealt professionally.

SOCIAL POSITION AND ORIGIN: The class background of our managerial groups offers insights into the approach they would tend to take toward many problems—particularly toward those of dealing with their labor force. This is not to say that those managers who had previously been manual workers would necessarily show greater care for their employees than would others with a different background. But there is the presumption that on an average they would have more empathy, although not necessarily sympathy, with them and with their attitudes.

Probably even more important, class background gives a good indication of the degree of mobility among managers. It helps to show by what route they reached their posts.

This background is presented in Soviet statistics by two measurements: "social position" and "social origin." "Social position" refers to the principal work in which the manager had earlier been engaged,[24] while "social origin" is a reference to the way in which

[23] Cf. a sample of chief engineers taken in 1935. Forty percent had occupied administrative posts in the economy before 1918, and 70 percent had held such positions during the Civil War period. (TsUNKhU, *Sostav rukovodiashchikh rabotnikov*, pp. 15-17.)

[24] "Social position" has been defined differently for members of the Communist Party than for the rest of the population. The statistical source giving the percentages for "social position" states that the definition used for Party members is that of their "position" at the time of entering the Party. However, it is most probable that this is only roughly accurate, and that the definition actually used was that given by the Communist Party itself. According to the latter, a member's "position" is to be determined by the last principal job held by him before he became a member of the

the manager's parents earned a living. Both of these measurements divide people into three categories—workers,[25] peasants,[26] and white-collar personnel.[27]

Divided according to "social position" in a 1936 study, almost two thirds of the directors were found to have been workers and somewhat over one third were listed as white-collar personnel. The heads of glavki showed an exactly opposite composition, a reflection of the fact that they came to an overwhelming degree from the intelligentsia of the prerevolutionary and Civil War Bolsheviks. Ninety-two percent of the chief engineers were classified as white-collar. Foremen, as might be expected, showed the highest proportion of workers—77 percent.[28] In all groups the proportion of peasants was insignificant; for directors it was less than 1 percent.[29]

Social origin data for 1936—presenting the family background—

Party; but this does not apply to the category of "workers," which also includes those whose occupation after joining the Party falls under this heading. Thus the "worker" category is larger than it would be if the same methodology were used for this grouping as is employed in forming the other two. Those who joined the Party while they were students, military personnel, or elected officials are grouped according to their previous work. *Ibid.* See also, Otdel rukovodiashchikh partiinykh organov TsK VKP(b) (Sector of Guiding Party Organs of the Central Committee of the Communist Party), "Instruktsiia k zapolneniiu partiinykh dokumentov novogo obraztsa" (Instructions for Filling Out the New Party Documents), *Part. Stroit.*, 1936, No. 5, p. 54. For non-Party people, "social position" refers to their work before entering the Soviet apparatus. "Workers" are those who uninterruptedly did hired physical labor in industry, agriculture, or transport for at least three years; "peasants" are those who worked in agriculture as collective farmers or independent peasants for no less than three years. Since the majority of managerial personnel studied are Party members, it is the Party definition of "social position" which applies to most of them.

[25] Doing hired physical work in industry, transport, or agriculture.

[26] Working, but not for wages, in agriculture, hunting, or fishing. All collective farmers are included in this category.

[27] These include all administrative workers, engineers, technicians, bookkeeping personnel, doctors, lawyers, teachers, etc. The three groupings are defined in instructions approved by the TsK VKP(b) on November 23, 1939, and published in *Partiinoe khoziaistvo; sbornik dokumentov i materialov* (Party Housekeeping; a Collection of Documents and Materials), (Moscow: 1945), pp. 7-8, and in the Post. of the TsK VKP(b) of March 13, 1928, "Ob opredelenii sotsial'nogo polozheniia kommunistov i prinimaemykh v partiiu" (On Defining the Social Position of Communists and of Those Taken into the Party), *Part. Stroit.*, 1936, No. 5, pp. 58-59.

[28] This last figure refers to the percentage of foremen whose immediate previous job was that of manual worker. In heavy industry, 54 percent of all foremen came up from the ranks of manual workers after 1927. (*Z.I.*, January 11, 1935, p. 3.)

[29] This absence of peasants is perfectly natural among the leadership of industry, particularly since the large influx of peasants into industry had begun at most seven years earlier.

offers a different picture only with regard to the peasantry. Peasants played a major and very similar role in all groups, running from 23 percent to 29 percent of the total. Among directors, those of worker parentage were slightly over twice the number of those of white-collar parentage, while the heads of glavki and chief engineers had two and two-thirds to three times as many white-collar people as those of worker origin. Of particular interest is the somewhat younger group of department superintendents; for of these, there were one and a half times as many of white-collar as of worker origin. But even where white-collar origin was strongest—among heads of glavki and chief engineers—it was no more than 56 percent of the group.[30]

PERIOD AT THE SAME POST: This categorization is the most basic index of the mobility within the industrial leadership. The high mobility among all management groups which is indicated by both 1934 and 1936 data would seem to give rise to major elements of inefficiency. For each industrial unit has its own peculiarities which take time for even the most skilled manager to master. This was recognized by the Central Committee of the Communist Party in 1929 when it insisted that directors of firms should be kept at the same posts for longer periods than was then the custom.[31]

Despite this Communist Party decree, few managerial personnel have remained for long at the same post. Studies in 1934 and 1936 showed that only 3 to 8 percent of directors had held the same post for over five years, 16 to 20 percent for three to five years, and another 40 to 55 percent for one to three years. Twenty-five percent to 35 percent had held down their jobs for less than one year.

Such brevity of tenure would appear to be due more to transfers to other roughly equivalent posts than to rises and declines in per-

[30] A 1934 study shows virtually no one in any management group as being of peasant origin. Its division of each category into worker and white-collar personnel is roughly the same as that shown by the 1936 material presented above. Thus a tremendous growth in all groups of those of peasant origin is indicated by a comparison of the two sets of figures. But as there seems no reason to expect that a jump occurred from almost zero to 23 percent and over, I would conclude that the 1934 data was collected poorly or that a peculiar definition was used for "peasant." The 1936 proportion seems far more in line with what could be expected, and thus it is the 1934 rather than the 1936 study which should be ignored.

[31] Post. of the TsK VKP(b), *Pravda*, September 7, 1929, p. 1.

sonal careers. This is indicated both by a sample study of my own, which will be discussed below in this chapter, and by the fact that chief engineers—despite the fact that 70 percent of them had held leading posts in the economy since Civil War days—had roughly the same distribution of time of service at the same post as had directors. Department superintendents (these latter for 1936 only) also had the same pattern of rates of turnover, and glavki chiefs leaned only slightly toward greater length of service.[32]

SUMMARY OF 1934-36 MATERIAL: Let us now combine these different statistical characterizations of managerial personnel so as to derive a picture of each group. This description, it should be remembered, applies directly only to the 1934-36 period.

Directors. The personal background of the vast majority of this group was that of manual hired laborer, and the fathers of half of them had also been workers. Thus they personally epitomized the Soviet slogan of "Dictatorship of the Proletariat." They were a group composed almost entirely of Party members. Directors were young to middle-aged people of 30 to 50, and the average one joined the Party in his early twenties during the period of the Party's rise to power and Civil War struggle to maintain itself. In 1934, half had no formal education whatsoever, and only one quarter were graduate engineers; but this was a rapidly changing picture, with the proportions shifting to 40 percent and 45 percent respectively by 1936. This sharp rise in the percentage of those with higher education was not nearly so much due to the influx of young graduates as to the education of those who had already established themselves as skilled administrators. In 1934, two thirds of the directors had been in their particular branch of industry for over five years, and one quarter for more than ten years. Thus they were far from being new recruits to industry from Party or other work. On the other hand, one third had held their present posts for less

[32] Figures for 1934 show a much higher turnover for heads of glavki. But these figures are not comparable to those assembled for managerial personnel of firms, as the glavki were mostly new creations of the early thirties. Glavki heads may have earlier held virtually identical posts under different titles. To a certain extent, this causes even in the statistics for 1936 a bias toward brevity of work at the same post. It is for this reason that I conclude that glavki heads remained at their posts for longer periods than did plant management personnel, although the statistics indicate this to only a minute degree.

than one year, and another half of the original total had held them for only one to three years. Thus their mobility from job to job was extremely high.

Chief engineers. In sharp contrast to their immediate superiors, almost all of these first assistants in the firms had a white-collar background. Only half of their parents, however, were white-collar. Two thirds of them were not Party members, and this proportion held equally well for the younger men as for the older ones. Even those who belonged to the Party were relatively late arrivals, their date of entrance being spread rather equally from 1917 to 1934. Although their age distribution was like that of the directors, the average chief engineer who was a Party member had joined four years later than had the average director. Ninety percent of them had a regular engineering education. Seventy percent had held administrative posts during the Civil War period. Those who had worked in their given branch of industry for over ten years comprised 50 percent of the total—or twice as high a proportion as that holding among the directors. Thus it is clear that chief engineers were essentially engineers with a middle-class background and with comparatively lengthy experience in operating industrial units. While the directors generally had begun their careers on a Party basis and only later achieved status and know-how in industry, the chief engineers were men of the same generation who had begun in the engineering schools and then had gone into industry. Even the Party members among them had joined mainly when the Party was firmly established and when membership was an important aid to their industrial careers.

Department superintendents. This group of intermediate management was made up of men younger than those composing the top management of the firms. Ten percent were under 30, and 60 to 70 percent under 40. Almost half of this intermediate management were of white-collar origin, and only half were members of the Party. Their educational qualifications were relatively high: 55 percent in 1934, and 80 percent by 1936 had finished regular engineering courses. Both at this time and in later years, intermediate management was characterized by a rather low percentage of Party membership. This fact seems to prove that recruitment to this level has not been on a Party basis. Evidently, the slogan of promotion of "non-Party Bolsheviks" appears to have been realized here. Department superintendents were predominantly Soviet-trained intelligentsia. Yet it is interesting to note that almost half were of white-collar origin, a reflection of the great advantages held by the small prerevolutionary intelligentsia in giving their children a higher education despite Governmental efforts to discriminate in favor of workers and peasants.

Heads of glavki. These were occupants of posts of great responsibility, and had the necessary political and technical qualifications. Virtually all were Party members, over one third having joined before 1917 and the rest in the period of the fight for gaining and retaining power. Thus their length of Party membership was considerably higher than that of any other group. Almost two thirds had a standard higher education. Of all the managerial groups, they had the greatest seniority in their industrial branch; 60 percent had worked in their given branch of industry for over ten years. As is not surprising in view of their many and varied qualifications, they were an older group than the others. Almost two thirds were over 40, and 10 percent above 50. The personal background of more than two thirds of them, and the family background of over half, was white-collar; this, indeed, is what would be expected in terms of the educational demands made upon them. Judging by political experience, education, technical experience, and age, they were indeed the "senior management" of Soviet industry.

CHARACTERISTICS AS SHOWN IN A SAMPLE MADE BY THE WRITER

The above information regarding management is taken from official Soviet studies of 1934-36 which correlate rather well with each other. Now we shall try to push somewhat beyond these statistics both in regard to the scope of the questions raised and to the period studied. This will be done on the basis of a sample composed solely of firm directors, and obtained by me from a reading of the daily press of heavy industry from 1934 through June, 1941. A detailed description of the sampling method used and the results obtained is given in Appendix B.[33]

[33] The sample includes 505 directors who at some time during the years studied

The directors included in my sample have been separated into three groups. Group I includes all those who were directors of firms during the period from January, 1934, through March, 1937; Group II includes all directors in the April, 1937-June, 1938, period; and Group III all those of the July, 1938-June, 1941, period. Directors who headed a plant during two or three periods will be included in more than one group. This time-division is based on the fact that the middle period is that of the great purges of directors in which many were ousted as "spies, wreckers, and saboteurs."[34] By a pre-Purge, Purge, and post-Purge categorization we can best test the effect of these purges on the composition and background of directors.[35]

SHIFTS FROM POST TO POST: Statistics for 1934 and 1936 show that directors, like all other firm management personnel studied, had held their posts for only a very brief time. Seventy-five percent had headed their firms for less than three years, and one quarter to one third for under one year.

My sample indicates that this great mobility continued right through the prewar period. The mobility of directors was the same in the Third Period as in the First, and in the Second Period (the Purge) was far higher.

Evidently, little attention was ever paid to the 1929 Party decree demanding that directors be retained longer at their posts. Managers were given little chance to develop a proprietary feeling for "their" firm. They were treated as important personnel in a

headed 224 firms. While the sample is heavily weighted toward the inclusion of directors of large plants, there is nothing to indicate that this bias affects the particular frequency distributions which I have drawn from the sample.

[34] The April, 1937, date for the beginning of the Purge Period is chosen because a reading of the daily industrial press shows that it was in this month that plant directors began to be seriously affected. While major purge trials had occurred considerably earlier, the repercussions do not seem to have reached the level of plant directors until then. June, 1938, is chosen more or less arbitrarily as the cut-off date, for the reduction in the rate of removals by purging does not seem to have been sudden, and no precise month could be chosen with accuracy.

[35] It should be noted explicitly that we are not testing the effect of the purges on managerial efficiency. We are not investigating the effects on production of the great increase in rate of turnover among managerial personnel. We are not inquiring into the effect of the purges on the morale and initiative of management personnel. All that we shall try to examine are the areas of continuity and change in the personal backgrounds of directors in the different periods.

huge industrial organization covering the entire country, and were likely to be transferred anywhere within it.

When we look at the paths by which directors reached their positions we see that the latter periods showed a striking change in the pattern of advancement. Eighty percent of the directors during the First Period had been at least moderately successful in fields other than industry (e.g., as Communist Party or city government officials or as military commanders) before beginning their industrial careers. In both the Second and Third Periods, however, only one third of the directors had had such a start. Thus, with the Purge, we see a sharp drop in the proportion of those who had made their mark before ever entering industrial management. The later directors were predominantly men whose careers had always been in industry.[36]

Another way of gaining insight into the paths followed by those who became directors is to inquire as to the post they held immediately before the directorship which brought them into our sample. Unfortunately, the subsamples containing such information are too small to be divided into more than three groupings of immediately preceding posts—jobs within a firm and below the level of director, directorships of other firms, and positions in industrial organs above the firm level (mainly in glavki and commissariats). In the First Period, our directors are divided equally among the three groups; in the Second and Third, the third grouping drops to below one fifth of the total while the other two rise to a level of about 40 percent each.[37]

The most noteworthy feature of the sample material bearing on

[36] The percentage figures cannot be considered as being at all exact, due to the tiny size of the sample about which we have information. However, the drop from the First Period to the other two is so sharp as to seem fairly reliable. In addition, and this is of great importance, the results are quite in conformity with what we are led to expect from other information. E.g., see S. M. Schwarz in G. Bienstock, S. M. Schwarz, and A. Yugow, *Management in Russian Industry and Agriculture* (London, New York, Toronto: 1944), pp. 104-24.

[37] A statistical test of significance between the First Period and the other two shows that such differences in groupings would occur 5 to 10 percent of the time due to chance, even if the distribution in the different periods was actually the same. Thus the difference in the percentages could not be taken as significant by itself. But knowledge of the existence of a campaign during 1931-33 of transfers of personnel from high trust, glavk, and commissariat positions to directors' posts, and the fact that no equivalent transfer campaign occurred later, causes me to accept the percentage changes from the First Period at face value.

this question is the high proportion of directors—ranging in the three periods from 31 percent to 46 percent of those about whom we have information—who had been transferred from an identical post in another firm. Often, of course, these transfers were really promotions since the directors moved to more important plants; less frequently they were demotions. Sometimes they were caused by the desire to place a capable man at the head of a firm which was doing badly, while his old plant, where everything was under control, could safely be given to another executive. But irrespective of the particular reason, it is clear that no great weight was given to the Party decision that directors should remain for a reasonably long time at the head of the same firm. Moreover, directors seem normally to have been transferred alone to their new firm. Occasionally a director would bring his own staff with him, but such a move tended to arouse hostile comment.[38]

The considerable size of the group which had earlier worked in organs above the firm level is an expression of several distinct policies. The high percentage in the First Period is essentially due to the great effort at the beginning of the thirties to bring top young executives out of trust-glavk-commissariat work and into the management of important firms which were newly built or poorly operated.[39] The continuation of directors with this background into the two latter periods partly reflects the demotion of those who could not make the grade as heads of higher units. But it also represents Soviet administrative policy for binding together all levels of the industrial hierarchy ranging from shop to commissariat through the interchange of personnel in both directions.[40] Just as a man might get his chance as director through having been a successful department superintendent of a firm, so too he might be appointed director after having served in a minor post in the glavk.

The sample of those who had previously held lesser posts within a firm is too small to be subdivided in a statistically reliable fash-

[38] Cf. the case of Director Belenkovich, reported in Z.I., March 12, 1937, p. 3, and that of Director Nude, reported in Z.I., March 14, 1937, p. 3.

[39] TsUNKhU, Sostav rukovodiashchikh rabotnikov, p. 16.

[40] Cf. Z.I., January 24, 1935, p. 4. Also, "Ocherednye zadachi organizatsii proizvodstva v 1938 g." (The Next Tasks in the Organization of Production in 1938), Org. Uprav., 1938, No. 1, p. 17.

ion. Nevertheless, a rough breakdown can be presented. Over half of the directors had earlier been chief engineers or technical directors. The other 50 percent are divided fairly evenly between former department superintendents and those who had held one of an assortment of "other" posts. The large proportion of directors who had earlier been chief engineers—and the fact that this figure remained high in each of the three periods—may seem surprising in view of the marked statistical dissimilarity between directors and chief engineers during the 1934-36 period. However, it is quite apparent that directors could have been—and were—selected from among chief engineers without at all reflecting the characteristics of that group as a whole.

A similar procedure to the one described above for classifying directors according to their previous posts has been used for distinguishing between the various sequential histories of former directors. For each of the three periods, I have set up four categories for directors who were dismissed or shifted from their posts, i.e., those dismissed or transferred to a job within a firm lower than that of director; those transferred to another director's post; those transferred into organs above the firm level; and, finally, those transferred to "other" work.

Taking as a base the number of directors in the sample for each period who are known to have been transferred to a specific post or to have been dismissed, the proportion of those whose dismissal or transfer falls into each of the above four categories remained highly stable as between the three periods. However, the percentage of those dismissed or lowered in rank in heavy industry as a whole may well have increased during the Purge Period, although this is not definitely indicated by my sample.[41] Those dismissed, or lowered in grade but kept at work in a plant, ranged from 38 percent to 46 percent of the total. Transfers to the post of director of another firm were also high: 24 to 35 percent. Transfers into or-

---

[41] Taking as a base the total removals for each period shown in my sample, the percentage of such dismissals or transfers about which I have information making possible their categorization falls to its lowest point, 44 percent, in the Second Period. There is reason to think that a higher proportion of those politically purged than of those dismissed for incompetence were replaced without a newspaper account of the reason for the change or of their future status.

gans above firm rank ranged from 18 percent to 31 percent, while the "other" category numbered a negligible 5 to 8 percent.

The transfer of a director into a glavk or commissariat was usually a promotion. The post of director was a common stepping stone to the top management positions of heavy industry as a whole, that is, the posts of commissar, assistant commissar, and glavk head.

In fact, of all directors listed in the First Period, 6 percent of them reached one of these senior management positions at some time before June, 1941. Of the directors in the Second and Third Periods, 11 percent and 12 percent respectively reached these posts.[42] It can readily be seen that a successful director could regard his career as having great possibilities, and a glance at the statistics shows that these possibilities were indeed real.

CHANGES WITHIN THE 1934-41 PERIOD: It is clear, both from my own sample and from other generalizing reports, that significant changes did occur in the composition of plant directors. However, these were changes which would seem the inevitable accompaniments of a more stable industrialized economy and of a longer period in power for the ruling party.

As has been described above, the educational level of directors sharply increased during the period. From being the exception it became the rule for a director in heavy industry to be a graduate engineer.

At the same time, the proportion of directors who had first made their mark outside of industry sharply declined. As the directors of the earlier thirties either advanced to new heights or fell out of the running in this highly mobile hierarchy of executives, their places tended to be taken by men brought up in industry's own ranks. Soviet-trained engineers became the directors; they were either men who had graduated when still youths and had worked their way up in the engineering-management ranks, or men who having proved their ability as skilled workmen and foremen, had been sent to engineering colleges and then had returned to indus-

[42] It should be remembered that there was a great increase during the latter thirties in the number of glavki and commissariats.

try with a solid combination of a work-and-education background. In either case, the director was a better trained technician than his predecessor had been. More and more as the years went by, he was an executive who possessed the knowledge and experience which Stalin had declared essential for really exercising "one-man-authority-and-responsibility."

The Purge Period only intensified this development. The Soviet people themselves speak of the period from early 1937 through the middle of 1938 as one of widespread and rapid advancement of personnel throughout all industry,[43] and certainly such promotion was an essential counterpart to the removal of former executives. But it should be remembered that the mobility had been great before the Purge and continued equally so thereafter.

Other features, uncorrelated with the change in favor of the engineer-director whose entire career had been in industry, remained highly stable. There was no change regarding the posts from which men became directors.[44] Similarly, the next posts to which former directors were transferred remained the same.[45]

CONCLUDING REMARKS

The executives of Soviet heavy industry contrast sharply with the managerial group of modern industry elsewhere in the world. Political reliability is stressed as an even more important qualification than expert knowledge. There is no place in management's ranks for those who view their work from a technical as opposed to a political standpoint. The accent is on youth, rather than on older men who have steadily advanced to the higher grades. An official's life is far from secure; a director may rocket up to the post of commissar or suddenly be demoted or dismissed. All that he

[43] Cf. the order No. 85 of the Commissar of Machine Construction of February 20, 1938, *Mash.*, February 21, 1938, p. 1. See also, the lead editorial in *Ind.*, December 31, 1937, p. 1.

[44] Except for a reduction in those coming from higher organs. The high percentage of these directors in the First Period had been due to 1931-33 policy which even then had been considered as temporary.

[45] Solomon Schwarz considers that from the mid-thirties on there were relatively few manual workers who found their way into managerial ranks either by direct promotion or through the medium of an engineering education. (Bienstock, Schwarz, and Yugow, *op. cit.*, pp. 121-22.) My reading, however, lends no support whatsoever to this point of view. The continuous reports of promotion from the ranks seems to indicate the direct opposite.

can be sure of is that there is little chance that he will direct the same plant for long.

It can be argued that some of the distinguishing characteristics of Soviet executives and of their work-environment have been largely a result of the newness of the regime and of its sharp break from Russia's past. The political approach may be considered as an out-growth of the dangers threatening the Communist Party regime both externally and internally. Youth of management can be viewed as a combined product of the political events which elimi-nated prerevolutionary managers, of the great industrialization which took place, and of the political purging which has occurred.

That these factors were of major importance cannot be denied. But to see them as all-important causes appears to me quite as fallacious as it would be to ignore them. The Soviet industrial ex-ecutive has been quite unlike his counterpart in other countries mainly because of the administrative system within which he has operated. Standards of recruitment have been entirely different, and so have been the demands made upon the officials.

For example, let us take the political qualifications required of candidates for managerial positions in industry. Soviet theoreti-cians completely reject the concept that the industrial executive should be judged purely as a technician. They insist that the execu-tive's personal approval or disapproval of policies enunciated by higher authorities is highly relevant, and they deny that his task is to implement whatever program may be handed to him.

Instead, they start from the basic premise of the unity of econom-ics and politics. While admitting that questions of economics can be distinguished from those of politics for purposes of classroom study, they consider them inseparable in life itself.[46] It is said that every major decision reflects the political conditions of the country, and thus that alternatives must be evaluated from the point of view of politics and not solely of economic effectiveness.[47] Soviet leaders insist that the following problems must always be posed: What will be the direct and indirect effects of a particular decision on the

[46] I. Stalin, Concluding remarks of March 5, 1937, to the Plenum of the TsK VKP(b), Z.I., April 1, 1937, pp. 1-2.

[47] I. Stalin, Lenin i Stalin, Volume II (Moscow: 1936), p. 364, as quoted by K. Ostro-vitianov in "Politika i ekonomika v sotsialisticheskom obshchestve" (Politics and Economics in Socialist Society), Problemy Ekonomiki, 1939, No. 6, p. 33.

political conditions within the country and in the world as a whole? Will the decision advance or impair the "victory of socialism"? They declare that such political questions should always take priority over those limited to economics,[48] such as: What is the relative cost in rubles of two alternative policies? Will a budgetary loss or profit arise from the manufacture of particular products in a given area?[49]

But if, to paraphrase Stalin, "it is necessary before taking any decision [of general State significance] to evaluate it from a political point of view,"[50] then who is in a better position to make this evaluation from the political viewpoint than the single political party of the country, the party which has taken upon itself responsibility for guiding all the efforts of the nation?

At this point in our study, the materials to be presented later may be anticipated by the statement that success criteria for management are not sharply defined, and that a clear announcement of the relative weight to be given to the various desiderata is normally lacking. Thus it has been considered by Soviet thinkers as imperative that lower officials should approach problems from the same point of view as does the country's top leadership. Guidance through issuance of policy-statements would be impossible if all officials did not interpret these programs and their emphases in a reasonably similar fashion.

For these reasons, the Communist Party is viewed as the natural recruiting ground for industrial executives. How better realize the goal of having all officials share a common philosophy, a single approach to all policy problems? Who can better interpret the Party program than Party members themselves? Moreover, according to Soviet writers, a policy of recruiting executives from within the Party is justified by the Party objective of uniting the "best" and most politically active people within its ranks. One legal textbook states bluntly that the Communist Party places its own members in

---

[48] *Ibid.*

[49] The significance of "political" as opposed to "purely economic" criteria of decision making, a delicate and difficult problem, will be analyzed in Chapter XIV. The question of the importance of such "political analyses" by executives on the plant level will be examined in the light of Soviet experience.

[50] Stalin, as quoted by Ostrovitianov, *op. cit.,* p. 33.

leading posts of government work and exercises strict Party discipline over all their actions.[51]

Yet the Party urges that the filling of managerial positions from its own ranks should not be overdone. It argues that "non-Party Bolsheviks," possessing initiative and organizational ability, should have equal opportunity for advancement to leadership posts. Formal Party membership should not be a criterion of promotion.[52]

Nevertheless, while it is insisted that "non-Party Bolsheviks" be given responsibility, the "Bolshevik" part of the term has never been played down. Of the two criteria for choosing personnel for leadership posts, Stalin has placed political reliability first and fitness for the concrete job second.[53] In what was obviously intended as an amplification for industry of this then unpublished remark, an industrial leader's political reliability was defined as consisting of his political preparation and seasoning, his activity and skill in educating people in the spirit of devotion to Soviet power.[54] Earlier, Stalin had called for a technical intelligentsia created from the working class, rather than from the prerevolutionary intelligentsia, and therefore capable of understanding and applying Soviet policy.[55]

There has been constant reference to Commissar Ordzhoni-

---

[51] *Sovetskoe gosudarstvennoe pravo* (Soviet State Law), issued by the Ministry of Higher Education of the USSR as a textbook for law schools and law faculties (Moscow: 1948), pp. 285-86. It should be noted that Soviet works which are officially listed as textbooks thereby gain an authoritativeness far beyond what they would otherwise have.

[52] Iu. Kaganovich, "Smelee vydvigat' bespartiinykh na rukovodiashchuiu rabotu" (For the Bolder Advancement of Non-Party People to Administrative Work), *Part. Stroit.*, 1938, No. 11, p. 30. Resolution on Organizational Questions of the XVIIth Congress of the VKP(b), *XVII s"ezd VKP(b)*, p. 673. Post. of the TsK VKP(b) of March 4, 1938, *Part. Stroit.*, 1938, No. 6, p. 62.

Superficially considered, the recruitment of key executives from the Party's own ranks seems irreconcilable with the demand for equal opportunity of advancement for "non-Party Bolsheviks." But when we remember that the Party prides itself on being the home of those who combine the proper personal qualities with politically mature "Bolshevik" views, the two themes fall into line. It is primarily junior personnel, or those senior executives who are not faced with daily "political" questions (e.g., a plant's chief engineer as opposed to its director), who can be the "non-Party Bolsheviks."

[53] Concluding remarks of March 5, 1937, to the Plenum of the TsK VKP(b), *Z.I.*, April 1, 1937, p. 1.

[54] Lead editorial of *Z.I.*, March 17, 1937, p. 1.

[55] *Voprosy Leninizma*, 10th edition, pp. 456-59.

kidze's slogan for industrial leaders: *"Party activity and belief—that is the main thing."* "That business executive, that director, that department superintendent who can . . . wholly preserve his Party spirit in a Bolshevik fashion—he'll go far. But nothing will come of those who get lost from this path. *Party activity and belief—above all and before all."*[56] The non-Party leader is usually conceived of as a Bolshevik who will later be admitted into the Party. From 1939 on, the Party Rules ceased to discriminate against white-collar workers and executives as candidates for Party membership.[57] Presumably this change caused an increase in the proportion of junior executives who were Party members. Top officials, men who have been leaders over a period of time, have, as we have seen, almost always been Party members.

In my view, this emphasis on the "Bolshevik" character of all executives arises from the fundamental nature of the Soviet administrative system. It arises both from the Soviet emphasis on the unity of economics and politics, and from the conception that the executive must be able to interpret properly national policies and be given reasonable independence and authority in carrying them out.

[56] G. K. Ordzhonikidze, *Izbrannye stat'i i rechi 1911-1937* (Selected Articles and Speeches 1911-1937), edited by A. I. Mikoian, L. Z. Mekhlis, L. P. Beriia and Z. G. Ordzhonikidze (Moscow: 1939), p. 292. Italics in original.

[57] Rules of the VKP(b), adopted by the XVIIIth Party Congress. *(VKP[b] v rez.*, 6th edition, Moscow: 1941, pp. 756-57.) Prior to this time, the Party Rules had made it more difficult for such personnel than for manual workers to join the Party and more easy for them to be removed from membership. (Cf. the Rules adopted in 1934 by the XVIIth Party Congress, *ibid.*, pp. 589-90.) The Rules adopted in 1925 by the XIVth Party Congress (*ibid.*, pp. 80-81) were discriminatory regarding admission into the Party but not with regard to exclusions from the Party.

IV: Formation of Plans

A FUNDAMENTAL FEATURE of Soviet heavy industry is the planned character of its operations. Decisions as to the proper development of the various branches are made by the Council of Commissars. While indirect methods such as that of price policy are used for achieving desired goals, reliance is to a very great extent placed upon the setting of specific tasks for subordinate bodies. Thus commissariats, glavki, and firms all have their plans of work which have been approved by higher bodies, and they are judged according to the fulfillment of their plans' principal indices.

At the summit of the system stands the Council of Commissars. Its task is to approve the annual and quarterly plans of the commissariats and of their major units. Immediately below are the Economic Council and the State Planning Commission, both attached to the Council of Commissars and doing the work of preparing and sifting programs for its final approval. These three bodies supervise the entire economy, and so are in a position to coordinate the plans of the many different commissariats.

The splitting up of commissariats since the end of 1936 vastly increased the importance and difficulties of centralized planning by the Council of Commissars and its agencies. While the needs of one branch of heavy industry and the production of another branch could be coordinated within the Commissariat of Heavy Industry itself so long as it headed both branches, the State Planning Commission and the Economic Council had to asume the task once the branches were placed in different commissariats. Thus the Economic Council was created and the role of the State Planning Commission was enlarged.[1]

[1] Cf. E. Lokshin, "Organizatsionnye problemy promyshlennosti SSSR" (Organiza-

Planning for Soviet industry has in reality been a continuous process rather than one which could be incorporated into sharply distinct plans made for specific periods. But for purposes of presentation, it is convenient to distinguish between that planning which is embodied in five-year, annual, and quarterly plans and that which is not given this official character. Only the first type will be discussed in this chapter. By a similarly arbitrary division of the material, there will be no treatment here of the formation of plans for procurement or for marketing of products. Moreover, our interest is not in plan formation in general, but solely in the plans developed for the firms and in the firms' role in planning. Other aspects of plan formation will be treated only incidentally.

FUNCTIONS OF PLANS

Soviet plans have been made for periods of unequal length, those for the briefest time spans being the most concrete. While the Five-Year Plans have been given by far the greatest publicity, it is the annual and quarterly plans which have been more closely enforced, and which have served as the basis for industrial operations.

Soviet plans have a number of purposes. They serve to present a goal and an inspiration to the general public; they pick out the chief points of concentration for the coming period; finally, they integrate the economy and set separate tasks for each of its elements.

The Five-Year Plans seem to be devoted primarily to the first two purposes. Since they cover a sufficient number of years for economic changes within the period to be noticeable to the average man, it is naturally they which have been given the greatest publicity, and the Soviets have talked of successes primarily in terms of these Five-Year Plans. But it is precisely this same time span, with the uncertainty as to specific developments which is implicit in its length, that makes these Plans poor tools in the work of making concrete the tasks of firms and in the detailed integration of the many branches of industry.

Thus no serious planning difficulty is implied in the fact that the Five-Year Plans have been formally accepted considerably after the

tional Problems of the Industry of the USSR), *Problemy Ekonomiki*, 1939, No. 4, p. 51. Also see "Rabotu Gosplana—na uroven' novykh zadach" (The Work of the State Planning Commission—on the Level of the New Tasks), *Planovoe Khoziaistvo*, 1948, No. 2, p. 19.

beginning of the periods which they were to govern. The Second Plan ran from 1933 through 1937, but was only formally accepted by a Party Congress in early 1934.[2] Furthermore, it was intended that it be concretely implemented on the firm and trust level only by June, 1934.[3] The Third, starting in 1938, was not adopted until 1939.[4]

Despite the absence of specificity in the Five-Year Plans, considerable attention has been given to their formation. The Second Plan was worked on for eighteen months to two years, and twenty-four All-Union conferences and consultations as well as dozens of commissariat and regional conferences were held to aid the State Planning Commission in working out the Plan.[5] While this Plan did not contain any production figures for individual firms, five-year projects for those within the Commissariat of Heavy Industry were to be worked out in 1934 on the basis of it.[6] It is in this fashion that the broad outlines of the projected development of the economy have been set forth.

But the plans upon which the industrial system actually has depended are the annual ones. A further refinement is the quarterly plan, but this has not normally been intended to be other than an elaboration of the annual. Both annual and quarterly plans for the commissariats are approved by the Council of Commissars, those for the glavki by the commissariats and those for the firms by the glavki.[7] The plans consist of directives as to production quotas,

---

[2] *Vtoroi piatiletnii plan razvitiia narodnogo khoziaistva SSSR*, Tom pervyi (The Second Five-Year Plan for the Development of the National Economy of the USSR, Volume One), (Moscow: 1936), p. 3.

[3] *Z.I.*, March 3, 1934, p. 4.

[4] Resolution adopted on March 20, 1939, by the XVIIIth Congress VKP(b), "The Third Five-Year Plan for the National-Economic Development of the USSR," *XVIII s"ezd Vsesoiuznoi Kommunisticheskoi Partii (b)* (XVIIIth Congress of the All-Union Communist Party), stenographic report (Moscow: 1939), pp. 648-67. The report which served as the basis for the Resolution set forth certain changes in the basic theses of the Five-Year Plan from their earlier provisional statement. Cf. V. Molotov, "Report of March 14, 1939, to the XVIIIth Party Congress on the Third Five-Year Plan for the Development of the National Economy of the USSR," *XVIII s"ezd VKP(b)*, pp. 292-93.

[5] Ts. Gal'perin, "Iz opyta sostavleniia vtorogo piatiletnego plana" (From the Experience of Establishing the Second Five-Year Plan), *Planovoe Khoziaistvo*, 1936, No. 3, p. 70.

[6] *Z.I.*, March 3, 1934, p. 4.

[7] This hierarchical system is not rigidly followed. Plans for some highly important firms may even be approved by the Council of Commissars itself.

types and qualities of goods to be produced, labor productivity to be achieved, the size and average pay of the labor force, the total wages and salaries to be paid, the average cost of products, and the size of the capital investment for the period.[8] Procurement and marketing agreements between firms are signed on the basis of annual plans; and materials, working capital, and moneys for construction and equipment are allotted on the basis of the plans.

FORMATION OF ANNUAL PLANS

In drawing up the plans, a fundamental contradiction inherent in centralization must be faced. While the national plan must be determined centrally in order to achieve both over-all national goals and internal consistency within the economy,[9] it is also true that if planning is not done by personnel of the actual production units, it will tend to be unrealistic. While setting impossible tasks for at least some units, such planning will at the same time ignore genuine possibilities for advances. Soviet theorists state this problem as the need for "planning from above and from below."

The process of making annual plans has been roughly the following.[10] Before the end of the old year compilations of existing industrial data are made and estimates are derived for the remaining months before the beginning of the period to be covered by the new plan. On the basis of this picture of the economy, the Council of Commissars lays down the broad political and economic aims of the new plan[11] and the technical policies to be followed.[12]

Founded on these instructions of the top Governmental body,

[8] Cf. *Narodnokhoziaistvennyi plan na 1936 god* (The National Economic Plan for 1936), 2d edition (Moscow: 1936).

[9] By internal consistency is meant the correct relationships of supply between the different sectors of the economy. For example, steel-using industries cannot be expanded without a compensating growth in steel production.

[10] Ia. Luganin, "Administration and Planning of Industry in the USSR," manuscript translation from the original Russian of the Soviet author, no Russian copy being available. (The manuscript was seen at the now defunct American Russian Institute in New York City.) Events described show it was written after March, 1946. A general reading of laws and articles roughly confirms much of the description given by Luganin.

[11] The approximate increase of industrial output, the percentage of output to be devoted to capital accumulation, the priority items of the plan, etc.

[12] Determination of technological processes to be inaugurated, the program of industrial mechanization, etc.

planning is carried on simultaneously by the State Planning Commission and by each commissariat. While the State Planning Commission develops preliminary plans of production and supply for each branch of the economy, the commissariats draw up their separate first-draft plans and inform the firms of their respective tasks under them. The firms work out schedules of fuel, materials, and equipment needed to fulfill these programs, and offer suggestions for changes in the proposed production. On the basis of such "planning from below" the commissariats amend their drafts and submit them to the State Planning Commission, which in turn checks the drafts against its own plans and draws up a composite plan for submission to the Council of Commissars. When the final national plan is approved, the commissariats revise their draft-tasks for firms and these draw up final annual plans which must be approved by the commissariats.[13]

Here we have a triple process of planning from above, counter-planning from below, and final determination of the plans from above. But this procedure is one which tends to be lengthy, while if the plans are actually to guide the economy it must be exceedingly rapid. Planning cannot be begun too early or its assumptions as to the state of the economy at the beginning of the planning period will be seriously in error. It cannot last too long or the plan will not be ready in time for the period it is intended to govern. Many of the compromises and difficulties in Soviet planning can be described in terms of the conflict between the pressure for speed of operation through "planning from above," and the truer expression of actual conditions which is achieved by "planning from below."

For while the Soviet leaders acclaim expansions in "planning from below" as important successes,[14] the maximum time which they have found possible to allot to the entire planning procedure

[13] Regional planning organizations include in their own plans all firms within their geographic areas. See "Novoe polozhenie o raionnykh planovykh komissiiakh" (The New Statute on the District Planning Commissions), *Planovoe Khoziaistvo*, 1938, No. 1, pp. 126-29. Also, I. Gaisinovich, "Sistema pokazatelei narodnokhoziaistvennogo plana raionov na 1937 g." (The System of Indices for the National Economic Plan of Districts for 1937), *Plan*, 1937, No. 2, p. 30.

[14] Cf. the article by V. Kiselev, head of the sector on methodology of the Planning Section of the Commissariat of General Machine Construction, in *Mash.*, October 14, 1939, p. 2.

is four to five months,[15] a period which often curtails the realization of "planning from below."[16] Often such planning cannot be developed until higher organs lengthen the period to be devoted to the planning process.[17]

Despite the difficulties, plant managements often have played an active role in determining the "limits" (tasks and the resources available for fulfilling them) to be set for their plants.[18] Their reason for interest in these "limits" is obvious, and informal relations with higher organs have greatly facilitated the possibilities for such participation. But their actual influence has differed with time and according to their particular branch of industry. The varying patterns can be seen in examples taken from two industries and two different years.

In preparing the first variant of the 1939 plan for the Glavk of the Metallurgical Industry, firms were asked to present the Glavk with their own programs for production output, with proposed coefficients of use of specific raw materials and fuels, and with other indices as well. But as the largest firms had not presented this material by the middle of September, 1938, the Glavk proceeded to make its plan without them.[19] Similarly, the Glavk of the Copper Industry did not receive from its firms any proposed construction projects or production plans which it could use as a basis for its own preliminary plan for 1938; but it did have such data for 1939.[20]

Ideally, one would think that plans should be made by mutual consent of higher and lower bodies. But Soviet planners seem to consider this unnecessary. For they recognize that there is a strong tendency for each organization to consider its plan from its own, rather than from the national, point of view. Often firm directors consider it "charity" on their part to accept a plan containing ambitious elements which they have the power to eliminate.[21] This attitude was strongly condemned in the late thirties and in the

[15] Cf. A. I. But, *Planirovanie v tsvetnoi metallurgii* (Planning in Nonferrous Metallurgy) (Moscow: 1946), pp. 7-8.

[16] Cf. *Ind.*, September 17, 1938, p. 2.

[17] Cf. the article of V. Kiselev in *Mash.*, October 14, 1939, p. 2.

[18] Cf. *Soveshchanie khoziaistvennikov 1934 g.*, p. 177. Article by Director I. G. Makarov in *Z.I.*, August 24, 1935, p. 2. Letter signed by Director I. Loskutov and other executives of the Gor'kii Molotov Auto Plant, in *Mash.*, December 30, 1938, p. 2.

[19] *Ind.*, September 17, 1938, p. 2.

[20] *Ind.*, September 18, 1938, p. 1.

[21] Cf. *Z.I.*, May 8, 1934, p. 3.

forties, and its continued prevalence caused higher bodies to impose their own concepts of proper "limits."

At the same time, firm managements have been in a position to fight against what they consider as poor planning by their glavki. They may condemn their own glavk's plan in the leading industrial press.[22] They may appeal—and with success—over their glavk's head to the commissar.[23] A nationally famous case particularly exemplifies the prestige of plant suggestions, and the weapons a plant management possesses with which to fight for its own ideas as to its proper annual plan. The director of the largest rubber-fabricating plant in the country was removed in a disciplinary action for fighting against his firm's plan even after it had been confirmed by the highest bodies of the country. Yet as a result of his fight, the head of the glavk which had established the production plan was ordered to assume temporarily the duties of director of the plant.[24] Thus the man who had approved the plan which had been condemned by the director as impossible to fulfill was required to take on the job of carrying it out. In such an environment, the management of a firm may not be able to determine the tasks set for it, but it does have strong weapons with which to combat the imposition of impossible programs.

In conclusion, the role given to "planning from below" is essentially that of a corrective to the "planning from above." Objections can be made to portions of the proposed tasks for the firm, suggestions offered for substituting one type of product for another, statements presented showing required investment and supply. But the setting of tasks is basically done from above, where there is a greater knowledge of the needs of the economy and of the capabilities of the entire industry.[25]

It is in the detailing of the plans for their own firms that personnel within the plants have played their main planning role. The annual "technical-production-financial" plans of the firms are the culmination of the annual national plans. They are the basis of

[22] Cf. the letter of Director Loskutov and other executives of the Gor'kii Molotov Auto Plant, in *Mash.*, December 30, 1938, p. 2.

[23] Cf. *Z.I.*, August 24, 1935, p. 2.

[24] Prikaz (Order) No. 32 of the Commissariat of Heavy Industry (hereafter cited as the NKTP) of January 8, 1934, *Z.I.*, January 9, 1934, p. 1.

[25] Cf. V. Kontorovich, *Tekhpromfinplan promyshlennogo predpriiatiia* (The Technical-Industrial-Financial Plan of the Industrial Firm) (Moscow: 1948), pp. 19-22. But, *op. cit.*, pp. 7-8. *Ind.*, September 9, 1938, p. 2. *Mash.*, December 9, 1938, p. 2.

the production work of the firms and are the foundation of the firms' quarterly and monthly planning and of their daily scheduling.[26]

The management of the firm is responsible for drawing up the firm's final plan. But this technical-production-financial plan is based on "limits" set by the glavk or commissariat, and must finally be approved by the same body. It is only a slight exaggeration to state that the "limits" present all the basic tasks and indices of the firm's plan,[27] while the plan itself provides detailed measures for carrying out these tasks.[28]

Nevertheless, some of the planning for the firm's plan is done before the receipt of these "limits." This preliminary planning deals with the use of production resources and with technical development.[29] Such planning can be done before the receipt of "limits" since it is not tied too intimately to the size and nature of the tasks given. It is considered that such planning within the firm should begin in the middle of the old year and that more detailed planning should proceed in the final quarter.[30]

[26] Cf. P. A. Shein, *Material'no-tekhnicheskoe snabzhenie mashinostroitel'nykh zavodov* (Materials-Technical Procurement of Machine Construction Plants), (Moscow-Leningrad: 1947), p. 102. Also, But, *op. cit.,* pp. 7-8.

[27] In nonferrous metallurgy, the "limits" have been as follows: 1. *Size, quality, and assortment of production.* The quantity of production is given both in natural terms (e.g., kilograms, meters) and in money value. 2. *Capital expenditures* expressed as a listing of the main units to be constructed or of the machinery to be bought. 3. *Labor and wages.* The number of workers are broken down into different categories, and the annual sum of wages for each category is given. Also, a figure is presented for productivity per worker to be achieved.

4. *Costs.* Either the percentage that costs are to be reduced during the year is stated, or unit cost for a limited assortment of products is given.

5. *Materials supply.* Funds of materials, fuel, and equipment are presented. 6. *Financing.* The firm's working capital is given and also the extent of financing of capital construction from other sources. (But, *op. cit.,* pp. 8-9.)

These detailed "limits" are not universal, each commissariat and glavk determining its own. But they seem to represent the general pattern. (For comparison, see *Mash.,* December 9, 1938, p. 2.)

[28] The firm's technical-production-financial plan deals with the same subjects as the "limits" given above, only in a much more refined fashion and with breakdowns to the plant-department level. It is also highly concerned with planning the technical development of the firm during the year. (Kontorovich, *op. cit.,* pp. 19 and 233-35. Also, Shein, *op. cit.,* p. 103.)

[29] These include such items as detailing the present losses in use of resources and their causes and formulating measures to combat them, finding production bottlenecks, working out methods for technical improvements, and checking machinery and developing schedules for its regular repair. (Cf. Kontorovich, *op. cit.,* p. 22, and But, *op. cit.,* pp. 7-8.)

[30] Cf. Kontorovich, *op. cit.,* p. 22, and Shein, *op. cit.,* p. 102.

So far we have discussed only the "planning from below" which is engaged in by firm managements. But the desirability of participation by both workers and executives in such planning—acting as individuals rather than as occupants of particular posts—has also often been stressed in Soviet leaders' statements. Molotov has pointed to such participation as a powerful weapon for improving economic leadership, and has asserted that no capitalist country is able to use it.[31] Stalin has asserted that it is impossible for Soviet leaders to make correct decisions, carry them out, or check on their fulfillment without the direct aid of the masses.[32]

Thus in the making of plans, participation from below is encouraged. For example, Molotov's report on the Third Five-Year Plan was published at the end of January, 1939. Thereafter for over a month there was a discussion of the Plan in the press, with participants making suggestions for their various industries and individual plants. At the Party Congress in March, Molotov declared that the discussion had brought forth some valuable corrections and additions, which would be considered in the final Communist Party resolution about the goals of the Plan.[33]

Participation within the firm has occurred primarily in the working out of the firm's plan on the basis of its "limits." The firm management, the Party organization, and the trade union are all held responsible for mobilizing the employees for such participation in evolving measures to fulfill the assigned tasks.[34] This mobilization is organized through the creation of brigades in different departments and shops to design each section's place in the over-all plan of the firm.[35] The prime emphasis has been placed upon the participation of engineers and technicians and the best Stakhanovite workers.[36]

In the Soviet view, participation is a vital tool in improving the effectiveness of plans. If particular extensions of participation fail in this, they are dropped or given only minor attention. For while

[31] Report to the February-March Plenum of the TsK VKP(b), Z.I., April 21, 1937, p. 3.
[32] Concluding words of March 5, 1937, to the same Plenum, Z.I., April 1, 1937, p. 2.
[33] V. Molotov, Report of March 14, 1939, to the XVIIIth Party Congress, *XVIII s"ezd VKP(b)*, p. 292.
[34] Cf. Kontorovich, *op. cit.*, p. 20.
[35] *Ibid.*, p. 21.
[36] Cf. *Ind.*, September 9, 1938, p. 2.

the Soviet leaders talk of participation as an end in itself—as the very embodiment of democracy—they demand that it carry its own weight in improving industrial production. Thus, in practice, it is those who are technically skilled or are crack workers with an eye to the plant's problems who have been mobilized to participate in planning. Primarily, their contribution takes the form of suggestions as to how best to fulfill the tasks given their unit.[37]

CONCLUDING REMARKS

Throughout this chapter, we have seen that the process of Soviet plan-formation in industry has comprised two conflicting tendencies. "Participation"—embodied in the concept of "planning from below"—has served as a fundamental theoretic underpinning of the process. But pursuit of this principle has raised many practical problems which have led in practice to sharp modification of participation programs.

Soviet writers lay considerable stress on planning by plant management, but time pressures have forced this planning primarily into the channel of carrying out tasks set from above. Participation by workers is given great importance in theoretic statements; but in practice, it has been limited to those who can make the greatest technical contributions. The group of participants in the planning of production work has been kept relatively small, and even it has been given, primarily, only limited tasks of working out detailed plans for the shops and departments. Since mass participation in planning must inevitably slow up the work, its use has been restricted to those areas where it has been felt to be functional in terms of direct results. Its utilization has been measured in terms of gains and losses of production in the immediate planning period.

In short, the Soviet combination of "planning from below" with "planning from above" appears to have placed primary emphasis upon the efficiency advantages of the latter. This emphasis has reduced the actual role in planning of plant management below that indicated as desirable by Soviet theorists. Nevertheless, contrary to some current notions, planning has still been an important function of plant management.

[37] Cf. Chapter XIII.

V: Limitations of the Plan

FROM THE GREAT STRESS placed upon five-year, annual and quarterly plans both in Soviet and foreign literature, it would be easy to think of them as covering all the operations of the plants and as being highly precise programs which "good" administrators are duty-bound to execute with exactitude. Such conclusions would be quite erroneous.

In the first place, plans are neither comprehensive nor precise. Secondly, economic and political conditions change too rapidly for any plan to be able to express, half a year after the time when it was composed, the needs of the moment. Soviet recognition of these two factors has kept them from even trying to use plans as blueprints. "Revisions" and "reinterpretations" of the plan are not the exception but the rule.

It is the task of this chapter to demonstrate that Soviet plans have not set forth detailed goals which were intended to remain constant throughout the period covered by the plan, and that Soviet planning cannot be considered as primarily embodied in the approved plans. We shall see that these plans represent only the starting point of a continuous planning process. It is essential that the reader form a correct picture of the nature and limitations of planning if he is to have a proper understanding of the true functions of plant management.

THE EMPHASIS ON FLEXIBILITY

At least in the machine-construction industry, there has been a strong tendency for the plans to express total production only in monetary terms. A few main types of machinery to be produced have been named in the annual plans; the others have

been determined during the actual planning year by negotiations between producer and consumer firms and have been listed in contracts between them.[1] In 1937, no more than 1 to 2 percent of the production of one of the major firms building electrical equipment was planned according to categories.[2]

Not till late 1939 did the Commissariat of General Machine Construction begin the planning of auxiliary and secondary production for its firms.[3] Formerly, the firms handled this work without any plan. Plans have been made for the production of only a few types of spare parts;[4] others were produced in whatever proportion the firms and glavki decided throughout the year. Firms have in general been left on their own with regard to accepting orders from other producers for parts and semifabricates. Not before 1947 does such work seem to have been generally included in the firms' plans.[5]

Furthermore, no one expects plans to be precisely fulfilled. In an expanding economy, and one with constant changes in types of production, such expectations would be totally unreasonable. The uncertainty of these expectations is further increased by the fact that plans for labor productivity, consumption of fuels and materials per unit of product, and unit costs are all made on the assumption of steady improvement over the situation existing at the time the plans are drawn up. While some firms will exceed their plans, it is certain that others will fall behind. And although failures to meet plans are not condoned, they must be taken into account.

To meet the problems caused by overfulfillment by some firms and underfulfillment by others, reserve stocks are considered necessary.[6] Coke reserves, for example, permit steel production to proceed faster than planned even if coke production lags behind. Furthermore, stocks of fuels and materials take up slack in the regional variances from the plan which would otherwise necessitate great

---

[1] Cf. *Z.I.*, August 17, 1937, p. 2, and *Z.I.*, March 4, 1937, p. 2.

[2] The Kuibyshev Electrical Plant. (*Z.I.*, August 5, 1937, p. 2.)

[3] *Mash.*, October 14, 1939, p. 2.

[4] Cf. *Z.I.*, February 15, 1937, p. 2.

[5] Post. No. 3110 of the Council of Ministers of the USSR of September 2, 1947, reported on in Kontorovich, *op. cit.*, p. 58.

[6] L. Maizenberg, "O khoziaistvennom plane" (On the Economic Plan), *Planovoe Khoziaistvo* (Planned Economy), 1940, No. 10, p. 19.

excess shipping (e.g., if coke production in one area exceeded, and in another fell behind, the plan).

But clearly there are sharp limits to a policy of reserves if only because of storage problems. Besides, despite theoretic acceptance of a policy of reserves, the Soviet people seem to have been hard pressed to produce sufficient fuels and materials to keep up with their growth in capacity for producing finished goods.[7] Under these circumstances, it does not seem likely that they were able to accumulate massive fuel and material reserves during the thirties.

Failures in Soviet plan fulfillment can be met not only out of reserves of materials and products, but also through utilizing idle plant capacity. For while there are pious statements that proper planning requires full use of existing equipment, it is clear that this has not been a fundamental principle employed in the setting of production "limits." Firms, over their own protests, have been given smaller programs than those they had actually fulfilled the previous year.[8] Even a plant producing equipment badly needed by such a priority industry as oil was given a production program which left 40 percent of its machinery idle in the second shift, and 80 percent idle in the third. In describing this situation in a newspaper article, the firm's director explained the existence of this unused capacity by the fact that the existing use of machinery was sufficient to meet the production quotas set in the firm's plan. In fact, the director did not urge an increase in the plan's goals but rather proposed the elimination of the third shift.[9]

But although there are certain reserves of equipment and plant capacity available to fill up gaps in plan fulfillment, major ill effects still result from the insufficient coordination of the production of interdependent industries. There has, for example, been considerable unplanned idleness of plants. A glaring case of this is in the cement industry. From 1936 to 1940, the productive capacity of the industry rose by 22 percent, but during the same pe-

[7] Cf. G. Smirnov, head of the State Planning Commission of the USSR, "K itogam pervogo polugodiia 1937 goda" (On the Results of the First Half of 1937), *Plan*, 1937, No. 13, pp. 5-7. Commissar F. A. Merkulov, Speech to the XVIIIth Party Congress, *Ind.*, March 22, 1939, p. 4. *Ind.*, June 3, 1940, p. 1.

[8] Cf. the article by V. A. Pavlov, Director of the October Victory Factory, in *Z.I.*, February 14, 1937, p. 2.

[9] A. Rastorguev, Director of the Borets Plant, writing in *Ind.*, July 3, 1940, p. 2.

riod, the annual use of this capacity fell from 88 to 64 percent.[10] Idleness of open-hearth furnaces of the Glavk of the Metallurgical Industry was 22 percent during 1936 and the first three quarters of 1937.[11] Planning has meant far from a precise synchronization and full use of the economy's resources.

In view of this lack of exactitude in planning (or—to phrase it differently—due to the absence of perfect knowledge by the planners of future developments), it is scarcely surprising that the Soviet leaders have always stressed the desirability of overfulfillment of plans, a practice which would be disastrous to a closely integrated design.[12] The famed disregard for the integrative aspect of the Five-Year Plans which has been expressed in the slogan of "The Five-Year Plan in four years," has had its counterpart in the attitude shown toward annual plans. The production programs have been officially categorized as the minimum obligatory tasks, to be exceeded if at all possible.[13] Plants frequently have pledged to produce goods above the amount included in their plans.[14]

As might be expected, the field of planning for the firms is lined with pitfalls mentioned year after year but never corrected. Thus there is much more room and need for "operational decisions" by glavki and commissariats, and for independent decisions by firm

[10] Malenkov's Report to the XVIIIth Party Conference, *Ch.M.*, February 16, 1941, p. 2.

[11] Order of L. M. Kaganovich, Commissar of Heavy Industry, *Ind.*, November 21, 1937, p. 2.

[12] Soviet stress on overfulfillment of plans is sometimes considered to be caused by the emphasis which has been placed upon a program of military preparedness and an extremely high level of national investment. Cf. H. Schwartz, *Russia's Soviet Economy* (New York: 1950), pp. 116-17. Oskar Lange has written that ". . . overfulfillment of the plan, not less than under-fulfillment, must be considered as a disturbance which upsets the plan. . . . The fact that overfulfillment of the production plans is regarded as a virtue, instead of as an upsetting of the general economic plan, shows clearly that Soviet economic planning did not serve the objectives of a harmonious socialist welfare economy, but served political and military objectives to which all other aspects of economic planning were sacrificed."—O. Lange, "The Working Principles of the Soviet Economy," *U.S.S.R. Economy and the War* (New York: 1943), p. 43.

In view of the material presented above, such an interpretation would appear unfounded. For an elaboration of this point, see the concluding section of Chapter VII.

[13] Resolution of December 25, 1935, of the Plenum of the TsK VKP(b), *Z.I.*, December 26, 1935, p. 1.

[14] Cf. the resolution adopted by a meeting of the workers of the Moscow Red Proletariat Plant on March 23, 1939, published in *Mash.*, March 29, 1939, p. 1. *Z.I.*, March 28, 1937, p. 3.

managements, than would appear on the surface. This is the case even after discounting the areas of the firm's work for which no detailed plans are laid.

Plans for the firms usually seem to have been drawn up in final shape only after the planning period actually started, indicating that the Soviet problem of operating within rigid deadlines had not been solved. The movement toward "planning from below" has exacted its price through slowing down the process of plan formation. Frequently, glavki have begun by giving the firms solely a quantitative quota of production, and only after the beginning of the planning year—sometimes after half of the year was over—were other "limits" set for costs, labor force, etc.[15] The final annual calendar plans for firms have been approved even later. In 1938, it was said that they were normally completed only in March and April of the planning year.[16] Even by August 15, 1938, 29 percent of the firms of the Commissariat of Heavy Industry had not yet had their 1938 plans approved.[17] In 1940, the same situation still seemed to prevail.[18]

The various "limits" set for the firms have sometimes been mutually contradictory. Limits for man-hours of labor have been reduced while the corresponding items in the cost limits were left at the same level.[19] The various limits for a single firm have often been worked up independently by different people in the glavk without being reconciled with each other.[20] In the Glavk of Heavy Machine Construction in 1938, limits of working force, wages, etc., were given to firms purely in dependence on the totals allotted to the Glavk as a whole. Planners of the Glavk frequently expressed their sympathy to firm directors when these limits bore no relation to production tasks, but their "help" went no further.[21]

[15] Cf. N. Koltunov, "Svoevremenno dovodit' plan do predpriiatiia" (For the Working Out on Time of the Plan for the Firm), *Plan*, 1935, No. 6, p. 42. Article by V. Perlin, head of the planning-production sector of the Magnitogorsk Stalin Firm, in *Ind.*, September 17, 1937, p. 3. *Mash.*, December 9, 1938, p. 2.

[16] L. Vilenskii, "Finansovye voprosy promyshlennosti" (Financial Questions of Industry), *Planovoe Khoziaistvo*, 1938, No. 10, p. 66.

[17] Prikaz of Commissar L. M. Kaganovich, *Ind.*, September 9, 1938, p. 2.

[18] Cf. *Ind.*, May 27, 1940, p. 3.

[19] Cf. *Ind.*, September 17, 1937, p. 3.

[20] Cf. *Z.I.*, August 17, 1937, p. 2.

[21] S. Akopov, Director of the Urals Ordzhonikidze Machine Construction Plant, writing in *Mash.*, December 22, 1938, p. 2.

Even when "limits" are set and plans approved, they are still subject to change. Certain alterations are made only for purposes of better evaluation of the firms' work, such as the customary revisions of planned cost and planned profit at the end of the year in line with changes in prices, freight rates, Bank interest, taxes, etc.[22] But other changes basically alter the entire production of the firm. Such changes have usually been caused by alterations in the plans for the economy as a whole or by the development of new interrelations between sectors of the economy, rather than by reconceived estimates of the firm's productive capacity. Thus during nine months of 1938, a major machine-building firm had its production plan changed five times, and the list of types of machines to be produced was completely revised.[23] A major auto plant had its program altered sixteen times in the second and third quarters of 1940.[24] An important brake-producing firm was in November, 1936, given an annual program of 95,000 brakes for 1937. In early January, the figure was pushed up to 138,000; by January 13, it was brought down to 108,000. On March 11, a final variant was set of 88,000—considerably below the original figure. The effect of such changes on the work of a plant can be seen from the fact that when this brake firm was given the task of producing 138,000 brakes, it greatly increased the production of its copper foundry, and when the program was reduced, it had to shut down the foundry for almost a month in order to cut the stock of castings to a normal ratio to production.[25]

Quite aside from regular changes in the annual plans, such as those described above, there are the "operational corrections" in firms' production plans which are ordered by the glavki. These revisions are intended to insure that production stay in line with changing requirements, but they can make complete hash of a firm's plan. In 1936 and 1937, such operational orders altered 20

[22] Instructions of the Commissariat of Finance, approved in Post. No. 2192 of the SNK SSSR of December 31, 1936, *BFKhZ*, 1937, No. 2.

[23] The Red October Plant. (*Mash.*, December 9, 1938, p. 2.)

[24] The Moscow Stalin Automobile-Tractor Plant. (V. Sitnin, "Krupnyi rezerv material'nykh resursov" [The Large Reserve of Materials Resources], *Planovoe Khoziaistvo*, 1940, No. 12, p. 42.)

[25] The L. M. Maganovich Brake Firm. (Article by P. Bakaleev, head of the planning-production sector of the firm, in *Z.I.*, August 11, 1937, p. 3.)

percent of the production of a leading machine-building plant.[26] Usually these corrections have been additional orders, and it is the rare firm which has been relieved of previous production demands when presented with these new ones. This is true even where the glavk has known that the firm would have to ignore planned orders and violate contracts with customer firms in order to satisfy the new requirements. Additional operational corrections have been made by glavki because they received materials other than those needed for fulfillment of the plan, and their firms' plans have been "corrected" so that production might fit the materials available.[27]

The "operational" as opposed to the "planning" system of production has even reached the point where managements have complained that one of the most serious obstacles in their work is the absence of long-range planning of the firm's development. Such an improvisational policy, it has been said, prevents any proper organization of production.[28] Firms have grown "like Topsy" for lack of genuine plans extending over several years.

In addition to these Soviet-recognized weaknesses in the planning system, a further source of erratic plan fulfillment lies in the obligation placed upon all plant managements to follow unswervingly the priority policies laid down by the top Party and Government bodies. The choice of "key sectors" of the economy has been called a leading Leninist-Stalinist principle of socialist planning.[29] Plant directors are expected to know which branches of the economy have priority, and to act in such a way as to favor these branches above all others. When the "key sectors" principle conflicts with the firm's plan, it is the plant management that must decide which to follow.

The following case, prominently treated at the time in heavy in-

---

[26] The Kuibyshev Electrical Plant. (*Z.I.*, August 5, 1937, p. 2.)

[27] Cf. *Z.I.*, August 5, 1937, p. 2. G. Privorotskii, "Nekotorye voprosy razresheniia sporov po promyshlennomu snabzheniiu" (Some Questions in Deciding Disputes Regarding Industrial Procurement), *Arbitrazh (Arbitration)*, 1937, No. 5, p. 15. *Z.I.*, August 21, 1937, p. 2 V. Kurganov, Director of the Kiev Bolshevik Chemical Machine Construction Plant, writing in *Mash.*, May 8, 1939, p. 2.

[28] *Z.I.*, August 11, 1937, p. 3, and Director S. Akopov writing in *Mash.*, December 22, 1938, p. 2.

[29] Cf. A. Kurskii, *Sotsialisticheskoe planirovanie narodnogo khoziaistva SSSR* (Socialist Planning of the National Economy of the USSR), (Moscow: 1945), pp. 34-35. Also Maizenberg, *op. cit.*, p. 15.

dustry's daily newspaper, indicates that the manager is expected on occasion to favor the "key sectors" principle over his plan. G. Frezerov, the director of a tool-producing plant, was chastized by the Commissar of Heavy Industry himself for not violating his contracts with other firms in order to take on a purchase-order of a firm in the oil industry. The director intended to take three months to fulfill this priority order, but was summoned by the Commissar of Heavy Industry and given ten days within which to fill it—a time limit which compelled his plant to drop all other work. Despite Frezerov's fulfilling this purchase order on time, he was reprimanded for not having originally given it top priority. Must the Commissar interfere in each order for each plant? it was asked.[30]

Thus we see that the plant director may be expected to follow national priority policy on his own responsibility even when, as in this instance, he could do so only by breaking the law and exposing himself to criminal charges for violation of procurement contracts with other organizations.[31]

THE THEORETIC STRESSING OF RIGIDITY

Throughout the above section, we have seen the powerful elements of flexibility which are present in Soviet planning. No period's plan is sacrosanct, certainly not the Five-Year Plan and not even the annual or quarterly ones. When the plan of either a firm or the nation clashes with the needs of the moment, it is the plan which must give way.

Yet while this has been the practice of Soviet industry, Soviet doctrine has been far more rigid. Opposition to proposals for the plan is in order up to the moment when the plan is approved. After that, the plan's unassailability can be summed up in the oft-repeated pronouncement: "The Plan is Law."

In early 1934, the director of the largest rubber-fabricating firm in the country openly challenged the annual plan for his firm after

---

[30] Z.I., May 22, 1936, p. 3.

[31] Post. of the TsIK (Central Executive Committee) and SNK SSSR No. 57/131 of February 18, 1931, Sobranie zakonov i rasporiazhenii raboche-krest'ianskogo pravitel'stva SSSR (Collection of the Laws and Orders of the Worker-Peasant Government of the USSR), 1931, article 109. (Hereafter cited as SZ.) This law remained in force and was still referred to in 1944 in Grazhdanskoe Pravo, pp. 373-74.

it had been approved by the Council of Commissars, the highest body in the land. Calling a conference of all Communist Party members in the firm, he tried to demonstrate that the plan for tire production was totally impractical. The fault lay, he proclaimed, in that the Government had allotted less funds for capital investment than he deemed necessary to carry out the program. As the only alternative to failure to fulfill the year's plan, he offered the hope that the lack of tractor tires for the spring sowing campaign would cause such a national scandal that the firm would be granted the necessary funds.[32]

This speech of the director was bitterly attacked as mobilizing the masses against the plan instead of for it.[33] Half a month later, the director was removed from his post and ordered to be given a job no higher than that of foreman. In dismissing him, the Commissar of Heavy Industry issued the much echoed pronouncement: "The Plan is Law."[34]

This precept is intended to apply to all levels of the industrial hierarchy. In a decree of November 29, 1937, frequently referred to thereafter, the Council of Commissars ordered that commissariats and glavki should not give overly large tasks to their firms. It was forbidden for the total of these tasks to exceed the production required by the plan of the parent organ. In the same fashion, firms have not been allowed to give their departments production tasks the sum of which exceeds the firm's own plan. All plans are to be rigidly controlled from above.[35]

CONCLUDING REMARKS

How can we interpret this sharp contrast between doctrine and reality? Let us turn for aid to an examination of both the functional and dysfunctional aspects of the doctrine.

[32] Z.I., January 2, 1934, p. 4.
[33] Ibid.
[34] Prikaz No. 32 of the NKTP of January 8, 1934, Z.I., January 9, 1934, p. 1.
[35] Mash., December 26, 1937, p. 1. Maizenberg, op. cit., pp. 22-23. V. Kontorovich, Voprosy planirovaniia predpriiatiia (Questions of Planning for a Firm), (Moscow: 1941), p. 6. In the postwar period, however, ministries have been permitted by law to give to their firms monthly production tasks whose sum could exceed the approved quarterly plans by up to 10 percent. See "Planirovanie v poslevoennyi period i novaia struktura Gosplana" (Planning in the Postwar Period and the New Structure of the State Planning Commission), Planovoe Khoziaistvo, 1946, No. 5, p. 19.

Precise, self-consistent planning and strict fulfillment of plans would, if practicable, raise greatly the efficiency of Soviet industry. It would provide a detailed synchronization of the different branches, eliminating stoppages for lack of supplies as well as the useless piling up of stocks of goods destined for industrial use. Firm managements could effect considerable economies of labor and machine time if they were able to lay out production schedules months in advance and if there was a stability of expectations with regard to tasks and the means available to carry them through. It is in pursuance of this goal of efficiency through rigidity of plans once made that the "Plan is Law" type of thinking is enunciated.

But the need for flexibility in fulfilling plans is too great to be denied. What is the use of carrying out a plan already outdated by events, demanding products which have since become of second priority? Where is the sense in a plan comprised of detailed orders when there is no concrete basis for setting such orders a year in advance? When a supplier firm does not fulfill its planned production, should a plant dependent upon it continue blindly along until pulled up short by the lack of materials? When it is known that no plan can be fulfilled precisely, should the central authorities reject the efforts to overfulfill wherever possible? With these conditions, is it a mistake to operate under such a psychologically powerful slogan as "The Five-Year Plan in four years"?

Soviet leaders desire both flexibility and the efficiency which is a product of stability of expectations. In practice, their emphasis is overwhelmingly on the side of flexibility. But is it unwise for them to mention every so often the need for stability? Perhaps it helps in holding to some sort of a mean.

One method employed for combining stability of expectations with flexibility is that of establishing informal ties between executives of different organs.[36] The formation of such relations among all planning bodies from the State Planning Commission to the commissariats and the firms is urged.[37] And in fact, such exchange of information and opinion among personnel from the various

[36] I do not mean to imply that the basic reason for informal relations is the desirability of the above combination. Rather my point is solely that such informality helps to resolve the problem discussed above.

[37] Cf. Ia. Luganin, "Administration and Planning of Industry in USSR," manuscript, p. 98. See footnote 10 on p. 64.

levels of the hierarchy seems to have occurred.[38] This is true both with regard to the process of forming annual and quarterly plans and to the making of those "operational decisions" which continuously revise the plans.

Through informal consultations and discussions of proposed changes, officials are somewhat protected from sudden surprises. But this functional aspect of informality carries with it a serious cost. Personal relations between officials become of major importance; friendships and quarrels can spell the difference between success and failure. The individual does not exercise authority simply by virtue of his post; to a considerable extent, his ability to function effectively depends upon his having a pleasant personality and good connections.

Thus a multitude of stresses and strains, which would be minimized in a system marked by formality and emphasis upon the post rather than upon the man filling it, exists in Soviet administration.

Just as it is possible to overestimate the significance of planning in Soviet heavy industry, so it is easy to underestimate it. One might conclude that there is no real planning. Such a conclusion would be untrue even if by "planning" is meant solely the five-year, annual, and quarterly plans, for these do serve as the main basis for production scheduling. And if planning is understood as coordination and commanding from above, there is no doubt as to the planned character of industry. There seems no reason for considering only the plans for fixed periods as "planning"; we should also include the changes in such plans, so long as they are made by higher bodies in accord with a rough over-all pattern of coordination.

Such a conception of Soviet planning leaves wide open the question of how the economy is actually administered. What sorts of commands are given throughout the year to plant managements, and which are considered to be the most important, and thus the governing ones, when they conflict with one another? What are the standards by which a management's success is judged? Since these questions are not answered by a study of the plans themselves, we must go beyond them to an analysis of the actual administrative methods and criteria employed.

[38] Cf. *Ibid. Ind.*, September 9, 1938, p. 2. *Ind.*, September 17, 1938, p. 2. *Mash.*, October 14, 1939, p. 2.

VI: Centralized Operational Direction of Firms

THIS CHAPTER is intended to demonstrate the administrative methods used to guide industrial firms. The Soviet planning system is not composed solely of formal plans. It is also made up of the total collection of operational orders given to firms throughout the year. It is with these latter that we shall now concern ourselves.

Our immediate problem is the following: What types of orders are given to firms by higher bodies and under what conditions? The categories set forth below have been worked out as an answer to this question.

Behind the maze of categories in the following sections there stands a relatively simple thematic structure which the reader would do well to bear in mind The orders and instructions of the highest administrative bodies have ordinarily fallen into two groupings. One is that of general policies intended to orient all economic organizations at any level, and the second is that of tasks given to intermediate bodies which they in turn are expected to subdivide among their individual firms. The distinguishing feature in the system of orders of top bodies is the heavy reliance upon the enunciation of national policies or "priorities." Intermediate administrative organizations, in contrast to their parent bodies, have concentrated upon issuing direct and specific instructions.

Throughout this chapter, the reader should keep in mind the following question: What are the functional and dysfunctional aspects of each of the categories of orders given to firm management by higher authorities? It is in terms of this question that we can best understand the reasons for the use under particular conditions of specified methods for the direction of firms.

TOP ORDERS COVERING INDUSTRIAL FIRMS

NATIONAL CAMPAIGNS: One major method of national economic leadership is through the medium of national campaigns. These are organized efforts to push ahead some State program and enlist the united efforts of all Soviet organizations concerned. Having the support of high Government decisions and therefore legal backing, they are also given great publicity in the press. Party and mass organizations are rallied behind them. Campaigns are initiated where considerable resistance to some program is expected, either because of special interests which are injured by new regulations, or because of the need to overcome quickly conservatism in a given field.

A major and periodic campaign is that for increased norms of output per worker and reduced rates per piece produced. With the rise of the Stakhanovite movement in late 1935, production per man-hour rose sharply in much of industry. With 56 to 57 percent of the workers under the various glavki of the Commissariat of Heavy Industry being paid by piece rates,[1] and with this wage system similarly prevalent throughout industry, maintenance of existing piece rates would have meant great monetary inflation.[2] Thus a major campaign of revision of output norms and piece rates was conducted in 1936 under orders of the December, 1935, Plenum of the Central Committee of the Communist Party.

The Central Committee's decision was of a highly general nature. It called for conferences in 1936 of the different branches of industry to help work out new norms, differing from plant to plant according to production possibilities. It provided that Stakhanovites were to be widely drawn into the work of setting up the new norms for each job, but that it was to be the responsibility of the

[1] M. Firin, "Organizatsiia zarabotnoi platy v tiazhëloi promyshlennosti" (The Organization of Wages in Heavy Industry), *Planovoe Khoziaistvo*, 1937, No. 1, pp. 112-14.

[2] The inflation would have resulted from the fact that an immense part of the increased production was not of consumer goods. Furthermore, a policy of unchanged rates would have caused great difficulties in the countryside, where real earnings would have had to decline under the resulting inflation (unless the inflation was multiplied by raising agricultural prices as well). Since production increased erratically in the various industries as a result of differing degrees of efficiency gained from new equipment and from new methods of work organization, dissatisfaction among industrial workers would also have been rampant under such an inflation.

firm directors to see that the revision was properly executed.[3]

During 1936, tasks for norm revisions were spelled out. Each branch of industry was given an over-all percentage increase in work norms, and through the branch conferences and glavki each plant was given its task in keeping with but differing from the over-all percentage. The firm management had the responsibility of deciding norm revisions for each job.

In 1937 in the Commissariat of Heavy Industry, there was not scheduled any general revision of work norms although there were efforts to improve the work already done in fixing the norms.[4] The year 1938 also slipped by, and only in 1939 was there another general norm revision. The year 1940 saw a third such campaign.

Why did these general campaigns take place? The answer lies in the impossibility of enforcing continuous rather than sporadic revision of work norms. Norm revisions were declared to be products of better equipment, supply, and work organizations, and there was a standing rule that when any job was mechanized or rationalized, the firm management should immediately raise the work norm correspondingly.[5] But in practice this was not done. In 1940, it was declared that it was only in periods of general campaign-type revisions that work norms were actually changed.[6] Improvements in technology and work organization meant higher earnings or a lighter work load until the next campaign, and thus norms could be sharply raised during a campaign because they took in the slack which had accumulated.

The reluctance of management to hold down worker earnings was partly a reflection of the shortage of labor and of the fear that continuous norm revision would create great difficulties in maintaining a stable labor force. There was also a natural reluctance to embark on such an immense added job as the revision of thousands of norms in each plant. The reduction in labor cost was apparently not sufficiently important to managements to spur them into ac-

[3] Resolution of December 25, 1935, of the Plenum of the TsK VKP(b), printed in Z.I., December 26, 1935, p. 1.
[4] Cf. Z.I., April 10, 1937, p. 1.
[5] Mash., January 20, 1939, p. 3.
[6] E. Vasil'ev, "Sotsialisticheskaia distsiplina truda" (Socialist Discipline of Work), Planovoe Khoziaistvo, 1940, No. 9, p. 26.

tion. But whatever the reason, it was only through these campaigns that work norms could in practice be increased.

While such campaigns seemed essential to higher authorities, they clearly had grave disadvantages. Management's knowledge that new campaigns would be forthcoming encouraged it to maintain existing norms in the interim and to store up rationalization gains.[7] Despite efforts to individualize norm increases, there was a natural tendency in a campaign to raise all norms indiscriminately.[8] Immense numbers of work norms had to be reviewed in a few months during each campaign. In 1939, there were two million such norms in the Commissariat of Intermediate Machine Construction alone.[9] Individual plants had tens of thousands of norms to review.[10] Small wonder that norm making, done at such a feverish pitch, was at a low level and was considered one of the weakest elements of the plants' work.[11]

Another type of national campaign was that of extending the progressive piece-rate system: the system of raising the rate paid the worker per unit as his production rises above a set level. The December, 1935, Plenum of the Central Committee of the Communist Party ordered that this wage system be made into the leading type in industry,[12] since it offered the greatest monetary incentive to high production. As a major form of encouragement, it ordered that while norms for straight piecework were to be raised, those for progressive piecework were to be held constant and that instead the fund of wages available was to be increased.[13] Reports on the 1936 Branch Conferences of Heavy Industry indicate that

[7] Cf. *Ibid.*

[8] Cf. *Mash.*, January 20, 1939, p. 3, where it is stated that even when old norms are not being fulfilled they must still be raised.

[9] *Mash.*, May 11, 1939, p. 2.

[10] Cf. *Z.I.*, April 21, 1937, p. 1.

[11] Cf. the article by R. Khisin, senior engineer of the Bureau of Technical Norm Setting and Capacity of the Commissariat of Heavy Machine Construction, in *Mash.*, May 9, 1939, p. 2. The article by N. Kochnov, Assistant Commissar of General Machine Construction, in *Mash.*, May 11, 1939, p. 2.

[12] A. G. Samulenko, "Stakhanovskoe dvizhenie i otraslevye konferentsii v khimicheskoi promyshlennosti" (The Stakhanovite Movement and the Branch Conferences in the Chemical Industry), *Org. Uprav.*, 1936, No. 3, p. 30.

[13] Plenum's Resolution of December 25, 1935, *Z.I.*, December 26, 1935, p. 1.

this instruction was carried out, except where labor productivity rose because of technological changes.[14]

As a result of this campaign, 30 percent of all employees of the Commissariat of Heavy Industry were being paid progressive piece rates in December, 1936.[15] By then, the harmful effects of this successful campaign were already being felt. Widespread application of this system led to overexpenditures of wage funds allocated to firms, and thus to complaints of "mistakes in application."[16] In 1939, the Commissar of Machine Construction condemned the widespread use of progressive piece rates and insisted that in the future they should only be employed in bottleneck jobs where production needs demanded this additional incentive.[17] He ruled that his personal approval was required for keeping any job on this wage system.[18] In February and March, 1939, the percentage of pieceworkers paid by progressive piece rates fell from 45 percent to 15.6 percent in Heavy Machine Construction, and from 25.8 percent to 11.8 percent in Medium Machine Construction.[19] The campaign for progressive piece rates had vastly overreached itself and was now decidedly dead.

A campaign which seems to have avoided the rigid bureaucratic features of the two described above was the new Stakhanovite movement which arose in 1939. This was a movement to encourage workers to operate several machines simultaneously instead of one, and to persuade other workers to master two trades and to combine them in their daily work.

These joint campaigns were propagandized on the basis of raising Soviet labor productivity to the American level. It was explained that the percentage of auxiliary and servicing workers was far higher in Soviet than in American heavy industry, and that this was one of the main reasons for American average labor productivity in 1937 being two to two and a half times as high as Soviet pro-

[14] Cf. *Z.I.*, March 4, 1936, p. 2.

[15] *Z.I.*, April 10, 1937, p. 1.

[16] *Ibid.*

[17] Article of V. K. L'vov, Commissar of Machine Construction, in *Mash.*, January 16, 1939, p. 3. Also, I. Iunovich, "Voprosy truda i zarabotnoi platy v mashinostroenii" (Questions of Labor and Wages in Machine Construction), *Planovoe Khoziaistvo*, 1939, No. 6, p. 79.

[18] *Ibid.*

[19] Iunovich, *op. cit.*, pp. 79-80.

ductivity.[20] The "combining of trades" was intended to reduce sharply the auxiliary labor force as well as to cut worker idleness caused by delays in waiting for other workers who ordinarily supplemented their operations.

In 1935, an article had appeared in the national trade-union magazine advocating precisely such "combining of trades" and giving examples of its successful practice in coal, ferrous metallurgy, and machine-construction plants.[21] But there was no follow-up for four years. What had happened in the meanwhile to cause the 1939 campaign?

In the first place, the need for economizing labor power had grown with the vast increase of industrial capacity compared to the available labor force. Secondly, the stress since 1935 had been on further "division of labor," and a simultaneous counter-campaign for "combining trades" would have been confusing. Thirdly, there had been considerable training on the job in heavy industry, and the labor force now had much more know-how. An extreme division of labor could be justified in the early thirties on the basis of its being easier to train workers to carry out a single type of operation than to perform several types,[22] but by 1939 those exaggerations which caused idle labor time were no longer considered necessary.

Thus when in mid-1939 the Urals Ordzhonikidze Plant of Heavy Machine Construction instituted the new Stakhanovite movement of multimachine operation and combination of trades, it received immediate attention. In July, the Commissar of Heavy Machine Construction ordered it introduced throughout his commissariat;[23]

[20] A. Grigor'ev, "Novye formy sotsialisticheskogo truda" (New Forms of Socialist Labor), *Planovoe Khoziaistvo*, 1939, No. 9, pp. 32-33. S. Kheinman, "Ob izlishkakh rabochei sily i o proizvoditel'nosti truda" (On Excess Labor Force and on Labor Productivity), *Problemy Ekonomiki*, 1940, No. 11/12, pp. 107-21.

[21] M. Firin, "O sovmeshchenii rabot" (On Combining Trades), *Voprosy Profdvizheniia* (Questions of Trade Unionism), 1935, No. 5-6, pp. 58-66. (Hereafter cited as *Vopr. Profdvizh.*)

[22] Cf. John D. Littlepage and Demaree Bess, *In Search of Soviet Gold* (New York: 1937), pp. 247-48. Littlepage, an American mining engineer who worked in the Soviet gold industry from 1928 to 1937, considered that under Soviet conditions of inadequate worker training, much greater division of labor was justified from the viewpoint of production efficiency than would be the case in a country industrially more advanced.

[23] *Mash.*, September 18, 1939, p. 3, and September 24, 1939, p.3.

in October, it was ordered introduced in the Aviation Industry Commissariat and in the Commissariat of Medium Machine Construction.[24] Soon all heavy industry had taken it up.

Yet from the start it was treated gingerly in recognition of its possible ill effects on production. Although the Commissar of Heavy Machine Construction ordered the widespread introduction of multimachine operation, he warned that each machine must produce at least 100 percent of its old norm per machine-hour. He advised that any machine falling below this level must be returned to the old system of one-machine-one-operator.[25] The Commissar of the Aviation Industry had similar qualifications in his order for the extension of the movement. However, he insisted that management must solve the problems involved, and he permitted managers considerable freedom in determining premiums and in permitting temporary high earnings for workers successful in switching over to the new system.[26]

Thus in this last campaign, the dangers of overextension were stressed from the beginning. There was more fear of going too far than fear of conservatism blocking the movement unless all stops were pulled.

A fourth type of general campaign has been that connected with laws inflicting hardships on elements of the population. These laws have been enforced quite rigidly.

In June, 1940, all industry was ordered to switch from a 41-hour to a 48-hour week.[27] This extension of each workday and of the number of workdays per week was intended to be introduced immediately, although it necessitated a complete reorganization of work schedules. Only eight days after the issuance of the decree, a portion of a metal plate-rolling department in the Dnepropetrovsk Petrovskii Plant was taken to task for still operating on the old system. The department head attempted to justify this minor lag by his inability to reorganize work schedules so rapidly, but he was

[24] *Mash.*, October 6, 1939, p. 3.
[25] *Mash.*, September 18, 1939, pp. 2-3.
[26] *Mash.*, October 6, 1939, p. 3.
[27] Where previously employees had commonly worked seven hours a day, five out of every six days, they now switched to eight hours a day, six out of seven days. Those who had previously worked shorter hours, now had their workday lengthened correspondingly.

hauled over the coals in the national press for his "violation of the law."[28] The results of this extreme rigidity in requiring immediate observance of the decree irrespective of scheduling possibilities can be seen from the fact that for two months thereafter production in many firms fell off despite the 17 percent increase in work-hours.[29] Only subsequently was the confusion in scheduling straightened out sufficiently to regain former production levels in these plants.

Yet, despite the damage done by this blanket and concrete order to all plants and industries however heterogeneous, would it have been politically feasible in terms of worker morale to have increased working hours in some shops and plants before they were raised in others, especially since they would have been raised sooner in plants where management was most skillful in readjusting schedules? The blanket order avoided this "discrimination," and had the additional advantage of placing maximum pressure upon management to use all its ingenuity in the rapid rescheduling of shifts.[30]

All in all, the campaign method of exercising national leadership appears to have been a blunt but powerful tool for putting through new policies. It could be used as a sledgehammer to drive ahead where a more delicate instrument would have been of no use. On the other hand, it developed an impetus of its own during the campaign swing and could not be handled with precision. While even an opposite approach might have been more useful in improving efficiency in some individual cases, yet all economic organizations and problems tended to be dealt with in terms of the campaign's own objectives.

NEW SYSTEMS: Besides conducting national campaigns, top governmental bodies have exercised leadership through the establishment of broad regulations covering many heterogeneous industries. No single commissariat controls a sufficient area of industry to issue such general rules, and thus only such bodies as the Eco-

---

[28] *Ind.*, July 4, 1940, p. 3.

[29] Vasil'ev, *op. cit.*, p. 23.

[30] The question remains of why a time lag was not established between the announcement of the new regulation and its enforcement. This is something which I cannot answer, except to presume that Soviet leaders felt that more production would be gained than lost by immediate application of the new system of work scheduling.

nomic Council or the Council of Commissars have the necessary authority.

An example of this sort of regulatory system is the new way of handling amortization and capital-repair funds which was set up in January, 1938. Before this, firms had paid their amortization accounts—a percentage of the stated value of their plant and equipment—into Long-Term Banks, and these moneys had been used in a centralized fashion for new capital construction as well as for capital repair. In practice, this resulted in serious neglect of capital-repair needs of the firms.[31]

In order to give proper weight to capital repair, the Council of Commissars established a new system.[32] New norms were set up for amortization accounts of the different commissariats (a specific annual percentage of the value of plant and equipment being set for each). Of this, roughly two fifths to one half was allocated for capital repair. The commissariats, in turn, were to establish individualized norms for each firm for total depreciation as well as for capital repair. While the nonrepair part of the depreciation fund was to go into a centralized account, the capital-repair fund for each firm was to be left at the disposal of that firm's director.[33] In 1941, glavki and commissariats were still forbidden to redistribute these capital-repair funds among their firms.[34] In this fashion, it was intended that capital repair throughout all industry should be rescued from its complete subordination to the interests of new construction.

PRIORITY TASKS: Another method of leadership is that of choosing particular aspects of industrial work which should be given heavy stress by all units.

Stalin has described this method of leadership as that of selecting the key task whose accomplishment will draw in its wake the solu-

[31] Cf. an account of the report of the Commissar of Finance to the Council of Commissars' meeting of November 28, 1937. (*Ind.,* December 1, 1937, p. 4.)

[32] Post. of the SNK SSSR of January 8, 1938, *Mash.,* January 9, 1938, p. 1.

[33] Expenditures from the repair fund, however, required higher approval. (Instructions of Gosbank, approved on April 15, 1938, by the Economic Council, *BFKhZ,* 1938, No. 17. M. Vidgor, "Voprosy finansirovaniia i kontrolia kapital'nogo remonta" [Questions of Financing and Supervising Capital Repair], *Den'gi i Kredit,* 1940, No. 8-9, p. 59.)

[34] Vidgor, *op. cit.,* p. 61.

tion of the remaining problems. An essential function of leadership, he said, is to recognize the crucial elements in each period.[35] Thus at the end of 1935, the extension and development of the Stakhanovite movement was considered as the prime task. In early 1939, there was a need for strengthening labor discipline at work (eliminating unjustified absences and latenesses of workers).

An example of priority selection can be seen in the instance when the Red Proletariat Machine-Building Plant resolved in 1939 on a program of plan overfulfillment which included 30 percent overfulfillment of the program for automatic machinery. This element, the plant collective's resolution stated, was included because Stalin had indicated the need for such machines.[36]

Another case in point was the 1939 declaration by the Eighteenth Congress of the Communist Party that economizing on fuel and electricity was a major task of all firms in industry, transport, agriculture, and the communal economy. This decision was given considerable newspaper publicity.[37] In addition to calling the general attention of firm managements, equipment designers, and others to the problem of conserving fuel, this top order was reflected in actions by other bodies. In April, 1939, the Economic Council for the first time permitted the State Bank to give special credits to firms to enable them to introduce rationalization measures for economizing fuel, and in May, 1939, the Bank ordered its branches to give such credits.[38] The command of the highest policy-making body in the land, a Party Congress, found its implementation in the activities of many organizations, working separately, but all knowing that neglect of this aspect of economic work would be taken as disobedience to "Party discipline."

The priority type of leadership, which declares certain aspects of work to be of major significance, would seem to avoid the tendencies toward red tape and restrictions on local autonomy which

[35] I. Stalin, Speech of March 3, 1937, to the Plenum of the TsK VKP(b), *Z.I.*, March 29, 1937, p. 7. This statement was referred to as late as 1940 by L. Maizenberg, "O khoziaistvennom plane" (On the Economic Plan), *Planovoe Khoziaistvo*, 1940, No. 10, p. 15.

[36] Plant resolution, printed in *Mash.*, March 29, 1939, p. 1.

[37] Cf. the lead editorials in *Mash.*, June 28, 1939, p. 1 and *Ind.*, January 28, 1940, p. 1.

[38] Circular No. 5398 of the State Bank of May 22, 1939, *BFKhZ*, 1939, No. 17/18.

are inherent in concrete orders by higher bodies. Nevertheless, the problem of causing overstress is equally serious.

At the end of 1936, the chief of the metallurgical sector of the Industrial Section of the Central Committee of the Communist Party brought up this problem in relation to metallurgy. All attention was being placed upon the heart of the metallurgical industry, that is, the blast furnaces, open-hearth departments, and metal-rolling departments. But the result of this concentration of attention, he declared, was that the auxiliary departments were neglected and remained weak. This created the serious danger of total disruption of Stakhanovite work in the main departments for lack of semifabricates, tools, and repair work.[39] "Priority concentration" on "principal" as opposed to "auxiliary" departments had backfired.

As a reaction to this sort of overstress, tasks have sometimes been declared to have "priority" solely in order to give them some place in a firm's programming. This has been done in order to prevent their utter neglect in the face of emphasis on the more important tasks.

A good example is the handling of consumers' goods by firms of the metallurgical and machine-construction industries. Because higher authorities judged firms mainly by their success in turning out the principal products of their industry, the firm managements tended to neglect consumers' goods. Plans for production of consumers' goods by these industries went unfulfilled in at least 1934, 1937, and the first five months of 1938.[40] Therefore, higher authorities had to emphasize as an auxiliary task the production of consumers' goods, particularly from industrial wastes and scrap. In 1936, the Council of Commissars ordered firms to build large departments for producing consumers' goods from waste, instructed the State Bank to give full credits for this construction, and gave firm managements considerable control over the profits made by the new departments.[41] Despite the very generous profits possible,

[39] A. Il'in, "Partiinaia rabota na zavodakh metallurgii" (Party Work in Metallurgical Plants), *Part. Stroit.*, 1936, No. 24, p. 57.
[40] *Z.I.*, January 16, 1935, p. 1. *Mash.*, February 28, 1938, p. 1. *Mash.*, July 15, 1938, p. 2.
[41] Post. of the SNK SSSR No. 1193 of July 7, 1936, *BFKhZ*, 1936, No. 22/23. *Z.I.*, June 12, 1936, p. 3.

as was indicated by the fact that the Donbas metallurgical firms in 1936 earned almost a 50 percent profit on their total sales of consumers' goods,[42] the firm managements a year later were still ignoring the order to build such departments.[43] Clearly the weight of the "priority" nature of main metallurgical items and machines depressed the output of consumers' goods. The only way in which the firms could be made to produce them at all was to stress continually the "priority" nature of these goods as well.[44]

PRIORITY SEGMENTS OF THE ECONOMY: The selection of industries which are to be given first attention with regard to supplies, labor force, etc., is another method by which top leadership is exercised.

In 1939, ferrous metallurgy did not fulfill its production plan. While the output of such a heavy metal consumer as the machine-construction industry had increased 14 to 15 percent as measured by Soviet indices, and that of defense industry by 47 percent, metallurgical production grew by only 5 percent during that year. It had become a serious bottleneck to industrial expansion.[45]

In the second quarter of 1940, the Central Committee of the Communist Party and the Council of Commissars issued a joint decree on the subject. The result was a rapid change in attitude throughout the economy toward metallurgical firms. As one metallurgical organization reported, fuel and transport—the lack of which had earlier slowed up its production—now suddenly appeared in oversupply.[46] Nothing was too good for ferrous metallurgy.

Similarly, firms of defense industry were singled out at the end of the thirties for well publicized awards of special premium funds, and hundreds of individual decorations at a time were presented to members of their work force. Even legal organs have paid special attention to priority segments. In the enforcement of a law declaring poor-quality production a criminal offense, the Supreme Court of the Soviet Union directed the public prosecutors and the lower

[42] Article by K. Petrov, head of the industrial sector of the Donets Office of the State Bank, in Z.I., March 23, 1937, p. 2.
[43] Z.I., August 20, 1937, p. 1.
[44] Cf. also, Z.I., May 11, 1934, p. 1; May 16, 1934, p. 1; and June 8, 1934, p. 1.
[45] Ind., June 3, 1940, p. 1.
[46] Ind., July 27, 1940, p. 3.

courts to concentrate on the priority segments of heavy industry, and especially on defense industry, and to reduce their stress on the less important industrial branches.[47]

This emphasis on priority segments clearly has considerable advantages. It is probably the quickest method for eliminating bottleneck sectors of the economy. It is the surest method of fulfilling and overfulfilling basic aspects of the national plan, although at the expense of other aspects. But its disadvantages are also serious. For to the degree that this method is geared to bottleneck areas, it creates new bottlenecks in the industries which are neglected, and as it stresses heavy industry and defense, it leads almost inevitably to a failure to fulfill the plan for consumers' goods.

CLEARING UP A SPECIFIC PROBLEM: Under the Soviet administrative system of "democratic centralism," higher organs are held responsible for the activities of units under them. Top organs are therefore ever ready to issue orders for the solution of serious and widespread problems existing anywhere. Normally, however, the task of making these orders concrete is left to the lower bodies.

A typical sort of order was that of the Commissariat of Heavy Industry in 1935,[48] intended to correct the general plan failure in the internal mobilization of firms' resources (turning up surplus materials and equipment).[49] The order placed pressure on all managements to improve the situation. Within two and a half weeks, all directors were to send to the glavki complete lists of surplus equipment and materials in their possession. They were also to review their plants' plans for the purchase of materials and equipment for the last two quarters of 1935, and to secure cancellation of all unnecessary procurement contracts; new orders and contracts were to be signed only under the personal review and authority of the plant director. The glavki were ordered to send responsible personnel as aids to those managements which were backward in mobilizing internal resources.

This order was intended to pressure the firms into the fulfill-

[47] Post. of the 47th Plenum of the Supreme Court USSR of June 9, 1934, *BFKhZ*, 1934, No. 20.

[48] I am considering the Commissariat of Heavy Industry as a higher organ prior to its subdivision at the end of 1936.

[49] Prikaz No. 962 of the NKTP of August 8, 1935, *BFKhZ*, 1935, No. 23.

ment of this task and to make their top managements personally responsible for work they would otherwise have shifted to the shoulders of subordinates.

A 1936 order for reducing the great waste of metal in the machine-construction industry used an additional method.[50] Here pressure was applied through ordering firms and glavki to review all norms of metal consumption and to present new norms to the Commissariat within three months. But in addition, a premium system was set up composed of 25 percent of the ruble value of the metal economies.

Top organs do not often give orders directly to specific firms, except in the case of firms of such major importance in the national economy as to be linked directly to them without intermediaries. When such direct orders are given to a firm having a glavk above it, it is because one of its problems has earlier evoked the attention of the higher organ.

As an example there is a 1935 order of an Assistant Commissar of Heavy Industry to a plant director to fire the chief engineer of his smithy department. Normally, the Commissariat would not have issued such an order. But the engineer had refused to accept a purchase request which another firm had tried to place with him. He had been called before the Assistant Commissar to explain his refusal, and had stated that the plant lacked the equipment needed for producing those items. Thereupon the Commissariat sent a special investigating commission to his department, but the engineer refused to accept the commission's conclusions. At this point, the Assistant Commissar maintained his own and the commission's authority by ordering this departmental chief engineer to be fired.[51]

EXPERIMENTATION: When top bodies are considering new methods, it has not been uncommon for them to try them out in a few firms before ordering a general change-over. Thus, in 1936, open-hearth furnaces in two metallurgical firms were reconstructed so as to raise their productive capacities to over 130 percent of the steel capacity generally accepted for furnaces of that size. The Commis-

---

[50] Prikaz No. 1448 of the NKTP of August 29, 1936, Z.I., September 1, 1936, p. 1.
[51] Z.I., April 1, 1935, p. 4.

sariat permitted this experiment which had been requested by the managements of these two plants, but considered that the extension of the new open-hearth methods to other firms would be premature until they had justified themselves here.[52]

Similarly, experiments have been undertaken with regard to rules of supervision over firms. In late 1934 and early 1935, there was much agitation by firm managements for greater freedom from detailed supervision over the number of workers they hired and the wages they paid.[53] Under existing law, the labor force of each firm was divided into five different categories, and higher organs were to set a separate monthly wage fund for each category and determine the number of personnel to be employed in it.[54] In early 1935, under prodding by firm managements, the Commissariat of Heavy Industry and the Commissariat of Light Industry freed a few firms in a number of different branches of industry from these requirements.[55] The experimental firms were naturally those whose managements had fought strongly against the old system and were deeply committed to making the experiment succeed.[56] This 1935 experiment seems to have been unfruitful, and in 1940 firm managements were still bitterly complaining of the old wage-fund system. But other experiments conducted on the command of top bodies were successful and were extended to industry in general.

TASKS TO BE FURTHER BROKEN DOWN: As one would expect in any hierarchical system, a major form of top leadership is that of giving a task to a particular commissariat which in turn subdivides it among its glavki; they in turn further subdivide it among the firms.

We have seen that all production plans are approved in this fashion. In the campaigns for revising work norms, commissariats are given an average task of norm increases to deal out among

[52] A. Tochinskii and V. Rikman, "Novye tekhnicheskie normy v chërnoi metallurgii" (New Technical Norms in Ferrous Metallurgy), *Planovoe Khoziaistvo*, 1936, No. 6, p. 44.
[53] Cf. articles in *Predpriiatie* (The Firm) during this period.
[54] Post. No. 269 of the SNK SSSR of February 21, 1933, *SZ*, 1933, article 75.
[55] *BFKhZ*, 1935, No. 36. *Z.I.*, September 1, 1935, p. 3, and September 10, 1935, p. 3. N. Gruev, "Neskol'ko zamechanii ob uproshchenii sistemy planirovaniia" (Some Remarks on the Simplification of the Planning System), *Predpriiatie*, 1935, No. 15, p. 11.
[56] Cf. *Z.I.*, May 8, 1935, p. 3.

their firms.[57] Tasks of reducing electricity consumption by industry have been handled similarly.[58]

LEADERSHIP OF FIRMS BY THE INTERMEDIATE ADMINISTRATIVE LEVEL OF GLAVKI AND COMMISSARIATS[59]

RUN-OF-THE-MILL ORDERS: The main form in which firms are led concretely is through direct instructions from glavki and commissariats. This is how production "limits," supply allocations, investment funds, etc., are set, the glavki making the final allocation of tasks which stem originally from the Council of Commissars. Special production orders are also given—some to be begun within two days of receipt of the order.[60] In this fashion the firms are directly integrated into the total industrial system.

When firm managements complain that all of their autonomy is being sapped away, that they are constantly at the mercy of bureaucratic issuers of instructions in the glavk and commissariat, they are referring primarily to direct orders. Unquestionably, this grievance reflects a serious and ever-present problem implicit in the very nature of integration through specific instructions. Yet the industrial structure is built in such a fashion that these instructions cannot be eliminated if the firms' operations are to be controlled from above in any detail under conditions of ever-changing specific goals.

GENERAL INSTRUCTIONS AND REGULATIONS: In addition to specific instructions to individual firms, there are the more generalized instructions which leave details to the firms themselves. Such for example was the order of the Commissariat of Machine Construction to organize periodic inspections of machinery, tools, jigs, and fixtures in all plants by commissions composed of Stakhanovites, designers, and technologists.[61]

---

[57] Cf. the discussion of the Postanovlenie of the Economic Council of January 4, 1939, concerning the Commissariat of Machine Construction, in Iunovich, *op. cit.,* pp. 74-75.

[58] Cf. the Post. of the SNK SSSR of October 13, 1936, *BFKhZ,* 1936, No. 28/29.

[59] The commissariats are considered as intermediate organs after the end of 1936, when the Commissariat of Heavy Industry began to be subdivided.

[60] Cf. *Z.I.,* May 14, 1937, p. 2.

[61] Prikaz of January 2, 1939, *Mash.,* January 3, 1939, p. 1. This order was intended to extend this form of Stakhanovite movement which was already functioning in many machine-construction plants.

General regulations are likewise issued. An example of this was the order of the Commissar of Machine Construction which was intended to solve a serious difficulty in relative wages.

A major problem long facing industry had been the large differential in pay between piece- and timeworkers. This differential was considered desirable in order to encourage workers to request and welcome transfer to piecework. But since many workers—particularly in repair work and technical control and inspection—had to remain on timework, there was much bitterness over their low earnings. Commenting on this in late 1938, the assistant head of the Section of Wages of the All-Union Central Council of the Trade Unions said that there existed a differential of 40 percent to 50 percent in base pay (hourly pay for timeworkers and hourly average rate for pieceworkers according to which their piece rates were set).[62]

Tackling this problem in early 1939, at the time of ordering a general work-norm revision in the Commissariat of Machine Construction, the Commissar instructed that essential timeworkers were to be shifted to the same base pay as pieceworkers. The jobs for which the wages were to be thus raised were to be determined by the head of each glavk—on the basis of the criterion of improving the work of the plants.[63] Here, as generally in this type of order, the task of working out concrete applications of the general rule was left to lower bodies.

Such instructions and regulations clearly leave far more autonomy to lower bodies than do specific orders. At the same time, these rulings are much less general than equivalent ones of higher bodies such as the Economic Council.

AID TO FIRMS: A major function of glavki and commissariats is that of giving technical aid to firms in working out the concrete problems which confront them. Firms turn to glavki for aid in solving such problems as that of why there is a high percentage of waste in their production.[64] Glavki have been strongly criticized in

[62] *Mash.*, October 23, 1938, p. 2.
[63] Prikaz No. 12 of Commissar of Machine Construction, V. L'vov, of January 5, 1939, *Mash.*, January 8, 1939, p. 2.
[64] Cf. *Ind.*, June 20, 1939, p. 3.

the national press when they have not given such help in the working out of organizational measures.[65]

In describing the nature of proper aid, Commissar I. Likhachev of Medium Machine Construction stressed the importance of organizing a technical council attached to the commissar which would have the task of extending and standardizing successful technological processes, and of applying the lessons learned in one industry to others which were less efficient. The second major method of commissariat aid which Likhachev stressed was that of sending large brigades, comprising men with many specialties, into backward firms to solve their specific difficulties.[66]

Such a brigade of specialists was sent to the Urals Dzerzhinskii Freight and Passenger Railroad Car Firm by Commissar Likhachev. The core of the brigade was composed of 15 designers, metallurgists, technologists, and production organizers of different firms of the Commissariat. In addition, up to 50 others—mostly leading Stakhanovites—took part in the work of the brigade from March to May, 1939. The brigade devised over 260 technical measures for the firm as a whole, of which 160 were already in operation by the beginning of May. Among other things, it worked out new methods for reducing waste in a specific department and in addition was called on to demonstrate to the conservative department head that these methods were practical for his department. By June, 1939, a second brigade with 53 specialists was sent out by the Commissariat to continue the work in this same firm.[67] In this fashion, technical resources far beyond that of any single firm were mustered for the analysis of individual production problems.

ORGANIZATION OF COORDINATING BODIES: For certain purposes commissariats and glavki, instead of themselves resolving problems common to many firms, have found it preferable to organize coordinating bodies to work out the solutions. When the Commissar of Machine Construction wished to tackle the problem of reducing cross-freightage in interfirm supply of parts and semifabricates, he ordered the creation of local commissions in the leading industrial

[65] Cf. lead editorial in Z.I., January 9, 1937, p. 1.
[66] Likhachev, writing in Mash., May 15, 1939, p. 3.
[67] Mash., June 15, 1939, p. 3.

centers and obliged the directors of firms to take an active part in the work of these commissions. His only other recorded action was to create a central commission to supervise these local ones.[68] While I have no information as to the actual functioning of these commissions, it seems probable that in reality they were principally meeting grounds for the individual firm managements of the area, and that the issue of success in reducing cross-freightage was in their hands.

Conferences of directors have been called to discuss specific problems.[69] The December, 1935, Plenum of the Central Committee of the Communist Party ordered the convocation of Branch Conferences of managers, engineers, and Stakhanovites during 1936 to revise industrial work norms.[70] These conferences seem to have been genuine working groups rather than mass meetings called to hear higher instructions and invoke public enthusiasm. The following material indicates this clearly.

From January to March, 1936, there were four conferences of representatives of ferrous metallurgical firms, with 700 engineers, foremen, Stakhanovites, and scientific personnel taking part.[71] In the period from February through May, there were over 20 Branch Conferences of machine-construction firms. Two authors who described the work of these conferences were critical of them for each following its own bent without regard to the materials and experience of other branches. They attributed this to lack of leadership of the conferences by the Commissariat.[72] A report on the work of the conferences of many branches indicated lively debates within the conferences regarding standardization of organizational methods for handling norm fulfillment. The report also noted that opposing decisions regarding the same point were taken by the different conferences, and that some questions were avoided because of strong differences of opinion between managements of firms which made the issues too hot to handle.[73] In general, deci-

---

[68] *Mash.*, April 26, 1938, p. 1.

[69] Cf. *Z.I.*, March 29, 1934, p. 2, and May 21, 1935, p. 2.

[70] Plenum resolution, *Z.I.*, December 26, 1935, p. 1.

[71] Tochinskii and Rikman, *op. cit.*, p. 40.

[72] A. Braude and R. Dorogov, "K itogam otraslevykh konferentsii mashinostroeniia" (On the Results of the Branch Conferences of Machine Construction), *Plan*, 1936, No. 11, p. 5.

[73] *Z.I.*, March 4, 1936, p. 2.

sions of the Branch Conferences were approved by the Commissariat. But not all were confirmed,[74] and it was even pointed out that some decisions were contrary to law.[75] All this seems to indicate that these branch meetings were truly conferences in which experience was compared and firm personnel played a real role in making decisions regarding standardization of practice.

STANDARDIZATION: Soviet authorities are anxious to standardize industrial practices, selecting those methods which prove best in practice and ordering their establishment in all appropriate firms. The intention is that each firm management should not only be able to learn from its own experience but be compelled to profit from the experience of others.

The standardization of progressive piece-rate systems was a major question before the 1936 Branch Conferences of the Commissariat of Heavy Industry. There were differences of opinion and practice on the question of how to define the period spent in production by the worker. Should it include only actual work-time, or also time lost in rest periods, in waiting for materials, in waiting for machinery repair, etc.? This question has no effect on earnings in straight piecework, but it is of major significance in a progressive piece-rate system where the rate increases as production rises above the norm. The different conferences standardized the system for all plants within each branch, but differed among themselves as to preferred methods of defining the period spent in production. Thus different systems were designated for firms of different branches.[76] Only in 1937 was a single system set up for the entire Commissariat of Heavy Industry.[77]

In the Ferrous Metallurgical Conferences, it was decided that the percentage of norm fulfillment should be determined on a monthly rather than on a daily basis. Similarly, it was decided to liquidate the experimental system used in some firms of paying progressive rates starting from the first ton of metal produced instead of for only the metal produced above the norm, and all plants had to con-

[74] Cf. Edict No. 177 of the NKTP of March 9, 1936, *BFKhZ*, 1936, No. 11.
[75] "Konsul'tatsiia" (Consultation), *Plan*, 1937, No. 2, pp. 54-56.
[76] *Z.I.*, March 4, 1936, p. 2.
[77] *Z.I.*, April 9, 1937, p. 2.

form to this ruling.[78] Another experiment tried in some firms of having, for the most important categories of workers, two- and three-stage progressive rates for varying degrees of above-norm production was ordered extended to all firms of ferrous metallurgy.[79]

It is recognized by Soviet authorities that standardization should not be pushed too far. In 1934, a member of the Central Committee of the Communist Party who was a high official in the Commissariat of Heavy Industry pointed out that it was impossible to set up a single type of organization for all of industry, and that the glavki were the proper bodies to carry out systematization[80] since they had relatively homogeneous firms under their control. When the commissariats were later broken up, they too began to standardize. Thus in 1939, the Commissariat of Medium Machine Construction and the Commissariat of the Aviation Industry set up standard systems for payment of Stakhanovites operating several machines or combining a number of trades; but the systems of the two commissariats differed sharply.[81]

Yet even standardization for similar bodies can be rigid and ill applied to the needs of individual firms. A complaint was voiced in 1940 by the directors of four firms that one of their plants had had to change its smoothly functioning table of organization to conform with a "model system" adopted by the Commissariat, although this change enlarged the administrative staff without increasing efficiency.[82] Whether or not this particular complaint was justified, it is clear that such abuses could easily occur.

CONCLUDING REMARKS

Now that we have classified the types of orders given to firms by higher bodies, we face the problem of presenting conclusions as to the nature of central control over the economy. We

[78] Article by Gurevich, head of the Glavk of the Metallurgical Industry, in *Z.I.,* March 20, 1936, p. 2.

[79] I. Gorelik, "Pervye itogi vnedreniia novykh norm v chërnoi metallurgii" (First Results of the Introduction of New Norms in Ferrous Metallurgy), *Plan,* 1936, No. 10, p. 4.

[80] M. M. Kaganovich, "Perestroika upravleniia predpriiatiem—boevaia zadacha tiazhëloi promyshlennosti" (The Reconstruction of the Administration of the Firm—an Emergency Task of Heavy Industry), *Org. Uprav.,* 1934, No. 3, p. 4.

[81] *Mash.,* October 6, 1939, p. 3.

[82] *Pravda,* September 10, 1940, p. 2.

shall try to evaluate the strengths and weaknesses of the Soviet form of centralized administration.

We shall do so first with regard to orders of top bodies (the Central Committee of the Communist Party, the Council of Commissars, the Economic Council, and the Commissariat of Heavy Industry before its subdivision in late 1936). We have seen that their instructions ordinarily have been of a general nature, the details being left to lower bodies to formulate or to the firms themselves to work out. True, there were exceptions. Sometimes specific orders were given to individual firms, but this occurred only when their activities had been called to the special attention of the higher body and had been discussed in detail within it. Some details were made specific in the laying down of broad regulations or in the giving of instructions to cope with particular problems, but usually details were left to the commissariats and glavki. Occasionally broad orders were made highly concrete—as with the switch from the 41- to the 48-hour week in 1940, but this seems to have been because bad morale would have resulted from varying rules in different industries.

The activities of top bodies have normally been twofold. (1) They have laid down general policies—as in pushing national campaigns; establishing priority aspects of work, priority segments of the economy, and priority tasks for specific industries; creating new regulatory systems; and establishing broad methods for solving major problems. (2) They have set tasks for the body immediately below in the industrial hierarchy, this body in turn breaking up the tasks among organizations subordinate to it. The highest organs also have ordered experiments—but this has occurred when no lower body had the authority to experiment in this fashion on its own.

Clearly there is nothing which lies outside of the authority of these top organs; there is no absolute "autonomy" of any lower group. Bodies like the Economic Council can interfere anywhere, and do so when trouble-spots appear. This is fundamental to the Soviet concept of "democratic centralism." But apparently these top organs have not used their power to "meddle" in details. They do not set up highly detailed regulations for heterogeneous groups of lower bodies, for they have recognized that details must vary with the concrete conditions of work. They do not tie up the economy in red tape, nor make it wait at every step for the issuance of rules from above, nor require it to follow hosts of specific orders.

So much for the strength of this part of the system. It has, however, been bought at the price of serious weaknesses. For in addition to setting tasks which were afterward subdivided by intermediate bodies among the firms, and establishing policies which were made concrete by other organs, Soviet top organs have also begun campaigns and established priorities which are binding on all bodies from the highest to the lowest. Desiring to push forward certain elements of the economy as well as certain tasks, they have compelled all bodies to stress them. These priorities have been considered as far more binding than specific tasks set for lower organizations; specific rules could be and were expected to be violated for the sake of these broader considerations. But since the requirement of "laying stress" and "giving priority" is an extremely crude method of direction—quite unresponsive to the question of "how much stress?"—it is scarcely surprising that the emphasis has often gone too far. The "campaign" method of operation, for example, has led to firms each having to revise tens of thousands of work norms in a period of a few months, and inevitably the revisions have been crude and unreflective of the real work conditions. This method of direction has even led to some "priorities" being set simply in order to counterbalance the overemphasis on other elements and on other tasks.

To a certain extent, the excesses of these "campaign" and "priority" methods can be laid to the immaturity of the Soviet Union's industrial system and reflect the need for raising from a very low level the quality of management's work in such crucial areas as quality of product and considerations of cost. Heavy stress has been placed on individual factors simply because they were being badly neglected or constituted bottlenecks. As the system matures, we may expect "campaigns" to be planned more moderately and with more attention to the effects of extremism. (Witness the 1939 campaign for the combining of trades and the operation of several machines by a single worker.)

But while excesses may be shorn away with time, the fundamental disadvantages of "priority" methods have been deeply imbedded in the practice of Soviet industrial administration. This seems to be due to the lack of a clear criterion of "success" for the administrative apparatus on any level. As will be shown subsequently, no quantitative appraisal of the different factors entering into the work of firm management is given to it from above, and management itself has to decide in each specific case the relative importance of the many "success" and "plan-fulfillment" criteria, and what weights to give them in the making of any particular decision. Since the many criteria are not evaluated relatively in standard quantitative terms by any organ in the country, firms need some substitute guide for proper evaluation on their part of the country's needs of the moment as interpreted by the top bodies. This guidance has been provided by "priority" methods. It is doubtful whether such procedures can be eliminated so long as Soviet administration does not have, and seems to reject in principle, any single and quantitatively expressed criterion of over-all "success" of firms.[83]

On the intermediate administrative level of the glavki and post-1936 commissariats, the methods of direction used have been quite different. Generalized instructions and regulations were issued by these bodies as well as by those above them. But "priority" and "campaign" practices were largely eschewed. In their place stood a tremendous body of direct instructions to firm managements.

That was because glavki, and even commissariats after their further divisions in 1939, have been considered to be organs close to the firms, aware of their concrete problems, and therefore able to issue specific orders, set precise tasks, and give concrete aid. They are held to be near enough to production to be able to pick out the best methods used in firms, standardize them, and order their application in all other plants. It is expected that through them industry will be more highly integrated than is possible solely by means of general instructions and priorities.

To the extent that these intermediate bodies are really close to production problems and able to analyze the specific difficulties of their firms, this type of administrative practice seems sound. The rub is, of course, that in reality they have often had far from sufficient intimacy with their firms. Where this has happened multitudes of orders have been issued and regulations promulgated

[83] The question of "success criteria" will be developed at length in following chapters.

which were totally inapplicable to the real problems and, insofar as they were obeyed by firm managements, were capable only of tying the economy into knots of bureaucratic red tape. Unsuited to solving the actual problems, they crippled management's initiative in undertaking their own solutions.

Soviet administrators have been highly aware of this problem. On an official level, it has been met by continual and growing emphasis on the need for giving genuine authority and even "autonomy" under most conditions to the lowest level of management —the foremen.[84] Unofficially, it has been met by the common practice of winking at the frequent disobedience to such orders by firm managements. This has reached such a point that management personnel have openly and unashamedly written in the national press of ignoring the detailed instructions given them.[85]

It would seem to me that it is on this—the intermediate—level of Soviet industrial administration that the dangers and ill effects of a system of detailed orders are most pronounced. But it appears quite possible that these deficiencies may be due primarily to growing pains of the economy. As managerial personnel become better trained, and as the glavki and commissariats come more and more into touch with the concrete problems of their firms, it may well be that red tape and inappropriate orders will be reduced to relatively unimportant proportions. That it will always be a problem of some magnitude seems, on the other hand, indisputable.

Our treatment of the nature of central control over industrial firms has covered only by implication the basic question of the degree of centralization found in Soviet industrial administration. To what extent has the firm management enjoyed "independence"? What has been the nature of this "independence"? Without an analysis of the degree of decentralization in Soviet industry, a study of the methods of centralization would be pointless indeed. It is to the explicit examination of the fundamental problem of the autonomy of firm managements that we shall now proceed.

[84] Cf. *Z.I.*, August 28, 1934, p. 3. Post. No. 900 of the SNK SSSR and of the TsK VKP(b) No. 900 of May 27, 1940, *SPR*, 1940, article 361. Post. No. 1639 of the Economic Council of Oct. 3, 1940, *SPR*, 1940, article 694. Report of Malenkov at the XVIIIth Party Conference in February 1941, *Ch.M.*, February 16, 1941, p. 3.

[85] See Chapter VII.

VII: Plant Management's Independence

A COMMON APPROACH to the problem of the degree of autonomy of lower organs is that of "division of functions," the definition of powers reserved exclusively for these bodies. But such an approach would be none too fruitful if applied to Soviet industry, operated according to the principles of "democratic centralism." For here the firms are closely integrated into the total administrative structure of heavy industry. Indeed, there are no aspects of the work of firm managements into which higher organs cannot enter. Judging solely by the criterion of "division of functions," we would have to say that there is virtually no autonomy whatsoever in Soviet heavy industry.

Such a view would be borne out by the complaints of plant managements in the national press concerning the insignificant autonomy left to them. Directors have complained of being snowed under by orders of all types from higher bodies such as glavki.[1] A glavk head admitted that in large plants with up to 20,000 to 25,000 workers, cases arise literally every day requiring changes in what the Army calls the table of organization of personnel. Yet the directors have no right to make changes, and must appeal each case to the glavk and justify their proposed measures.[2] In 1935, firm managements were given permission to purchase equipment and inventory on their own responsibility if the value of each unit purchased was not over 200 rubles. When one considers that this sum was no more than half to three quarters of the average monthly earnings of a foreman in heavy industry, the accompanying newspaper statement that this was a triumph for managerial auton-

[1] Cf. Director S. Birman's article in Z.I., January 27, 1934, p. 2.

[2] S. Reznikov, head of the Glavk of the Metallurgical Industry of the South and Center, writing in Pravda, October 4, 1940, p. 3.

omy seems to be a good indication of the significance of such "autonomy."[3] In the metallurgical industry during 1940, the heads of even the tiniest metallurgical departments were appointed by the glavki heads rather than by the firm directors.[4] All directors of heavy industry were at one time forbidden to leave their plants on business without the personal permission of the commissar or the head of their glavk.[5] Even where a special fund out of firms' profits (the "director's fund") was set up to provide for premiums and other incentives, and where firm managements and the local trade union bodies were intended to have control over these moneys, some glavki in practice took on themselves the determination of the sums to be given out in individual premiums to workmen and insisted that the managements get permission from them for each premium grant.[6]

Often directors are given more autonomy than is shown above. But where this is the case, it is only because their glavk and commissariat do not choose at the moment to exercise authority over the particular matter. At any moment a higher body can interject itself into the area of "autonomy."

But while firm managements do not have special areas of authority in which higher organs are forbidden to poach, they exercise considerable independent decision-making powers in the process of carrying out higher orders. This is demonstrated in the case to be discussed below of the introduction of intrafirm dispatching at the Kaganovich First Ball-Bearing Works.

From 1934 on, serious efforts were made to introduce dispatching systems into the firms of heavy industry. (By dispatching is meant a continuous control over the production work of all units within the firm by a central organ of management, so that work will be done according to a detailed time schedule coordinating

[3] Post. of the SNK SSSR of September 19, 1935, *SZ*, 1935, article 417. **Lead editorial** in *Z.I.*, September 22, 1935, p. 1. TsUNKhU Gosplana SSSR, *Zarabotnaia plata inzhenerno-tekhnicheskikh rabotnikov i sluzhashchikh v sentiabre-oktiabre 1934 g.* (Salaries of Engineering-Technical Workers and White-Collar Workers in September-October, 1934), (Moscow: 1935), Table I, pp. 12 and 22-25.

[4] Glavk head S. Reznikov, writing in *Pravda*, October 4, 1940, p. 3.

[5] Prikaz No. 1029 of the NKTP of December 4, 1933, *Prikazy i rasporiazheniia NKTP* (Orders and Instructions of the Commissariat of Heavy Industry), 1933.

[6] Cf. *Pravda*, October 17, 1940, p. 2.

operations throughout the plant.[7] In this fashion, stocks of materials and parts, tools and machinery, and labor can be used most effectively for continuous production of finished products, the various shops and departments working as a unit rather than as independent entities. It is the task of dispatchers to coordinate the subunits and to maintain a constant production flow.) Various orders were issued by the Commissariat as well as by the individual glavki insisting on the introduction of dispatching,[8] and by 1937 about 100 firms had such a system.[9] Among the firms in which the Commissariat ordered the inauguration of dispatching was the First Ball-Bearing Works, but the failure of this plant's management to make and carry out the proper implementing decisions doomed the new system to purely formalistic realization. The Commissariat's decision by itself could effect no real change in the existing methods of operation. This example of the very real autonomy of firms in the execution of orders from above will bear analysis.

In 1934, just before dispatching was introduced into the Works, production there was organized in the following fashion.[10] The departments producing the rollers, the ball bearings, and the separators each had a production process completely independent of the work of all other departments. Those departments producing the containing ring were, however, all dependent upon one another for semifabricates, and one half of the plant's labor force was engaged in this work. Thirdly, there were the assembly departments which depended upon the others for parts. In order to have smooth production, daily scheduling was of the utmost importance. Instead, however, planning was on a monthly basis.

[7] Otdel organizatsii proizvodstva NKTI and TsIO NKTP, "Osnovnye polozheniia po organizatsii dispetcherskoi sistemy upravleniia na mashinostroitel'nykh predpriiatiakh" (The Main Conditions for the Organization of a Dispatching System of Direction in Machine-Construction Firms), *Org. Uprav.*, 1934, No. 4, p. 3.

[8] Cf. M. M. Kaganovich, "Perestroika upravleniia. . . ," pp. 3-14. Prikaz No. 320 of the NKTP of February 26, 1936, "O sostoianii dispetcherizatsii i meropriiatiiakh po dal'neishemu i razvitiiu" (On Establishing Dispatching, and Measures for its Furthering and Development), *Org. Uprav.*, 1936, No. 2, pp. 3-6.

[9] "Organizatsiia proizvodstva v tretei piatiletke i zadachi TsIO" (The Organization of Production in the Third Five-Year Plan and the Task of the Central Scientific-Research Institute for the Organization of Production), *Org. Uprav.*, 1937, No. 4, p. 9.

[10] This analysis is a summary of the article by L. M. Baikova, "O dispetcherizatsii na zavode 'Sharikopodshipnik'" (On Dispatching in the Plant Ball-Bearing Works), *Org. Uprav.*, 1937, No. 3, pp. 73-80.

The plant's Planning-Production Sector designated the departments' monthly production tasks for each of the items they were to produce and determined the amount of each item to be sent to the other departments within the month. There was no planning of cycles of beginning and completing batches within a department, of norms of unfinished production, of hours or even days for delivering semifabricates to another department. Interdepartmental coordination was sporadic and only for particular batches, and it took the form of conversations between head personnel as to which orders to push ahead and which to postpone. With such a loose coordination of departments, it is not surprising that equipment was idle for lack of semifabricates, and that production was jerky and unsatisfactory.

When in 1934 a dispatching system was set up in the plant on orders of the Commissariat, special dispatching rooms for the departments and for the plant's central apparatus were established, and dispatchers were appointed. The plant management, in thus following higher orders, considered that its duty was done and that the dispatchers would now rapidly establish order; the *deus ex machina* had been found.

But the essential preconditions for a special dispatching system had not been created. No norms had been worked out for needs of materials, fuels, and semifabricates per unit of production of each department; nor had time schedules been established for the production or transfer of products as items moved from department to department. There was no systematized information as to required machine time per operation, or as to transport time, or the time for delay in stock which was to be expected for each part. Thus the chief dispatcher and his shift dispatchers had to adjust themselves to the existing planless system. The dispatchers became, in practice, "pushers." Within a single department and between departments they followed key orders and saw that they were given priority. Thus they only added to the plant's confusion.

Deprived of the possibilities of working out their original assignment, the dispatchers remained on the fringe of administration. Created as parallel organs to the planning bureaus within each department, the dispatching bureaus tried to carry out their tasks without reference to them. But as it was the planning bureau in each department which made the operational work plans, set tasks for each machine, and handled supplies and repair work, the dispatchers were utterly isolated and powerless. This was reflected in the fact that the engineers and experienced workmen who at first were named to the dispatching bureaus were after a few months replaced by simple "pushers" who were quite ignorant of production practice and needs.

Thus by mid-1937, after three years of "carrying out" the Commissariat's order to introduce dispatching into the plant, the system remained purely formalistic and ineffectual and was, therefore, completely discredited.

It should be noted that the plant's management appeared to have accepted willingly the order to introduce dispatching. The difficulty was that it could only have carried it through successfully if it had first worked out the norms and time schedules required for a functioning dispatching system. But the management could not have accomplished this without moving trained technical personnel from their old jobs. Almost certainly, the plant would for a time have shown less success in meeting production orders.

The Commissariat's original decree had left firm management with the task of designing the multitude of measures required to make the new system a success. Thus it implicitly left to the management the responsibility of deciding whether the game was worth the candle, whether a proper dispatching system was worth the heavy expenditures of money and man power which would have been required. Apparently, the management decided that it was not necessary to obey the Commissariat regarding the introduction of dispatching, that the temporary difficulties in "plan fulfillment" which would inevitably have resulted were more important in the over-all weighting of the plant management's "success." Management had no formal "autonomy" regarding the introduction of a dispatching system; nevertheless, it had the power and obligation to make an "independent" decision as to the amount of man power to devote to fulfilling the command given it.

It is due to the existence of such managerial power that in investigating the problem of autonomy we must go beyond the question: In which areas of work are firm managements left free of instructions from above? Having answered that there are no such

areas, we must further ask: Where and to what extent do managements exercise independence of decision making?

FIELDS OF INITIATIVE OF FIRM MANAGEMENT

REGARDING PROBLEMS IN EARLY STAGES: Although emphasis
in Soviet industry has been on coordination and standardization of
practices, there has at the same time been a strong and constant
predilection in favor of experiment. While, as we have seen in the
preceding chapter, experiments might be ordered from above
when firms did not themselves have sufficient authority to institute
them, it has been those firms whose managements have fought for
the new ideas which have customarily been chosen to carry on the
experiments. More normally, new ideas have been tried out by individual firms without higher approval.

In 1934, the Menzhinskii Aviation Firm began paying its workers according to a new system in which the pay scale was tied to
the quality of production as well as to the usual quantity indices.
All sorts of practical problems were met—how many quality grades
should be used; what effect this would have on total wages paid
out and on other costs; what additional incentives could be used
for high-quality production and how these could be geared into
the premium system; and how the new system could best be introduced.

The plant's new wage system seemed successful, and by November, 1934, the newspapers of six other firms began demanding the
introduction of the new system into their plants. On December 10,
the head of the Glavk of the Aviation Industry ordered all directors to adopt the experience of this plant to their own firms. Managements in other industries took up the campaign.[11] This acceptance of the Menzhinskii Plant's example took place despite the
fact that the plant had been able to develop its premium system
only by violating its plan through overexpenditures of its planned
wage fund.[12] So many firms wrote to the Menzhinskii Firm's management asking about its system that on April 16, 1935, the firm
created a special consultative bureau. Within twelve days, representatives of twenty-five different plants personally appeared before

[11] *Z.I.*, April 29, 1935, p. 2.
[12] *Z.I.*, September 4, 1935, p. 3.

the bureau with questions.[13] Thus it was at the practical initiative of an individual plant that a major campaign began in Heavy Industry. Other campaigns also began in individual firms, and their experience with new methods formed the original basis for many such movements.

While standardization of practice is desired by higher bodies, they consider that it should be based on prior experience. All the standardization work in 1936 of progressive piece-rate systems followed this precept. It has been common practice that firms should be given full freedom to establish temporary norms of work for new items of production, and that only after the firm has gained experience with the new products should a higher body approve the work norms and piece rates.[14] When all industry was shifted from the 41- to the 48-hour work week in 1940, firms were left on their own in making up new work schedules. Two leading metallurgical firms immediately introduced different schedules. One changed from a system of four brigades for a production unit to three, and the other introduced a seven-brigade system. Each method had its own strengths and weaknesses, and only experience could show which was preferable. Executives in metallurgy throughout the country were vitally interested in the determination of which organizational system was better, and there was pressure for a quick decision by higher authorities and for standardization of practice.[15] But prior experimentation by the firms was nevertheless considered essential.

It is clear that this sort of autonomy by firms must be short-lived with regard to any particular matter. It can last only so long as experience has not accumulated sufficiently to permit proper standardization. But since new problems are constantly arising, this type of autonomy is still of major importance to firms. Standardization of practice is accompanied by the birth of new problems requiring experimentation in the handling of which autonomy is temporarily granted.

In addition, it should not be thought that standardization is al-

[13] *Z.I.*, May 6, 1935, p. 3.

[14] Cf. Prikaz No. 23 of the Commissariat of Construction Materials USSR, summarized in *Ind.*, February 10, 1940, p. 3.

[15] *Ind.*, July 5, 1940, p. 2, and July 7, 1940, p. 1.

ways rapid. In 1936, the various Branch Conferences determined the method to be used by the firms in their branch for figuring the percentages of norm fulfillment of all workers on progressive piece rates. In 1937, the Commissariat of Heavy Industry ordered a single such system for all the firms of the Commissariat. But in late 1938, even the firms under a single glavk used markedly varying methods for figuring norm fulfillment of straight pieceworkers.[16] Standardization in this field was still far from complete.

SUGGESTIONS TO HIGHER BODIES: As we have seen in Chapter IV, managements have some say with regard to the annual planned "tasks" given their firms. They suggest their investment[17] and procurement needs. They may offer complete reorganization schemes as when, in 1935, a group of engineers and economists of the Stalingrad Dzerzhinskii Tractor Plant drew up a plan for the total reorganization of the plant and its production, and presented the plan in the national industrial press.[18] Machine-construction plants develop new designs which may be accepted for production in many other firms as well.[19] This sort of initiative of management, however, is totally divorced from the possession of independent authority—except insofar as the suggestions carry weight due to their source.

APPLICATION OF HIGHER DECISIONS TO CONCRETE CONDITIONS: It is probably in this area that firm management exercises most of its autonomy. For, clearly, higher decisions are worthless unless applied, and, as was shown above in this chapter in the case of the introduction of dispatching into the First Ball-Bearing Works, such application requires considerable initiative and know-how which often are lacking.

At the December, 1935, Plenum of the Central Committee of

---

[16] Article by S. Pogostin, senior engineer of the Sector of Personnel and Wages of the Commissariat of Heavy Industry, in *Ind.*, September 5, 1938, p. 2. The significance of this for the worker was that the percentage of norm fulfillment had a marked effect on his prestige and status in the plant, as exampled by its use in the determination of which workers should be designated as Stakhanovites.

[17] Cf. Prikaz, No. 245 of the NKTP of February 26, 1935, *Z.I.*, February 27, 1935, p. 1.

[18] *Z.I.*, December 9, 1935, p. 3.

[19] Cf. the article by Director I. Lisin and Technical Director S. Zak in *Z.I.*, June 14, 1936, p. 3.

the Communist Party, the Party demanded the end of the practice of basing work norms on "experience" rather than on scientific study of production possibilities.[20] The carrying out of this demand has often been repeated by high industrial officials, and the continued dominance of such "practical" norms has been regretted.[21] Yet in 1939, in the Commissariat of General Machine Construction, 66 percent of all work norms were "practical" ones, 12 percent were based on time and motion studies, and only 23 percent were based on a full analysis of production and on a methods study.[22] The reason for this failure can be seen in the fact that there were 2,026,000 separate work norms in this commissariat alone.[23] Clearly, the revision of these on a properly scientific basis was an enormous job—and it was only on the initiative of firm managements that it could be done at all.

Similarly, firm managements must decide which decisions actually to carry out. For example, design work and the use of experimental departments by machine-construction firms have been continually stressed, and it has been considered essential that they should originate a large proportion of the country's new models. In a 1936 Branch Conference of the heavy machine-building plants, it was decided that thenceforth they should be obligated to reexamine all orders for machinery given to them by consumer plants, and wherever possible to design equipment more suitable to these plants' production processes. But, in practice, the machine-building plants ignored the designing of new equipment. They felt it more important to concentrate on getting out production, and used their "experimental departments" for regular production work. Without the facilities for building and trying out individual models and for remedying errors of design, the firm designers were of course stymied. As a result, the firms felt that strong design departments were as unwarranted as proper experimental departments, and so transferred their best engineers to production.[24]

[20] Resolution of December 25, 1935, *Z.I.*, December 26, 1935, p. 1.

[21] Cf. *Ind.*, September 5, 1938, p. 2, and September 15, 1939, p. 2, and *Mash.*, May 11, 1939, p. 2.

[22] N. Kochnov, Assistant Commissar of General Machine Construction, writing in *Mash.*, May 11, 1939, p. 2. The sum of the percentages differ from 100 percent due to rounding off.

[23] *Ibid.*

[24] Cf. *Z.I.*, March 14, 1936, p. 2.

HANDLING PROBLEMS WITH WHICH HIGHER BODIES ARE NOT COPING:
Many problems—even those of major importance—are not analyzed
and grappled with by higher bodies. While in individual cases
there may be many different reasons for this, the underlying cause
seems to be the inability to solve all questions simultaneously. This
group of problems, left perforce to autonomous handling by the
firms, is a phenomenon in Soviet industrial administration which
can be expected to diminish as industrial practice and administration become more mature.

In 1938, for example, the director of a major machine-construction plant complained in the press that there were no up-to-date
higher instructions or norm materials governing the payment of
the engineering-technical personnel of his firm, and that in practice
the management decided all wage questions regarding this major
group of personnel "according to its own understanding." When
the plant directed questions to the Commissariat on this matter, no
answer was received.[25]

In 1937, all plants of heavy industry were ordered to improve the
quality of their work norms for pieceworkers. But nothing was said
about the norms and premium systems for timeworkers. The Moscow Kuibyshev Electrical Combinat decided on its own to revise
premium systems in order to give timeworkers greater incentives.[26]

Even entire areas of activity may be left virtually uncontrolled.
The importance of supplying parts and semifabricates to firms by
other plants in the same industry has been stressed in the Soviet
press. But supervision over this work by higher bodies has been
highly sporadic, and has generally been neglected.[27] It was not until 1947 that fulfillment of such orders for "interfirm cooperation"
was generally included in the definition of "plan fulfillment" for
the firms.[28]

[25] Director K. Zadorozhnyi of the Novo-Kramatorskii Stalin Plant and Venderovich,
writing in *Mash.*, January 10, 1938, p. 3.
[26] *Z.I.*, April 15, 1937, p. 2.
[27] Cf. Brigada TsIO (Brigade of the Central Scientific Research Institute for the
Organization of Production). "Spetsializatsiia i kooperirovanie v glavsredmashe"
(Specialization and Cooperation in the Glavk of Medium Machine Construction) *Org.
Uprav.*, 1937, No. 6, p. 86. Also, G. Dobrovenskii, "Kooperirovanie promyshlennosti"
(Cooperation of Industry), *Problem Ekonomiki*, 1938, No. 3, pp. 32-37.
[28] Post. No. 3110 of the Council of Ministers of September 2, 1947, reported in
Kontorovich, *Tekhpromfinplan*, p. 58.

GENERAL INITIATIVE DUE TO OVER-ALL RESPONSIBILITY: Up to this point we have specifically discussed managerial initiative in particular areas. There is, however, a driving force in the Soviet system which compels management to exercise initiative in all phases of managerial activity: to initiate new methods, to search out new possibilities for increased production and reduced cost, and even to violate orders and aspects of their plan which are harmful to the firm. This force is the knowledge that "success is never blamed," while the manager who is not "successful" in his over-all results is rarely considered to have a legitimate excuse.[29]

In fact, the Soviet code of "self-criticism" has tended to view efforts to blame failures on other people or organizations as rationalizations and as irrelevant to the bare fact of failure. In 1934 the top management personnel and the Party secretary of the Khar'kov Electromechanical Firm, in a letter to the press, explained the plant's bad record by the lack of good equipment.[30] The letter was published, but was severely criticized by the newspaper's editor. It is the management's task to work out a concrete program for overcoming the plant's backwardness, he wrote, yet the authors of the letter simply offer excuses.[31] A proper Soviet newspaper letter was written by Director M. B. Grosman. In discussing the plant's failure to produce satisfactorily, he pointed out that supplies allotted to him were not received. But, he wrote, he would shoulder the blame for failure in not having overcome this obstacle.[32] Failure was failure, and excuses were irrelevant.

The drive for "success" has vastly enlarged the area of initiative of firms. For, indeed, it forces management into undertaking all sorts of activities irrespective of whether they are formally under other organs.

This can be seen in many areas. For example, the development of a sufficiently large and trained labor force has been a constant problem. Planned recruitment from agriculture under contracts with collective farms has long been stressed.[33] City councils and

[29] The concept of success will be treated in considerably more detail below.
[30] Z.I., June 17, 1934, p. 1.
[31] Ibid.
[32] Z.I., June 11, 1934, p. 2.
[33] N. Aristov, "Organizovannyi nabor rabochei sily" (Organized Recruitment of Labor Force), Planovoe Khoziaistvo, 1939, No. 11, pp. 89-92.

local Communist Party committees have helped recruit personnel for firms.[34] But managements still have depended heavily and probably mainly on "hiring at the gate."[35]

Similarly, major equipment is supposed to be purchased from machine-construction firms according to investment allotments. But when these firms refuse to accept orders because they are overloaded, or when delivery would be too greatly delayed, the firms needing the machinery often have produced it themselves.[36]

AUXILIARY FUNCTIONS: In addition to the functions directly connected with production and further construction, plant managements have a host of other duties. These have included such duties as designing new models and equipment, due to the feeling of top authorities that scientific institutions are not close enough to production to handle the problem by themselves.[37] But the main force developing initiative for most of management's auxiliary work is not so much pressure from higher organs as the fact that production itself would suffer if this work were neglected.

For example, managements have had great difficulty in getting a sufficiently large labor force, keeping down turnover of workers, and finding those with the necessary skills. Up until 1937 (when rationing had been abandoned and it was easier for workers to get goods if they had the money), firms operated Sectors of Workers' Supply for their own personnel. At the end of 1934, there were 13,600 such stores within plants of heavy industry which serviced 4,650,000 workers.[38] In order to supply their Plant Sectors with foods to sell and to serve in plant dining rooms, the firms also owned and operated State Farms. On April 1, 1935, there were 200,000 people working on the State Farms of the Commissariat of Heavy Industry,[39] and directors were advised to concern them-

---

[34] Cf. *Z.I.*, July 10, 1935, p. 2.
[35] Cf. Aristov, *op. cit.*, p. 92.
[36] Cf. *Z.I.*, *February* 8, 1937, p. 2.
[37] Cf. Prikaz No. 873 of the NKTP of July 16, 1935, *BFKhZ*, 1935, No. 22.
[38] Speech of Piterskii, head of the Glavk of Sectors of Workers' Supply, at the First Plenum of the Council of the Commissariat of Heavy Industry, printed in *Z.I.*, May 12, 1935, p. 1.
[39] TsUNKhU, *Trud v SSSR*, p. 49.

selves with these State Farms just as though they were departments of their firms.[40]

Firms having good Sectors of Workers' Supply could more easily attract and hold workers than could other plants. There was a similar incentive for proper building and operation of kindergartens for children of plant workers after these kindergartens were turned over to firm managements in 1936.[41] In the same fashion, firm managements built and operated the housing for a high proportion of their total labor force. On January 1, 1935, 56 percent of all workers in the Commissariat of Heavy Industry were housed in their firms' own buildings.[42] While much of the money for this housing came from the State budget, free funds at the disposal of the plant managements[43] were also used. The firm with good housing to offer had a decided edge on its competitors in enlisting and retaining efficient labor.

If skilled labor was to be obtained, it was up to the firms to institute courses for training workers on the job. Such courses were required by the Commissariat of Heavy Industry, and it was the directors who were given the task of organizing and conducting them.[44] There was both the direct responsibility for properly operating the courses and the knowledge that poor operation would find its reflection in the production of a later period.

The general responsibility of management for its employees was pointed out by the Commissar of Heavy Industry in 1934.[45] In this speech the Commissar instructed directors to devote resources to schools, community dining rooms, etc. True, such care of the

[40] Cf. Z.I., April 2, 1935, p. 2.

[41] Prikaz No. 1517 of the NKTP of September 11, 1936, BFKhZ, 1936, No. 28/29.

[42] I. Lifshits and S. Abramov, "Za kul'turnuiu eksploatatsiiu zhilishchnogo fonda v tiazhëloi promyshlennosti" (For a Cultured Use of the Housing Fund in Heavy Industry), Vopr. Profdvizh., 1935, No. 5-6, p. 51. Of the Commissariat's housing, however, 20 percent of the space consisted of barracks. See also, the NKTP otchetno-ekonomicheskii sektor (The Commissariat of Heavy Industry Accounting-Economic Sector), Tiazhëlaia promyshlennost' SSSR za 1931-1934 gg. (Heavy Industry of the USSR During 1931-1934), materials for the report of the Commissar of Heavy Industry, S. Ordzhonikidze, to the VIIth Congress of Soviets of the USSR (Moscow: 1935), p. 144.

[43] In the form of the director's fund from 1936 on.

[44] Cf. Prikaz No. 1043 of the NKTP of July 31, 1934, BFKhZ, 1934, No. 23. Also, Prikaz No. 165 of the NKTP of January 26, 1936, Za Promyshlennye Kadry (For Industrial Cadre), 1936, No. 2, pp. 7-8. (Hereafter cited as Za. Prom. Kadry.)

[45] G. K. (Sergo) Ordzhonikidze, speech at the Conference of Workers of Heavy Industry on September 20, 1934, Z.I., September 22, 1934, p. 2.

population was the job of other State organs, but, in places other
than the old and well-established cities, these organs had little
resources. Therefore, he said, it was up to the firms dominating
new communities such as Magnitogorsk to take over the job others
could not handle.[46]

Indeed, directors have complained that sometimes they are
forced to assume all the work of city government. One district authority insisted that a firm supply the local baking plant with fuel
because its workers bought most of the bread. It insisted that it was
up to the firm's management to care for the local population.[47]
The director could scarcely have avoided complying, for the penalty would have been loss of his labor force and failure to fulfill his
annual plan.

MANAGEMENT'S INDEPENDENCE OF ACTION

Since plant managements are judged by their over-all "success,"[48] it is hardly surprising that they should regard many problems from the point of view of the good of their own plant. In
a fashion similar to that of capitalist businessmen they seem to look
upon rules and laws not too strictly enforced as intended only for
the gullible.

In Chapter VIII we shall see how widespread have been the
violations of supply allocations. Similarly, labor force plans drawn
up by higher bodies are often broken by firms the day after they
are established.[49] When there is no follow-up control, plants may
utterly ignore Commissariat instructions to rush particular priority orders.[50] Priority tasks set for the firms of a given commissariat by the Economic Council itself have been completely disregarded despite a worsening situation.[51] In 1937, Molotov
complained that even leading officials of the commissariats "forget"

[46] In 1933, according to John Scott who worked in Magnitogorsk, the director of
Magnitogorsk actually ran the entire city's administration. Scott, *Behind the Urals*
(Cambridge, Mass.: 1942), p. 81.
[47] Article by Director S. Akopov in *Mash.*, December 22, 1938, p. 2.
[48] See the following chapters for further evidence.
[49] *Mash.*, December 9, 1938, p. 2.
[50] Cf. *Z.I.*, August 12, 1937, p. 1.
[51] Cf. the article by N. Guliaev, assistant to the head of the Credit Administration of
the Commissariats of Heavy Industry and of Machine Construction, in *Mash.*, December 11, 1938, p. 2.

decisions of the Party and Government which are basic to their work.[52]

These violations are so well recognized as semi-legitimate that directors have written articles in the national press describing how they have violated both the law and their glavki instructions, announcing that they consider these violations as quite proper, and stating that they intend to continue and even extend them in the future.[53] (This open violation of regulations is, of course, not peculiar to the Soviet economy. In the United States, railroad and bus unions have not infrequently threatened to bring transport lines to a standstill solely by rigid obedience to the rules of the companies themselves.)

Thus it can be seen that, when directors feel that they must break existing rules and laws in order to operate, they need not normally fear prosecution for such actions. At the same time, they are exposed to punishments should their violations be judged seriously harmful.

The need for a manager to hold a boldly independent attitude was pointed out in a discussion article by engineer V. Spiridonov. Spiridonov declared that the zealous plant director must be willing to take the responsibility of using State funds for purposes other than those for which they were allocated. If he judges that insufficient money has been allotted to capital repair, he should use current-repair funds to carry out the necessary work. Spiridonov's clear implication was that only the ne'er-do-well manager would always obey the rules and laws under which he is supposed to work.[54]

[52] V. M. Molotov's Report to the Plenum of March 28, 1937, of the Central Committee of the Communist Party, *Z.I.*, April 21, 1937, pp. 2-3.

[53] In February and March, 1935, there was a whole series of such letters in *Z.I.* with regard to wage fund violations. Cf. the article by Director E. Kovarskii in the issue of February 28, 1935, p. 3, and the one by Director P. Zhbakov in *Z.I.*, March 26, 1935, p. 3. Such brazen confessions by top management continued even during the heart of the Purge Period, as witness the article by V. Perlin, chief of the Production-Planning Sector of the Magnitogorsk Stalin Firm in *Ind.*, September 17, 1937, p. 3. In the post-Purge period, such articles as that of Director Akopov in *Mash.*, December 22, 1938, p. 2, continued the tradition.

[54] *Mash.*, July 24, 1938, p. 2. It is in the light of such material as has been presented in this chapter that we should read statements of non-Soviet writers on the rigid bureaucratization of Soviet industry. Hubbard, for example, writes of industry that ". . . no Soviet official will do anything without a written order; . . . equally, everybody who gives an order puts it on paper for a record." Leonard E. Hubbard, *Soviet Labour and Industry* (London: 1942), p. 123.

Just as the successful manager must be willing to take a bold position with regard to rules and laws, he must also stand forth independently when caught between conflicting higher organizations. The storms which he may be called upon to brave are often severe ones.

For over a year a Moscow director, S. A. Freiman, was threatened with legal action when he found himself in the middle of a quarrel between the Moscow City Council and his own Glavk. A house, formerly not under the plant, was transferred to the firm's ownership by an arbitrator of the Moscow City Council. Then the house was ordered repaired, and the firm's management was instructed to pay 40,000 rubles for this work. Director Freiman, however, would not pay, pleading that his Glavk refused to allocate him the necessary money as it denied that the house belonged to the firm, and that he could only get it by illegally taking it from funds specifically allocated to other purposes. The case dragged on, and finally Director Freiman was sentenced by a Moscow court to six months of labor at his place of work with a 15 percent deduction from his pay. The court suspended sentence for four months, but the sentence was then to go into effect unless the repairs had meanwhile been completed.[55] It is not recorded if the Glavk and the Moscow City Council finally settled matters, or if Freiman actually had to decide which law he preferred to break.

Director Gorlanov was similarly caught between the demands of local authorities and the duties of his job. Local Party and Government officials had long diverted a machine-construction plant of the Irbitskii District of the Sverdlovskii Region from its proper functions to that of exclusively servicing the community's needs. In late 1934, the Commissariat of Heavy Industry changed the plant leadership and appointed Gorlanov. Local authorities treated him most suspiciously as a "Moscow director." When he refused demands for plant moneys to be used for local sanitation, agricultural needs, the newspaper, the militia, etc.—all of which grants would have been quite illegal, although common—the local Party and Government officials took their revenge. In less than three months they had "investigated" the firm and on the basis of this

[55] *Z.I.*, May 18, 1935, p. 1.

had ousted Gorlanov from the Communist Party. In addition, they had demanded his removal as director and the local Party secretary had quite illegally suspended him from work.[56] What happened to Gorlanov thereafter is not recorded, but irrespective of the outcome, he took the only position which could possibly have won him success in the eyes of the Commissariat. His boldness in standing up to the local authorities was an essential requirement for the proper fulfillment of his job.

Operating in this environment, it is scarcely surprising that plant directors have developed some of the feeling of independence which typifies businessmen in capitalist countries. When they have entered conferences, even with the Commissar, they often have seemed to go in as powers in their own right—possibly to be cajoled and persuaded, but not commanded.

At the VIIth All-Union Congress of the Soviets, the Commissar of Heavy Industry reported on progress in 1934. He gave the coefficients of blast-furnace use for several firms, cleverly mentioning that of the Petrovskii Firm in an order of firms where it would appear at its worst.[57] When the Commissar gave the coefficient of 1.24 for his firm, Director Birman interrupted from the floor of the Soviet to say that the coefficient was down to 1.15 in December. With this interruption the Commissar snapped the trap, demanding of Birman that he promise to achieve a coefficient of 1.15 throughout 1935. Politbureau member Voroshilov laughingly shouted out, "You're trapped, Birman!" and the hall filled with laughter and applause. Birman had to give his word to achieve this coefficient throughout 1935.[58] In many later speeches[59] Birman denied that he had been tricked by the Commissar and claimed that he would have promised this coefficient in any case, but his frequent repetition only emphasized that nobody believed him.

In the May, 1935, First Plenum of the Council of the Commissariat of Heavy Industry, the same Commissar Ordzhonikidze devoted himself to obtaining pledges from directors that they would

---

[56] Z.I., July 5, 1935, p. 3.

[57] The coefficient of blast-furnace use is a positive function of the area of the blast furnace divided by the furnace's production. (Z.I., November 18, 1935, p. 1.)

[58] Stenographic report of that portion of the meeting, Z.I., February 2, 1935, p. 3.

[59] Reported in Z.I., during 1935.

reduce costs sufficiently so as not to require State subsidies. As various directors spoke at the Plenum, Ordzhonikidze would try to put each on the spot and extract a pledge. They would attempt to squirm out. When the First Assistant Commissar said that various directors had made such pledges, Ordzhonikidze returned to his pet query of the day: "And how about Birman?" "Birman is a stubborn fellow," the Assistant answered, "and it is not easy to draw a pledge from him. But I think that by uniting all our common efforts we'll be able to do it."[60] But Birman refused, and it was only three and a half months later that he finally agreed to make the pledge and that subsidies for his plant were thus ordered ended.[61]

From this it can be seen that the Commissar's relationship with major directors was scarcely that of a man who gave orders arbitrarily. He entered conferences as a big businessman in a capitalist country might enter a conference with the heads of many smaller firms which were independent and yet needed his good-will for continued successful operation—as a man who could wield much authority but still had to exercise all his business acumen and persuasive ability to achieve the results he wanted. Similarly, the directors acted independently. At this First Plenum they boasted of their plants' accomplishments, and were frequently caught in distortions or outright lies by the Commissar, but they appeared not to be fazed by this, and continued in new boasts. No one seemed surprised at "convention-type" glorifying. The atmosphere could be likened to that of an American sales convention.

It is impossible for me to say if this managerial independence is as characteristic of the latter thirties as of 1934 and 1935. The 1936 Plenum of the Council of the Commissariat of Heavy Industry was devoid of the argument and persuasion of the First Plenum.[62] In late 1937, heavy industry glavki and commissariats were reorganized for closer and more direct supervision over the

[60] *Z.I.*, May 11, 1935, p. 1.

[61] Prikaz No. 1015 of the NKTP, *Z.I.*, August 30, 1935, p. 1. Examples such as this make it difficult to understand Bienstock's comment that "not many managers have the will to struggle for 'autonomy' . . . ," G. Bienstock, S. M. Schwarz, and A. Yugow, *Management in Russian Industry and Agriculture* (London, New York, Toronto: 1944), p. 11.

[62] Cf. speeches printed in *Z.I.*, in June 1936.

firms. But violations of higher orders by management continued unabated. If firms may have lost some of their independence, they retained enough to be far more than administrative units under tight central control.

ATTITUDES ARISING FROM MANAGERIAL INDE- PENDENCE

Along with the independent position of firm managements, there developed a set of corresponding attitudes on the part of managerial personnel. Actions and decisions tended to be evaluated from the viewpoint of what would help the individual firm to "succeed" in the eyes of higher authorities. To paraphrase one Soviet correspondent: The general good of the economy would be given lip service—but often little more.[63] Thus plant managements tended to press for smaller annual tasks from higher authorities. As the head of the Planning Sector of one firm expressed it: "Why should I go in for charity and advise [the higher bodies] . . . of the production possibilities of the plant?"[64] Directors often "played safe." If they had good luck in the year's work and overfulfilled their quotas—fine; if they merely achieved them—they had accomplished the expected.[65]

On the other hand, exaggerated requests would be made for investment funds from the State Budget. In 1934 it was planned to enlarge considerably the capacity of the Moscow Stalin Auto-Tractor Firm. Its director, Likhachev, presented an estimate of 897 million rubles as needed for the work. When Commissar Ordzhonikidze appointed two investigating committees, they recommended a sharp reduction in the appropriation. In addition to cutting the requested allocation to 465 million rubles, Ordzhonikidze reprimanded Director Likhachev and warned that the discovery of any other such padded request would lead to his removal.[66] With the exposure of Likhachev, the director of the second great automobile plant reacted quickly. He had submitted to Moscow a request for about 1 billion rubles for construction work.

[63] *Mash.*, June 1, 1938, p. 2.
[64] *Z.I.*, May 8, 1934, p. 3.
[65] Lead editorial in *Z.I.*, April 23, 1935, p. 1.
[66] Prikaz No. 245 of the NKTP of February 26, 1935, *Z.I.*, February 27, 1935, p. 1.

Now he hastily recalled the request for "review," and resubmitted it at 500 million rubles.[67]

In the same fashion, it has been necessary to offer firm managements incentives of some type in order to persuade them to do work which was clearly important. The attitude of the management of the GOMZ OGPU Optical Plant provides a good example of this. For goods already in regular production the plant in 1936 received a fixed price from which it was able to clear a profit. But in the case of new products for which the plant had not yet worked out regular production methods, the plant was paid a price equal to the cost incurred—whatever that might be. Since all profits had to come from old product lines, the management did all it could to avoid producing new items. Despite extremely rapid scientific advances in the field, the proportion of the plant's production which was composed of new products kept declining.[68] The importance of new production was quite irrelevant to the management so long as profits—far more important as a criterion of success—could best be earned by sticking to the old items.

Directors have often even further narrowed their interest in economic success. They have been solicitous of the success of their firms in the short run only. They have shown more of a loyalty to their own records than to the firms themselves, tending to "milk" off the qualities providing fundamental health to the firm for the sake of immediate production records. When we remember the description in Chapter III of the tremendous mobility of personnel at all levels of management, we can well understand directors' frequent indifference to the future of their plants.

As an instance, difficulties have been encountered in placing engineering graduates in plants of ferrous metallurgy. Despite the great shortage of engineers, directors refused to hire many graduates who were sent to them,[69] and it was necessary for the Commissariat of Heavy Industry to issue a special decree ordering plants to accept all graduate engineers directed to them.[70] Clearly,

[67] Director S. S. D'iakonov of the Gor'kii Molotov Auto-Tractor Plant. (*Z.I.*, March 18, 1935, p. 3.)

[68] *Z.I.*, May 16, 1936, p. 2.

[69] L. Raskin, chief of the Sector of Cadre of the NKTP, "Pobeda metallurgii—pobeda kadrov" (The Victory of Metallurgy is the Victory of Cadre), *Za Prom. Kadry*, 1935, No. 3, p. 12. Also, *Ind.*, December 28, 1937, p. 4.

[70] Prikaz No. 779 of the NKTP of June 25, 1935, *Za Prom. Kadry*, 1935, No. 12, p. 13.

the reason for such refusals was that young engineers, in the Soviet Union just as in the United States, often require considerable practical experience before they are worth their salt.[71] Managers were told that they could have a well-trained engineer two years later if they took a raw graduate now and trained him in the plant.[72] But the argument—although unquestionably sound—seems to have been unconvincing to many directors who were far more aware of the trouble and expense involved in providing such training.

An even greater problem has been encountered in the inadequacy of repair work. In 1934 the September conference of executives of the Commissariat of Heavy Industry called for greater care for equipment and better repair work.[73] In 1938 there were still complaints that repair was neglected and that departments which were supposed to handle repairs for the firm were used instead for regular production.[74] In 1940 repair work generally was still considered totally unsatisfactory.[75]

One of the reasons for this condition was pointed out by a Soviet author.[76] The degree of repair work done is not considered any index of the success of management. While this fact would be irrelevant if repairs were absolutely required for current production, in actuality their delay often need not seriously injure production for months or even years. In addition, it should be noted, one of the major consequences of the delay of repairs is that equipment is worn out far more quickly than normally, and since all major equipment is replaced from Commissariat or State Budget grants, the firm management cannot consider this a cost to the firm.

Many directors have regarded themselves as the absolute bosses of their own firms. An engineer, who demanded housing in a plant building on the basis of a decree of the Commissariat, was told by the director that he, the director, was the master of his plant and would distribute housing as he saw fit.[77] A lead editorial in the in-

[71] Cf. Z.I., March 28, 1936, p. 3.
[72] Raskin, op. cit., pp. 12-13.
[73] Z.I., December 10, 1934, p. 1.
[74] Cf. lead editorial in Mash., September 22, 1938, p. 1.
[75] B. Smekhov, "Planirovanie remonta osnovnykh fondov" (Planning Repair of Fixed Capital), Planovoe Khoziaistvo, 1940, No. 10, pp. 50-61.
[76] Ibid.
[77] Z.I., March 28, 1934, p. 3.

dustrial press spoke of directors disregarding "on principle" orders
from their glavki.[78] Firm managements virtually broke off "diplo-
matic relations" with other firms and glavki,[79] and were reproached
for considering themselves as feudal lords quite outside Soviet
law.[80]

Accustomed to considerable independence, directors at every opportunity have advocated further autonomy. They have complained bitterly about the glavki setting hosts of detailed planning
requirements and reprimanding directors who did not fulfill them
even though the directors were, on the whole, successful.[81] They
demanded that "success" be defined solely by a few key tests.[82] They
wished to be relieved of supervision by their glavki over many basic
aspects of the firms' work.[83] These protests have occurred at all
times, and were published in the national press throughout the entire period included in this study.

Such letters of directors have been interpreted by G. Bienstock,
writing in the United States, as reflecting the existence of sharp
limits to the autonomy of plants.[84] To this writer, however, it appears that these letters indicate managerial strength as well as weakness. They seem to have been written in the spirit of struggle
against efforts further to integrate plants into a closely controlled
industrial system, and to demand extension and legal recognition
of the criterion of "over-all success" for plants rather than of the
theoretically binding criteria of fulfillment of all aspects of all
plans.

It should not be thought that the currents in the Soviet economy
which tend to make managements think primarily in terms of
their own firms have had things all their own way. The official
morality has always been opposed to this type of thinking, and has
stressed the over-all national interest rather than the interests and
"success" of the firm alone.[85] The emphasis upon placing State in-

[78] Z.I., June 6, 1937, p. 1.
[79] Lead editorial in Z.I., June 29, 1937, p. 1.
[80] Z.I., June 29, 1937, p. 1.
[81] Cf. the article of Director N. Egorov, Pravda, September 26, 1940, p. 3.
[82] Cf. the article of four Leningrad directors, Pravda, September 10, 1940, p. 2.
[83] S. Reznikov (head of the Glavk of Metallurgical Industry of the South and Center,
and a former director himself), writing in Pravda, October 4, 1940, p. 3.
[84] Bienstock, Schwarz, and Yugow, op. cit., pp. 9-12.
[85] Cf. the lead editorial in Z.I., November 12, 1934, p. 1, and the lead editorial in Z.I.,
March 18, 1937, p. 1.

terests above those of any firm has been steadily increased. The extremely high rate of mobility found among all firm personnel has, in a way, increased the influence of this propagandized morality. Managerial executives would scarcely seem to have had time to develop a loyalty to one firm before they were moved on. This high mobility should have tended to make them feel part of a large organization comprising the industry as a whole rather than simply executives of a single firm.

Yet the fact is that these counterpressures do not seem to have overcome loyalty to firm interests. This seems due to industrial executives being evaluated according to the over-all effectiveness of the units for which they are responsible. This method of judgment tends to make "moral considerations" highly abstract and relatively meaningless. For loyalty to one's own record as an up-and-coming executive has meant loyalty to the immediate production record of the organization one heads. The successful manager plays the game according to the rules which are actually—and not just legalistically—in force. Those who do otherwise must soon disappear from the ranks of top management. Just as under the capitalist economic system, only realists can rise to the top and stay there.

CONCLUDING REMARKS

Managerial initiative functions within the bounds provided by instructions and "priorities" of top and intermediate bodies. Two major channels for the expression of initiative are suggestions to higher bodies regarding tasks and allocations for the particular firm, and the application of orders from above to the concrete problems of the firm. The second channel is present in any large administrative system, and the first in most.

A third major outlet is in initiating new practices and methods. For although Soviet leaders believe in standardizing practices within an industry, they are equally in favor of prior and fairly free experimentation by the different firms. In addition to deciding on methods in cases where higher bodies feel that there is not yet sufficient experience to permit standardization, firms also exercise autonomy in areas of work which higher authorities are not yet supervising, presumably because they consider that the results would not warrant the effort.

At this point it may be well to raise the question of whether management's frequent disobedience of rules and of orders from above has been a reaction to the specific character of Soviet industrialization. It can be argued that the continued planning and programming of a very high rate of military preparedness and of development of heavy industry has created problems for firm managements which they could not solve in a legal and orderly fashion. The pressure of a high investment policy may be said to have kept planned inventories too low, thus forcing management continually to strive to build up inventories in any fashion possible.[86] The same pressure may be thought to have kept the annual plans at far too ambitious a level, thus compelling the firms both to struggle for a reduction of their plans and, once the plans were approved, to concentrate on fulfilling only those indices which were given the most attention by higher authorities. Thus, for example, managements concentrated on the quantitative level of output even at the expense of the quality, assortment, and cost standards set forth in their plans.[87] According to this argument, the *raison d'être* of these "overambitious" plans, and thus the indirect cause for management's violations, can be found in the desire of the Soviet leaders to industralize the economy as rapidly as possible and simultaneously to build up the rate of military expenditure. It is the pursuit of these twin objectives which has established the climate of the Soviet economy within which firm managements have had to operate.[88]

In my view, the above argument is probably fallacious. For if the Soviet economy had not been geared to the development of heavy industry and military preparedness, it would presumably have been oriented toward as rapid as possible an expansion in the production of consumers' goods. While such a change in objective would have had major ramifications throughout Soviet society, it is difficult to see why it should have relieved the pressure on plant managements. If Soviet leaders felt that a policy of low inventories was effective in speeding the development of heavy industry, why would they have believed it to be any less effective in increasing the production of consumers' goods? If highly ambitious plans

---

[86] Cf. Chapter VIII for examples of such actions.
[87] Cf. Chapter IX.
[88] For a closely related argument, cf. footnote 12 in Chapter V.

were conceived of as the best method for realizing one objective, why would they not also have been thought best for achieving the alternative goal? Only if it is posited that the alternative of expansion in the output of consumers' goods would have been pursued less vigorously than was the actual policy, could one properly conclude that pressure on plant managements would have been relaxed. But it seems difficult to see why the Soviet leaders would have "taken pity" on the managers and accordingly have set forth less ambitious plans for their firms.[89]

Thus it would appear to me that whatever the policy underlying the direction in which Soviet industrial production was expanded, or even the relative expansion of production and employment in industry as compared to agriculture, plant managements would have faced the same pressures from higher authorities and would have reacted in the same fashion. They would have adopted the same combination of disobedience to instructions in order better to achieve "over-all plan fulfillment" and disobedience in order to present the façade of "plan achievement" at the price of chicanery.

A second question which naturally arises is whether expressions of initiative by firm managements were eliminated during the period of the great Purge in 1937-38. Management then faced the serious risk that failure—always highly possible in an experiment—would be taken as proof of "wrecking." In other fields, indeed, the Purge definitely discouraged the taking of responsibility, even by Party members.[90]

While the Purge doubtless exercised a heavy influence on management in the direction of extreme caution in exercising initiative, it also seems to have applied counterpressure in the opposite direction. This counterpressure as it acted within the State Bank

[89] It is beside the point to claim that more might have actually been accomplished with higher inventories and more modest plans. All that is relevant here is what Soviet leaders considered to be the facts of this matter. There is no reason to believe that their ideas on this subject would have changed with a shift in the basic objective toward which production was directed.

[90] E.g., in the sponsorship by Communist Party members of new candidates for Party membership. Cf. M. Shamberg, assistant head of the Sector of Leading Party Organs of the Central Committee of the All-Union Communist Party, "Protiv volokity pri prieme novykh chlenov v VKP(b)" (Against Red Tape in Admitting New Members into the Communist Party), *Part. Stroit.*, 1938, No. 7, pp. 20-21.

apparatus can be seen very clearly from a reading of the Bank magazine.[91] A host of new ideas for Bank practice were worked out and adopted during 1937. After the February-March 1937 Plenum of the Central Committee of the Communist Party, which seems to have given the green light for widespread purging, a meeting of State Bank officials was called to discuss the results of the Plenum. Many of the officials were here taken to task for continuing practices inaugurated by those who had previously headed the Bank and were now labeled as "wreckers." It was said that the practices which they had begun should have been treated with great suspicion not only because they had yielded bad results but also because of the fact that "wreckers" had originated them.[92] The inference was clear that continuation of old methods might well be taken as evidence of "wrecking" on the part of the new officials.[93]

Despite the very valid fear that failure might be interpreted as "wrecking" and be punished accordingly, industrial plant managements continued outright disobedience to higher orders throughout this period, glavki silently countenanced these violations,[94] and directors responsible for them were retained at their posts and later even promoted to high Commissariat work.[95] When plant managements continued such practices as keeping false books in order to evade higher supervision,[96] it seems unreasonable to think that such managements would be held back from legally permitted experiments on the ground that failure might result in political accusations. On the other hand, it seems quite probable that less daring managements were thus dissuaded from experiment.

[91] *Kredit i Khozraschët* (Credit and Business Accounting) for 1937.

[92] The meeting occurred during March 19 to 23, 1937. Cf. "Aktiv pravleniia gosudarstvennogo banka" (The "Active" of the Administration of the State Bank), *Kredit i Khozraschët*, 1937, No. 7, pp. 23-39.

[93] One might suspect that the pressure for "change" would be such as to cause the widespread adoption of "new" methods—even where the "newness" was purely nominal. There is, however, no evidence that practices were widely pushed simply because they were departures from the procedures followed by the former "wreckers." In any case, pressure for change would cause executives to try to develop new methods, and certainly an efficient new method would be generally preferable to an inefficient one.

[94] Cf. *Ind.*, September, 17, 1937, p. 3. Prikaz No. 502 of the NKTP of June 7, 1937, *BFKhZ*, 1937, No. 18.

[95] Report of an investigating brigade of the Commissariat newspaper *Za Industrializatsiiu, Z.I.*, September 2, 1937, pp. 2-3. *Mash.*, January 29, 1939, p. 4.

[96] An example of this was the situation in the Magnitogorsk Stalin Firm in late 1937. (*Ibid.*)

From all this it seems reasonably safe to conclude that while experimentation and initiation of new methods may well have been seriously reduced during the Purge Period, they still remained as important forms of managerial activity. While initiative was dangerous, so was the absence of initiative.

With "success" the sole lasting criterion of a manager's effectiveness, it is small wonder that he feels compelled to break rules which get in his way. For, ordinarily, he will not be judged harshly for violating regulations so long as his plant "gets out the production."

Thus, managerial initiative plays a great role in the Soviet industrial system. It is at this point that the most vital elements counteracting overcentralization and routinization are found. It is the plant managements which are most important in discovering and working out new organizational methods. It is in the plants that grass-roots ideas originate; they may later be taken up by higher bodies and spread to all industries or they may be condemned in official instructions. Nevertheless, it is here that they get their first test and hearing.

Certainly the presence of this initiative is a powerful factor keeping the industrial system alive and growing, but the main force behind it is the "success" evaluation of management. Yet it is precisely this vague criterion which necessitates campaigns and "priority" orders by higher bodies, elements of the Soviet system which I have described in the previous chapter as being a major weakness. Thus a prime strength and a weakness of the economic administration are closely intertwined, and there have been no serious Soviet efforts to separate them. Whether their divorce would have been possible is open to serious doubt, but this is a matter to be postponed for the Conclusion.

VIII: Procurement and Marketing: The Fusion of Centralized Guidance and Independent Plant Action

THIS CHAPTER illustrates in a major area both the continuous nature of the planning process and the combination of central planning and plant independence which has evolved in practice. We shall see that in the field of procurement it is the firm management which has been held basically responsible for getting the supplies which have been allotted to it by higher authorities. While an enormous centralized superstructure has been organized to procure and market goods, the firm must in the last analysis depend upon its own efforts.

This chapter serves a twofold purpose. On the one hand, it illustrates the themes of the previous four chapters. On the other, it describes in detail two aspects of prime importance for industrial production anywhere—procurement of the factors of production and marketing of the products.

THE ALLOCATION SYSTEM

The national "materials schedules"[1] stand at the apex of the planning system for procurement and marketing. The Council of Commissars, and after its formation the Economic Council, have had the task of approving both annual and quarterly schedules for major products. These schedules are the forms through which are determined the quantity of products to be produced during the period and the amounts to be used and accumulated for reserves throughout the economy. The task of each schedule is to make the

[1] Material'nye balansy.

two sides of the equation equal for the particular product treated. For if consumption should be planned to be greater than production plus existing reserves, the plan could not be fulfilled; while if production were planned to be greater, unneeded surpluses would pile up. The schedule of each product consists of three elements: the amount of production of a product; the structure of its consumption-pattern (for production, construction, etc.) and the norms governing its use in major fields (e.g., amount of coal to be used in producing each ton of steel); and finally, the distribution of the product among different branches and regions.[2]

But such materials schedules, obviously requiring enormous work to develop, have been drawn up only for key goods. In mid-1937, there were about 250 such materials schedules,[3] and by 1940 there were still only 450.[4]

The use of these materials schedules is the key method for integrating the work of different branches, and naturally the schedules grew in importance as the branches were divided up among many commissariats.[5] The schedules are intended to serve both as guides to production and allocation of needed items[6] and to choice of materials by the consuming organizations themselves when alternatives are feasible. As such, they comprise the foundation for procurement and marketing plans for the whole economy.

All producers' goods and materials are distributed to consuming bodies in one of two ways: by centralized or decentralized distribution. Consumers' goods are divided up in similar fashion among distribution agencies. Centralized distribution is a system of direct

[2] Cf. B. Sukharevskii, "Material'nye balansy promyshlennoi produktsii v narodnokhoziaistvennom plane" (Materials Schedules of Industrial Production in the National Economic Plan), *Planovoe Khoziaistvo*, 1937, No. 11-12, p. 27.

[3] Of these, 90 were for different types of machines and equipment, 45 for ferrous metals and metallurgical items, and 16 for construction materials. See "Do kontsa likvidirovat' posledstviia vreditel'stva v planovykh organakh" (Toward Completely Eliminating the Remnants of Wrecking in the Planning Organs), *Planovoe Khoziaistvo*, 1937, No. 5-6, p. 11.

[4] Three hundred of these were for fuels and materials. A. A. Iotkovskii, *Material'noe snabzhenie i sbyt produktsii promyshlennogo predpriiatiia* (Materials Procurement and the Marketing of the Products of the Industrial Firm), (Leningrad: 1941), p. 7.

[5] E. Lokshin, "Organizatsionnye problemy promyshlennosti SSSR." (Organizational Problems of the Industry of the USSR), *Problemy Ekonomiki*, 1939, No. 4, p. 51.

[6] Through 1937 at least, however, they did not greatly affect production decisions but were rather used solely as the basis for distribution. ("Do kontsa likvidirovat' . . . ," p. 11, and Sukharevskii, *op. cit.*, pp. 28-29.)

allocation of supplies; the decentralized form is a modified open market which, however, operates at standardized prices.

Centrally distributed supplies are in turn divided into two groups: "funded" and "quota." The funded goods are those for which the Economic Council approves annual and quarterly materials schedules. The commissariats are the "main fundholders," since they are allotted given amounts and assortments of materials and equipment.[7] They in turn subdivide their funds among the glavki, and these among the firms. Thus each firm has a definite supply for the quarter and for the year as a whole. "Quota" supplies—only slightly less vital—are handled in an identical fashion except that each schedule is drawn up by the commissariat which is the main producer of the product, and it is this commissariat which allocates supplies to all principal consumers.[8]

Goods distributed decentrally have no such allocation system. If they are produced by national commissariats, supplies may be allotted to each region and here sold to firms in accord with the suggestions of local planning commissions. Or they may be bought up by organs of consuming commissariats and glavki which then sell them to their own firms. Other decentralized goods may be sold directly by the producing plant to other firms.[9]

In the total supply structure, the predominant role has been played by centralized distribution.[10] Through 1937, almost all main types of materials and virtually all the products of heavy industry were funded.[11] In 1938 the list of funded items was short-

[7] Like all such hierarchical rules in the USSR, it has exceptions. Some of the largest firms are also "main fundholders."

[8] Iotkovskii, *op. cit.*, pp. 17-21. A somewhat different set of definitions is given by P. A. Shein in *Organizatsiia material'nogo snabzheniia sotsialisticheskogo prompred-priiatiia* (Organization of Materials Procurement for a Socialist Industrial Firm), (Moscow: 1939), pp. 10-12, but they appear from other evidence to be incorrect or confused.

[9] There is a certain overlapping of the centralized and decentralized distribution systems. Goods which are normally funded may be handled in a decentralized fashion in regions where there are a great many consumers, each needing only tiny quantities. But the significance of this overlapping is small. (Iotkovskii, *op. cit.*, p. 21.)

[10] Iotkovskii, *op. cit.*, p. 17.

[11] G. Sakharov, "Snabzhenie i sbyt v tiazhëloi promyshlennosti" (Procurement and Marketing in Heavy Industry), *Biulleten' Gosarbitrazha* (Bulletin of the State Arbitration System), 1934, No. 14, p. 7. B. N. Iakobson, "Problemy organizatsii i plani-rovanie promsnabzheniia v tret'ei piatiletke" (Problems of the Organization and Planning of Industrial Supply in the Third Five-Year Plan), *Snab. i Sklad.*, 1937,

ened,[12] but there is no indication that they were transferred to any but the "quota" list.[13] It would seem that decentralized supply has mainly come from cooperatives, local firms, and other organizations not under a national industrial commissariat.[14] Thus firms of heavy industry have marketed virtually all their production in a centralized fashion, and appear to have received the vast majority of their supplies in the same manner. (For the firms, the difference between "funded" and "quota" supplies is unimportant; in both cases they receive allotments and go through the same steps to get them.)

Just as production planning has its aspect of "planning from below," so too has the planning of procurement. Firms present both annual and quarterly statements of their requirements for centrally distributed goods to their own glavki and to the producing commissariats. Glavki compose statements of needs for presentation to the commissariats, and the commissariats compile them for submission to the State Planning Commission and to the Economic Council. The statements all show the quantity and quality of materials and fuels needed, and attempt to justify the requests by demonstrating their basis in standard norms of materials per unit of product, while at the same time indicating measures to be taken for economizing on materials, using waste products and local resources, etc.[15] They also point out possible substitutions of some materials for others.[16] Thus, while allocation of supply is from the top down, firms and even plant departments have some voice in it.

Once organizations have received supply allotments, they must sign contracts with the producing bodies for delivery of the goods. Centralized allotments are like priority orders in the United States during the last war—they give the holders of these allotments the

No. 9, p. 4. "Khronika: V Gosplana SSSR" (Chronicle: In the State Planning Commission of the USSR), *Planovoe Khoziaistvo*, 1938, No. 5, p. 167.

[12] "Khronika: V Gosplana SSSR," p. 168.

[13] For examples of funded, quota, and decentralized supply items, cf. Iotkovskii, *op. cit.*, pp. 19-21.

[14] Cf. I. S. Person in "O tovarooborote sistemy Soiuzsnabsbyta za 1936 g." (On the Trade Turnover of the System of All-Union Procurement-Marketing Agencies During 1936), *Snab. i Sklad.*, 1937, No. 4, p. 24, where he states that about three quarters of the decentralized purchases of the All-Union Procurement-Marketing Agencies of the Commissariat of Heavy Industry came from these sources in 1936.

[15] Shein, *Organizatsiia snabzheniia*, pp. 75-77, and Iotkovskii, *op. cit.*, pp. 15-16.

[16] *Ibid.*

right to purchase goods, but they do not guarantee their delivery. Firms must proceed to make contracts according to which their allotted supplies will actually be delivered by producing or by go-between organizations. Similar contracts have usually also been made for decentralized supplies.[17]

FLEXIBILITY AND STABILITY

The problems involved in reconciling the desire for plan stability with the requirement of flexibility are just as difficult for Soviet planners to solve in the field of centralized supply as in production. Production plans for all bodies down to the firm level are both annual and quarterly, and so are the allotments of supply which are linked to them. The contracts between firms and other organizations are made on an annual basis, and call for fixed deliveries at specified times with financial penalties for infractions.

Conflicts between the desired flexibility in industry and the annual marketing and procurement plans constantly arise. For example, what happens when the quarterly production plan for a unit shifts from the lines indicated by its annual plan, and away from the marketing commitments provided by the organization's contracts? What happens when a consuming organization has its quarterly plan and thus also its quarterly supply allotment fixed in complete variance to its existing annual contracts? Or worse yet, when the plans of either are "corrected" within the quarter? Since supplier and purchaser are dependent upon one another, a change in the program of either can have disastrous effects upon the other. Can the injured party collect damages when its contract is broken by command of a higher body?

Soviet law and its practice strongly favor flexibility. Contracts must be in accord with plans, and if the plan for either party is altered in line with decisions of the Council of Commissars or of the Economic Council, then the contract must be changed accordingly.[18] Likewise, in practice, a commissariat has usually been able

---

[17] Cf. Chapter X for further details on contracts.

[18] *Arbitrazh v sovetskom khoziaistve* (Arbitration in the Soviet Economy), collected by V. N. Mozheiko and Z. I. Shkundin (Moscow: 1948), 4th edition, pp. 35-36. A. V. Venediktov, *Dogovornaia distsiplina v promyshlennosti* (Contract Discipline in Industry), (Leningrad: 1935), pp. 132-33.

to switch about as it wishes the distribution of its supply allotment among its firms.[19] Thus a plant management can have no more confidence in its materials base remaining unchanged than it can in the stability of its production program. On the other hand, commissariats have been forbidden to annul production orders needed to fill quarterly procurement plans of other organizations for funded items.[20] Firms whose production plans are changed by their glavki or commissariats cannot in practice always cancel orders already under way, and so surpluses of unused specially prepared materials and semifabricates may pile up in their warehouses.[21]

From this it can be seen that some attempt is made to give assurance to a firm that it will be able to receive its fuels and materials and market its goods in the quantities and structure which were planned at the beginning of the year, but that a far greater stress has been placed upon plan flexibility. Much as is the case with production planning, the planning of procurement is more a continuous process than a matter of rigid plans for specific periods.

MARKETING AND PROCUREMENT PROBLEMS OF FIRMS

A tremendous apparatus has been established to distribute products within industry. Not only does every firm have its own individual marketing and procurement sector, but both glavki and commissariats have special procurement and marketing organs. In 1936, about 70,000 people were working solely in that part of the procurement and marketing apparatus of heavy industry which existed above the firm level.[22]

Firms have been serviced by a host of overlapping bodies. They might get their materials and market their products through their

---

[19] Cf. B. Siptits, "Voprosy, trebuiushchie ofitsial'nogo raz"iasneniia" (Questions Requiring Official Determination), *Arbitrazh*, 1936, No. 19, pp. 10-11. Prikaz No. 764/A of the NKTP of December 4, 1938, *Ind.*, December 8, 1938, p. 3. Prikaz No. 962 of the NKTP of August 8, 1935, *BFKhZ*, 1935, No. 23.

[20] Post. No. 1278 of the SNK SSSR of December 2, 1938, *BFKhZ*, 1939, No. 3.

[21] V. Sitnin, "Krupnyi rezerv material'nykh resursov" (The Large Reserve of Materials Resources), *Planovoe Khoziaistvo*, 1940, No. 12, pp. 41-43.

[22] I. Saltanov, head of the All-Union Procurement-Marketing Agency of the Commissariat of Heavy Industry, writing in *Z.I.*, June 23, 1936, p. 3.

commissariat's procurement and marketing agency, through their glavk's organs which have performed the same function, or even through the organs of the commissariats or glavki of their customers and suppliers.[23] The confusion involved has been very great. But with all this servicing apparatus, it has still been the firms themselves which are ultimately responsible for the marketing of their products and the procurement of the necessary fuels and materials.

The rest of this chapter will be devoted to the problems with which the firms are faced and to their methods of solving them.

The marketing of firms' products is a relatively simple task due to the heavy demand for goods. Yet a firm may have considerable work to do even in this field. Contracts must be worked out and signed with marketing and procurement organs and with other firms. Suits for nonfulfillment of scheduled shipments must be settled. The problem of collecting payment for articles shipped is often a grievous one.[24] Machine-construction firms which follow schedules of shipment made up by their glavk marketing organ frequently have found themselves faced with serious problems: consumer firms have not made their orders specific, they have not signed contracts, they are regular delinquents in paying for shipments. To avoid halts in production and financial embarrassments, these producer firms frequently have handled shipments along lines entirely contrary to the instructions of their marketing organ.[25] Advertisement of machines and machine tools by the producing firms has been very common,[26] and while these ads do not indicate any difficulty in selling the equipment, they do show an attitude of responsibility by the individual firm for the marketing of its own products.

But while marketing has not been too serious a problem for firms, the procurement of needed supply has been one of the most vexing areas in the entire work of management.

A firm must pay damages for shipments it has contracted to make and cannot, even though such nonfulfillment is directly due

---

[23] The procurement and marketing apparatus above the firm level is described in Appendix C.

[24] See below in this chapter.

[25] Cf. *Mash.*, October 14, 1938, p. 3.

[26] Cf. *Mash.*, 1937-39.

to nonreceipt of goods centrally allotted to it.[27] But while firms can and do sue glavk and commissariat procurement and marketing organs for nonfulfillment of their contracts, often no damages have been collected.[28] This absence of financial responsibility on the part of these organs has been sufficiently widespread to cause the head of the marketing-procurement sector of a leading Moscow firm to ask in mid-1938: What is the use of a contract with these organs?[29] In practice, indeed, the actual procurement of centrally distributed supply allotments must be attributed more to the work of firms than to that of supply organs.[30]

Commissariats and glavki have been permitted to reduce the production programs of their firms without bearing any responsibility for surplus materials which continue to be delivered to the firm according to contract. Due to such a reduction in its plan, a watch plant in the first quarter of 1940 had piled up stocks of watch jewels sufficient for 387 days of production, and it was powerless to cease receipt of further shipments.[31] Far more commonly, however, production programs have been enlarged with no corresponding increases in supply allotments.[32] Or supply allotments themselves have been cut. This happened, for example, when a major rubber-goods plant failed to fulfill its production program for the first quarter of 1940, and its management hoped to make this up in the third quarter. The commissar of that industry encouraged the firm in this endeavor, but warned the management that it would not receive full norms of rubber and textile supplies for items not covered by the quarterly plan—even though they were within the annual plan. Thus only by extraplan economizing on raw materials could the firm hope to fulfill its annual plan.[33] Small

[27] Editorial thesis formulated on the basis of decisions of the State Arbitration Tribunal attached to the Council of Commissars of the USSR, presented in "Arbitrazhnaia praktika" (Arbitration Practice), *Arbitrazh*, 1938, No. 2, pp. 26-28.

[28] For the prevalent acceptance of this situation, cf. S. Bratus' and M. El'evich, "Sbyti i otvetstvennost' po dogovoram" (Marketing Organs and Responsibility for Contracts), *Biulleten' Gosarbitrazha*, 1935, No. 8, pp. 7-8.

[29] *Ind.*, July 26, 1938, p. 3. See also "Khronika: V Gosplana SSSR," p. 169.

[30] G. A. Dlugach, "Snabzhenie tiazhëloi promyshlennosti cherez otraslevye snaby" (Procurement for Heavy Industry Through Branch Procurement Organs), *Snab. i Sklad.*, 1936, No. 1, p. 22.

[31] Sitnin, *op. cit.*, p. 43.

[32] Cf. *Z.I.*, April 22, 1937, p. 3.

[33] The firm involved was the Red Triangle Plant. (*Ind.*, July 25, 1940, p. 2.)

wonder that the director of a machine-building plant complained that the problem of getting needed supply was the most complex one facing all firm managements in his industry.[34]

At the same time, firms are not left entirely on their own in getting supplies. Not only do they receive aid from their glavk and commissariat procurement organs, but they can also appeal to outside agents. A firm producing 69 percent of the country's aluminum was forced to shut down partially for lack of coal, and could get no aid from its own glavk. But a plea to the Commissar of the Fuel Industry brought the needed fuel.[35] The newest zinc plant in the country was scheduled to undertake a five-day Stakhanovite period, but suffered from lack of electricity. It was the Regional Committee of the Communist Party which got it the required supply.[36] In fact, the Central Committee of the Communist Party has severely reprimanded regional committees for allowing major firms in their districts to suffer from lack of raw materials.[37]

Poor supply can and does have disastrous effects upon the production of firms. During 1936, Leningrad industry, recipient of 9 to 15 percent of all metal consumed in the country, failed to receive 15 percent of the weight of "funded" metal allotted to it.[38] An abrasives plant was almost completely idle throughout the first half of 1938 due to lack of electricity and fuel.[39]

Even the most important firms of the country have had their work interrupted.[40] Receipt of supply in improper assortment for different categories (e.g., of metals) leads to the accumulation of

[34] Director B. Gutnov, in *Z.I.*, October 30, 1935, p. 2.

[35] Reference is to the Dneprovskii Aluminum Plant. (*Ind.*, June 20, 1939, p. 3.)

[36] Reference is to the Cheliabinskii Kirov Zinc Plant. (Article by the plant's director Lutsuk, in *Z.I.*, February 5, 1936, p. 3.)

[37] Decree of the TsK VKP(b) of November 9, 1939, in "V Tsentral'nom Komitete VKP(b)" (In the Central Committee of the All-Union Communist Party [Bolshevik]), *Part. Stroit.*, 1939, No. 21, pp. 57-58.

[38] B. N. Iakobson and L. M. Rozenberg, "Eshchë ob organizatsii i praktike metallo-snabzheniia" (More on the Organization and Practice of Metal Procurement), *Snab. i Sklad.*, 1937, No. 6, p. 23. Also, *Z.I.*, April 22, 1937, p. 3. The 15 percent figure would be far higher if it included the sum of all nonshipments broken up into different categories, for procurement plans for some types of metals were overfulfilled. (The authors of these articles considered the situation in Leningrad to be characteristic of that in metals procurement throughout the USSR at that time.)

[39] Reference is to the Cheliabinskii Abrasives Plant. (Article by P. Tubanov, head of the Abrasives Glavk, in *Mash.*, October 15, 1938, p. 2.)

[40] Cf. *Z.I.*, January 27, 1936, p. 3, and February 28, 1937, p. 2.

heavy stocks of some types accompanied by stoppages in production due to the absence of others, to wasteful use of materials when none but the more expensive categories are available for work that could as well be done with cheaper types, to extra wage bills where substitute materials require additional fabrication, and to unplanned assortment of production since goods must be produced which can be made with the materials at hand.

The difficulties of firms in getting supplies should not, however, give the impression that managements have been eager to accept whatever materials are offered. The problem of supply has been essentially that of being shipped a poor assortment of categories rather than an insufficient total. This is shown by the fact that on July 1, 1940, each of the three machine-construction commissariats, the commissariats of ferrous and nonferrous metal production, and the chemical commissariat all had larger stocks on hand (when measured in ruble value) than their plans allowed them.[41]

Thus, it is not surprising that on occasion, when some goods have been in temporary oversupply and storage space was short, firms have had to be compelled to accept larger stocks than they wished.[42] There has been regular rejection of shipments of goods, and producers have brought suits against firms because of this. In 1937, one quarter of the disputes which came before the State Arbitration Tribunals were caused by organizations refusing to accept goods shipped to them.[43]

A goodly proportion of these supply difficulties would seem to have been inevitable. An economy operating at comparatively full capacity, and with relatively small reserves, must either suffer from a scarcity of fuels and materials or from their unplanned accumulation. For it would be clearly unreasonable to expect either absolute accuracy and integration of production and consumption

[41] Nine percent excess for machine construction, 11 percent for ferrous metallurgy, 22 percent for nonferrous metallurgy and 7 percent for the chemical industry. (Sitnin, op. cit., p. 40.)

[42] Cf. Z.I., August 12, 1935, p. 3.

[43] There were 65,774 such cases that year, making up 25.6 percent of the total. This compares with the figure of 32.4 percent as the proportion of suits over failure to ship goods for which contracts had been signed. See F. Goloshchekin, Chief Arbitrator attached to the Council of Commissars of the USSR, "O rabote Gosudarstvennogo arbitrazha v 1937 g." (On the Work of the State Arbitration System in 1937), Arbitrazh, 1938, No. 7, pp. 5 and 10. There is nothing to indicate that this was an exceptional year with regard to these figures.

plans or their perfect fulfillment. As finished-goods industries, and particularly machine construction, grew more rapidly in the thirties than did the output of coal and steel, shortages of fuels and materials were the accompaniments of full capacity production.

But there have been a number of specific weaknesses in the Soviet supply system which have greatly complicated supply problems. Chief among such deficiencies are the following:

Firms have been required to submit statements of their requirements to the marketing organizations distributing fuels and materials. In order to allow time for preparing production plans, these statements have been due before the beginning of the planning period, usually 10 to 75 days ahead, depending upon the branch.[44] The difficulty with this procedure is that frequently the firms had not yet received their production tasks at the time when they were obliged to submit their supply requirements.[45] Even more frequently, of course, they have not known what their allotments of centrally distributed materials would be. Yet preliminary statements to the marketing organs have been specifically demanded.[46] When these statements have been drastically changed at a later date, it has been all very well to rebuke the firm managements for not knowing their own needs,[47] but this has not eliminated the necessity for reversing instructions which went out to producer firms on the basis of the stated requirements.

The allotment of centrally distributed materials has been extremely haphazard. Often plants received allotments proportional to the planned ruble value of their production, quite irrespective of the types of units to be produced.[48] The whole field of raw-materials stocks has been dealt with most unsystematically.[49] In order to be sure of having sufficient materials, firms have often requested larger supplies than needed and even presented falsely reduced

[44] V. Aizin, "Pravovoe znachenie zaiavok" (The Legal Significance of Statements), *Arbitrazh,* 1937, No. 20, pp. 12-14. Also, Iotkovskii, *op. cit.,* p. 15.

[45] Cf. Iakobson, "Problemy organizatsii . . . ," p. 4. Sitnin, *op. cit.,* p. 41.

[46] Aizin, *op. cit.,* pp. 12-13.

[47] That this might be done in such cases is shown in the speech of P. Marin, head of the Procurement Sector of the Dinamo Kirov Firm, *Ind.,* December 18, 1939, p. 3.

[48] *Mash.,* December 9, 1938, p. 2.

[49] Cf. B. Iakobson's article in *Z.I.,* April 22, 1937, p. 3, and the article by A. Fleishman, aid to the director of the Kuibyshev Electrical Combinat, in *Z.I.,* July 26, 1937, p. 3.

statistical data as to inventory. The procurement organizations usually have had only scanty information on which to base their evaluation of these requests, and thus they have cut down orders indiscriminately or by a set percentage. Naturally, this formalistic approach has encouraged firms to submit still more exaggerated orders the next time.[50]

Allotments of supply have been frequently made only after the beginning of the period for which they were intended. Thus by March 20, 1937, only 40 to 50 percent of the store of materials centrally supplied on an annual calendar-year basis to Leningrad heavy industry—and only 25 percent of the metals—had been allotted to individual firms.[51] Such delay in dividing allotments among firms not only has kept all of their planning uncertain, but occasionally even has led to refusals of producers to ship needed goods to them.[52]

Even when allotments have been given out, glavki and commissariats have reserved the right to revoke them and to redistribute the freed supplies among their other firms.[53] Moreover, managements have often not even been informed of cancellation of shipments. One executive of a large combinat producing electrical equipment wrote that his plant stationed many employees in supplier firms simply in order to keep in touch with developments, as the suppliers refused to answer letters or telegrams.[54]

ILLEGAL METHODS OF PROCUREMENT

With these difficulties in getting materials, it is scarcely surprising that supply work should be a fertile field for chicanery. Even the commissariats have submitted larger requests than necessary.[55] Glavk and commissariat procurement organs have custom-

[50] Sitnin, *op. cit.*, pp. 41-42. Pikus, "V tekhnicheskoi li gramatnosti snabzhentsev reshenie voprosa?" (Is the Solution of the Question Contained in the Technical Understanding of the Procurement Agents?), *Predpriiatie,* 1934, No. 8, p. 5.

[51] *Z.I.*, April 22, 1937, p. 3.

[52] Cf. *Ind.,* November 3, 1937, p. 3.

[53] Siptits, *op. cit.*, p. 11.

[54] A. Fleishman of the Kuibyshev Electric Combinat, writing in *Z.I.*, July 26, 1937, p. 3. Cf. also *Z.I.*, September 2, 1937, p. 3.

[55] Cf. S. Volikov, head of the Glavk for Marketing Metals, writing in *Ind.,* August 12, 1938, p. 3.

arily filled their warehouses with goods, a high percentage of which were obtained illegally.[56] The Glavk of Metallurgy has illegally sold ferrous metals to the Commissariat of Light Industry, and has in turn received consumers' goods for sale to its metallurgical workers.[57] When higher organs carry on in this fashion, it is scarcely surprising that firm managements have followed suit.

Frequently—and probably typically—a successful supply head of a firm has been considered as the man who could deliver the goods, quite irrespective of how he got them. In fact, the firm director has rather preferred that he should not bother higher organs too often, but instead get materials "on his own."[58] In 1934, one director even boasted in a national newspaper of his success in buying metals illegally.[59]

One often-used method for procuring illegal supplies has been to pay black market prices to the producing firms. Metallurgical plants, for example, would label a portion of their production as scrap or damaged goods, and so be permitted to sell it in decentralized fashion outside of the allotment system. Prices, of course, would be higher than the legal ones for first grade metals.[60]

A second common means has been to divert materials allocated for one purpose (e.g., construction or repairs) to another use (e.g., production) in the same firm. In this fashion, the firm management has eased its task in fulfilling or overfulfilling one portion of its plan through the neglect of another part.[61]

A third approach has been the exchange of work done by one firm for materials held by another. Orders are accepted by the supplier plant only if the other firm agrees to provide it with some

[56] The 1938 study conducted by the Glavk for Marketing Metals, reported on by S. Volikov in *Ind.*, December 31, 1938, p. 2.

[57] Report of the meeting of December 27, 1937, of the Economic Council, *Ind.*, December 28, 1937, p. 2.

[58] S. Gurov, "O lovkosti ruk i o 'znakomom parne' " (About Sleight of Hand and "Clever Fellows"), *Predpriiatie*, 1934, No. 5-6, p. 8.

[59] M. Grosman, director of the Khar'kov Hammer and Sickle Machine-Building Plant. (*Z.I.*, June 11, 1934, p. 2.) In the latter thirties, however, such open lawbreaking was more frowned upon.

[60] This was accepted as an established fact by the Economic Council at its meeting of December 27, 1937. (*Ind.*, December 28, 1937, p. 2.) Such practice was only possible, of course, where no central prices had been established for that type of scrap.

[61] Cf. M. M., "Zadachi promsnabzheniia" (Tasks of Industrial Procurement), *Snab. i Sklad.*, 1937, No. 11, p. 26.

of its products[62] or with other materials specifically allotted for its own production needs.[63]

A fourth has been the exchange of materials between firms. Buying whatever ferrous metals are offered, even in categories utterly useless to them, firms have then proceeded to barter them with other firms. As the metals are funded, the practice is illegal, but higher organs appear to have viewed it sympathetically since firms have thus received the materials they needed.[64] Such barter has inevitably led firms to accumulate useless stocks on hand as "trading material," and attempts of higher organs to buy up these stocks have met with great resistance.[65]

Finally, there has been the constant overstatement of requirements of centrally distributed materials.

THE IMPORTANCE OF PERSONAL RELATIONS

So necessary is the "personal touch" in getting supplies, that firms have commonly retained full-time "pushers" at important plants and supply organs. These have had the task of getting their firm the supply to which it is entitled, but which it would probably never see except for the representative on the spot.[66] When firms have not had such "pushers," their glavki have on occasion recommended that they send them out.[67] The cost and waste of manpower involved in the institution of "pushers" can be easily imagined. In 1940 the situation became so bad at ferrous metallurgical plants that the Economic Council itself had to forbid the presence of "pushers" in these particular plants.[68]

A striking example of the importance of personal relations is contained in a recent Soviet novel. A Sakhalin fishery badly needs trucks and tractors for temporary use in the lumbering work which is a preliminary to the building of houses for the workers. Until a

[62] Cf. *Z.I.*, September 28, 1935, p. 3.
[63] Fleishman of the Kuibyshev Electrical Combinat, writing in *Z.I.*, July 26, 1937, p. 3.
[64] Cf. *Z.I.*, January 29, 1936, p. 2, and June 4, 1937, p. 3.
[65] Cf. the article by N. Guliaev, assistant head of the Credit Administration of the Commissariats of Heavy Industry and of Machine Construction, *Mash.*, December 11, 1938, p. 2.
[66] Cf. *Z.I.*, July 26, 1937, p. 3.
[67] Cf. Director N. Egorov's article, *Pravda*, September 26, 1940, p. 3.
[68] Post. No. 1484 of the Economic Council of August 29, 1940, *SPR*, 1940, article 578.

new director arrives, the problem of getting this transportation has appeared insolvable. The new director, however, is a close friend of an Army colonel in the vicinity, and in the name of friendship is loaned even more equipment than is required. This incident is described by the novelist without any hint of disapproval.[69]

From all this it should be apparent what a tremendous role the firms themselves play in marketing their products and in procuring the necessary materials. There is no room for a bashful management which patiently waits for the huge supply and marketing system to provide it with its needs. Either a firm sees to its own requirements or a change in management will soon be in order.

CONCLUDING REMARKS

It would be easy to draw the conclusion that the Soviet supply system is a total failure, and that this is why its rules are evaded. But although it is probably the weakest area in Soviet industry, such an opinion would be unwarranted.

In the first place, I have been dealing mainly with the faults of Soviet procurement rather than with its successes, and thus have inevitably given a blacker impression of the system than is justified from an objective standpoint.

Secondly, the many violations and illegal actions of firms should be considered as part and parcel of the system as it actually functions. While common practices are illegal and officially frowned upon, the frown is paternal and higher bodies look the other way or actually give aid to the violators. To consider such actions as a breakdown of the system is to miss the whole point of how the economy functions.

Why then make such necessary practices illegal? Because one does not easily throw away the efficiency advantages of systematic allocation and marketing. Shortcuts and violations of the planned routine are thus forbidden, the Soviets here paying lip service to the functional features of systematization. More, declaring common practices to be illegal serves to keep in the forefront the need for strengthening preferred and orderly procurement and market-

[69] A. Chakovsky, *It Is Morning Here*, translated into English by B. Isaacs, in *Soviet Literature*, 1950, No. 9, pp. 87-91.

ing methods. Managements which go too far may have their knuckles rapped.

But the strict enforcement of such systematization would most likely cause greater wastes than it would eliminate. Orderly centralized procedure requires a degree of stability which has not existed in Soviet industry. Thus, in actuality, it is the firms themselves which have been made responsible for the procurement of allotted materials and their managements have developed their own methods for getting them. Higher organs have not tried to enforce the legal and "rational" procurement methods; they have recognized that this would destroy the flexibility of the system. They have had to find a compromise between the "efficiency" rules and the flexibility of entrepreneurial activity.

IX: The Measurement of Success: I

IN EARLIER CHAPTERS, we have shown how managements work with the single end of achieving "over-all success" for their firms. It is with this in mind that they break rules and laws, that they adopt "independent" attitudes and practices. We shall see below that controls, and particularly punishments and incentives, are directed to a great extent toward making them strive for this "single" aim.

But we have yet to face explicitly the basic question: What is a "successful" plant management? On what basis is one director praised and promoted to a higher post and another "removed for inability to cope with his responsibilities"? When an executive faces the almost daily problem of determining which of the plant's tasks should be stressed and which should be slighted, how does he go about making a decision? What are the various elements entering into the determination of success, and what are their relative importance?

In a capitalist enterprise, the definition of "success" is clear-cut. It is a matter of dollars and cents; the management which can earn high profits—and by a policy which does not undermine the future profitability of the firm—is unequivocally more successful than one whose profits are lower or nonexistent.[1] The "correct" way of

[1] This generalization is based on the assumption of identity of interest between the management and the entire body of owners of the enterprise. It clearly does not include cases where management's prime interest is in "milking" a corporation and the main body of stockholders, or in manipulating the corporation's affairs in the interests of stock speculation.

Even with this reservation, however, the generalization may be disputed. One may point to such goals as power, prestige, and security as playing important independent roles in determining the actions of even those companies in which the managers are also the owners. One may deny that "long-run profitability" is any more definite a criterion for decision making in the capitalist firm than is "plan

analyzing any managerial problem is by asking what effect alternative solutions will have on present and future profits.

The Soviet director has what at first sight might appear to be an equally decisive test question: What effect will alternative decisions have upon his firm's plan fulfillment? He who "fulfills and overfulfills" his plan is successful. But by itself, this criterion has little content and offers no help in solving concrete problems.

We have seen in Chapters IV and V that a firm's plan is far from the precise arrangement of figures and percentage-improvements which appears in the files of higher organs. Planned tasks are a minimum assignment; the slogan of "The Five-Year Plan in four years" is an ever-present echo in management's ears. There are "priority" tasks, the overfulfillment of which is considered as more important than the 100 percent attainment of each element of the firm's plan. In brief, the official plans are only the starting points for a process of order giving by higher bodies which goes on at all times rather than periodically, and which has as its goal the direction and integration of the economy in a flexible fashion—adjusted to the myriad of changes which occur during any annual or even quarterly period. The plan formalized at the beginning of each year in no way serves as the single measure by which to judge the firm's work.

The complexity of the problem of defining "success" is shown in the following examples.

Over many years, the Magnitogorsk Stalin Firm had violated its financial plan and the State laws. It had accumulated huge debts to suppliers because its funds were tied up in illegal capital construction and in supplying consumers' goods to its workers. It had

---

fulfillment" in the Soviet firm. However, an evaluation of these objections would be far outside the scope of this study. For our purposes, it would seem enough that belief in the all-importance of the profit motive seems to be widespread among all segments of the population in capitalistic society. The main currents of economic theory, whether they be classical, Keynesian, or Marxist, all take the primacy of the profit motive as a fundamental assumption. In view of this widespread acceptance of the generalization we are here employing, it would appear to be a reasonable one to use until more convincing evidence is presented to the contrary.

Nevertheless, the reader should be aware of the fact that a case can be made for the argument that a capitalist firm management has no clear-cut single criterion of success which can serve it as a guide to action. An exponent of this view would find a clear parallel to the problem of determining what is a successful Soviet firm management in the problem of deciding what makes a successful capitalist management.

given nonexistent items as "security" for loans from the State Bank.[2] Yet although these conditions were exposed in a national magazine, the firm's director was still retained at his post, and in less than two years was given the second highest job in all Heavy Industry.[3] The reason was clear: on the whole, his management had been successful.

When Director Shtein reorganized the Red Profintern Plant so effectively that its production quotas could at last be fulfilled, he violated the labor laws in the process. He was strongly attacked for this both by the national trade-union newspaper and by an inspection brigade of the All-Union Central Council of Trade Unions. But he won equally powerful supporters, and finally the Central Committee of the Communist Party itself vindicated him.[4] For Shtein, the rise in production was the criterion of success.

But this was not the criterion used in judging the management of the Makeevskii Kirov Firm. This plant fulfilled its tonnage quotas, but in doing so violated its quality and assortment programs. As a result, the old leadership was removed.[5]

It has never been a simple matter to decide which of several firms worked better during a given period; there have been long arguments as to which plant should be declared the winner of various interfirm competitions.[6] In a typical competition, the rules would provide a long list of indices to be used by the judges. Such indices were production of finished goods in the planned assortment, an even flow of production as between different ten-day periods and as between months, planned mastery of new types of products, improvement in product quality and reduction in waste, economy of materials through improved design and through changing of technological processes, fulfillment of labor productivity tasks and lowering of unit cost, keeping within the established wage fund, and increase in the number of worker suggestions for improvements in work methods and conditions and their adoption into op-

[2] I. Dubnov, "Rabota vslepuiu" (Working Blindfold), *Kredit i Khozraschet*, 1935, No. 9-10, pp. 58-59.

[3] The director was A. P. Zaveniagin, whose career was described in Chapter III. (Prikaz No. 233 of the NKTP of March 15, 1937, *Z.I.*, March 16, 1937, p. 1.)

[4] *Z.I.* and *Trud* (Labor) for April and May, 1935.

[5] *Ind.*, May 23, 1938, p. 1.

[6] Cf. the articles which appeared in *Z.I.* of January, 1936, disputing the result of a metallurgical contest.

eration.[7] But the rules of these competitions have given no indication of how each of the indices of success should be weighted in the decision as to the best firm.

NONFINANCIAL CRITERIA: THEIR IMPORTANCE RELATIVE TO ONE ANOTHER

Of the many nonfinancial criteria used during the 1934-41 period, that of "value of product" seems to have been far and away the most important.

In 1936, the director of a fairly prominent plant described a problem faced frequently by managements. Towards the end of the month, he said, the plant dispatcher frequently comes to the director and asks which of two items should be produced in the remaining days. If one is chosen, the "value of product" task of the firm will be fulfilled, but an important new product within the planned assortment will be neglected. If the other is designated, the quantitative task for the month will not be achieved. Wrote the director: "If there is a considerable lag [in production] from 100% . . . and if the fate of the program depends on such a choice, there would hardly be anyone who would hesitate. The production of the new product would be left to the following month."[8]

In early 1938, the Commissar of Heavy Industry announced that the work of firms for that year would be judged not only according to output, but also by their success in lowering costs and achieving proper quality.[9] The implication of this order was that these were considerations which had previously not been important in evaluation.

As early as 1936, the Government tried to reduce somewhat this stress on quantity. The Council of Commissars and the Central Executive Committee of the USSR issued a joint proclamation establishing a new criterion as the main one to be used for evaluating the success of each industrial firm. This new criterion was the output of those finished and marketable products which properly met the plan's quality and assortment requirements. It was intended to

[7] Cf. *Mash.*, May 23, 1938, p. 1.
[8] Director E. Kovarskii, writing in *Z.I.*, October 8, 1936, p. 3.
[9] Prikaz No. 20 of the NKTP of January 21, 1938, *Ind.*, January 29, 1938, p. 1.

take priority over the former criterion of "value of product"—
which included unfinished goods and entirely ignored assortment
and quality.[10] The shift in criteria was ordered as of October 1,
1936, for all industrial firms.[11]

But the new index never caught on. The old one continued dominant, and in practice the new criterion of success was held to a
decidedly secondary position in spite of all protests.[12] Throughout
industry, but particularly in the Commissariat of Machine Construction, firms overfulfilled their production quotas in the first
half of 1938 by means of violating their assortment plans and disregarding quality.[13] In 1940, a leading economist complained that
in the evaluation of firms' work often little attention was paid to
quality improvements or to cost reductions.[14] As late as 1944,
premiums given to engineering and managerial personnel were
based solely upon the index of production-quantity, and not at
all on quality, cost, or assortment standards.[15]

The success criterion of quantity is normally defined in terms
of a plan period of a quarter or a whole year. But this is not always
the case. On occasion, plant records for a month or even a day may
be given greater stress by management. In fact, the production of

[10] Z.I., September 9, 1936, p. 1. Also, "Khronika: V Gosplana SSSR" (Chronicle: In
the State Planning Commission USSR), Planovoe Khoziaistvo, 1938, No. 3, p. 165. The
shift was to be from the "valovaia produktsiia" index to that of "tovarnaia produktsiia." A further difference between the two indices is that the first is measured in
constant prices, mainly according to 1926-27 values, while the second is in current
prices.

[11] Z.I., September 8, 1936, p. 2, and September 9, 1936, p. 1.

[12] Cf. "V Gosplana SSSR," Planovoe Khoziaistvo, 1938, No. 3, p. 165. V. Tokarev, "O
metodakh otsenki vypolneniia plana po assortimentu" (On Methods of Evaluating the Fulfillment of the Plan According to Assortment), Planovoe Khoziaistvo,
1938, No. 8, p. 64. R. Kholodnyi, "Planirovanie tovarnoi produktsii" (Planning
Marketable Production), a discussion article, Planovoe Khoziaistvo, 1940, No. 4, p. 48.
A. Birman, "Nekotorye voprosy ukrepleniia khoziaistvennogo raschëta v promyshlennosti" (Some Questions of Strengthening Business Accounting in Industry), Problemy Ekonomiki, 1941, No. 1, p. 112.

[13] Sh. Turetskii, "Usilit' vnimanie k kachestvennym pokazateliam" (In Order to
Concentrate Attention on Qualitative Indices), Planovoe Khoziaistvo, 1938, No. 11,
p. 67.

[14] Sh. Turetskii, "Ekonomika proizvodstva i kachestvennye pokazateli plana"
(Economy of Production and the Qualitative Indices of the Plan), Planovoe Khoziaistvo, 1940, No. 8, pp. 21-22.

[15] A. Zverov, Commissar of Finance of the USSR, "Sovetskie finansy i Otechestvennaia
voina" (Soviet Finances and the Patriotic War), Planovoe Khoziaistvo, 1944, No. 2,
p. 47.

a whole plant may be allowed to fall in order to permit a few individuals to set work records. Thus in April and May, 1936, many metallurgical plants experienced an absolute drop in production. One director explained this failure in his plant by the fact that he and his management had in the previous months neglected repair for the pursuit of monthly production records.[16] Other directors have organized their plants so as to make one-day records, and immediately afterwards suffered reduced production because proper routine had been destroyed.[17] Some managements concentrated on giving individual workers conditions in which they could establish national records,[18] although the mass of workers paid for this in poorer work conditions, and thus the production of the plant as a whole suffered. In all these cases, the managements concerned evidently felt that their success would be measured more by the making of records than by their total production results.

Although prime stress has been laid on the quantity of production, this does not mean that other facets of industrial work can be safely ignored by executives. In 1940, the Commissar of Nonferrous Metals was ousted from his post and demoted to a lesser job because he had overstressed the importance of quantity. It was established that he had on occasion permitted violations of quality standards in order better to fulfill his Commissariat's quantitative production program.[19]

Quality of product, reduction of scrap and waste, proper assortment of products according to plan—all these tests of a management's success were emphasized throughout the whole 1934-41 period. Directors and others were sentenced to prison terms for violating quality standards.[20] Directors were removed for paying out too much money in wages in comparison with production results,[21] others for neglecting to carry out cheap and minor mechanization which would have eliminated heavy manual labor.[22] Great emphasis was placed on the need for management to econo-

[16] Director Birman, speech at the 1936 Council of the NKTP, Z.I., July 3, 1936, p. 4.
[17] Cf. Ind., September 28, 1937, p. 1.
[18] Cf. Post. of the TsK VKP(b) of December 28, 1937, Mash., December 29, 1937, p. 1. Also, "Ocherednye zadachi organizatsii proizvodstva v 1938 g.," p. 16.
[19] Ind., July 10, 1940, pp. 1 and 4.
[20] Cf. Ch.M., November 5, 1940, p. 4.
[21] Cf. Mash., January 3, 1939, p. 2.
[22] Lead editorial, Z.I., June 22, 1936, p. 1.

mize fuel, power, and materials and not to use more of these items per product unit than was allocated by the firm's plan.[23] There have even been cases where entire industries have been directed to concentrate primarily on such aspects of work as that of conserving metal, instead of on the increase of production.[24]

Thus, while managements have kept their eye primarily on the graphs of quantity produced, only the foolhardy director would stress this aspect to the exclusion of the other main ones mentioned or even of a host of minor indices which might on occasion plague him.

From the multitude of relevant success indices, the reader may have formed the impression that firm managements must operate blindly, guided by no standards, and trusting to luck that all will work out. This would, however, be incorrect. The preeminence of such indices as quantity, quality, and assortment of production, and of remaining within the firm's allotments of materials and fuels has brought some order into the otherwise chaotic picture. The presence of "campaigns" and "priorities" stressing one or more factors also has aided management in deciding which elements of its work are at the moment most important.

But relative emphases cannot be expressed quantitatively. The director cannot readily decide if it is worth while to use a little more fuel per product unit than was planned in order to increase production slightly. If a lot more fuel was needed for only a little more production, or a little fuel for a big increase, the decision would be easy. But it is the borderline cases which cannot be decided on "rational" and "economic" grounds because there is no common denominator in terms of which to express both the fuel and the product. It is for this reason that a commissariat senior engineer could write in 1939 that his commissariat had no technical-economic criteria for determining whether one technological process for manufacturing a given item was better than some other. If 150 engineers are set to work to develop a manufacturing proc-

---

[23] Cf. the campaign conducted throughout January, 1940, in *Ind.*

[24] Directions to the Stakhanovite movement of the machine-construction industry by the December, 1935, Plenum of the TsK VKP(b). In practice, however, the Stakhanovite movement ignored this order. (Cf. lead editorial of *Z.I.*, August 5, 1937, p. 1.)

ess, he wrote, 150 different variants will be received, and each will be hotly defended as the best by its originator.[25]

FINANCIAL CRITERIA AS COMPOSITE TESTS OF EFFECTIVENESS

Noncomparability between the different tests of success of a firm has been recognized as a problem by Soviet theoreticians and industrial leaders. They have stressed the desirability of having some composite index which would reflect many aspects of the work of a firm, just as profit does for a capitalist enterprise.

A possible means of setting up such a criterion of success is to reduce all elements to the single factor of money. To a certain extent, Soviet theoreticians have followed this procedure.

Marx had used the concept of "value" as a common denominator underlying all commodities, the "value" of a commodity being the amount of labor required to produce it.[26] As a first approximation, he considered that the price of a commodity represents its value.[27]

In the same fashion, Soviet theoreticians declare that all expenditures of labor—either directly, or indirectly in the form of machinery, materials, etc.—are expressed in rubles as a unifying measure. Since this is the case, "Money of a socialist state functions above all as a *weapon . . . of supervision over the expenditures of social labor.*"[28] The cheaper the money cost of a commodity, the less social labor has been spent in producing it. Here is a common de-

[25] R. Khisin, senior engineer of the Bureau of Technical Norm-Making and Capacity of the Commissariat of Heavy Machine Construction, writing in *Mash.*, May 9, 1939, p. 2.

[26] In the determination of a product's value, labor of different degrees of skill must be reduced to a single level with the skilled types counting as multiples of the unskilled. Moreover, only "socially necessary"—and not wasted—labor is considered as contributing to the "value" of a commodity.

[27] There have been many criticisms of Marx's use of the concept of "value" and of its relation to price. However, since Soviet theoreticians reject these criticisms, it seems irrelevant to discuss their pros and cons in this outlining of Soviet theory.

[28] E. Bregel' and A. Tsagolov, "Naznachenie i funktsii deneg v sotsialisticheskoi ekonomike" (The Assignment and Functions of Money in a Socialist Economy), *Planovoe Khoziaistvo*, 1940, No. 12, p. 72. (Italics in original.) See also K. Ostrovitianov, "Sotsialisticheskoe planirovanie i zakon stoimosti" (Socialist Planning and the Law of Value), *Voprosy Ekonomiki* (Problems of Economics), 1948, No. 1, p. 38.

nominator for the materials, fuel, capital equipment, and direct labor used in production.[29]

Soviet reliance on the unitary measuring stick of money was greatly strengthened by Stalin's famous 1931 speech, noted in Chapter II, in which he stressed the need for introducing and strengthening business accounting in all firms. Stalin insisted that managements must constantly consider the relationships between their money income and expenditures and that they must reduce money costs so that their firms would show a money profit instead

---

[29] The Soviets recognize that neither an item's cost nor its sales price accurately represents the amount of labor which has gone into its production. If their pricing system accurately represented the "value" of all products, then the least cost would mean the least expenditure of social labor. But the pricing system does not precisely represent "value" and is not intended to do so. While one ton of coal may have the "value" of two tons of peat, encouragement of the use of peat by industry may seem desirable (e.g., because of the general coal shortage and the resultant need for encouraging industrial consumers to use a more troublesome form of fuel). If, then, coal is set at four times the price of peat, their relative prices depart from their relative "values"—but the interests of the economy are furthered by this deviation. Thus the separation between price and "value"—but in a planned direction and to a planned extent—is considered desirable. (Cf. Bregel' and Tsagolov, *op. cit.*, pp. 75-76.)

However, such deviation lessens the validity of the conception of cost as expressive of social labor. This has been a major argument for the elimination in general of State subsidies for fuels, materials, semifabricates, and capital goods. Subsidies, Soviet authors argue, should be as rare as possible. Cf. Sh. Turetskii, "O khoziaistvennom raschëte" (On Business Accounting), *Planovoe Khoziaistvo*, 1939, No. 1, pp. 113-30.

Soviet authors point out another major reason for the failure of money to accurately represent "value." Misrepresentation is seen as inherent in the surplus value arising from living labor. For a firm's wage bill does not represent both the value of the "labor power" used and the surplus value emanating from it, but rather the value of the "labor power" alone. Thus wages paid out by a firm do not correspond to the "labor" embodied in its product. As a result, a firm striving to reduce costs will slight the reduction of the use of "living labor," since this is priced roughly at the lower "value" of the "labor power." Materials, on the other hand, are priced in correspondence to their full "value." Cf. A. I. Notkin, *Ocherki teorii sotsialisticheskogo vosproizvodstva* (Outline of the Theory of Socialist Reproduction), (Moscow: 1948), pp. 89-94. Also, A. Emel'ianov, "O metodakh opredeleniia ekonomicheskoi effektivnosti primeniia mashin v sovetskom khoziaistve" (On Methods of Defining the Economic Effectiveness of the Application of Machines in the Soviet Economy), *Voprosy Ekonomiki*, 1949, No. 11, pp. 108-9.

However, this second reason why money is an inaccurate expression of "value" tends to lose its importance if industrial machinery, raw materials, and fuels are priced below their "full value" and if the prices of consumers' goods are compensatingly raised above their "value." Since deviations of Soviet prices from "value" have primarily been in this direction, the second argument developed above appears, even when judged from a Marxist position, to have less significance than one would otherwise think. (This point was suggested by Professor John Maurice Clark.)

of having to feed out of the State Budget through subsidies. He set as a major task the lowering of costs and the earning of profits by all industries.[30]

However, while Soviet thinkers accept monetary results as an important test of economic success, this is by no means their only such criterion. They have pointed out that indices expressed in natural units such as production and materials consumed are still necessary, even though money is a common denominator for all of them.[31] The work of one firm affects others, and Soviet writers insist that it is only from a narrow, merchant's viewpoint that profitability can be viewed in other than its national and long-term aspect. The earning of profit by a given firm is important, but may readily be sacrificed to other goals.[32]

In the postwar period, efforts have been made by Soviet economists to develop financial criteria for evaluating the comparative advantages of alternative investments. Their search is for one unitary measuring rod. But the discussion in the Soviet press has been to the effect that what can be found at best is a test which summarizes the relative financial costs and returns of different investments, and that these should comprise only one factor in any decision as to investment policy.[33] With regard to the production activity of going firms, there has not even been a suggestion of looking for a single criterion of efficiency. A firm's management is judged by its ability to fulfill, and if possible to overfulfill, its annual plan with all the manifold criteria of such fulfillment.

Two financial indices of the success of firms have nevertheless been developed. While only limited confidence has been placed in

[30] I. Stalin, Speech of June 23, 1931, to the Conference of Business Executives, *Voprosy Leninizma*, 10th edition, pp. 461-63.

[31] G. Kozlov, *Khoziaistvennyi raschet v sotsialisticheskom obshchestve* (Business Accounting in a Socialist Society), (Moscow: 1945), pp. 19-20.

[32] Cf. P. Vasil'ev, in his review of *Organizatsiia proizvodstva v mashinostroenii* (Organization of Production in Machine Construction), in *Org. Uprav.*, 1938, No. 1, p. 73. Also, the reply by B. Katsenbogen, head of the authors' brigade which assembled the reviewed book, in *Org. Uprav.* 1938, No. 1, p. 79. Furthermore, D. Chernomordik, "Effektivnost' kapital'nykh vlozhenii i teoriia vosproizvodstva" (Effectiveness of Capital Investments and the Theory of Reproduction), *Voprosy Ekonomiki*, 1949, No. 6, pp. 81-82. The section on profitability quoted in these articles from a January, 1933, report by Stalin seems to me to be taken quite out of its original context (cf. *Voprosy Leninisma*, 10th edition, pp. 497-98), but it represents the usual Soviet interpretation from at least 1938 to the present.

[33] Cf. Chernomordik, *op. cit.*, especially pp. 80-81 and 89.

them, and indeed the partial index of "value of product produced" seems to have been given greater importance right through the period covered in this study, yet these composite criteria have grown steadily in importance in Soviet industry.

The percentage of reduction in money costs per unit of product has been a major element of all plans. Particularly in the latter period of 1938-41, cost reduction received great emphasis. In 1941, the principal speaker at the XVIIIth Party Conference called it ". . . a major index characterizing the quality of the entire work of the firm."[34] The principal natural elements entering into this composite index of cost were the hours worked by employees and the raw materials, parts, fuel, and electricity bought from other firms.[35]

But cost reduction is still only a partial index. Tasks are assigned and results measured for products which were produced in both the previous and present years, but new products are commonly excluded.[36] In addition, the extent of production is virtually excluded from the index, and this exclusion is true not only of the quantity produced, but also of its quality and assortment. Only to the extent that increased production reduces the overhead costs per unit of product[37] does the amount of production affect the cost-reduction index.

A second financial index, which includes most elements of the firm's work, is profitability. A comparison between profits actually achieved and those planned for the year should indicate how successful the firm has been. Particularly after the XVIIIth Party Congress of 1939 has this index of success been stressed.

But the over-all index of profitability seems to have been too all-inclusive to inspire much faith. Plants have suffered losses instead of making planned profits for such reasons as that they did

[34] Malenkov, Report to the XVIIIth Party Conference, *Ch.M.*, February 16, 1941, p. 3.

[35] In the 1937 plan for all industry, almost 46 percent of the cost reductions were scheduled to come from economies in the use of raw materials, fuel, and electricity. See "Za povyshenie kachestva raboty promyshlennosti" (For Raising the Quality of the Work of Industry), *Planovoe Khoziaistvo*, 1937, No. 1, p. 6.

[36] Turetskii, "Nekotorye voprosy narodnokhoziaistvennogo planirovaniia," p. 74.

[37] This is because fixed administrative costs and amortization of buildings and equipment are divided up more finely and a smaller burden is placed on each unit of product.

not receive coal and had to use more expensive wood and peat for fuel.[38] Reduction of experimental work has been an alluring method for managements to use in increasing the year's profits.[39]

It is probably because of the weaknesses in the profitability criterion that the index of cost reduction has been retained and even given increased importance. With the greater stress on finances which followed the 1939 Party Congress, profitability received added emphasis. But the industrial press still seemed to prefer the index of cost reduction, and mentioned it more frequently as a proper test of success.[40] For cost reduction included only those elements of industrial work which had been most neglected—the economizing of production factors. It could be used as a valuable addition to the other major tests—production quantity, quality, and assortment—rather than as a substitute for them. Profitability, on the other hand, combined most aspects of plants' activities, and heavy emphasis upon it would have meant a reduction in the importance of the production indices.

Thus profitability has been rejected as the basic criterion for evaluating managerial decisions and firms' work. In 1935, the Commissar of Heavy Industry criticized a director for determining questions on this basis. The director headed a synthetic rubber plant and produced considerable quantities of a waste from which he could have manufactured ether. But since the production and sale of ether as a by-product would not have covered its costs, and since it was not included in his plan, he did not set about producing it. This, said the Commissar, was giving an entirely undue weight to the criterion of profitability.[41] Similarly, in 1940, a leading economist stated that no single index of plan fulfillment could be used alone; there is no substitute for genuine analysis of all the elements entering into a firm's work, he said.[42]

[38] Cf. *Ind.*, May 22, 1938, p. 3.

[39] Director E. Kovarskii, writing in *Z.I.*, October 8, 1936, p. 3. At least in 1936, moreover, the quantity of plants' production was said to have been the main determinant of their profitability. See G. Poliak, "O fonde direktora promyshlennogo predpriiatiia" (On the Director's Fund of an Industrial Firm), *Planovoe Khoziaistvo*, 1938, No. 4, pp. 61-62.

[40] Cf. *Ind.* through 1939.

[41] G. K. Ordzhonikidze, Speech at the Council attached to the NKTP on May 12, 1935, in *Org. Uprav.*, 1935, No. 3, p. 10.

[42] Turetskii, "Ekonomika proizodstva i kachestvennye pokazateli plana," pp. 18-19.

X: The Measurement of Success: II

WHILE SOVIET WRITERS explicitly observe that financial measures of a firm's activities are not all-important in determining the management's success, we must push far beyond this bare statement if we wish to learn just how consequential finances really are.

On first impression, one might naturally expect that one of the most important forms of supervision by higher organs would be financial. Particular attention has been given by Soviet leaders to business accounting and to the proper observance by firms of "financial discipline." Higher organs find that financial control is in many ways easier to exercise than supervision over each of the manifold aspects of a plant's work. For example, incentives which are partially automatic can be linked to the financial success of managements.

This chapter will explore the incentives and controls which have been developed to prevent firms from trespassing the limits of solvency and to encourage them to strive for an affluent financial position. We shall examine managerial actions and attitudes regarding financial matters in order to evaluate the actual role and significance of financial incentives and controls.

THE NATURE AND SIGNIFICANCE OF THE FIRM'S INCENTIVE FOR FINANCIAL HEALTH

FIRMS' NEEDS FOR FINANCES: In Chapter II, we saw the manner in which firms are given a certain financial independence. Each is allocated a sum of money for working capital, and this is deposited to its account at the State Bank. Expenditures on wages, materials, fuels, etc., are debited against this account, and receipts from sale of products are credited to it. Additional financial resources are supplied by State Bank loans and are deposited to the firm's credit. The Bank account[1] can only be debited by the State Bank with the firm's permission, and the firm can use it as it sees fit.[2] The firm has other financial resources—both a second Bank account to be used for specific purposes and to be credited only from specified funds,[3] and cash kept on hand—but both of these items are very minor.[4]

The sufficiency of a firm's Bank account is determined by two factors. One is the amount of working capital which is allocated by higher bodies. The standard for determining this amount is the following: It should be sufficient so that the plant can pay its current expenses as they arise, but it should not be so great as to remove the pressure for a rapid production-sales cycle.[5] This is a standard of allocation which requires a high degree of precision for successful application. Yet methods used for determining allotments of working capital have been in practice exceedingly crude.[6]

The second factor determining the adequacy of the account is the efficiency of the plant itself. For if less fuel or materials or labor hours than was planned are used per product unit, the account will grow. The faster the production cycle, the smaller will be the amount of capital tied up in wage and materials expenses before being released by sale of the finished product. Throughout the duration of the planning year, the firm retains considerable

---

[1] The raschëtnyi schët.

[2] After August, 1939, as will be shown below, an exception was made with regard to the payment of wages.

[3] The tekushchii schet.

[4] Cf. *Kreditnyi slovar' dlia bankovskikh i finansovykh rabotnikov* (Credit Dictionary for Bank and Financial Workers), (Moscow-Leningrad: 1935), for a brief description of the different financial accounts of firms. At least for some firms, there exist also special accounts composed solely of Bank credits. See M. M. Usoskin, *Kratkosrochnyi kredit v narodnom khoziaistve SSSR* (Short-Term Credit in the National Economy of the USSR), (Leningrad: 1948), pp. 48 and 53.

[5] G. Kozlov, *Khoziaistvennyi raschët v sotsialisticheskom obshchestve* (Business Accounting in a Socialist Society (Moscow: 1945), pp. 35-36.

[6] M. Greidenberg, "Problema oborotnykh sredstv promyshlennosti" (The Problem of Working Capital of Industry), *Plan*, 1935, No. 24, pp. 21-24. L. Vilenskii, "Finansovye voprosy promyshlennosti" (Financial Questions of Industry), *Planovoe Khoziaistvo*, 1938, No. 10, p. 69. Article of A. Strukov, senior economist of the Commissariat of Finance of the USSR, *Mash.*, September 26, 1939, p. 2.

amounts of its savings, and part of the profits can be carried over into future years through the director's fund.[7]

A major means of linking the physical production of plants with their financial condition has been the practice of concluding contracts between firms and the organizations with which they trade. These contracts are enforced by a system of Arbitration Tribunals which have covered all State and cooperative firms and organizations. This system is designed to settle contractual disputes and to insure that violations of purchasing and marketing agreements will be punished by financial sanctions against the guilty party, the injured organization receiving the money fines as compensation for the losses suffered. Thus the procedure of carrying out almost all procurement through contracts between organizations—and of enforcing these contracts where necessary by arbitration—is intended to make money a common denominator for all failures to fulfill planned production, procurement, and sales. The firm's Bank account is debited or credited after the settlement of each contractual dispute.

Despite the fact that controversies between firms about contract violations are supposed to be settled privately and without arbitration wherever possible,[8] there were 130,000 arbitration disputes in 1936 which came before the Arbitration Tribunals of the Commissariat of Heavy Industry.[9] The size of this figure can be better appreciated when one considers that disputes between firms of different commissariats, or between firms of the same glavk, were ineligible for submission to these tribunals. In nine months of 1933 there were at least 500,000 disputes submitted to all the Arbitration Organs of the country.[10] During 1937, a single metallurgical firm appeared in over one hundred cases before the Central Arbi-

[7] Iu. Shenger, "O denezhnykh rezervakh sotsialisticheskogo khoziaistva i ikh roli v kreditnom planirovanii" (On the Monetary Reserves of the Socialist Economy and their Role in Credit Planning), *Planovoe Khoziaistvo*, 1937, No. 11-12, p. 119.

[8] Cf. Prikaz No. 105 of the NKTP of January 31, 1937, *BFKhZ*, 1937, No. 4. Prikaz No. 764/a of the NKTP of December 4, 1938, *Ind.*, December 8, 1938, p. 3.

[9] V. Mozheiko, "Metody sutiazhinchestva" (Methods of Going to Law about Nothing), *Arbitrazh*, 1937, No. 12, p. 27.

[10] Gamburg, Assistant Chief Arbitrator attached to the SNK SSSR, "O praktike shtrafov v organakh arbitrazha" (On the Practice of Fines in the Arbitration Organs), *Biulleten' Gosarbitrazha*, 1935, No. 2, p. 3.

tration Tribunal of the Commissariat of Heavy Industry alone, not counting the suits it took part in before other tribunals.[11]

That the arbitration of contracts is almost solely a financial question is shown by the fact that the arbitration system has usually been unable to help injured parties except with financial recompense. In regard to cases of nonshipment of goods according to contract, an arbitration decision that the goods must be shipped is considered superfluous as the obligation exists already. Yet the arbitrators have not had the power to extend this obligation beyond the planning year.[12]

Arbitrators have been officially permitted and urged to use measures additional to financial exactions in order to punish firm managements which commit serious violations of contracts. The statute of the State Arbitration Tribunals states that one of their principal functions is that of advising the economic organs above the offending firm of the violations, and even of informing the Public Prosecutor in appropriate cases.[13] But in actuality, very few tribunals have written to the Public Prosecutor, the higher economic organs, or to the Communist Party bodies.[14]

Forty percent to 60 percent of claims for damages as well as of those for sanctions provided in the contracts have been granted by the arbitration tribunals.[15] Thus, sufficient damages have been awarded to make it worth while to bring up a case, but enough

[11] L. T-ov, "O rabote predpriiatiia po materialam arbitrazha" (On the Work of the Firm According to Materials of Arbitration), *Arbitrazh*, 1938, No. 6, p. 18.

[12] Privorotskii, "Nekotorye voprosy razresheniia . . .," p. 15.

[13] Instruction letter No. GA-13 of the State Arbitration Tribunal attached to the SNK SSSR of August 14, 1940, in *Arbitrazh v sovetskom khoziaistve*, pp. 244-45.

[14] *Ibid.* "Kadry-arbitrazham" (Arbitration Cadre), *Biulleten' Gosarbitrazha*, 1934, No. 6, p. 1. "Organy arbitrazha v 1933 g." (Arbitration Organs in 1933), *Biulleten' Gosarbitrazha*, 1934, No. 6, pp. 14-15. V. A., "Zametki o signalizatsiiax" (Notes on Reporting), *Arbitrazh*, 1937, No. 7, pp. 10-11. K. Aleksandrovskaia, "Signalizatsii mestnykh organov Gosarbitrazha" (The Reporting by Local Organs of the State Arbitration System), *Arbitrazh*, 1939, No. 8, p. 19.

[15] Goloshchekin, "O rabote Gosudartvennogo arbitrazha v 1937 g.," p. 10. "Rabota organov Gosarbitrazha v pervom polugodii 1935 g." (The Work of the Organs of State Arbitration in the First Half of 1935), *Biulleten' Gosarbitrazha*, 1935, No. 18, p. 30. F. I. Goloshchekin, "Piat' let Gosarbitrazha" (Five Years of State Arbitration), *Arbitrazh*, 1936, No. 10, p. 2. "Nekotorye vyvody k itogam raboty Gosarbitrazha za 1 kvartal 1936 g." (Some Conclusions on the Results of the Work of the State Arbitration System during the First Quarter of 1936), *Arbitrazh*, 1936, No. 13, p. 4.

claims rejected to cause the respondents to fight unjust demands. That cases have been very widely fought is shown by the high proportion of appeals from the decisions of the primary tribunals: 13 to 20 percent of their decisions have been appealed, and roughly 5 percent of the original decisions reversed.[16]

The results of arbitration of contractual disputes have been of considerable importance to the managements concerned.[17] Large enough sums were involved—billions of rubles annually—to affect heavily the solvency of their firms. Managements have feared payments of damages as a threat to the profitability of their plants and to their Bank accounts. Collections of damages and fines from respondents have sometimes been great enough so as by themselves to insure a fairly healthy financial condition for the "injured" firms.[18]

A Soviet firm's insolvency is evidenced by its inability to pay its debts. Creditor organizations attach its Bank account, and so make it impossible for the firm to use it freely.[19] All claims have their order of priority according to the type of debt from which they stem, and must be paid off accordingly.[20] In the meantime, the firm continues to produce, but each individual transaction now requires the State Bank's approval so as to insure that it is directed to improving the firm's financial position and to fulfilling the firm's

[16] "Sistema Gosudarstvennogo arbitrazha v 1934 g." (The System of State Arbitration in 1934), *Biulleten' Gosarbitrazha*, 1935, No. 9/10, p. 47. N. Kheifets, "Zhaloby na resheniia" (Complaints about Decisions), *Arbitrazh*, 1936, No. 8, p. 24. "Pis'mo glavarbitra NKTP t. Zangvilia" (Letter of the Chief Arbitrator NKTP, Comrade Zangvil'), *Arbitrazh*, 1936, No. 14, pp. 50-51. "Soveshchanie glavnogo arbitra pri SNK SSSR s glavnymi arbitrami soiuznykh respublik" (Conference of the Chief Arbitrator attached to the SNK SSSR with the Chief Arbitrators of the Union Republics), *Arbitrazh*, 1938, No. 9-10, p. 6.

[17] The two main types of disputes handled have been those caused by nonsupply of contracted goods and those occasioned by the refusal of purchasers to accept products which they had ordered. In 1937, apparently a fairly typical year, 32 percent of the cases before the State Arbitration Tribunals fell into the first group, and 26 percent into the second. Ten percent were disputes over the quality and assortment of products. (Goloshchekin, "O rabote Gosudarstvennogo arbitrazha v 1937 g.," pp. 5-6.) Quality disputes increased from a low of 3 percent in 1934 to 10 to 12 percent in 1940. (Gamburg, "Rabota organov arbitrazha" [Work of the Arbitration Organs], *Biulleten' Gosarbitrazha*, 1935, No. 9/10, p. 34. *Arbitrazh v sovetskom khoziaistve*, p. 217.) The remaining grounds of dispute seem to have been pretty well scattered.

[18] Turetskii, "Ekonomika proizvodstva i kachestvennye pokazateli plana," pp. 18-19.

[19] Cf. *Z.I.*, July 3, 1934, p. 2.

[20] Post. of the TsIK and SNK SSSR of February 6, 1929, *BFKhZ*, 1929, No. 10.

plan. An insolvent firm has lost the right to free maneuverability of its current income.

The director of a Soviet firm whose Bank account has been attached can be put in the same position as a capitalist entrepreneur operating on a shoestring. Director Mozgolov, who was in this position for several months, had to spend most of his time trying to scare up enough money with which to operate. Each day was a new battle to finance his plant's running costs.[21]

PREVALENCE OF FINANCIAL DIFFICULTIES: Insolvency has been a far from rare occurrence. When one considers that working capital is allocated so that firms should have barely enough if all goes according to plan, and that the methods used for determining the required amounts have been extremely rough, it is not surprising that many firms have suffered financial embarrassment. As of August 1, 1939, 27 percent of all the clients having accounts in the State Bank owed overdue debts to one or more suppliers. In heavy industry, the percentage was still higher for entire commissariats.[22] As of March, 1937, almost half of the industrial firms which came under a special study had overdue debts outstanding; 19 percent of the firms had debts overdue for more than thirty days.[23] In the first half of 1934, more than half of all the cases which came before the Arbitration Tribunals were suits for the collection of unpaid debts.[24]

Many firm managements even seem to have voluntarily permitted their firms to become insolvent. During the first half of 1936, the Leningrad office of the State Bank kept a systematic check on 75 large firms of heavy industry. Together they showed a profit of 18 percent above that planned for the period. Yet almost all of the firms failed to pay their bills and had their Bank accounts attached at some point during the half year. The main reason for

[21] Z.I., March 27, 1935, p. 2.
[22] M. Usoskin, "Voprosy kreditovaniia i raschëtov v sviazi s neplatëzhami" (Questions of Crediting and of Accounts in Connection with Nonpaying Organs), Den'gi i Kredit, 1940, No. 4-5, p. 18.
[23] Iu. Shenger, "Organizovat' bor'bu s debitersko-kreditorskoi zadolzhennost'iu (In Order to Organize the Fight Against Non-Bank Debts), Kredit i Khozraschët, 1937, No. 19, p. 9.
[24] "Ofitsial'nyi otdel," Biulleten' Gosarbitrazha, 1934, No. 18, pp. 29-31.

their inability to remain solvent was that they accumulated far
more materials and products than had been planned for in their
allotment of working capital.[25] The same reason was also cited in
later years for different plants.[26] Other profitable firms chose insolvency when they decided to use their working capital to finance
repair work for which no funds had been scheduled.[27] One profitable firm had its Bank account attached continuously for four and
a half months—except four times for several hours each time.[28]

Why did firms choose to exceed their planned allotments at the
expense of their solvency? Certainly not because managements
were indifferent to the additional State Bank controls or to the bad
reputation they thereby received, but rather because the alternative was worse. The danger of failing to get supplies in the future
caused accumulation of surpluses when they were available; insufficient allocations for capital repair or new construction presented a serious threat to production which had to be met in some
fashion. When feasible, managements preferred to retain the independence of an unattached account. But clearly they were not
wedded to such independence when it conflicted with what they
considered as more basic prerequisites for successful operation.

In order to make insolvency particularly unpleasant, suppliers
have been authorized to cut off shipments to firms which do not
pay their bills.[29] Supplier firms, however, have been extremely re-
luctant to take such a drastic step.[30] One reason is that the purchasing plants can draw them into lengthy arbitration.[31] More impor-

[25] Article by D. E. Mezhov, Manager of the Leningrad Provincial Office of the
State Bank, Z.I., September 3, 1936, p. 3.
[26] Cf. K. Petrov, head of the industrial sector of the Donets Office of the State
Bank, writing in Z.I., March 23, 1937, p. 2, and Mash., May 30, 1939, p. 3.
[27] Cf. the report of a newspaper investigatory brigade, Z.I., September 2, 1937, pp.
2-3. That this was not the common thing is shown, however, by the general neglect
of plant repair which was discussed in Chapter VII.
[28] Mash., May 30, 1939, p. 3.
[29] Cf. Prikaz No. 1267 of the NKTP of December 4, 1935, approved by the SNK SSSR
on December 9, 1935, Z.I., December 10, 1935, p. 1. V. Sobol', "Ob oborotnykh
sredstvakh" (On Working Capital), Problemy Ekonomiki, 1937, No. 3-4, p. 151.
Mash., October 14, 1938, p. 3.
[30] Sobol', op. cit., p. 151. F. Lobanov and P. Mitropol'skii, "Likvidatsiia neplatëzhei
—odna iz tsentral'nykh zadach Gosbanka" (The Liquidation of Nonpayments is One
of the Central Tasks of the State Bank), Kredit i Khozraschët, 1937, No. 22, p. 13.
"Za reshitel'nuiu perestroiku bankovskoi raboty," p. 3.
[31] Cf. Z.I., August 15, 1935, p. 2.

tant, a firm adopting such a policy might find itself unable to locate acceptable customers.[32] But the main reason for this reluctance is that higher authorities clearly have intended the practice to be reserved for emergency use only.[33] The national supply plans, which in turn determine the possibilities of firms fulfilling their production plans, are not to be lightly interfered with for financial reasons alone. Thus the threat of cutting off shipments to insolvent firms is not likely to cause them much anxiety.

FINANCIAL PROSPERITY AS AN INCENTIVE TO MANAGEMENT: As we shall see below and in the following chapter, managerial promotions and bonuses have not been tied to the financial prosperity of the firms. Only to the extent that a firm's financial condition affects its over-all "plan fulfillment" does it influence the size of the salary and bonus paid to the director and other members of management.

Nevertheless, management has had a major interest in earning high profits. It has been impelled to try to cut costs and make profits because the money saved could be used for purposes which it itself determined to be important. Expenditures which management is legally empowered to make are impossible without these extra earnings, and the same is even more true of illegal expenditures on extra materials, fuels, etc.

In 1936, a "director's fund" was set up for each industrial firm.[34] This fund was to be composed of 4 percent of all earned profits which had been planned for in the firm's annual plan and 50 percent of all profits which were above this amount. The moneys in the fund were to be spent by the director, with the approval of the plant's trade-union committee and according to a system established by the commissar, on housing, services, and individual pre-

[32] Lobanov and Mitropol'skii, op. cit., pp. 13-14.

[33] Cf. ibid. B. Berkovskii, "Otvetstvennoe khranenie tovarov i kreditovanie na summy v puti" (The Storage of Goods with Responsibility for them and the Crediting of Goods en Route), Kredit i Khozraschët, 1937, No. 6, pp. 4-5. G. Shvarts, assistant chief of the Central Planning-Economic Administration of the State Bank, "Voprosy ukrepleniia platëzhnoi distsipliny" (Questions in the Strengthening of Payment Discipline), Den'gi i Kredit, 1939, No. 7, p. 37.

[34] Post. of the TsIK and SNK SSSR of April 19, 1936, BFKhZ, 1936, No. 12. Earlier, much the same purpose had been accomplished by a multitude of separate funds.

miums to workers, and on unplanned and additional capital construction and rationalization measures.[35]

This fund has proved very important to directors. Its value does not seem to have lain in any relationship between the firm's fund and premiums to top executives.[36] Rather it has rested in the extra maneuverability gained by management through this reservoir of uncontrolled money. For one thing, it has been one of the two financial sources into which directors could delve to carry out unplanned construction and to purchase small equipment.[37] For another, special premiums for workers and the building of more housing, plant dining rooms, etc., have helped to attract and hold skilled workers. Many firms have been unable to make such expenditures for lack of sufficient profits.[38]

Data on the use of directors' funds bears out the above characterization of them as sources of money with which managements can maneuver. The law setting up the fund provided that at least 50 percent of the moneys should be used for housing the firm's personnel.[39] Yet in 1936 only 3.7 percent of the moneys of five industrial commissariats were used for housing construction, and in 1940 only 27 percent on both construction and repair.[40] On the other hand, while the use of the fund for production needs was mentioned last among its purposes in the founding law, 50 percent of the moneys were used for production in 1936 and 14 percent in 1940.[41] At least in 1936 there was not too strong a correlation between the rubles per worker in a firm's director's fund and the

---

[35] The director's fund was abolished during the war, but reinstituted at the end of 1946. (A. Arakelian, *Upravlenie sotsialisticheskoi promyshlennost'iu* [Administration of Socialist Industry] [Moscow: 1947], p. 134).

[36] Cf. *Pravda*, October 17, 1940, p. 2. At least in the Commissariat of Light Industry, however, expenditures for management of a "social-cultural" nature—such as those on housing—have come from the director's fund. (Prikaz No. 456 of the Commissariat of Light Industry of June 22, 1936, *BFKhZ*, 1936, No. 25/26.)

[37] Post. No. 726 of the SNK SSSR of April 19, 1936, *BFKhZ*, 1936, No. 15.

[38] Cf. *Ind.*, January 18, 1940, p. 2.

[39] Post. of the TsIK and SNK SSSR of April 19, 1936, *BFKhZ*, 1936, No. 12.

[40] G. Poliak, "O fonde direktora promyshlennogo predpriiatiia" (On the Director's Fund of an Industrial Firm), *Planovoe Khoziaistvo*, 1938, No. 4, pp. 64-65. Arakelian, *op. cit.*, pp. 133-34.

[41] *Ibid.* While the differences between the 1936 and 1940 figures are very marked, I am unable to say which is a more typical year, or even whether the figures illustrate a trend. So far as I have been able to determine, statistics for other years are not available.

firm's expenditures per worker, from the fund, on service to its employees.[42] Writing in 1938 a Soviet economist pointed out that the fund had been diverted into a major source of unplanned capital investment by managers.[43]

The degree of incentive for management embodied in the director's fund has, however, been very uneven. Those firms which were planned to operate with losses might sharply reduce the amount of subsidies required, and yet not earn any such fund.[44] Even among those firms which were planned to be profitable, the size of the planned profits differed sharply. Thus plant executives could not help but feel that the size of the director's fund did not correspond to the accomplishments of the firm.[45]

Moreover, while the size of a firm's director's fund is dependent on its profits, the right to use the fund for greater maneuverability has not been solely related to the firm's financial success. For the fund could only be employed by the firm management with the permission of the director's superior (normally the head of the glavk), and this permission was to be given only if the quantity, assortment, and quality plans were fulfilled.[46] While the director's fund has served primarily as an incentive to management in developing a strong financial position for the firm, there is no indication that it has offered any great temptation for doing this by the neglect of basic elements of the firm's plan.

In addition to the director's fund, there are other similar sources of financial maneuverability. Reduction in the labor required per unit of product permits increased premiums to be paid at least temporarily to the work force. Particular firm successes have been

[42] Poliak, *op. cit.*, p. 67.

[43] *Ibid.*, p. 66.

[44] Commissar V. A. Malyshev, Speech at the meeting of May 28, 1939, of the Supreme Soviet of the USSR, *Mash.*, May 30, 1939, p. 2. Of the prewar years, only 1936 was an exception to this. (Post. No. 52/724 of the TsIK and SNK SSSR of April 19, 1936, *BFKhZ*, 1936, No. 15.)

[45] Director G. Tsvetkov, writing in *Mash.*, January 26, 1939, p. 2. The postwar law on the director's fund established that the percentages of both planned and unplanned profits to go into the director's fund should differ sharply as between ministries. (Arakelian, *op. cit.*, pp. 134-35.)

[46] Instructions of the Commissariat of Finance of the USSR for applying the Postanovlenie of the TsIK and SNK SSSR of April 19, 1936, *BFKhZ*, 1937, No. 2. More precisely, these instructions provided that permission was required before the legally established percentage of a firm's profits could be transferred by the management into the firm's director's fund.

rewarded by higher authorities with grants of large sums to be distributed by management to outstanding workers.[47] Production of consumers' goods from industrial wastes has yielded profits which could be used for unplanned construction and purchase of equipment as well as for premiums.[48]

The incentive for management to earn these funds permitting greater maneuverability is very strong. Such moneys are of considerable help in achieving "success" and the material and intangible rewards which go with it. In addition, they give management "independence." To a far greater degree than would otherwise be possible, directors with large funds can make autonomous decisions in the management of their firms. Certainly the impetus to become —even partially—the master of one's destiny cannot be considered a weak one.

CONTROLS OVER FINANCIAL DISCIPLINE

GLAVK AND COMMISSARIAT SUPERVISION: Just as firms are given planned tasks for production, quality, etc., so are they also presented with financial tasks. Their annual plan will include an item for planned profits for the year, or for a maximum planned subsidy if it is a firm which is not expected to come out financially ahead. It will also include figures for cost reductions per product unit. Higher industrial organs check on the fulfillment of these indices just as they do on the other indices of the plan.

Glavki and commissariats have their own financial plans to fulfill, and these are a composite of all the tasks of their firms. Thus the glavki chiefs have a personal stake in the condition of their firms' finances. But they have an equal incentive for insuring that plants produce the planned quantities and meet all the other nonfinancial tests of success. Their interest in financial matters is no greater than their interest in other aspects of the firms' work.

There have been complaints that glavki and commissariats have paid no more attention to financial questions than did their firms. It is said that they have not checked on financial discipline, and have readily pulled their firms out of money difficulties by means of

[47] Cf. Post. No. 577 of the SNK SSSR of April 28, 1939, *SPR*, 1939, article 200.
[48] Post. No. 726 of the SNK SSSR of April 19, 1936, *BFKhZ*, 1936, No. 15, and Post. No. 934 of the SNK SSSR of June 2, 1940, *SPR*, 1940, article 390.

extra subsidies.[49] Certainly not all commissariats and glavki acted in this fashion, but such complaints indicate that these organs have not shown any special concern for financial discipline.

THE STATE BANK: This institution has had the greatest responsibility of all State organs for the maintenance of financial discipline by the firms. All but the smallest transactions must pass through the Bank branches rather than be handled directly in cash.[50] The Bank supervises the use of working capital by plants and issues loans to cover a significant portion of their needs. Yet in spite of these opportunities for supervision, the Bank has been unable to exercise strict control over firms of heavy industry, and indeed it seems as if its main supervisory function has been that of advising the glavki and commissariats of financial violations.

Among the direct financial controls possessed by the Bank, by far the strongest has been its power to grant credits. Firms are supposed to be provided by their commissariat with sufficient working capital to cover their normal needs during seasons of the year when these are at a minimum. Seasonal growth in expenses is to be covered by Bank credits.[51] But while this seasonal role of credits has been established in Soviet law and theory since 1931,[52] in practice the Bank has also been expected to finance virtually all shipments of products during the time they are en route. By 1943, a Soviet author could state that any firm which shipped more than 15 to 20 percent of its production without receiving such bill-of-lading credit for it thereby indicated that its management was willfully refusing to use credits to the proper extent.[53]

The significance of Bank credit as an instrument of control over

[49] Cf. Kh. Rozenberg, assistant head of the Financial Sector of the Moscow Stalin Auto Firm, writing in *Mash.*, July 8, 1939, p. 2.

[50] E. Bregel' and A. Tsagolov, "Naznachenie i funktsii deneg v sotsialisticheskoi ekonomike" (The Assignment and Functions of Money in a Socialist Economy), *Planovoe Khoziaistvo*, 1940, No. 12, p. 81.

[51] B. Berkovskii, "Kreditovanie promyshlennosti i kontrol' rublem" (The Crediting of Industry and the Control by the Ruble), a discussion article, *Kredit i Khozraschët*, 1937, No. 5, p. 4.

[52] Post. of STO of July 23, 1931, *SZ*, 1931, article 316.

[53] N. Veitsman, *Analiz khoziaistvennykh pokazatelei predpriiatiia* (Analysis of Economic Indices of the Firm), (Moscow: 1943), pp. 62-63. The very high proportion of such bill-of-lading credits in the prewar period shows that this statement could almost certainly have been made then with equal accuracy.

firms has been weakened by the structure of the credits. Over half of the loans to heavy industry's firms have been granted on bills of lading.[54] Yet these credits to producers, covering finished goods from the time they are shipped until they have been paid for, have been given automatically. The Bank has only been interested in assuring itself that the goods were actually shipped, and thus that the loans had proper security behind them. This form of credit has not been used at all as a method of control over the financial activities of firms.[55]

Aside from financing shipments of finished products, Bank credits are used to provide some of the moneys needed for stockpiling materials and semifabricates, and for carrying on the firm's books unfinished production and finished goods until they are sold.[56] Such credits are essentially seasonal in nature. But heavy industry as a whole has shown relatively little seasonal fluctuation in its financial needs. It has been characterized by an absence of seasonal production processes and by very little need for agricultural raw materials.[57] Thus, while January Bank credits have run about 20 percent of the total working-capital needs of industrial firms of light industry, they have comprised only 6 to 8 percent of the funds used by heavy industry's firms.[58] Plants of heavy industry have not depended on loans as a major source of their financing.[59]

---

[54] Data for January 1, 1938 (V. Sitnin and Z. Simkin, "Usilit' kontrol' rublem v tiazhëloi promyshlennosti" [In Order to Strengthen Control by the Ruble in Heavy Industry], *Planovoe Khoziaistvo*, 1940, No. 12, p. 24). That this situation continued is shown by the article "Gosbank v period zaversheniia stroitel'stva sotsializma" (The State Bank in the Period of Completing the Building of Socialism), *Den'gi i Kredit*, 1939, No. 4, p. 12.

[55] V. Zhdanov, "Iskorenit' avtomatizm v kreditovanii raschëtnykh dokumentov v puti" (For the Elimination of Automatism in Crediting Bills of Lading), *Den'gi i Kredit*, 1939, No. 6, p. 39. S. Orlov, "Eshchë o kreditovanii tranzitnykh otgruzok" (More on Crediting of Shipments en Route), *Kredit i Khozraschët*, 1937, No. 12, pp. 25-26. Sitnin and Simkin, *op. cit.*, p. 25.

[56] E. Mitel'man, "Nado li detsentralizovat' planirovanie kreditov?" (Must the Planning of Credits be Decentralized?), *Kredit i Khozraschët*, 1936, No. 14, pp. 13-14.

[57] Mitel'man, "Nado li detsentralizovat' planirovanie kreditov?" p. 13.

[58] Sitnin and Simkin, *op. cit.*, pp. 23-25. E. Kasimovskii, "O kreditovanii gotovykh izdelii" (On the Crediting of Finished Goods), *Den'gi i Kredit*, 1940, No. 6-7, p. 18. There seems to have been no important difference here in the situation in the machine-construction industry and in the rest of heavy industry.

[59] In 1939, an increase in the proportion of credits to total working capital was introduced in the machine-construction industry. The purpose was to extend Bank control over the firms by forcing managements to liquidate loans and borrow anew every fifteen days. This new system was only put into effect in fifty firms, however.

To the extent that the State Bank has provided heavy industry's firms with working-capital credits other than those given to finance shipments of finished products, these credits have normally been granted on the basis of "credit limits." These "limits" define the amount of money which may be loaned against materials on hand, against fuels in stock, etc. Each of these forms of security is treated separately, and thus it is intended to prevent firms from accumulating, for example, more fuels than planned and from financing them by credits which were meant for the storing of raw materials.[60]

"Credit limits" have been set by the central office of the State Bank. However, the limits for each firm were established on the basis of statements prepared by its glavk. Normally the Bank has used no other materials for determining the limits. Thus, in practice, each commissariat was given limits which it subdivided among its glavki, and these in turn were divided among the firms.[61] Planning of credits for the firms was, therefore, not really a function of the State Bank; it was a job of the same glavki which did all the nonfinancial planning for these firms.[62]

In what fashion, then, has the Bank exercised any real authority over the granting of these "planned credits" to firms? The central office, of course, has exercised none; it could not have any real knowledge of the problems of each firm in the economy and scarcely has pretended to have any. Local offices of the Bank, however, have been empowered to cut off credits to any firm which en-

(Sitnin and Simkin, *op. cit.,* pp. 25-28. V. Sitnin, "Gosbank i mashinostroenie" [The State Bank and Machine Construction], *Den'gi i Kredit,* 1940, No. 1, p. 12.) A Soviet author, reporting in the Bank magazine on this experiment, declared that there seemed to be no significant increase in control. (Sitnin, "Gosbank i mashinostroenie," pp. 12-14.) A comparison of the proportion within the machine-construction industry of stocks on hand covered by credits in 1940 with that in 1936-38, shows that this experiment was not extended throughout the industry. ("Za reshitel'nuiu perestroiku bankovskoi raboty," pp. 1-2. Sitnin and Simkin, *op. cit.,* p. 25.)

[60] Usoskin, *Kratkosrochnyi kredit v narodnom khoziaistve SSSR,* pp. 40-48.

[61] S. Gol'dberg and Ia. Fishkes, "Upravlenie ne znaet finansov zavodov" (The Administration Doesn't Know the Finances of the Plants), *Kredit i Khozraschët,* 1936, No. 12, pp. 13-14.

[62] By 1948, and possibly much earlier, it seems that this practice was accepted into the formal structure of the establishment of credit limits, and the Bank lost all responsibility for the task. (Cf. Usoskin, *Kratkosrochnyi kredit v narodnom khoziaistve SSSR,* p. 47.)

gages in such practices as piling up excessive stocks of materials, or using working capital for investment purposes.[63] They have been instructed to reduce credits if a firm fails to fulfill its production plan.[64] Indeed, Bank branches have at least temporarily reformed some managements by the threat of ending their credits,[65] and have even carried out this threat in the case of other plants.[66]

But such independent action by Bank branches has been the rare exception. The magazine of the State Bank has repeatedly pointed out that credits normally have been granted automatically within the scope of the "limits" established by the glavk.[67] The Bank has not begun to use its power to abolish or reduce credits as a means of enforcing its demand that firms act in a responsible financial fashion.

The third type of loan—in addition to those for the financing of shipments and to "planned credit"—has been that of "unplanned credit." These loans are supposed to be given to firms at the discretion of the local branches of the State Bank, and are mainly intended to cover unexpected needs which have arisen through no fault of the firm itself.[68] Thus, in 1934 they were primarily used to finance the storing of finished goods which could not be marketed immediately because of the shortage of transport.[69] In 1937, local Bank branches were permitted to grant unplanned loans where needed for the payment of overdue debts to suppliers—but only after the borrowing firms had pledged to eliminate all above-

---

[63] Post. of the SNK SSSR of June 4, 1936, *BFKhZ*, 1936, No. 16/17. Berkovskii, "Kreditovanie promyshlennosti i kontrol' rublem," p. 5. Prikaz No. 3/2 of the Office of the Public Prosecutor of the USSR of August 26, 1934, *BFKhZ*, 1934, No. 31. Permission from the central office of the State Bank has, however, been required before a local office may cut off a firm's credit.

[64] Usoskin, *Kratkosrochnyi kredit v narodnom khoziaistve SSSR*, p. 47.

[65] K. Barvinskii, manager of the Cheliabinskii Office of the State Bank, "Izuchenie khoziaistva—osnova ulusheniia kreditnoi raboty" (The Study of the Economy is the Basis for Improving Credit Work), *Kredit i Khozraschët*, 1936, No. 9, p. 30.

[66] *Ibid.*, pp. 30-31.

[67] "Peredovaia" (Lead), *Kredit i Khozraschët*, 1937, No. 4, p. 2. Berkovskii, "Kreditovanie promyshlennosti i kontrol' rublem," pp. 4 and 7. Iu. Shenger, "Protiv mekhanicheskogo kreditovaniia" (Against Mechanical Crediting), *Den'gi i Kredit*, 1940, No. 10, pp. 9-10.

[68] Usoskin, *Kratkosrochnyi kredit v narodnom khoziaistve SSSR*, pp. 43-44.

[69] I. Dubnov and E. Mitel'man, "Kontrol' rublem v tiazhëloi promyshlennosti" (Control by the Ruble in Heavy Industry), *Kredit i Khozraschët*, 1934, No. 22, p. 3. Mitel'man, "Nado li detsentralizovat' planirovanie kreditov?" pp. 13-14.

plan stocks of materials within a specified period.[70] Such loans have also been used to provide firms with the means for financing rationalization measures which would quickly pay for themselves.[71]

The right to grant "unplanned credit" would seem to offer Bank branches the opportunity to exercise a measure of genuine control over their customer firms. A director who realizes that the head of the local branch has it in his power to pull him out of financial difficulties is likely to respond favorably to this official's suggestions as to measures which he should take to improve his firm's financial position. However, this possibility for Bank control has never been used. "Unplanned loans" were given publicity at various times, but they were never allowed to become an important source of financing.[72] The result, as was pointed out by one Soviet author, has been that directors have seen no necessity for paying overmuch attention to the ideas of local Bank officials.[73]

All in all, the Bank's main instrument of direct control over firms—its right to grant or refuse them credits—seems never to have been exercised significantly. Much has been written about it, and instances can be cited where it was used to reform the practices of individual plants. But a reading of the Bank and industrial press clearly shows that on the whole it has been ineffectual.

The State Bank has mainly concentrated its attention on making sure that its loans had proper security behind them. In practice, there was greater disapproval of the Bank "meddling" in economic administration than of its permitting financial discipline to go unenforced.[74]

When, on occasion, the Bank has attempted to follow a more vigorous control policy, it has had its knuckles severely rapped. During 1940, it adopted the line of reducing credits to those firms

[70] Iu. Shenger, "Organizovat' bor'bu s debitorsko-kreditorskoi zadolzhennost'iu," pp. 10-11.

[71] Cf. Circular No. 5398 of the State Bank of the USSR of May 22, 1939, *BFKhZ*, 1939, No. 17/18.

[72] Ia. Fishkis, "Ustranit' nedostatki v vydache ssud na vremennye nuzhdy" (For the Elimination of Deficiencies in the Giving of Loans for Temporary Needs), *Kredit i Khozraschët*, 1937, No. 18, p. 7. Berkovskii, "Kreditovanie promyshlennosti i kontrol' rublem," pp. 7-8. "Gosbank v period zaversheniia stroitel'stva sotsializma," p. 13. "Za reshitel'nuiu perestroiku bankovskoi raboty," p. 2.

[73] Berkovskii, "Kreditovanie promyshlennosti i kontrol' rublem," p. 8.

[74] For a 1941 statement of this position by a prominent financial writer, see Iu. Shenger's article "Protiv mekhanicheskogo kreditovaniia," pp. 9-10.

of heavy industry which had excess frozen stocks. But the only result was the further weakening of the Bank's influence. For, although the ruble value of credits would normally have risen in 1940
as production grew, it declined instead in most branches of heavy
industry and machine construction. From January 1 to October 1,
the proportion of stocks covered by Bank credits dropped from 8.9
percent to 7.5 percent in the three commissariats of machine construction, and from 11.9 percent to 8.9 percent in seven other
heavy industry commissariats. The place of legitimate Bank credit
in financing these stocks of materials and goods was partially taken
up by overdue debts to suppliers and to the Bank itself. These illegal sources of financing were supplemented by increases in the
working capital granted to firms by their commissariats.[75] As it
would have been quite impossible for the commissariats to have
increased the working capital of their firms unless the Council of
Commissars had first enlarged their own supply of such moneys, it
can be said that the State Bank's efforts in 1940 to use credit as a
means of control were frustrated not only by the firms and industrial commissariats but even by the top executive organ of the
Government.

Aside from attempts to use credit as a direct supervisory weapon,
efforts for enforcing Bank control over firms have been concentrated in the field of wages. As early as 1933, the Bank was given the
task of seeing that firms spent no more for labor than was called
for by their plans. Commissariats were to divide their annual and
quarterly wage funds among their firms, and the State Bank was
not permitted to give any firm money for wages—even though it
came from the firm's own Bank account—beyond the limits of its
allotted monthly and quarterly wage fund. Additional moneys
could be paid out only if the firm's production was above plan, and
if the planned expenditure of wages per product unit was not exceeded.[76] Thus, it was the Bank's task to supervise directly the fulfillment by firms of the wage plans fixed by industrial organs.

I do not have information as to whether the Bank actually refused to pay sums not provided in the approved wage funds, but in
any case this system of strict Bank control proved unsuccessful. For

[75] "Za reshitel'nuiu perestroiku bankovskoi raboty," pp. 1-2.
[76] Post. No. 269 of the SNK SSSR of February 21, 1933, SZ, 1933, article 75.

in mid-1935 it was abolished, and the Bank was instructed to pay out all moneys for wages which the firm managements themselves certified to be necessary.[77] Supervision over expenditures was lodged primarily in the glavki and commissariats which composed the wage plans for the firms, and the Bank's control duties were limited to seeing that the sums paid out to managements to cover wages were actually used for this purpose.[78]

From mid-1935 through 1937, the Bank exercised no supervision whatsoever over wage expenditures.[79] In auditing reports there was not even a subdivision for Bank expenditures on such control.[80] Only in 1938 did the picture begin to change. In June, firms were instructed to begin informing the Bank of their wage-fund allotments and of the proportion of their production plans which they had fulfilled.[81] The head of the Bank demanded that all branch heads report at least once a month to the leading regional Government and Communist Party officials on overexpenditures of wage funds by firms in their district.[82] But when the Bank found such overexpenditures, it could do no more than report them to the firms' glavki and to the regional Party and Government organs.

In late 1938, the Council of Commissars experimented with a considerable increase of Bank control over selected firms throughout industry.[83] The experiment was a success, and in late 1939 a new system of Bank control was introduced generally.[84] Once again, as before mid-1935, the Bank was to restrict its payments for covering wages to the monthly fund given each firm by its glavk

[77] *Z.I.,* June 17, 1935, p. 4.

[78] *Ibid.*

[79] Iu. Shenger, "Zadachi Gosbanka v bor'be s pereraskhodovaniem fondov zarplaty" (The Tasks of the State Bank in the Fight Against the Overexpenditure of Wage Funds), *Kredit i Khozraschët,* 1937, No. 23, p. 5. N. Zabozlaev, "Fondy zarplaty—pod bditel'nyi bankovskii kontrol'" (Wage Funds under Vigilant Bank Control), *Den'gi i Kredit,* 1938, No. 5, p. 32.

[80] G. Shabanov, "Aktiv'no borot'sia s pereraskhodom fondov zarplaty" (In Order to Actively Fight Against Overexpenditure of Wage Funds), *Kredit i Khozraschët,* 1937, No. 23, p. 7.

[81] Zabozlaev, *op. cit.,* p. 32. N. Zabozlaev, "Novoe v kontrole za fondami zarplaty" (What is New in Control over Wage Funds), *Den'gi i Kredit,* 1939, No. 1, p. 50.

[82] N. Zabozlaev, "Bol'she operativnosti v bor'be s pereraskhodami fondov zarabotnoi platy" (More of an Operational Character to the Fight Against Overexpenditure of Wage Funds), *Kredit i Khozraschët,* 1938, No. 4, p. 19.

[83] Zabozlaev, "Novoe v kontrole za fondami zarplaty," pp. 50-51.

[84] Post. No. 1215 of the SNK SSSR of August 15, 1939, *BFKhZ,* 1939, No. 29/30.

or commissariat. Overexpenditures up to 10 percent of the fund could be paid by the Bank if such violations were not repeated. If the firm produced more than was called for by its production plan, and did not violate in the process its wage norm per product unit, the Bank was to pay out the additional money required. But otherwise the head of the firm's glavk or the commissar himself would have to give permission for all extra payments. In addition, the commissar would have to cover the firm's above-plan expenditures from the commissariat's total wage fund for the month.[85]

In this fashion, the State Bank was given the task of enforcing the wage allotments of the plants. A Bank study, covering over 34,-000 industrial firms during seven months of the law's operation, showed a sharp reduction in the percentage of those exceeding their planned wage bills.[86] Figures for December, 1939, of three heavy industry commissariats show that three quarters of all excess expenditures by firms were made only with their commissariat's permission.[87] But the commissariats themselves could and did overexpend their own funds,[88] and considered keeping within wage bounds as only one of many indices of the success of both the firms and of the commissariat as a whole. Thus, even in the case of this tightest of Bank controls, the Bank supervision consisted mainly of calling the attention of the industrial glavki and commissariats to their firms' failures.

A major obstacle to pushing Bank control over wages too far was indicated in 1940 by a prominent Soviet economist. With wages singled out as a particularly crucial cost element, some plants reduced wage expenditures by purchasing semifabricates and services from other firms when normally they would have carried out this work themselves. The economist pointed by implication to the risks involved in expanding control over any one aspect of costs

[85] *Ibid*. A. Proselkov, a member of the Central Administration of the State Bank, "Kontrol' za raskhodovaniem fondov zarabotnoi platy" (Control over the Overexpenditure of Wage Funds), *Den'gi i Kredit*, 1939, No. 8, pp. 41-42.

[86] T. Orlova, "Bank v bor'be za ekonomiiu zarabotnoi platy" (The Bank in the Fight for Wage Economies), *Den'gi i Kredit*, 1940, No. 2-3, pp. 14-15.

[87] The Commissariat of Electrical Industry, of Construction Materials and of the Chemical Industry. The Bank itself permitted only 7 percent, and the glavki heads 19 percent (*Ibid.*, p. 18).

[88] *Ibid.*, p. 18.

such as wages, while all other aspects were not equally supervised.[89] As the firms were answerable to their glavki and commissariats and not to the State Bank, distortions increasing total costs were not likely to be pushed too far. But if Bank control over wages had been made very strong, it would have compelled the firms to take advantage of the absence of supervision in other financial areas, and so have led them to weaken their total financial position.

To sum up, the State Bank has exercised little independent control over firms. While it does have certain powers of independent control, these have seldom been used. When there was an attempt to employ credits for this purpose in 1940, the effort was utterly frustrated. The Bank branches have been denied any power even in such a minor aspect of control as that of investigating the legitimacy of the reasons for which purchasers refuse payment for goods ordered. They have been obliged automatically to honor any request to refuse payment.[90]

Bank supervision has been exercised mainly through recommendations to commissariats and glavki, to the Communist Party and State Control Commissions, and to the Public Prosecutor.[91] Thus the actual enforcement of financial discipline has been in the hands of organs which are quite as interested in nonfinancial indices of the success of firms as in the financial criteria.

MANAGERIAL ATTITUDES TOWARD FINANCIAL SUCCESS

In the light of this material on incentives for firm profitability and on controls against financial abuses, our natural inter-

[89] Sh. Turetskii, "Nekotorye voprosy narodnokhoziaistvennogo planirovaniia" (Some Questions of National Economic Planning), *Problemy Ekonomiki*, 1940, No. 7, pp. 74-75.

[90] Bank circular No. 2886 of April 15, 1935, referred to by S. Gur'ev in "Usilit' kontrol' nad otkazom ot adtsepta" (In Order to Strengthen Control over Acceptance-Refusals), *Kredit i Khozraschët*, 1937, No. 23, p. 17. M. Gomberg and I. Naumov, "Kreditno-raschëtnaia rabota" (Credit-Accounting Work), *Den'gi i Kredit*, 1940, No. 4-5, p. 77.

[91] E. Mitel'man, "Tovarnaia rabota banka" (The Goods Work of the Bank), *Kredit i Khozraschët*, 1934, No. 18, pp. 10-13. Shabanov, *op. cit.*, p. 7. "Za reshitel'nuiu perestroiku bankovskoi raboty," p. 2. *Finansirovanie i kreditovanie kapital'nykh vlozhenii* (Financing and Crediting of Capital Investments), edited by V. M. Buzyrev, issued as a study-aid for the financial-economic institutes (Moscow-Leningrad: 1941), p. 230.

est is in the response shown by firm managements. As is not surprising, managerial attitudes have been mixed.

Many firm managements have tended to give relatively little weight to financial criteria.[92] Many, as we have seen above, have not been too concerned when their firms were threatened with insolvency. Some have considered good organization and technique as goals in themselves rather than as means for achieving particular economic results.[93] Even in 1939, directors who placed little emphasis on financial considerations could still be considered highly successful. A national industrial newspaper pointed to I. Korobov, director of the Petrovskii Metallurgical Firm, as an able young executive who had achieved important improvements during his ten months as director. But like many other industrial leaders, the paper editorialized, he scorned financial matters; thus his plant suffered losses in the first half of 1939 despite its opportunities to be profitable.[94] For all of Korobov's financial failure, it should be noted, the newspaper hailed him as a top-flight director. Furthermore, he retained his post at least till the war. Financial failure was not considered too important.

Concern for profits seems to vary from firm to firm. In 1939, prices of metallurgical products were changed to encourage the production of the more difficult shapes and grades. Despite this price encouragement, the Ordzhonikidze Firm refused an order for a type of steel difficult to produce. The Konstantinovskii Frunze Firm not only produced this steel, but its director asked the Metal Marketing Organ for more such orders. In describing this series of events, an important glavk official gave a simple explanation: The director of the Konstantinovskii Firm was interested in earning profits, while the director of the Ordzhonikidze Plant was indifferent.[95] In other cases as well, he said, the management of the Ordzhonikidze Firm had rejected opportunities for earning considerable profits by undertaking more difficult tasks. Similarly,

[92] M. M. Kaganovich, "Perestroika upravleniia . . .," p. 6. Veitsman, *op. cit.*, pp. 33-34.

[93] M. M. Kaganovich, "Perestroika upravleniia . . .," p. 6.

[94] Lead editorial in *Ind.*, August 22, 1939, p. 1.

[95] P. Berzhkov, head of the rolling group of the Technical Sector of the Glavk of the Metallurgical Industry of the South and Center, writing in *Ind.*, August 25, 1940, p. 3.

other firms have even preferred loss items to profitable products which presented greater production problems.[96]

Why this difference between firms? To some extent, as the glavk official implied, it may be a reflection of the directors' personalities. One feels he is doing well enough and need not invite new headaches for new profits; the other is eager to take on responsibilities and win fresh plaudits. But this difference in attitude may also be caused by the two plants being in different positions regarding plan fulfillment. The Ordzhonikidze Plant's management might have felt that accepting the more complicated order would have meant failure to produce the planned quantities; Konstantinovskii's may have felt confident that it could fulfill the planned quantities even with these more difficult but profitable items. Thus the criterion of profit earning would quite naturally have had a different value to the two directors.

However, there have been enough managements strongly interested in earning profits so that proper pricing has been a question of major importance. (Prices of firms' products and of the materials and fuels consumed are mainly established centrally.[97]) It has been frequently pointed out by Soviet officials that proper price relationships can be of major importance in influencing firms to produce desired goods rather than less important ones.[98] When two directors of metallurgical firms publicly urged the revision of the relative prices of metallurgical products so as to increase the manufacture of deficit items, the head of the Steel Marketing Agency agreed. He announced that a new price list would be ready within one week to meet the problem of providing incentives for proper assortment.[99] During the first quarter of 1938, the lowest percent-

[96] *Ibid.*
[97] Post. No. 37 of the Committee of Prices attached to the Council of Work and Defense of February 26, 1932, in *Arbitrazh v sovetskom khoziaistve*, pp. 440-41. Also, A. Shneerov, "Ustanovlenie tsen i spory o tsenakh v praktike Gosarbitrazha" (The Setting of Prices and Price Disputes in the Practice of the State Arbitration System), *Arbitrazh*, 1938, No. 20, pp. 13-15.
[98] Commissar A. Mikoian, speech of March 13, 1939, at the XVIIIth Party Congress. (XVIII s"ezd VKP(b), p. 216.) A. Braude, an outstanding engineer, writing in *Z.I.*, February 15, 1937, p. 2. Director R. I. Puchkov, writing in *Z.I.*, June 6, 1936, p. 3.
[99] *Z.I.*, August 23 and 24, 1935, p. 1.

ages of plan fulfillment attained in metallurgy were primarily for those items which were unprofitable to produce.[100]

Just as proper pricing has encouraged production of deficit goods, it has helped reorient industrial consumption. Firms have economized on materials and metal shapes which were expensive, and have worked out methods for using cheaper substitutes.[101] At least some plants have kept their department heads informed of all changes in prices of materials, so that they could use the least expensive ones.[102] Once plant managements have employed their initiative in developing such methods, it is usually simple to get higher organs to allocate substitutes for the deficit materials scheduled for use under the plan.

To conclude, financial considerations have played a role in managerial thinking, but a far from dominant one. Financial success has stood as only one criterion among others both more and less important. For Soviet firm management, profitability has by no means performed the function of a single criterion of success in the way that it seems to for firms in capitalist countries.[103]

SUMMATION OF THE PROBLEM AND ITS PERSONIFICATION

The Soviet answer to the problem of how managerial success is to be defined can scarcely be considered as either satisfactory or settled. Independent and often contradictory indices are simultaneously used; the determination of success is viewed as a problem of "proper evaluation" of the net result shown by the various indices, and is thus arbitrary in that the evaluation differs with the person making the decision. While composite financial criteria exist and are much publicized, they are considered as auxiliaries rather than substitutes for the natural indices such as quantity, quality, and assortment. As we have seen above, financial tests of success are applied by the same economic organs which also use the

[100] Sh. Turetskii, "Voprosy tsenoobrazavaniia" (Questions of Price Formation), *Planovoe Khoziaistvo*, 1938, No. 6, p. 81.

[101] Turetskii, *Vnutripromyshlennoe nakoplenie v SSSR*, p. 340. Ia. Rubinshtein, department head in the Leningrad Bolshevik Firm, writing in *Mash.*, August 9, 1939, p. 3.

[102] I. Abramov, "Zavod im. Kominterna v bor'be za rentabel'nost' " (The Komintern Plant in the Fight for Profitability), *Plan*, 1935, No. 13, p. 9.

[103] For a discussion of this point, cf. Chapter IX, footnote 1.

nonfinancial criteria. Financial controls are, in the last analysis, exercised solely by these bodies. Thus there are no evaluating or supervising organs which both exercise real authority over industrial firms and are exclusively or even mainly concerned with finances, although none of them are indifferent to financial considerations.

THE DIRECTOR AND HIS CHIEF BOOKKEEPER: The problems implicit in this dual existence of both individual and composite criteria are personified within the firm by the relationship between the director and the chief bookkeeper. The director approaches problems from the same point of view as does the leadership of the glavk and commissariat above him—by using both types of indices and by making his own personal evaluation of their relative weights. The chief bookkeeper, on the other hand, is interested solely in financial tests—and it is up to him to judge all actions entirely by their effects on the firm's financial condition. It is natural then that the director and chief bookkeeper are often permanently at loggerheads.

The chief bookkeeper of a firm—who is responsible for all accounts and payments—has been given powers sufficient to maintain a position independent of the director. His signature is required for the payment of any money by the firm. While he must fulfill all orders of the director,[104] he is instructed to inform both the glavk and the Commissar of Finance of all commands which are illegal or contrary to established bookkeeping practice. Differences between him and the director are decided by the glavk. While the director suggests both his appointment and removal, it is the higher organ (usually the glavk) which actually decides such questions.[105]

The chief bookkeeper is supposed to be the "supervisor for the State" within the firm.[106] His task is to prevent expenditures for purposes other than those intended by the plan (e.g., the use of

---

[104] But not if the action will make the bookkeeper himself criminally liable.

[105] Post. of the SNK SSSR of Sept. 29, 1932, *BFKhZ*, 1932, No. 49/50, and its amendment by Post. No. 1249 of the SNK SSSR of June 21, 1935, *BFKhZ*, 1935, No. 22.

[106] F. Shenger, head of Central Bookkeeping for the NKTP, writing in *Z.I.*, March 14, 1935, p. 3. (Shenger is presumably a misprint for Shefer.)

working capital for construction purposes).[107] He is expected to halt the waste or misuse of funds and to be bold in his actions rather than operate as a "director's . . . bookkeeper."[108] He must submit both monthly and annual balances for his firm to the higher organs.[109] His books are to be audited at least annually.[110]

Thus, the chief bookkeeper of a firm is expected to prevent the director from breaking the laws in order to achieve greater "success." Audits of his accounts and documents, and the fact that he is open to criminal charges if he should be found to have neglected his control duties, help to keep him to this task.

But the chief bookkeeper has another function in the firm, and one of equal importance. Since all figures of the plant flow into the bookkeeping department, it is argued that the chief bookkeeper is the plant official most strategically placed for analyzing the total work of the firm and for pointing out its weak elements.[111] It is said that he should be the closest aid to the director, informing him daily of how the firm is functioning.[112]

However, as one bookkeeper pointed out, the two roles of aid to the director and watchdog over him are often mutually exclusive. The control function frequently leads to an inability of the director and bookkeeper to work together.[113] Glavk and commissariat officials have the same concept of success as does the director. Only in the bosom of his own firm, in the person of his "closest aid," does the director meet a power which must be reckoned with and which has quite different standards from his own.

Small wonder that a director tends to consider a vigorous chief bookkeeper who looks out for the "State interests" as a traitor to the firm, or that he should often respond by persecuting him[114] and

[107] *Ind.*, June 21, 1938, p. 3.

[108] Lead editorial in *Z.I.*, May 20, 1937, p. 1.

[109] Post. No. 1372 of the SNK SSSR of July 29, 1936, *SZ*, 1936, article 359.

[110] Post. of the SNK SSSR of April 15, 1936, *BFKhZ*, 1936, No. 12.

[111] F. F. Shefer, head of Central Bookkeeping of the NKTP, "Zadacha rentabel'nosti predpriiatii i rol' uchëta" (The Task of Firm Profitability and the Role of Accounting), *Org. Uprav.*, 1935, No. 4, pp. 12-15.

[112] G. K. Ordzhonikidze, Commissar of the NKTP, Speech at the Council of the NKTP on May 12, 1935, *Org. Uprav.*, 1935, No. 3, p. 9.

[113] A. Golubev, writing in *Pravda*, September 26, 1940, p. 3.

[114] Cf. the speech of F. F. Shefer at the Council of the Commissariat of Heavy Industry, *Z.I.*, May 14, 1935, p. 4, and July 6, 1937, p. 3.

by attempting to get him fired.[115] In contrast, the State considers the bookkeeping function so important that it was willing at the end of 1938 to invest over 150,000 of its short labor force in this occupation in the firms of heavy industry.[116]

The chief bookkeeper, doomed to work in his difficult position, may choose to renounce his control duties and operate solely as an aid to the director.[117] But we should note that the Soviet industrial press has pointed to many more cases of bookkeepers persecuted for their diligence than of those exposed as having abdicated their supervisory function. This can be explained by the fact that the chief bookkeeper's own advancement and premiums depend on his ability to maintain financial discipline; that he is open to criminal prosecution if he permits violations; that morality as exposited by the Communist Party and by all organized means of expression is on the side of strict enforcement.

However, the chief bookkeeper can do no more than inform the glavk of financial violations. It is up to the glavk and commissariat leadership to decide whether or not to crack down. Sometimes, indeed, they do. When one acting director tried to persuade the commissariat to transfer his annoying chief bookkeeper, he himself was ousted instead.[118] But as the higher leadership shares the director's lack of interest in the maintenance of financial discipline, it seems much more common for them to ignore the complaints of chief bookkeepers.[119]

Inconclusive evidence indicates—quite in line with what we would expect—that the chief bookkeeper's analyses of plant and department work tend to have been disregarded.[120] Why has he, then, been given control functions which place him in this anomalous state? Because otherwise financial discipline would be ignored far more than it has been. Without him, the composite financial cri-

---

[115] Cf. Ordzhonikidze, Speech at the Council of the NKTP on May 12, 1935, *Org. Uprav.*, 1935, No. 3, p. 10.

[116] *Ind.*, December 27, 1938, p. 1.

[117] Cf. *Mash.*, April 23, 1939, p. 2.

[118] Prikaz No. 24 of the NKTP of January 5, 1937, *Z.I.*, January 8, 1937, p. 3.

[119] Cf. lead editorial in *Z.I.*, April 12, 1935, p. 1.

[120] Cf. the article by I. Perlov, chief bookkeeper of the Glavk of Refractory Substances of the Commissariat of Ferrous Metallurgy, *Ind.*, August 14, 1940, p. 2. *Mash.*, April 23, 1939, p. 2.

teria would have considerably less significance for management
than they have actually had. Why are his powers not strengthened?
Because Soviet leaders do not wish the composite criteria to over-
shadow the many individual ones.

CONCLUDING REMARKS

The chief bookkeeper's permanent war with his director symbolizes the conflict in the thinking of Soviet industrial
leaders between the desire for a single test of success and standard for decision making, and the fear of renouncing the existing system of multicriteria. The advantages of a clearly defined
criterion in terms of which decisions can be made are vividly evident to them. Such a criterion would reduce arbitrariness as well
as vastly simplify and speed up the process of decision making. But
the failure—as they see it—of any composite index to give due
weight to all the individual factors in a situation, seems to them too
serious to permit wholehearted adoption of any unitary measuring
stick. They refuse to renounce the flexibility inherent in deciding
every question "on its merits"—and in terms of the ever-changing
stresses of different times and places—rather than according to
the weighting system given by the price structure of the moment.
The Soviet leaders can neither adopt the method of a single standard for decision making nor move too far away from it.

XI: A Note on Enforcement of Controls over Management

IN WHATEVER FASHION the success of firm management is measured, there is a need for enforcing management's obedience to the standards of higher bodies. The attainment of these standards must be rewarded and failure to attain them punished. It is to these rewards and punishments, and to some of the bodies responsible for enforcement of standards, that this chapter will be devoted.

PENALTIES FOR EXECUTIVES

The usual method used by economic bodies for handling managerial personnel who do not turn out successful work is demotion. Clearly, the main purpose of such demotions is to bring more capable managers into these posts. But demotion is a major punishment for an industrial executive. Men building careers are thrown sharply backwards. Conceivably, if ousted from their posts in one commissariat, they can find equivalent ones in another. The chances of this, however, are remote. Normally, they locate in the lowest managerial ranks, and may well remain there. Having met with failure in one post, an executive cannot easily move into another firm or district and continue his progress upwards.

The seriousness of removal from one's post is accentuated by its ramifications into other fields. A director who is ousted may well have his Party status called into question, particularly because he will no longer have "success" to excuse his prior inevitable legal lapses while a manager.

As seen in Chapter III, mobility of all managerial personnel has been exceedingly rapid. Higher bodies have responded to plan failures in a firm or industry by wholesale dismissals. In 1939, ferrous metallurgy did not fulfill its plan; as a result, 2,665 executives and specialists of firms were removed or transferred. During 1939 and the first quarter of 1940, 42 directors and 37 chief engineers of ferrous-metallurgical plants were replaced.[1] In the machine-construction industry, some plants year after year failed to fulfill their production programs. Instead of analyzing the situation and helping them, the Commissariat reacted solely by issuing new orders and removing directors and chief engineers.[2]

This manner of responding to failure has aroused protests. In 1939, the earlier heavy dismissals by the Commissariat of Machine Construction were criticized by one industrial commissar as having yielded no results.[3] There have also been attacks on the practice of promoting capable foremen to the posts of department heads and then removing them in a month or so because they could not handle the job. It has been pointed out that instead they should have been aided to fulfill their new functions more capably and to grow into their posts, that their removal simply meant promoting others who would also be likely to fail for lack of a proper chance.

While the penalty of dismissal has been applied quickly and with little hesitation, the weapon of criminal prosecution has been used sparingly. This is not the case with regard to political offenses, and in the hysteria of the large-scale purges many cases of simple inefficiency or of inability to fulfill impossible production tasks must have been interpreted as political crimes and punished accordingly. But in the hosts of cases where such overtones have been absent, legal proceedings against firm executives have been rare.

This can best be seen from the data of State Arbitration Tribunals. As was pointed out in the previous chapter, these Tribunals handle disputes between economic bodies regarding the signing of contracts and violations of existing contracts. It should be noted that all contractual violations are considered criminal offenses.[4] Yet of 362,000 cases brought before the State Arbitration organs in 1937, only 0.6 percent of the cases were called to the attention

[1] *Ind.*, June 3, 1940, p. 1.
[2] I. Likhachev (Commissar of Medium Machine Construction), writing in *Mash.*, May 15, 1939, p. 3.
[3] *Ibid.*
[4] See below in this chapter.

of the Prosecutor's office and the courts.[5] Data for one third of the State Arbitration organs in the first half of 1934 show that barely 0.7 percent of the cases were so reported.[6]

Thus, less than 1 percent of the arbitration cases have actually been filed with the prosecutors. Even with regard to this tiny percentage there have been complaints—whose accuracy has been attested to by the Chief Prosecutor of the Russian Republic—that the reports are often simply ignored by the prosecutors.[7]

Where prosecutions of managerial actions have occurred, there has been a marked tendency to prosecute lower-grade executives and to allow top management such as directors to escape with reprimands. This tendency was officially noted as widespread in 1934.[8] In 1935, when the Moscow plant Borets was faced with the prospect of a blocked Bank account due to inability to pay its debts, the head of the firm's financial sector fabricated accounts in order illegally to get money from the State Bank. The plant's chief bookkeeper aided in this deception. When the facts were uncovered, the financial chief was sentenced to three and one-half years imprisonment by the courts and the chief bookkeeper to two years. But the plant director—who could scarcely have helped knowing of the fabrication and in any case was responsible for all actions of his subordinates—was retained in his post and merely reprimanded as "socially to blame."[9]

However, criminal prosecutions of managerial personnel have been used in national campaigns to show that the State means business. When a strong labor discipline decree was issued at the end of December, 1938, the newspapers a half month later blossomed forth with orders of the different commissars turning over directors and other firm executives to the courts for criminal prosecution due to their nonenforcement of the law.[10] Similar

[5] Goloshchekin, "O rabote Gosudarstvennogo arbitrazha v 1937 g.," pp. 4 and 11.

[6] "Ofitsial'nyi otdel" (Official Sector), Biulleten' Gosarbitrazha, 1934, No. 18, pp. 29 and 32.

[7] S. Piastunovich, "Za deistvennost' signalizatsii" (For Real Reporting), Arbitrazh, 1939, No. 2, pp. 10-13.

[8] Post. of the 47th Plenum of the Supreme Court of the USSR of June 9, 1934, BFKhZ, 1934, No. 20. This was with regard to the enforcement of the law against poor-quality production.

[9] Z.I., July 10, 1935, p. 4.

[10] Cf. Prikaz No. 50 of the Commissariat of Machine Construction of January 16, 1939, Mash., January 17, 1939, p. 1.

methods were used to demonstrate that the law of July 10, 1940, prohibiting poor-quality production was really intended to be enforced.[11] These prosecutions seem to have been instituted mainly for their effect on other executives, as is shown by the wide publicity they were given.

INCENTIVES FOR EXECUTIVES

While penalties for unsuccessful work are employed in Soviet industry as in that of any other country, incentives are given at least equal weight. For plant executives, as for all other personnel in Soviet industry, these take many forms. The hope of speedily building a career and the realization that there is considerable opportunity for advancement is doubtless of major importance to the young men comprising the management group. Since a prime qualification of an executive has been that he be a good "Bolshevik"—whether Party or non-Party—ideological motivations have probably played a greater role for this group than for the rank and file of the population. Dedication to "building Socialism," and by 1939 to "building Communism," has been important. The desire for greater social recognition, for winning medals and orders, has its place and is given considerable scope for satisfaction. Finally, there is the pride in the shop and firm which is strengthened by intershop and interplant competitions, by the award of Red Banners, and by publicity given to successful plants.

While it is difficult to say much about these intangible incentives, their effectiveness should not be underestimated. A famous sociological study carried on over many years at the Hawthorne works of the Western Electric Company in the United States showed how important intangibles were in their effect upon the output of workers generally. Effective wage systems seem to have made for better work not primarily because of the direct monetary incentives offered, but rather through their effect on other than economic motivating factors.[12] Moreover, would not the importance of nonmaterial incentives be far greater to management personnel anywhere, particularly to those of the Soviet Union,

---

[11] Cf. *Ch.M.*, November 5, 1940, p. 4.

[12] F. J. Roethlisberger and W. J. Dickson, *Management and the Worker* (Cambridge, Mass.: 1939), pp. 531-33, 557, 575-77.

trained in and in part selected for their strong espousal of Communist Party doctrine which holds that the Soviet individual can only develop and find happiness by working for the betterment of his society?

But although Soviet industry leans heavily on intangible incentives, it equally stresses monetary rewards. Stalin insisted upon this in 1931,[13] and the emphasis has continued ever since. Equality in wages between personnel of different skills has been denounced as *petit bourgeois*. The piece wage has become the dominant form of labor payment. Wherever possible, it has been intended that lower management should be paid by piecework and that top management personnel, for whom this is impractical, should receive premiums as well as a set salary.[14] In 1940, premiums made up 11 percent of the total earnings of all engineering and managerial personnel of industry.[15]

Managerial personnel usually have a considerable material stake in moving upward in the industrial hierarchy. A comparison of managerial earnings with those of other personnel would be a separate study and cannot be attempted here. However, it may be noted that Soviet theorists all argue that earnings should rise sharply with responsibility.[16] In addition to managers receiving relatively high pay, they also have such privileges as the use of plant automobiles and chauffeurs, of plant housing, etc.[17]

For our purposes, it would be quite irrelevant to attempt to apportion the relative influence exercised on management by intangible and by monetary incentives, as these are intended to be supplementary and not competitive. Broadly speaking, an executive earns intangible awards of prestige and promotion for the same

[13] I. Stalin, Speech of June 23, 1931, to a Conference of Business Executives. (*Voprosy Leninizma*, 10th edition, pp. 451-52.)

[14] Cf. *Z.I.*, March 4, 1936, p. 2.

[15] Turetskii, *Vnutripromyshlennoe nakoplenie v SSSR*, pp. 292-93.

[16] That practice does not always accord with this, is shown by the frequent complaints of foremen that they earned less than skilled Stakhanovites under them. This was officially recognized as a problem which should be corrected in Postanovlenie No. 900 of the SNK SSSR of May 27, 1940. (*SPR*, 1940, article 361.)

[17] Data for September-October, 1934, on relative earnings is presented by TsUNKhU in *Zarabotnaia plata inzhenerno-tekhnicheskikh rabotnikov i sluzhashchikh*. But this material has the dual disadvantage of being for a period prior to the birth of the Stakhanovite movement—which may have sharply changed the picture—and of taking department heads and their assistants—combined into a single group—as the highest element of management studied.

actions which gain him money premiums. It is only his "social conscience" which might motivate him to different decisions where there is a conflict between the good of his firm and that of the country as he sees it. But here we have no conflict between intangible and material incentives, but rather one which cuts across these lines.

Just as the intangible incentives are designed to promote "overall success," so also are strong efforts made to direct material incentives into this channel. Salaries of all top management have been set by fairly high authorities.[18] The granting of premiums has been even more closely controlled. Directors, their assistants and aids, and their chief bookkeepers have been able to receive premiums only on special decree of the commissar of their industry.[19] Directors have been able to give premiums up to one month's salary to all other managerial personnel, but higher rewards have required permission of the commissariat.[20] Through this top control over money premiums, it has been possible to tie them to "overall success" rather than to individual indices of work. In addition to monetary premiums, special gifts such as cars are given to individuals by higher bodies as a reward for plan fulfillment.[21]

Material incentives to management have sometimes been used to stress particular aspects of their operations. For example, firm managements for a long time refused to use low-grade cotton in production, and surpluses even had to be thrown away. When, in 1938, bonuses began to be paid to managers in proportion to their use of these poorer materials, they quickly worked out methods for utilizing them.[22]

Yet even when such specialized incentive systems have been established, they have contained provisions intended to guarantee

[18] In 1936, it was ordered that no salary over 800 rubles could be paid without the Commissariat's approval. (Circular No. 013860 of the NKTP of July 22, 1936, *BFKhZ*, 1936, No. 22/23.)

[19] Post. of the TsIK and SNK SSSR of June 17, 1935, *SZ.*, 1935, article 277. The sparse evidence available indicates that an additional one month's salary has been a rather standard premium given to successful top management personnel. (Cf. *Mash.*, December 8, 1938, p. 2 and August 21, 1939, p. 1.)

[20] Post. of the TsIK and SNK SSSR of June 17, 1935. Also, *Pravda*, October 20, 1940, p. 3.

[21] Cf. *Z.I.*, January 12, 1935, pp. 1 and 4.

[22] Mikoian, Speech of March 13, 1939, at the XVIIIth Party Congress, *XVIII s"ezd VKP(b)*, p. 216.

against neglect of other major aspects of the firms' plans. Thus, in 1936, the Conference of the Auto-Tractor Industry decided that the main factor in giving premiums to managements of plant departments was to be the reduction of costs. But the Conference also declared that no premiums should be paid unless the production program were fulfilled 100 percent and in the planned assortment of items.[23] Similarly, a premium system for foremen of the whole Heavy Machine-Construction Industry provided fairly standard premiums for each percentage of overfulfillment of the production program. But these premiums could only be granted if planned quality and assortment indices were followed, and they could be withheld in case of overexpenditures of materials, fuel, or wages.[24]

This fairly cautious policy of combining "priority" and "over-all success" considerations in the granting of material awards has not, however, prevented individual incentives from being dysfunctional. For example, in 1940 it was desired to motivate directors and chief engineers of metallurgical firms to produce difficult and complex types of metals. This was done by paying them premiums for achieving "planned profits," and by pricing the desired items at levels which made them considerably more profitable than shapes and compositions simpler to produce. But the intent of this incentive system was largely frustrated by the resistance of department heads. For they received bonuses under quite a different system, being given premiums in accord with their ability to reduce costs. Since "planned cost" was set at the same figure per ton for all types of metals, it was clearly preferable for them to produce the simpler and cheaper types. That is why they objected strongly, and with considerable success, to producing the more complex items.[25]

ORGANS CONCERNED WITH ENFORCEMENT

Soviet thinking has always followed Molotov's dictum that

[23] Z.I., March 4, 1936, p. 2.
[24] Post. No. 900 of the SNK SSSR and the TsK VKP(b) of May 27, 1940, SPR, 1940, article 361.
[25] Article by P. Berezhkov, head of the rolling group of the Technical Sector of the Glavk of the Metallurgical Industry of the South and Center, Ind., August 25, 1940, p. 3.

plans are turned into scraps of paper unless they are enforced, that it is the controls which are the heart of the planning system.[26]

Soviet theorists have maintained that proper supervision is impossible without the participation of the mass organizations which are always on the spot and know the day-to-day affairs of the plant. Yet they have not neglected the role of official bodies. In this section, we shall consider the supervisory activity of only State organs and the press. But, as we shall see, even these are so organized as to be highly dependent upon mass organizations and individual volunteers.

Soviet firms are subject to inspections by all bodies having jurisdiction over them. Sometimes, indeed, these inspections are so frequent as to be ridiculous. Director N. Egorov complained that in five months of 1940 his plant was inspected once by a brigade of the commissariat, four times by representatives of the glavk, three times by representatives of the Commissariat of Finance, once by a commission of the District Government Committee, and three times by representatives of the Commission of State Control.[27] In 1938, the Commissar of the Machine-Construction Industry announced that the collegium of top executives of that commissariat would thenceforth meet at least once every five days, and that every other session would be devoted wholly to checking on fulfillment of Government and Commissariat decisions.[28]

But despite the considerable attention given to control activities by the glavki and commissariats, it has been emphasized that they are unable to supervise alone the work of the firms. In 1941, the major speaker at the XVIIIth Party Conference commented on this inability as a prelude to a call upon all Party organizations to help them in supervision.[29] The Commissar of Heavy Industry in 1937 told of the telegrams he received from trade-union officials when firm managements stepped out of line, and he requested increased reporting by trade-unionists of management violations.[30] As a mat-

---

[26] V. M. Molotov, Report on the Third Five-Year Plan to the XVIIIth Party Congress, *XVIII s"ezd VKP(b)*, p. 293.

[27] *Pravda*, September 26, 1940, p. 3.

[28] *Mash.*, August 27, 1938, p. 2.

[29] Malenkov, Report to the Conference, *Ch.M.*, February 16, 1941, p. 2.

[30] Commissar V. I. Mezhlauk's Speech of August 19, 1937, to the Congress of Trade-Unionists of Heavy Machine Construction, *Z.I.*, August 21, 1937, p. 1.

ter of course, commissariats and glavki in their supervision of management expect considerable aid from people regularly employed in the given plant.

COMMISSION OF STATE CONTROL: While most State supervision is carried out by intermediate organizations, the Soviet administrative system has a central supervisory body as well. For if the Council of Commissars is to issue orders and regulations on its own, it requires an enforcement organ. This function is served by the Commission of State Control attached to the Council of Commissars, a commission having permanent representatives distributed throughout the country who are appointed and removed by the Central Commission so as to insure that they be subservient to local authorities.[31] The main function of the Commission and its representatives has been to check on the fulfillment of decisions of the Council of Commissars and of the Economic Council. But in addition, it is supposed to guard against the waste of State funds, and to see that the commissariats and other organizations themselves exercise proper supervision over lower bodies and properly handle complaints from rank-and-file personnel.[32]

Thus the Commission of State Control has had the dual task of checking on the execution of principal Government decisions and on the proper exercise by other organs of their supervisory functions. Some decrees of the Council of Commissars and of the Economic Council have been specifically entrusted to the Commission for enforcement.[33] But as a rule, the Commission's representatives seem to have worked mainly with bodies above the level of the firm.[34]

[31] The Commission was created in 1934 by order of the TsIK and the SNK SSSR dated February 11, 1934. (*BFKhZ*, 1934, No. 6.) It was raised to Commissariat status by the Ukaz of the Presidium of the Supreme Soviet of the USSR of September 6, 1940. (*Ind.*, September 7, 1940, p. 1.)

[32] Decision of the Bureau of the Commission, approved by the SNK SSSR on February 28, 1938, *Mash.*, March 1, 1938, p. 1. Post. of the Commission, approved by the SNK SSSR, *BFKhZ*, 1936, No. 16/17. Ukaz of the Presidium of the Supreme Soviet of the USSR of September 6, 1940, *Ind.*, September 7, 1940, p. 1.

[33] Cf. Post. No. 1484 of the Economic Council of August 29, 1940, *SPR*, 1940, article 578.

[34] By early 1941, the new Commissariat of State Control was said to have begun to exercise what was called "anticipatory control" in the largest and most important firms of the country. (*Pravda*, January 7, 1941, p. 3.) This anticipatory control, which was first provided for in the Statute of the Commissariat adopted a few months

Despite dealing mainly with the higher administrative organs, the Commission representatives are supposed to lean on the "actives" or active workers of the organizations they check on and to mobilize them for correcting faults which are uncovered.[35] Thus, even here, mass participation is stressed.[36]

PUBLIC PROSECUTOR'S OFFICE AND THE COURT SYSTEM: Another organ of supervision over managerial personnel is the Prosecutor's office and the courts. These, of course, have only the right to investigate and prosecute legal offenses. But since the laws are so written that virtually every director inevitably makes himself liable to criminal penalties in the course of his daily work, the line between legal and purely administrative agencies becomes very fine.

Managers performing certain specifically prohibited acts are subject to criminal prosecution. Thus directors who fail to enforce the labor-discipline laws are held criminally liable,[37] as are those guilty of repeated overconsumption of electricity.[38] But in addition, there is a catchall law under which directors and other responsible officials who fail in any respect to fulfill contractual obligations with other firms or organs are held to have committed a crime.[39] Contracts have such a broad content that virtually every

earlier, was intended to check illegal expenditures by firms. It was to be exercised through checking estimates and expenditure documents before moneys were actually paid out. The controllers, who were to work in major firms and be responsible to the Commissariat of State Control, were to have the right to forbid any illegal expenditure by the firms. (*Ibid.* "Polozhenie o Narodnom Komissariat Gosudarstvennogo Kontrolia Soiuza SSR" [Statute of the People's Commissariat of State Control of the USSR], *Pravda*, October 16, 1940, p. 1.) However, this anticipatory control did not exist before October, 1940, at the earliest.

[35] Post. of the Commission of September 29, 1935, approved by the SNK SSSR, *BFKhZ*, 1936, No. 16/17.

[36] The reader will have noted that the work of the State Control Commission has been dealt with in a very scanty fashion. This is a consequence of the lack of satisfactory material on its activities. The absence of serious comment on this Commission in the Soviet press and periodicals, however, gives the impression that it did not exercise an important direct influence on plants during the period studied.

[37] Ukaz of June 26, 1940, of the Presidium of the Supreme Soviet of the USSR, *Vedomosti verkhovnogo soveta SSSR (Journal of the Supreme Soviet of the USSR)*, 1940, No. 20 and Post. No. 1502 of the SNK SSSR of August 21, 1940, *SPR*, 1940, article 543.

[38] Post. No. 2692 of the SNK SSSR of December 10, 1934, *SZ*, 1934, article 460.

[39] Post. No. 37/131 of the TsIK and SNK SSSR of February 18, 1931, *SPR*, 1931, article 109. That the law remained in force even after the War is shown by the

firm will violate some provisions during a year. Thus all responsible firm executives are permanently open to prosecution.

The right to prosecute or not as the Government sees fit is present in reality in any legal system. A close student of American police systems has concluded that "The policeman's art . . . consists in applying and enforcing a multitude of laws and ordinances in such degree or proportion and in such manner that the greatest degree of social protection will be secured." There cannot and should not be equal enforcement of all laws, he states.[40] But the widespread use of the courts as an agency by which economic organs discipline their officials is a practice strange to developed capitalist countries.

Yet evidently some Soviet agency must determine which executives are to be prosecuted, and the decision must be made on other than purely legal grounds. Normally, these powers have been retained by economic organs above the firms, such as the glavki. Thus, at least during the years 1934-37, prosecutors were forbidden to bring any engineers or executives to trial—except for delaying wage payments or for producing poor-quality goods—without the prior agreement of the economic body superior to the culprit's own organization.[41] In effect, the Prosecutor's office became an arm of the glavki and commissariats, to be used when these bodies wished to apply to some person stronger punishment than that of reduction of his earnings, demotion, or even dismissal.

Like other organs, the Prosecutor's office and the courts have chartered their course according to "priority" considerations. They have been instructed to center their law-enforcement activities on the most vital industries.[42] They have been ordered to establish

reference to it in *Grazhdanskoe pravo*, Volume I, pp. 373-74. Harold J. Berman, however, asserts that it is no crime in Soviet law for a firm simply to break a contract without malicious intent. See Harold J. Berman, *Justice in Russia* (Cambridge, Mass.: 1950), p. 79.

[40] Bruce Smith, *Police Systems in the United States* (New York and London: 1940), p. 21.

[41] Circular No. 10/67 of the State Prosecutor of the USSR of June 2, 1934, *BFKhZ*, 1934, No. 21 and the explanatory Circular No. 35/1 of May 25, 1937, *BFKhZ*, 1937, No. 23. Under special circumstances, however, prosecutors were allowed to bring cases before the courts without such agreement and on their own personal responsibility. (Cf. Circular of August 23, 1934, *BFKhZ*, 1934, No. 36.)

[42] Cf. Post. of the 47th Plenum of the Supreme Court of the USSR of June 9, 1934, *BFKhZ*, 1934, No. 20.

and maintain close ties with the trade unions and with the press in order to gain wide publicity for their work and achieve the maximum propaganda effect.[43] Mobilization of mass groups has been stressed.[44] For Soviet legal organs have—in the field of industry—been geared primarily to acting in the interests of production "success."

THE PRESS: We have described the State supervisory organs, but also of tremendous importance is the press. While only about forty newspaper copies a year per person were printed in 1940, there were 9,000 newspapers functioning. Four thousand of these were regional.[45] Non-State bodies such as trade unions and cooperatives own and operate newspapers, but their general policy is of course closely controlled. Local newspapers are, in fact, Communist Party organs.[46]

A major function of newspapers is to receive complaints from the population at large, investigate them, and make sure that action is taken. In addition, such papers as those of industrial commissariats have local correspondents in all the major plants of their industries throughout the country. It is frequently articles in the press which first uncover malpractices. Party units in firms have often been spurred to action by a newspaper report on conditions in their plants which they had formerly ignored.[47] Newspapers have published their own lists of firm directors who do not take resolute action in production campaigns.[48] When the management of one firm achieved great successes in current production through the neglect of necessary repair work, and when the plant and regional Party Committees supported its postponement of repair, it was a letter to the national industrial newspaper by a local correspondent which exposed the situation.[49] Six days after

[43] Cf. Post. of the 49th Plenum of the Supreme Court of the USSR of December 28, 1934, *BFKhZ*, 1935, **No. 5.**

[44] Cf. Post. of the 47th Plenum of the Supreme Court of the USSR of June 9, 1934.

[45] "O rukovodstve partiinoi pechat'iu" (On Guidance of the Party Press), *Part. Stroit.*, 1940, No. 9, p. 3.

[46] *Ibid.*

[47] Cf. *Z.I.*, February 20, 1934, p. 1, and Kriundel', secretary of the Party Committee of the Moscow Stalin Auto Plant, writing in *Mash.*, October 5, 1937, p. 3.

[48] Cf. *Z.I.*, February 4, 1934, p. 1.

[49] *Z.I.*, April 15, 1934, p. 2.

the letter was printed, the director was removed by the Commissariat.[50] Even important executives of firms have written to the newspapers for aid when the responsible organizations have given them the run-around.[51]

The question arises of the extent to which the general population participates in this letter writing. Letter writers inevitably expose themselves to retaliation from those they criticize. It may also be that in questions affecting major personnel or problems the Party unit on the corresponding level will designate or request some Party member to write an "individual" letter which actually represents the Party group's viewpoint.[52] Nevertheless, it seems clear that the press is used as a major instrument for enlisting general participation in the work of supervising industrial activity.[53]

If newspapers are to fulfill the important supervisory function which they are given by the Party and Government, a certain type of "freedom of the press" must be assured to them. This "freedom" in no way implies the right to differ from official policies, or even to refrain from actively propagandizing for them. Rather, it means the "freedom" to criticize deviations from central policy and to dig out deficiencies in all organizations but the very highest and to attack those people responsible. But to exercise such rights, newspapermen must be protected against reprisals from the powerful people they may attack.

In this sense, "freedom of the press" has been held very dear in the Soviet Union and seems to have been fairly well realized. Politbureau member L. M. Kaganovich cautioned all commissariats to support their newspaper editors when they discover faults in the commissariat. If they should fail to do so, he warned, the Central Committee of the Communist Party would itself take action to support the editors.[54] When the director of the machine-building firm Compressor was vigorously attacked in a letter in *Za Industrializatsiiu*,[55] a worker of the plant decided to go around during

[50] Prikaz No. 536 of the NKTP of April 21, 1934, in *Z.I.*, April 22, 1934, p. 1.
[51] Cf. *Z.I.*, January 24, 1934, p. 1. *Pravda*, January 24, 1939, p. 2.
[52] A. Inkeles, *Public Opinion in Soviet Russia* (Cambridge, Mass.: 1950), pp. 208 and 304.
[53] *Ibid.*, pp. 209-15.
[54] L. M. Kaganovich, Speech to the Plenum of the Party Control Commission on June 28, 1934, printed in *Part. Stroit.*, 1934, No. 13, pp. 1-10.
[55] *Z.I.*, March 12, 1937, p. 3.

lunchtime and read the letter aloud in several of the plant's departments. In one of the departments, the union organizer forbade him to read the letter; soon after, the worker was chastised by both the firm's union president and the Party secretary. The worker wrote to *Z.I.* of the incident, and the newspaper sent a reporter to investigate. It then printed the letter with a scorching editorial on the "toadies" of the director.[56] Such interference with the press was not to be taken lightly.[57]

[56] *Z.I.*, March 21, 1937, p. 3.
[57] For a full description of the supervisory operations and problems of the Soviet press, cf. Inkeles, *op. cit.*

XII: The Communist Party in the Life of the Firm

UP TO THIS POINT, we have viewed plant managements solely in relation to other industrial bodies. We have considered the integration of their work into that of the entire State administrative apparatus, but have found it convenient to postpone an explicit treatment of the activities of Communist Party organizations and of the nonmanagerial employees of the plant. However, it should be recognized that this division is of a highly formalistic nature; the Communist Party and organizations enlisting mass participation are basic elements in any type of Soviet supervision over management.

It is with the study of these organizations which stand apart from the State apparatus that this and the following chapter will be concerned.

As has been indicated earlier, Soviet leaders consider that industrial problems are rooted in a political base, and that therefore their solution requires Communist Party leadership. At the same time, proper administration is considered impossible without widespread participation by the masses of employees. Industrial executives are expected to be guided in their work by these two fundamental concepts which, as we shall see, have major significance in the Soviet treatment of the problems of industrial administration.

The work of the Party units in the firm cannot be considered totally apart from the question of the participation by nonmanagerial employees in the life of the firm. For a fundamental task of the plant Party unit is that of enlisting and embodying such participation. However, all participation of employees which does not

take place through the medium of activity within the Communist
Party will be held over to Chapter XIII.

MAJOR ROLES OF THE PARTY WITH REGARD TO THE FIRM

Soviet theory maintains that the Communist Party stands
at the very heart of the Soviet system. "The Party is the core of
power."[1] "The Party directive has . . . the force of law."[2] Not a
single decision on general questions of State activity should be
taken by Government organs without prior guiding instructions
from the Party.[3]

At the same time, Soviet leaders completely reject any identifi-
cation of the Communist Party with "State power." As regards governmental functions, the Party is the core of power but is not the
State power itself.[4] The Party directive does not by itself create
law, but defines its direction and purpose. The Party is considered
as the kernel of State power and the Party directive as the kernel
of law.[5]

Just as the Party is the kernel of Government power, so too it is
conceived of as the "soul" of all mass organizations. Its function is
not to appropriate their tasks, but rather to set the tasks and to
guide their fulfillment. The Party's ". . . significance consists in
uniting the work of all mass organizations . . . and of *directing*
their activity towards one goal. . . ."[6] Thus it is held that the
Party should constantly strengthen Government and trade-union
organizations, increase their authority, and, by directing their
work, carry out its decisions through them.[7]

Behind this view as to the role of the Communist Party lies a
conception of the nature of socialist society. All loyal and dependable elements of the population are seen as bending their efforts

[1] I. Stalin, *Voprosy Leninizma*, 11th edition, p. 124. This quotation was referred
to in 1946 by I. I. Evtikhiev and V. A. Vlasov, *Administrativnoe pravo SSSR* (Administrative Law of the USSR), (Moscow: 1946), p. 6. Text for law institutes and faculties.
[2] *Ibid.*, p. 245. This quotation was referred to in 1948 in *Sovetskoe gosudarstvennoe
pravo*, p. 286.
[3] *Ibid.*, pp. 124-25. This was referred to in 1948 in *Sovetskoe gosudarstvennoe pravo*,
p. 286.
[4] *Ibid.*, p. 124. This was referred to in 1946 by Evtikhiev and Vlasov, *op. cit.*, p. 6.
[5] *Ibid.*, p. 124. (Referred to in *Sovetskoe gosudarstvennoe pravo*, p. 286.)
[6] Stalin, as quoted in *Pravda*, March 9, 1937, p. 1. (Italics in the *Pravda* editorial.)
[7] *Pravda*, March 9, 1937, p. 1.

toward a single basic goal, summed up in such phrases as that of "building socialism." But since "building socialism" has many facets, different organizations are needed in order to direct and mobilize mass participation in working them out.

Soviet thinkers have recognized that there is a serious danger that organizations will build up their own special interests.[8] When one considers the host of organizations affecting the industrial work of the firm—the trade union of the plant, the "production actives" group, the inventors' and rationalizers' group, the City Council, other plants, procurement and marketing organizations, and a host of others—the need for an integrating body is clear. Thus the Communist Party is needed in order to guide all efforts toward the basic unitary objective. It is intended to be sufficiently unified and firm to be able to fill this role.[9]

Through its position above and apart from any other organization of the country, the Party is expected to be able to combat special organizational interests. While primary Party bodies may well identify themselves with the particular interests of their own plant or other economic organization, the danger of this happening is lessened by their being subordinate to regional committees. These are expected to be free of "departmental" interests and to employ "Party discipline" to combat attitudes arising from such interests. This discipline is implicit in the conception of the Party as a centralized hierarchy, reaching from the cell to the Central Committee and Politbureau.

In addition to integrating different organizations, the Party makes a vital contribution to Soviet administration by providing a common ideology and set of goals. A ubiquitous organization, active at all levels of the economy down to the shop shift, it is available to judge the correctness of the decisions and activities of all administrators from the viewpoint of the national leadership. The Party unit within the plant is always on the spot to give its own

[8] Cf. K. V. Ostrovitianov, "O zadachakh nauchno-issledovatel'skoi raboty v oblasti ekonomiki" (On the Tasks of Scientific-Investigatory Work in the Field of Economics), reworked stenographic report read at the general assembly of the Division of Economics and Law of the Academy of Sciences of the USSR on October 12, 1949, *Izvestiia Akademii Nauk SSSR, otdelenie ekonomiki i prava* (Bulletin of the Academy of Sciences of the USSR, Division of Economics and Law), 1950, No. 1, p. 28. The degree to which such interests have motivated managerial staffs was seen in earlier chapters.

[9] Cf. I. Stalin, Speech of February 4, 1931, *Voprosy Leninizma*, 10th edition, p. 442.

evaluation of the relative importance of the many factors going into managerial decisions. It is in theory the spokesman of the national Communist Party interests, and the sworn enemy of any director who tries to set himself up as an independent power. Simultaneously, the Party membership serves as an ideal source of recruitment for leaders who are expected to share the same goals and outlook as those of the nation's top leadership.[10]

Party influence over mass organizations and State bodies is exerted not only through Party determination of these organizations' tasks, but also through the supervision of their operations. It is the primary Party organizations of the firms which are the basic units in Party control. They have been ordered to systematically aid and strengthen industrial management. They have been given "the right of supervision over the work of the administration[s],"[11] and this has been defined as meaning the right to see written materials dealing with production, to hear reports from the managerial personnel, and to make recommendations to management as to specific measures for eliminating deficiencies and for a better carrying out of the firm's plan.[12]

This right of supervision has led to the practice of treating functionaries of the primary Party unit as important members of the management. In firms, they have typically taken part in conferences of industrial executives,[13] and affixed their signatures to socialist competition agreements between firms.[14] When plant managements have been unable to procure needed supplies, the plants' Party units have not infrequently used their authority to get them through Party channels.[15]

---

[10] Many organizations in capitalist countries also attempt to develop in their executives a common approach to problems. Within the Tennessee Valley Authority organization, for example, strenuous efforts have been made to indoctrinate those involved in administration on a policy-affecting level. Cf. Philip Selznick, *TVA and the Grass Roots* (Berkeley and Los Angeles: 1949), p. 21.

[11] *Rezoliutsii XVIII s"ezda VKP(b) 10-21 marta 1939 g.* (Resolutions of the XVIIIth Congress of the All-Union Communist Party [Bolshevik] of March 10-21, 1939), (Moscow: 1939), pp. 55-56.

[12] "Edinonachalie i pravo kontroliia" (One-Man-Authority-and-Responsibility and the Right of Supervision), *Part. Stroit.*, 1940, No. 18, p. 34.

[13] Cf. Prikaz No. 1256 of the NKTP of September 26, 1934, *Z.I.*, September 27, 1934, p. 1. *Mash.*, May 15, 1939, p. 2.

[14] Cf. *Z.I.*, September 10, 1936, p. 1.

[15] Cf. the letter by L. Epel'man, Party organizer for the Central Committee at the Middle Urals Copper-Smelting Plant, *Ind.*, June 23, 1940, p. 3.

However, the work of the primary Party organization within the plant goes far beyond that of control. The Party organization is primarily a mobilizing force and one which tries to link together the goals of management and workers. As such, its effectiveness is seen as depending upon the degree to which it rests on a mass basis.

The Party strives to improve the work of its own members, mobilizes Party and non-Party people for the fulfillment of production tasks, and holds production conferences of its own "actives."[16] A representative of the Central Committee of the Communist Party has defined the production task of Party committees of plant departments as that of arousing first all Communist workers, and then the non-Party people, for the removal of production blocks.[17] Politbureau member L. M. Kaganovich has pointed out the same thing for plant Party organizations and has insisted that they take the individual Communist as their starting point, on the ground that in the final analysis it is he who determines the success of the production plans.[18] When the top Party leadership plans the introduction of important measures, it is the Party rank and file which is entrusted with the educational and other preparatory work required.[19]

Since it is the intention to have a strong membership at all levels of the plant's work force, and to maintain control over both managerial policy and that of the trade union and other mass organizations, the Party unit of a plant is expected to be able to insure a basic unity between the goals of management and of the workers and to keep friction to a minimum. Party members, working alongside non-Party shopmates, are supposed to be highly effective in putting over by word and example new ideas of organization and production. Being workers themselves, they have entree where management personnel could not possibly have it.

[16] Arakelian, *Upravlenie sotsialisticheskoi promyshlennost'iu*, pp. 214-15.

[17] A. Il'in, head of the sector of metallurgy of the Industrial Section of the TsK VKP(b), "Partiinaia rabota na zavodakh metallurgii" (Party Work in Metallurgical Plants), *Part. Stroit.*, 1936, No. 24, p. 56.

[18] Cf. A. Sokolov, "Uzlovye voprosy partraboty na predpriiatiiakh" (Crucial Questions of Party Work in the Firms), *Part. Stroit.*, 1934, No. 20, pp. 22-23. Also, D. Kontorin, "O sekretare raionnogo komiteta partii" (On the Secretary of the District Committee of the Party), *Part. Stroit.*, 1936, No. 19, p. 17.

[19] V. Polonskii, a secretary of the Central Council of the Trade-Unions, "Stakhanovskoe dvizhenie i profsoiuzy" (The Stakhanovite Movement and the Trade Unions), *Voprosy Profdvizheniia*, 1934, No. 11-12, p. 21.

Sometimes the Party enlists participation in order to eliminate sources of worker complaints. In the newspaper of the Dinamo Plant, a letter was published complaining of the work of the plant's Workers' Supply Sector. The Party committee reacted by calling a conference of housewives and plant workers. Over one hundred questions were raised before and during the conference, and the plant management was compelled to give exhaustive replies to each. The results of the conference could be seen in improvement of sanitary conditions in stores, the elimination of queues of buyers, the setting up of model counters, etc.[20]

But more often, participation has been treated as a vital production-aid. The Party organization of a plant is expected to mobilize the participation of all employees in the resolution of production problems.[21] It has been declared that it cannot exercise proper supervision over production unless it is tied closely to the Stakhanovites and other worker "actives."[22] Stalin has declared that the Communist Party would be helpless if it lost its closeness to the general population.[23]

Director S. Birman, in an article written primarily for the purpose of arguing that plant directors should dominate their Party organizations rather than vice versa, yet found it necessary to criticize all executives who undervalued the role of Party mass work in the firm. He insisted that the most talented, educated, and technically advanced executives could not succeed without the enthusiasm of the workers and the continuous explanation to them of the tasks lying before them. No management can carry out the work needed for this, continued Birman, without the aid of the Party organization.[24] In an article devoted to criticism of his plant's Party unit, Director N. Goncharenko still paid tribute to the prac-

[20] "Ovladet' bol'shevistskim stilem organizatsionno-prakticheskogo rukovodstva" (For Mastering the Bolshevik Style of Organizational-Practical Leadership), Part. Stroit., 1934, No. 8, p. 4.

[21] Cf. Ind., February 5, 1940, p. 1 where there is a citation of the Postanovleniia of the TsK VKP(b) of November 4 and 9, 1939.

[22] S. Masterov, head of the organizational-instructional sector of the Leningrad City Committee of the Communist Party, "Kontrol' pervichnykh partorganizatsii v deistvii" (Supervision over the Primary Party Organizations in Action), Part. Stroit., 1939, No. 11, p. 52.

[23] I. Stalin, Concluding Remarks of March 5, 1937, to the Plenum of the TsK VKP(b), Z.I., April 1, 1937, p. 2.

[24] Z.I., January 18, 1934, pp. 2-3.

tical aid given by Party conferences organized around the questions of rebuilding the plant and of fighting against production losses.[25]

The bad results arising from the disregard of the Party unit by the management of a large Moscow plant point up the value of proper cooperation. The director of the plant worked out a system of organizational and technical measures designed to improve the quality of the plant's products, and issued appropriate orders to the various departments. But the Party committee of the plant did not know of the orders in time to enable it to mobilize the Communist production workers of the plant for their suggestions and aid in carrying out the management's decisions. The trade-union organization was occupied with matters totally unrelated to product quality. As a result, the plant administration was entirely isolated from the production workers and could make no progress in instituting its changes in work methods. Quite a good deal of time was lost before the Party organization was able to muster its forces behind the director's measures.[26]

The proper use of the Party organization was demonstrated in 1940 in the Middle Urals Copper-Smelting Plant, where the improvement of the metallurgical department was picked out as the key production task of the Party.[27] In previous years, efforts had been made to introduce scheduling into the department. But the schedules had been ineffective. It was held that the essential reason for their ineffectiveness was that they had not arisen from widespread discussions by the workers and junior management. This time, however, the Party organized conferences of Communist engineers and of Stakhanovites around the problem of scheduling construction work and the mounting of machinery, and then raised the question for discussion by an all-plant Party meeting. The Party and plant administration together set the appropriate schedules.

As the next stage in improving the metallurgical department, the Party unit sent the Communists with the most technical experience and organizational ability into the decisive shops. A Party group

[25] *Ind.*, August 9, 1940, p. 2.
[26] "Edinonachalie i pravo kontrolia," p. 36.
[27] L. Epel'man, Party organizer of the TsK VKP(b) in the plant, writing a letter in *Ind.*, June 23, 1940, p. 3.

was formed for the first time in one of them. A young engineer, till then working as shift engineer elsewhere, was chosen as Party organizer for this shop. The Party group, headed by this specially selected man, exercised daily supervision over the operations in this decisive area.

Similar work was done by the Party unit of a Leningrad tire plant, where an all-plant open Party meeting—to which 180 non-Party workers were also invited—was called to discuss the question of the quality of the tires. In preparation for this meeting, brigades were formed to investigate the various problems involved.[28]

The above-listed functions are the main ones of the Party which relate directly to the work of firm managements. Summarizing, they are coordinating the activities of the different organizations; supplying a common ideology and set of goals for all leadership personnel; providing a source of recruitment for top-level administrators; supervising all operations of the firm management; integrating management and all levels of employees into a single force; and finally, mobilizing mass participation and enthusiasm for the production tasks of the plant. Of all these, the function of mobilizing mass participation is the most fundamental—the successful fulfillment of which is treated by Soviet theorists as a prerequisite for success in the other fields.

THE PARTY UNIT OF THE FIRM AS A MASS ORGANIZATION

Soviet theorists stress the mass character of the Party organizations of the firms. This emphasis has a clear basis in efficiency concepts. For if the Party unit degenerates into the rule of a few officials, it is no better able to fulfill its tasks than would equally efficient Communists operating as industrial executives; the Party unit becomes superfluous. If the Party unit is divorced from the non-Party workers, it is unable to carry out its functions of mobilizing mass participation or of linking together management and employees.

The mere fact that a Party strongly based on mass participation would be highly functional to the Soviet regime is no proof that

---

[28] R. Shub, secretary of the plant's Party bureau, writing an article in *Ind.*, September 10, 1940, p. 3.

the Party has had this character. It is the reality rather than Soviet theory which is our main concern.

Unfortunately, evidence bearing on the degree to which this theory has been realized is exceedingly nebulous. Only detailed surveys on the spot during the period studied could have offered the possibility for an accurate judgment. Moreover, the situation doubtless differed radically from plant to plant. That is why it seems impossible to arrive at any founded conclusions. However, due to the subject's importance, I will present what relevant materials I have seen. These deal with the role of the Party rank and file in the lowest level of Party organizations, but offer no information as to the ties between the Party and the non-Party employees.

SIZE AND COMPOSITION OF PARTY UNITS: There are no figures available on the proportion of Communists to the total work force of the plants of heavy industry. The best materials at my disposal are percentages derived from my own sample of heavy industry plants.[29] Relevant data have been found for only eight of the 224 firms in the sample. But these eight had a total work force of 100,-000.

Of the eight firms, the lowest percentage of Communists was in the Magnitogorsk Stalin Firm, where 5 percent of the employees were Party members. The highest percentage—12 percent—existed in the Stalingrad Stalin Metallurgical Plant. In five of the other six plants, the proportion of Communists was slightly over 10 percent.[30]

From these figures, I would guess that roughly 10 percent of the employees of heavy industry firms belonged to Party organizations. When we consider that Party members are supposed to be a select

[29] The sample is described in Appendix B.
[30] The remaining six plants were the Leningrad S. M. Kirov Electric Power Plant, the Moscow Hammer and Sickle Metallurgical Plant, the Nikol'skii Plant, the Moscow Stalin Auto Plant, the Leningrad Stalin Metallurgical Plant, and the Electric Steel Plant. The figures, unfortunately, are somewhat mixed; the distinction between Party members and candidates is not always clearly made. The sources for the different plants, in order of listing and beginning with those mentioned in the text, are: *Ind.*, November 29, 1938, p. 1, and December 31, 1939, p. 2. Z. Sibiriachka, "Opyt organizatsii grupp sochuvstvuiushchikh na predpriiatii" (The Experience of the Organization of Groups of Sympathizers in the Firm), *Part. Stroit.*, 1934, No. 11, pp. 27-30. V. Tsvetkov, "Kazhdyi chlen partkoma—organizator, agitator, propagandist" (Each Member of the Party Committee is an Organizer, an Agitator, and a Propagandist),

leadership group, this proportion appears high enough to have given the Party its mass base throughout a plant if all other conditions were favorable. But whether such a base was actually established would depend to a large extent on the distribution of the membership.

Party theory is sharply in favor of wide distribution of Party members. One Party secretary boasted: "In our organization, there is not a single brigade or group in which no Communists are working."[31] In a decree of the Central Committee, the practice was criticized of accepting new members into the Party solely according to their personal qualifications. It was insisted that consideration should also be given to the problem of properly distributing Party membership throughout the work force and the population as a whole.[32] Where an insufficient percentage of a plant's Party members was engaged directly in production, the plant's Party organization has been criticized.[33]

On the other hand, practice appears frequently to have been quite different from theory. In one plant department, 75 percent of the Communists held management posts from assistant foreman on up.[34] In the Dnepropetrovsk region, the great majority of Party members in the two heavy industry plants covered by a regional questionnaire were engineering and technical employees.[35] In the Magnitogorsk Combinat, only 302 of 1,095 Communists worked directly in production.[36]

The tendency to develop disproportionate Party weight among management and engineering personnel[37] is not surprising. The

Part. Stroit., 1937, No. 13, p. 51. *Z.I.*, September 28, 1935, p. 2, and January 3, 1936, p. 3. *Z.I.*, July 21, 1934, p. 3. *Z.I.*, August 14, 1936, p. 3, and October 12, 1936, p. 3. V. Egorov, "Za stalinskoe vydvizhenie partkadrov" (For the Stalinist Advancement of Party Cadre), *Part. Stroit.*, 1937, No. 13, p. 40. *Z.I.*, September 24, 1937, p. 2; *Ind.*, October 4, 1937, p. 2 and April 2, 1938, p. 3.

[31] V. Volchenkov, "Partiinyi kontrol' deiatel'nosti administratsii" (Party Supervision over the Activity of the Administration), in *Partiinaia rabota na transporte* (Party Work in Transport), edited by V. E. Tsaregorodtsev (Moscow: 1948), p. 11.

[32] Post. of the TsK VKP(b) of November 16, 1939, in "V tsentral'nom komitete VPK(b)," *Part. Stroit.*, 1939, No. 21, pp. 59-60.

[33] Cf. *Ind.*, February 3, 1940, p. 3.

[34] Sokolov, *op. cit.*, p. 23.

[35] *Z.I.*, January 18, 1936, p. 3.

[36] *Ind.*, February 3, 1940, p. 3.

[37] G. Bienstock attests to the same tendency. See G. Bienstock, S. M. Schwarz, and A. Yugow, *Management in Russian Industry and Agriculture* (London, New York, Toronto: 1944), p. 25.

outstanding plant employees are the natural source of Party recruitment, but they are also the people who advance into more responsible industrial posts. Thus the Party faces serious difficulties in keeping its membership base among production workers. New recruitment is, of course, the obvious means for meeting this problem. But success in dealing with it doubtless varies sharply from firm to firm.

THE SOVIET FORM OF DEMOCRACY WITHIN THE PARTY: The mass participation existing within a Party plant unit must depend to a significant degree upon the amount of membership control which exists within the Party organization. Soviet leaders have been firm advocates of a particular type of "democracy." The extent to which this "democracy" has been realized within the Party units of the plants probably has a major effect on the extent to which Party rank and file are effectively mobilized for carrying out Party decisions.

Stalin has defined proper Party democracy as having nothing to do with "freedom for a few intelligentsia . . . to chatter on without end." Rather, he said, the desirable sort of democracy involves the "freedom of the Party masses to determine questions of building the Party, the growth of the activity of the Party masses, and the drawing of them into the Party leadership."[38] Democracy is not understood as permitting opposition in Party units to the policies of the national leadership. It is viewed as meaning a program of the greatest and most rounded activity by the rank-and-file members in order to better carry out these policies.

Seen in this way, the fight for "Party democracy" is essentially the fight for more rank-and-file participation in the decisions and work of the lower Party units. It has little or nothing to do with control by the Party membership over decisions of the top Communist Party organs such as the Politbureau.

Thus the significance of elections in the plant organizations of the Communist Party does not lie in their offering the Party membership an opportunity to choose between advocates of alternative

[38] I. Stalin, *Politicheskii otchët XV s"ezdu VKP(b)* (Political Report to the XVth Party Congress), p. 67, quoted in L. Tandit's article "Bol'shevistskaia vnutripartiinaia demokratiia" (Bolshevik Intra-Party Democracy), *Part. Stroit.*, 1938, No. 9, p. 40.

policies. Any such conflict of policy would be decided by higher Party bodies, and an advocate of the rejected program could scarcely run on an opposition ticket. Rather the significance of Party elections in the plants rests in the fact that they offer a convenient mechanism for selecting local leaders who can effectively carry out higher Party policies. Soviet top leadership has the greatest interest in seeing that men are chosen for lower leadership posts who are popular with the Party rank and file and are capable of commanding their confidence. So long as all candidates are equally devoted to the Party policies determined by higher Party organs, it is to their interest to encourage the choice of the candidate whom the membership desires.

It is in this light, I feel, that we should interpret the sharp denunciations by Politbureau representatives of the absence of this sort of "democracy," and their demands for corrective action. In early 1937, Zhdanov showed how most Party organizations had been continually violating democratic procedure. He stated that Party elections had not been generally held for years, and that when members left Party committees they were not replaced by new elections but through coopting by the remaining members of the committee. He declared that open voting, normally done by lists, was only a formality and turned even those elections which did occur into mere approvals of decisions as to personnel selection which were actually made elsewhere. He was very critical of a situation in which higher Party organs did not simply approve or disapprove changes in the leadership of lower bodies, but highhandedly made the changes themselves. He condemned the preparation beforehand of resolutions to be adopted by Party meetings, insisting that the resolutions should grow out of discussion and the exchange of opinion.[39]

The Central Committee of the Communist Party endorsed Zhdanov's report and ordered corresponding action. It demanded regular Party elections by secret ballot and voting on individual candidates instead of by lists.[40]

[39] Politbureau candidate A. Zhdanov, Report of February 26, 1937, to the Plenum of the TsK VKP(b), in *Z.I.*, March 11, 1937, pp. 1-2.
[40] Resolution of the TsK VKP(b) adopted February 27, 1937, in *Z.I.*, March 6, 1937, p. 1.

The extent to which "Party democracy" actually increased is too large a subject to be treated in this study. Its major significance for the development of mass participation by rank-and-file Party members should, however, be clear.

The role of Party secretaries and organizers is also crucial in determining the degree of participation in the day-to-day Party life. For these secretaries and organizers are the key figures in the Party units. Either they may act as capable organizers of Party mass work, in which case they are centers around which participation can develop, or they operate as officials who make decisions and issue orders on their own responsibility with at best purely formal approval by Party meetings.

Soviet theory clearly prefers the first type of secretary and organizer.[41] But the qualifications for work in industry are much the same for both—not only organizational ability and political training, but also the technical knowledge which makes possible proper participation in decisions and work relating to production. The Central Committee of the Communist Party has recommended that engineers should be chosen as Party secretaries in defense plants.[42] In 1939, it was stated that excellent results had been achieved by following this recommendation.[43] But secretaries of this type face strong temptation to act in a fashion similar to business executives whose qualifications they share. In the 1937 elections for the Party committee of the Moscow Hammer and Sickle Plant, the former secretary was eliminated from the list of candidates due to his rudeness, his airs, and his "separation from the masses"; all these had been testified to by 33 Party members during a two-hour discussion.[44]

The national leadership has been fully conscious of the danger of

[41] E.g., in a brochure containing official Communist Party answers to questions asked by Party officials, it is insisted that the type of control exercised by the primary Party organizations must be mass control. The reason given is that if only a narrow circle of people are drawn into the active work of the Party unit, no matter how capable these people may be, they will not be able to discover and correct difficulties as well as could be done if the experience of all the members of the Party unit was drawn upon. See *Voprosy partiino-organizatsionnoi raboty* (Questions of Organizational Party Work), (Moscow: 1948), p. 19.
[42] A. Ugarov, "Vybory partorganov v moskovskoi organizatsii" (Elections of the Party Organs in the Moscow Organization), *Part. Stroit.*, 1938, No. 9, p. 18.
[43] Zhdanov, Report to the XVIIIth Party Congress, in *Ind.*, March 21, 1939, p. 7.
[44] *Z.I.*, April 20, 1937, p. 4.

the degeneration of Party secretaries from their assigned role of mass-organizer. As a leading example of such backsliding, Zhdanov, speaking for the Politbureau, pointed to the existence of "triangles" in all plants. The "triangle" of a plant consisted of the director, the Party secretary, and the union president. The triangle would meet, make decisions, and issue directives. Zhdanov was critical of triangles primarily because they existed as family get-togethers, designed to make it difficult for either the Party or union members to criticize management. The Party and union top leaders worked, he said, hand in glove with the director, but in utter isolation from their memberships.[45] After this report of Zhdanov's, it seems that triangles were abolished. Whether this was a change in substance as well as in form is another question,[46] and one less easily answered.[47]

Which type of Party leader—the organizer or the official—has been more typical, I cannot say. The Party secretary who considers himself primarily an official clearly cannot be as successful as the effective organizer. On the other hand, it is an easier role to fill and one in which a modicum of efficiency can probably be more easily attained. Doubtless, both types have existed everywhere.

Summing up, we can say that development of "Soviet democracy" on the plant level of the Communist Party would be highly functional from the viewpoint of the Politbureau. The choice of the candidate for local office who is most popular and believed by those on the spot to be most effective must appear highly desirable

[45] Zhdanov's Report to the Plenum of the TsK VKP(b) on February 26, 1937, *Z.I.*, March 11, 1937, pp. 1-2.

[46] In late 1939, the secretary of the Leningrad Party Committee noted that in some Leningrad firms the selection of plant personnel was still made through agreement between the plant director and the secretary of the plant's Party organization. He attacked this practice on the basis that the plant's Party organization as a whole should take an active part in choosing plant personnel. (G. Smirnov, secretary of the Leningrad City Party Committee, writing in *Pravda*, September 27, 1939, p. 3.)

[47] Solomon Schwarz gives the impression that he seems to interpret Zhdanov's speech as signaling the end of the role of the Party in the management of firms, and as giving full power to the director. (Bienstock, Schwarz, and Yugow, *op. cit.*, pp. 43-44.) Bienstock also writes of the abolition of the triangle as though it represented the destruction of the power of the Party unit in the plant. (*Ibid.*, pp. 13-14.) Such an interpretation appears to me to have no justification in Zhdanov's speech and, as we shall see later in this chapter, no basis in Soviet practice after 1937. (Interestingly, its lack of foundation in Soviet practice seems to be recognized by Bienstock and Schwarz. Cf. *Ibid.* pp. 22-26.)

—so long as all candidates accept all Politbureau policies and adequately reflect its philosophic approach to problems. (The danger that local memberships may register opposition by choosing Party officials who either are not enthusiastic followers of the Party line or who are inefficient is lessened by the right of higher bodies to disapprove the selection of new Party officials when they have reason to doubt their reliability or effectiveness.) The participation of the total Party membership of a plant in making low-level Party decisions is a fruitful procedure—providing it occurs within the framework of policies determined by higher bodies.

Thus one can well accept the authenticity of the oft-repeated belief of Soviet leaders in the importance of developing "Soviet democracy" in the basic Party units. But it goes beyond the possibilities of this study to try to evaluate the extent to which it has been realized.

CONTROL OVER THE FIRM BY INTERMEDIATE AND HIGHER PARTY BODIES

Up to this point, we have been considering the role of the Party organizations operating within the firms themselves. But all higher and intermediate Party organizations, ranging from the Central Committee to the district and city committees, are also vitally interested in the operations of heavy industry. Our task in this section will be to deal with these Party bodies and whichever of their actions directly affect the operations of firm managements.

As one would expect, the Central Committee usually adopts decisions which relate to more than a single firm. Thus in December, 1933, the Central Committee condemned the sanitary conditions in many food-processing plants, singling out some of the plants by name. But it did not itself take concrete action regarding these firms; instead it held the industrial organs and the intermediate Party bodies responsible for improvement.[48] In 1941, the Central Committee ordered the industrial commissariats to increase the production plans for firms in cases where the firms' average monthly production plans for the first quarter of 1941 would otherwise have been lower than the actual production achieved in De-

[48] "V tsentral'nom komitete VKP(b)," *Part. Stroit.*, 1934, No. 2, p. 63.

cember, 1940.[49] The Central Committee has more than once publicly called to account regional Party committees for not successfully supervising major industrial firms in their areas.[50]

The Central Committee may also take action relating to an individual firm, although even here it normally leaves to intermediate Party bodies decisions as to specific measures. Thus in November, 1940, the Central Committee called the attention of the Party committee of the Molotov Region to the unsatisfactory work of the Stalin Machine-Construction Plant located in the region; it suggested that the regional committee adopt measures to achieve systematic work in the plant. Following upon this action by the Central Committee, the Party Regional Committee made a detailed analysis of the Stalin Plant.[51]

A good indication of the limited role of the Central Committee in dealing with individual firms can be found in an examination of the institution of Party organizers of the Central Committee. In order to strengthen the Party units in firms of major national importance, the Central Committee itself has approved the names of Party organizers to be sent to these firms to head their Party organizations.[52] These Party organizers of the Central Committee in 1941 numbered 236 in major firms of the Ukraine alone.[53] They have doubled as secretaries of the plant Party committees.[54] The Party organizers have been expected to be men exceptionally experi-

[49] A. A. Kuznetsov, secretary of the Leningrad City Committee of the VKP(b), "Ob itogakh XVIII Vsesoiuznoi konferentsii VKP(b)" (On the Results of the XVIIIth All-Union Conference of the All-Union Communist Party [Bolshevik]), *Partiinyi Organizator* (Party Organizer), 1941, No. 5-6, p. 24.

[50] Cf. Post. of the Party Control Commission of September 29, 1939, approved by the TsK VKP(b), "V tsentral'nom komitete VKP(b)," *Part. Stroit.*, 1939, No. 19, p. 64. Also, Post. of the TsK VKP(b) of November 9, 1939, in "V tsentral'nom komitete VKP(b)," *Part. Stroit.*, 1939, No. 21, pp. 57-58.

[51] Gusarov, Speech to the XVIIIth Party Conference, *Pravda*, February 18, 1941, p. 3.

[52] This has occurred in defense industries, ferrous metallurgy, and coal mining as well as possibly in other industries. Zhdanov, Speech to the XVIIIth Party Congress, *Ind.*, March 21, 1939, p. 7. "Dnevnik soveshchaniia: Glavnoe—rabota s kazhdym otdelnym kommunistom" (The Minutes of a Conference: The Main Item Is Work with Each Individual Communist), *Part. Stroit.*, 1935, No. 16, p. 9. P. Liubavin, secretary of the Stalin Regional Committee of the Ukrainian Communist Party, *Pravda*, June 15, 1939, p. 2.

[53] M. Burmistenko, Speech to the XVIIIth Party Conference, *Pravda*, February 20, 1941, p. 6.

[54] A. Ugarov, secretary of the Moscow Regional and City Committees of the VKP(b), "Vybory partorganov v Moskovskoi organizatsii" (Elections of Party Organs in the Moscow Organization), *Part. Stroit.*, 1938, No. 9, p. 18.

enced in Party affairs, and, generally, with a good technical training in the industry of the firm to which they were sent.[55]

Despite the fact that these Party organizers have officially represented the Central Committee in their firms, it does not appear
that they have been kept in a central pool and dispatched to the
firms in which they were most needed. Rather, local district committees of the Party have chosen personnel for the posts of Party
organizers of the Central Committee in the major firms of their
districts, the Central Committee of the Republic concerned has
approved the nominations, and, finally, the Central Committee of
the All-Union Communist Party has given its approval.[56] Thus it
would seem that it has been the local Party bodies, rather than the
Central Committee, which have normally decided on who should
be chosen as a Party organizer of the Central Committee.

The slight documentation which I have seen indicates that even
after the Party organizers have been chosen, they have been expected to work more closely with the regional and city Party committees than with the Central Committee. Thus M. Burmistenko
reported to the XVIIIth All-Union Party Conference that many of
the Party organizers of the Central Committee who were stationed
in major plants of the Ukraine were working unsatisfactorily. He
felt that the Ukrainian Communist Party was responsible for their
bad work. For, he said, many regional and city Party committees
were not supervising the work of these Party organizers of the Central Committee. He insisted that the regional and city Party committees should frequently hear reports from these Party organizers
and should generally supervise their activities.[57]

From all this it would appear that the Party organizers of the
Central Committee, despite being in form the representatives of
the Central Committee in major firms, in practice have been
chosen and supervised primarily by intermediate Party bodies. The
Central Committee's contribution would seem to have been pri-

[55] Zhdanov, Speech to the XVIIIth Party Congress, *Ind.*, March 21, 1939, p. 7.
Liubanov in *Pravda*, June 15, 1939, p. 2.
[56] Cf. M. Burmistenko, secretary of the Central Committee of the Ukrainian Communist Party (Bolshevik), "O podbore i vydvizhenii kadrov" (On the Selection and
Promotion of Personnel), *Part. Stroit.*, 1939, No. 15, p. 18. M. Burmistenko, "Smelee
vydvigat' kadry" (For a Bolder Promotion of Personnel), *Part. Stroit.*, 1939, No. 5,
pp. 17-18.
[57] Burmistenko, *Pravda*, February 20, 1941, p. 6.

marily to lend them its name and authority, and to have taken the precaution of approving the candidates presented by intermediate Party organizations. This seems entirely in line with the Central Committee's apparent policy of not working closely with individual firms, but rather of operating through intermediate Party and economic organs.

All Communist Party bodies, including the Central Committee, have had a fundamental and continuing interest in the choice and promotion of personnel in all areas of the society. In 1939, a basic task of Party organizations was stated as that "of strengthening their guidance over the selection and distribution of personnel in Government, economic, and other organizations, and of insuring that the heads of these organizations and departments conduct their personnel work correctly and in a Bolshevik fashion."[58] Party organizations have been instructed to concern themselves not only with the promotion of Party members but also with that of non-Party personnel.[59]

The Central Committee, acting mainly through officials employed in the apparatus directly responsible to the Secretariat of the Central Committee, has stood at the head of the Party's personnel operations and has coordinated them.[60] It is difficult to state the extent to which it has taken a direct part in determining the personnel composition of individual firms. However, we can define with reasonable safety the following minimum and maximum limits of such activity by the Central Committee and its apparatus. On the one hand, firm personnel below the level of senior

[58] "Podniat' delo podbora kadrov na nauchno bol'shevistskuiu vysotu" (In Order to Raise the Selection of Personnel to a Scientific and Bolshevik Height), *Part. Stroit.*, 1939, No. 13, p. 8.
[59] Malenkov, Report to the XVIIIth Party Conference, *Ch.M.*, February 16, 1941, p. 3.
[60] In the 1934 reorganization of the apparatus of the Central Committee, personnel functions were given primarily to branches of the apparatus organized along industry lines. But beginning in about early 1937, the Central Committee increasingly concentrated all personnel work into a single branch. This tendency was formalized in 1939 when the apparatus was reorganized along functional lines. (Resolutions of the XVIIth and XVIIIth Party Congresses, *VKP[b] v rez.*, 6th edition, pp. 584-86 and pp. 749-53. Zhdanov, Speech to the XVIIIth Party Congress, *Ind.*, March 21, 1939, p. 6.) A discussion of the organization and functions of the apparatus is contained in Louis Nemzer's article, "The Kremlin's Professional Staff: the 'Apparatus' of the Central Committee, Communist Party of the Soviet Union," *American Political Science Review*, Vol. XLIV, No. 1 (March, 1950), pp. 64-85.

management would not normally have been chosen or approved by the Central Committee or its apparatus.[61] On the other hand, directors of the leading heavy industry firms of the nation would almost certainly have come under the scrutiny of the Central Committee's apparatus before appointment.

The Central Committee's apparatus has taken a particularly active role in distributing each year's crop of college graduates among firms and other organizations throughout the Soviet Union. Thus in 1938, the Central Committee was said to have assigned 61,000 graduates—from a total for the country of 103,800—to work posts. Of these, 6,000 had had prior interviews with officials of the apparatus.[62] In 1941, the Central Committee took a hand when the Commissariat of the Chemical Industry did not send a single engineering graduate to the Bondiuzhskii Chemical Plant which had only one engineer-mechanic, although it had sent eleven to the Rubezhanskii Chemical Combinat in the first quarter of 1941 and planned to send ten more in the second quarter.[63]

In addition to personnel work, the Central Committee has been deeply concerned with enforcement of the execution of central Party decisions by all organized bodies in the Soviet Union. In 1934, two different types of bodies were established to perform this enforcement task. Inside the apparatus of the Central Committee, branches were organized along industry lines and each was instructed to enforce Party orders in its assigned segment of the economy.[64] Simultaneously, a Party Control Commission attached to the Central Committee was organized, one of its main functions being that of enforcing throughout the entire Soviet Union the decisions of the national Party organs and particularly of the Central Committee.[65]

The Party Control Commission has shown considerable concern

[61] This statement is based on the fact that primary and intermediate Party organizations have been held responsible for supervising the selection and promotion of junior management, engineers, skilled workers, etc.

[62] *Pravda*, March 5, 1939, p. 3. *Bol'shaia Sovetskaia Entsiklopediia* (The Large Soviet Encyclopedia), (Moscow: 1947), p. 1235.

[63] *Pravda*, April 29, 1941, p. 4.

[64] In addition, each branch was to organize Party work, see to the distribution and training of personnel, and carry on mass agitation and propaganda for improving production. (Resolution of the XVIIth Party Congress, *VKP[b] v rez.*, 6th edition, pp. 584-85.)

[65] *Ibid.*, p. 588.

for economic problems.[66] In fact, it seems to have been even more important and to have had greater authority in this area than the State Control Commission.[67] At least on occasion, it has investigated individual firms.[68]

For all the activities of the Central Committee and its organs, it must be remembered that the regional, district, and city Party committees have played a much larger direct role in the life of the firms.

In the field of industry, the main task of these intermediate Party committees has been stated as consisting in the selection of personnel and in supervision over the execution by firms of the instructions of their commissariats and glavki.[69] As the chief speaker at the 1941 All-Union Party Conference put it, ". . . commissariats alone are not in a position to supervise the work of firms and to check on the execution of decisions of the commissariats. Therefore the Party organizations should help the commissariats . . ." in this task of supervision.[70] "City and regional committees of the Party must, together with the commissariats, bear responsibility for the work of all industrial and transport firms in the city or region."[71]

The Voronezhskii City Committee spent days discussing the high production costs of the Dzerzhinskii Locomotive Repair

[66] Thus the head of the Commission in a speech of June 28, 1934, to the Plenum of the Commission presented two main groups of problems as those with which the Commission should be primarily concerned at that time. Both groups combined various eonomic problems. (L. M. Kaganovich, Speech of June 28, 1934, to the Plenum of the Party Control Commission attached to the Central Committee of the Communist Party, *Part. Stroit.*, 1934, No. 13, pp. 3-4.)

[67] Cf. Post. of the IIId Plenum of the Party Control Commission, *Z.I.*, March 17, 1936, p. 1. Also, the Post. of the Presidium of the All-Union Central Council of the Trade-Unions of July 13, 1934, *BFKhZ*, 1934, No. 22.

[68] M. Stepanov, member of the Party Control Commission, "Polnost'iu vypolnit' direktivu TsK o pishchevykh predpriiatiiakh" (For the Complete Fulfillment of the Instructions of the Central Committee Regarding the Food-Processing Firms), *Part. Stroit.*, 1934, No. 12, p. 10. In 1939, the Party Congress decided that responsibility for enforcement of Party decisions was too diffused. As part of the general reorganizational process taking place in the Party, the Party Control Commission was reorganized and given sole control over fulfillment of the decisions of the Central Committee. Resolution of the XVIIIth Party Congress, *VKP(b) v rez.*, 6th edition, pp. 749-53. "Usilit' kontrol' za ispolneniem reshenii partii" (For Strengthening Control over the Execution of Party Decisions), *Part. Stroit.*, 1939, No. 12, pp. 3-7.

[69] A. A. Kuznetsov, *op. cit.*, pp. 23-24.

[70] Malenkov, Report to the XVIIIth Party Conference, *Ch.M.*, February 16, 1941, p. 2.

[71] *Ibid.*

Plant. The reasons for the above-plan costs were explored, and it was noted that the Party organization of the plant had given no serious consideration to the cost problem. The City Party Committee ordered the administration and the Party organization of the plant to take action leading to the elimination of extra costs.[72]

When the Urals Machine-Construction Plant received an order from its commissariat for two plywood presses requiring new design, the district Party committee established daily supervision over the plant's fulfillment of its schedule of designing and building the presses.[73]

The Sverdlovskii District Committee investigated one of the largest plants of its district which was not fulfilling its plan, and found that the departmental administrative apparatus was overloaded. The District Committee recommended to the plant director that he cut his administrative staff and save up to 100,000 rubles annually.[74]

A secretary of the Moscow Regional Committee reported that the committee often helped firms with procurement problems when they proved unable to get out of difficulties by themselves.[75]

The Rostovskii Regional Committee coordinated the operations of a number of firms in its region in order to achieve planned production of priority harvesting equipment and spare parts. Discovering that a major firm of the region responsible for this production was not working on schedule, the regional committee investigated possibilities for improvement. It found that a bottleneck was the production of many small parts which could easily be produced in other plants of the region. Thereupon a conference of the directors and Party secretaries of a number of firms of the region was called, and sufficient help was mustered so that the harvesting machinery was produced on schedule.[76]

From these examples, it can be seen that intermediate Party committees perform some of the same functions vis-à-vis plant

[72] *Pravda*, January 7, 1941, p. 2.

[73] *Pravda*, May 19, 1941, p. 1.

[74] "Otchët otdela kadrov na plenume raikome" (A Report of the Personnel Branch to the Plenum of the District Committee), *Part. Stroit.*, 1940, No. 21, pp. 59-60.

[75] K. Makarov, writing in *Pravda*, May 26, 1941, p. 2.

[76] A. Rozhkov, "Promyshlennyi otdel obkoma" (The Industrial Branch of the Regional Committee), *Part. Stroit.*, 1940, No. 21, pp. 55-56.

managements as do the primary Party organizations. In addition, they supervise activities of the plant Party organizations, thus acting as a check on the work of the lower Party bodies and as a court of appeal from their decisions. Finally, they coordinate the work of many plants of their area in a fashion impossible for any other body.

THE COMMUNIST PARTY AND MANAGERIAL ONE-MAN-AUTHORITY-AND-RESPONSIBILITY

We have seen that Party organizations of the plants as well as higher Party committees are expected to supervise firm managements. Being the "core of power," the Party has authority over industrial production, and Party units are held responsible by higher Party organs for plan fulfillment.

However, plants are expected to be operated along the principles of one-man-authority-and-responsibility. As we saw in Chapter II, the firm director is given full powers and is subject only to glavk and commissariat orders. His commands are obligatory for all plant employees.

The need for reconciling the two principles of Party supervision and managerial one-man-authority has continuously plagued Soviet leadership.

THE RECONCILIATION IN THEORY: It is held that plant Party organizations should "exercise leadership over the social-political and economic life of the firm. . . ." The "creative activity and initiative of the masses in organizing and administering production" should be developed.[77] But the Party organization is expected to meet its responsibility of guiding the firm's work by acting through management rather than by by-passing it.[78] Party organizations are not to substitute themselves for organs of management.[79]

When new work norms were not being fulfilled by many metallurgical workers, the head of the metallurgical sector of the Indus-

[77] Post. of the TsK VKP(b) of September 5, 1929, *Pravda,* September 7, 1929, p. 1.

[78] I. Stalin, Concluding remarks of March 5, 1937, to the Plenum of the TsK VKP(b), *Z.I.,* April 1, 1937, p. 1.

[79] A. Shokhin, member of the Commission of Party Control attached to the TsK VKP(b), "Vrednaia podmena khoziaistvennykh organov" (Harmful Substitution for Economic Organs), *Part. Stroit.,* 1937, No. 6, p. 25.

trial Section of the Central Committee of the Communist Party laid the blame on the Party organizations of the various plant departments. He pointed out that the workers could not fulfill the norms without help in removing production obstacles. Some Party organizations, he said, took the position that solving the production problems was the job of plant executives. Other Party units tackled each problem individually, thus assuming detailed operational leadership over production. Both positions, according to this representative of the Central Committee, were equally incorrect.[80]

He held that the task of the Party was to arouse all Party members, and after them non-Party workers, to the need for resolving the production problems. The Party organizations should give concrete aid to lagging individual workers who are Party members or candidates, see that the trade-union bodies give similar help to non-Party workers, constantly check on management operations, organize production conferences through the trade unions, and see that instructors in more efficient work methods are used to teach the rank-and-file workers.[81] In short, the Party was to be an aid and check on management, but not a usurper of its functions.

THE CONFLICT IN PRACTICE: The theoretic division of functions between the Party organization and the plant management never seems to have been properly "understood" by those responsible for carrying it out. Even in late 1940, the magazine of the Central Committee of the Communist Party had to report that there were still Party officials who were asking: If there is to be one-man-authority-and-responsibility for the work of the firm, how is supervision by the Party organization to be combined with it?[82]

Since Party bodies are held responsible for the production work of their firms, there has been great temptation for them to take over the powers of firm management and to exercise them directly. Why be responsible for the errors of others, they naturally reason. The result is ". . . that many secretaries of Party committees have begun to resemble engineers . . . and bookkeepers

---

[80] Il'in, *op. cit.*, p. 56.
[81] *Ibid.*
[82] "Edinonachalie i pravo kontrolia," p. 34.

. . ." more than heads of Party organizations. Party units were turned into bodies narrowly concerned with production technique.[83]

A report of a meeting of the Bureau of the Serovskii City Party Committee showed that the Party Bureau was being used as a distributing agency for all sorts of materials and equipment. An order was prepared commanding one department of a plant to build 100 troughs for another department of the same plant. The secretary of the City Party Committee recognized that this was a violation of managerial authority, and so the order was changed to one recommending to the director that he have the task carried out. By this verbalism, managerial one-man-authority was maintained.[84]

In 1934, it was reported to be common practice that when anything went wrong in a plant department, an appeal would be made to the Party organization. The feeling was prevalent that the industrial executives were a gang of "bureaucrats" and opportunists, and that only the Party officials were correctly carrying out the Party policies regarding industry.[85]

Even in 1940, some Party units considered their job that of registering all the mistakes of management and making things as tough as possible for the director. At the first Party meeting called to introduce the new director of the Lower Tagil'skii Plant, one Party foreman expressed the prevailing sentiment in the statement: "We'll see how the new director works. . . . And doubtless we'll whip him along." The new director listened to this promise with the recollection that his predecessor had been illegally removed from his post by this same Party group, and then had been turned over to the courts for criminal prosecution.[86]

Occasionally, directors fought back. S. Birman, a highly independent director of a major metallurgical plant, urged that since the Party unit was an important link in the successful operation of the plant, the director's leadership should cover not only the industrial administration of the plant but the Party unit as well. The director requires complete one-man-authority-and-responsibility,

---

[83] Lead editorial in *Pravda,* March 9, 1937, p. 1.

[84] *Ind.,* August 25, 1940, p. 3.

[85] E. Babachenko, secretary of the Party committee of the Engels Plant, writing an article first printed in *Pravda,* July 21, 1934, and reprinted in *Z.I.,* July 22, 1934, p. 3.

[86] N. Goncharenko, director of the plant, writing in *Ind.,* August 9, 1940, p. 2.

he insisted.[87] Birman justified his suggestion by an illustration from his own plant's work. The previous February, he had requested the plant's Party organization to begin a mass campaign against workers quitting industrial work for the summer. But the Party unit, which was on the outs with him, did nothing until June when workers were already quitting in droves.[88] Nothing more was heard of Birman's idea, however.

While heavy accent on Party supervision tended to cause Party domination and usurpation of management functions, Party organizations of plants have sometimes jumped to the opposite extreme when they were strongly criticized for violating the principle of one-man-authority-and-responsibility. They have stood aside from economic work and limited their activity to that of propaganda and agitation.[89] They have begun to drop production questions from their agenda.[90] They have given none of the aid to management which they of all organizations are most capable of providing. However, Party units which thus neglected their duties seem to have been fewer than those which have fallen into the opposite deviation from the Party policy.

SHIFTING EMPHASES OF SOVIET THEORY: To combat the extreme manifestations both of Party supervision and of one-man-authority-and-responsibility, Soviet theoreticians have laid stress on the opposite principle in the hope of creating balance.

In early 1937, Stalin indicated that the Party organizations had gone to the extreme of emphasizing their functions in economic work and neglecting their other functions of political education and activity and of hunting out "wreckers and saboteurs."[91] The decisions of the Plenum of the Central Committee of the Party of February-March, 1937, were directed above all to turning the Party organizations towards political work and towards ending their self-substitution for management organs.[92] There can be no

---

[87] Director S. Birman, discussion article in *Z.I.*, January 18, 1934, pp. 2-3.
[88] *Ibid.*
[89] Zhdanov, Report to the XVIIIth Party Congress, *Ind.*, March 21, 1939, p. 6.
[90] "Edinonachalie i pravo kontrolia," p. 34.
[91] I. Stalin, Report of March 3, 1937, and Concluding Remarks of March 5, 1937, to the Plenum of the TsK VKP(b), *Z.I.*, March 29, 1937, pp. 1-3, and April 1, 1937, pp. 1-2.
[92] Shokhin, *op. cit.*, p. 25.

doubt that the result was to lessen Party interference in firm management.

In early 1939, the emphasis was reversed. The All-Union Congress of the Party gave the primary Party organizations the formal right of supervision over management. Soon afterward, it was noted that the Party organizations of many firms had reorganized their work in line with this Party decision.[93] The accent was back on Party supervision.

In 1941, the XVIIIth All-Union Party Conference continued this trend. It stated in a resolution that "Many local Party organizations . . . incorrectly suppose that they bear no responsibility for the work of industry and transport."[94] It ordered the introduction of additional full-time secretaries for industries in city and regional Party committees.[95]

A SITUATION OF INEVITABLE CONFLICT: It would seem that Party responsibility and supervision cannot be reconciled with managerial one-man-authority-and-responsibility by any formal division of functions between the Party organizations and management.

A Leningrad speaker at the 1941 Party Conference pointed out that local Party organizations often bring questions before commissariats only to find that they are submitted to endless consideration. When time presses, he went on, the Leningrad City Committee sometimes decides economic questions itself without waiting for a decision from the commissariat.[96]

Although the Central Committee of the Communist Party has reprimanded city Party committees for appointing and dismissing directors of firms which were under All-Union commissariats,[97] Politbureau candidate Zhdanov seems to have approved Party appointments of industrial executives when they turned out success-

[93] S. Masterov, op. cit., p. 52. N. Patolichev, secretary of the Iaroslavskii Regional Committee of the Communist Party, "O sochetanii partiino-politicheskoi i khoziaistvennoi raboty" (On the Uniting of Party Political and Economic Work), Part. Stroit., 1939, No. 14, p. 32. Article by D. Sarapulov, secretary of the Party committee of the New Kramatorskii Stalin Plant, Mash., September 15, 1939, p. 2.

[94] "O zadachakh partiinykh organizatsii v oblasti promyshlennosti i transporta" (On the Tasks of Party Organizations in the Field of Industry and Transportation), Partiinyi Organizator, 1941, No. 4, p. 29.

[95] Ibid., p. 33.

[96] Kuznetsov, Pravda, February 18, 1941, p. 2.

[97] Cf. Post. of the TsK VKP(b) of January 3, 1938, in Mash., January 5, 1938, p. 1.

fully. In his report to the XVIIIth Party Congress, he referred to the Leningrad Kirovskii Machine-Construction Plant as an example of correct linking of Party and managerial work. In his description of the Party activity there, he stated that the plant's Party organization had rooted out wreckers from management and had itself promoted 500 new cadre to the new management.[98] Thus it appears that even Central Committee members were not entirely clear as to the formal division of functions between Party and plant management.

With this absence of formal clarity, it is natural that emphasis has always been placed on the need for the closest ties and a comradely atmosphere between the management and the plant's Party organization.[99] There has been criticism of the constant "philosophizing" as to the form in which the Party organization may make "suggestions" to management. If the proper relationship between the two is created, it has been said, no problem arises over verbiage. But if director and Party organizer are at loggerheads, then no resolution of difficulties is possible.[100]

When the plant administration is represented in the Party leadership, coordination of the efforts of both would seem to have the best chance for success. In line with this, it appears to be typical for the plant director to be a member of the plant's Party committee. He is normally considered an important part of the plant's Party leadership.[101] When, in 1937, only two of the members of the previous Party committee of the Moscow Hammer and Sickle Metallurgical Plant were reelected, the plant director was one of them.[102]

It is possible for the Party organization of the plant and the plant's management each to fill amicably its respective functions. But since these heavily overlap, the situation is burdened with latent conflict. The industrial press is constantly filled with reports of this conflict coming to the surface. Yet if the Party is to fill its

[98] *Ind.,* March 21, 1939, p. 6.
[99] Post. of the TsK VKP(b) of September 5, 1929, in *Pravda,* September 7, 1929, p. 1.
[100] "Edinonachalie i pravo kontrolia," pp. 36-37.
[101] Cf. "Organizatsionno-partiinuiu rabotu—na uroven' politicheskikh zadach" (Toward Raising Organizational Party Work to the Level of the Political Tasks), *Part. Stroit.,* 1934, No. 5-6, p. 53. Also, P. Protsenko, "Usileniem partraboty obespechit' dal'neishii rost proizvodstva" (Secure the Further Growth of Production by Strengthening Party Work), *Part. Stroit.,* 1934, No. 15, p. 38.
[102] *Z.I.,* April 20, 1937, p. 4.

prescribed role in the operation of industry, such a condition of perpetual struggle seems inevitable. The tendency for managements both to operate autocratically and to overemphasize the special interests of their own firms is combated by giving great power to the Party organization in the plant, but this gain, from the Soviet viewpoint, is counteracted by the inefficiency arising from conflicting jurisdictions.

CONCLUDING REMARKS

In the Soviet scheme of industrial administration, the Communist Party's position is essentially justified by the concept that the administrator is at least as much a politician as he is a technician. Thus it becomes reasonable to set up a political organization to supervise his actions and to guide his political thinking. Drawing its membership within the plant from all ranks of employees, the Party is expected to bind management and the workers together through informal bonds, thus making both groups feel that their basic interests are identical. In linking the leading personnel of all organizations in the society, it is expected to combat and overcome the special interests of the many different bodies. These functions boil down to that of being an integrating force in industry.

Furthermore, it should be noted that local Government authorities do not seem to have concerned themselves with firms under All-Union commissariats.[103] Thus it has been the Party organs which have had to function as the sole genuine regional authorities over the firms of heavy industry. It is the regional Party organs which have coordinated the activities of firms of different industries within a given area both with the activities of other firms and with the area's resources.

These functional aspects of Party supervision have their dysfunctional counterpart. This is the introduction of the problem of divided responsibility, a difficulty of major proportions. There is no single line of authority, but rather a double system of overlapping jurisdictions.

The confusion arising from this system of multiple authority

[103] Cf. Dvinskii, Speech to the XVIIIth Party Conference, *Pravda*, February 20, 1941, p. 4.

has been handled by Soviet leaders in a somewhat compromise fashion. While the Party's supervisory powers have been stressed, there has been equal emphasis placed upon managerial one-man-authority. The principle most strongly emphasized at any moment has been that which in practice was being most neglected. It has seemed impossible to push either principle too far, under penalty of building up insuperable obstacles to successful administration.

XIII: Participation by Employees in the Life of the Firm: A General Treatment

THE OVER-ALL ASPECTS

SOVIET THEORIZING: Let us now investigate the participation of nonmanagerial employees in the administration of heavy industry.

Participation of the masses has always been a key Soviet theoretic doctrine. Already in 1919, the Party and Government leaders had declared that the sole means of cleansing Soviet institutions of bureaucracy was to draw ". . . the wide masses of the workers and peasants into the administration of the country and into the widespread supervision of the organs of administration. . . ."[1] In a 1937 speech, Stalin developed this theme. The strength of the Bolsheviks rests in their ties and their closeness to the masses, he said.[2] All leaders see events and individuals one-sidedly, from above; thus the leaders' point of view is limited. The masses also have a limited perspective, seeing things from below and without an over-all grasp of the situation. "In order to arrive at the correct resolution of a question, it's necessary to combine these two experiences. Only in that case will leadership be correct. That is what it means not only to teach the masses but to learn from the masses."[3]

Stalin proclaimed the need for mass participation in all aspects of leadership. For what does correct leadership mean? he asked. It means the correct resolution of questions; but this is impossible without considering the experience of the masses, who test on their

---

[1] Decree published April 12, 1919, and signed by Lenin, Stalin, and Kalinin. Quoted by N. Krupskaia in "Lenin i Stalin o bor'be s biurokratizmom" (Lenin and Stalin on the Fight Against Bureaucracy), *Part. Stroit.*, 1937, No. 2, p. 23.

[2] I. Stalin, Concluding remarks of March 5, 1937, to the Plenum of the TsK VKP(b), *Z.I.*, April 1, 1937, p. 2.

[3] *Ibid.*

own bodies the results of the leadership. It means the carrying out of the decisions; but this cannot be done without the direct help of the masses. Finally, it means the supervision over the execution of decisions; this also is impossible without direct aid from the rank and file.[4] For they know all the minor successes and failures as higher supervisors cannot possibly know them, and so are able to dig out many matters and, in a fashion impossible for higher-ups, show the way to correct mistakes.

What have the Soviets meant by "mass participation" in industry? Basically, they have viewed it as being expressed in four forms. One of these is supervision by the employees in a firm over the work of the management, and their strict criticism of all its deficiencies.[5] A second is the offering of suggestions—particularly through employee conferences.[6] A third is the direct performance of administrative tasks by workers who do this in addition to their regular work.[7] Finally, and as important as any of the other three forms, is the movement upward of rank-and-file workers into posts in management and into leading positions in Party and trade-union organizations.[8]

It is claimed that mass participation prevents the divorce of officials from practical life. The mass of workers, it is said, will have little patience with those officials who solely follow orders and show no initiative in solving problems. They will demand genuine leadership, and will not be satisfied with the issuance of orders and instructions. Moreover, it is held, they will reject application of a unitary standard to people whom they know as individuals, and will insist on an individualized approach.

PARTICIPATION THEORY IS NO FAIR-WEATHER COMPANION: Our main problem in the rest of this chapter will be to examine the

---

[4] *Ibid.*, pp. 1-2.

[5] Resolution of the XVIIth Party Congress of 1934, *XVII s"ezd VKP(b)*, p. 673.

[6] Cf. Malenkov, Report to the XVIIIth Party Conference, *Ch.M.*, February 16, 1941, pp. 3-4. N. M. Shvernik, Report to the XIth Plenum of the Central Council of the Trade Unions (abbreviated stenographic report), *Profsoiuzy SSSR*, 1941, No. 4, p. 14.

[7] Resolution of the XVIIth Party Congress of 1934, *XVII s"ezd VKP(b)*, p. 673.

[8] Cf. lead editorial in *Ind.*, December 31, 1937, p. 1. Also, I. Stalin, *Politicheskii otchët XV s"ezdu VKP(b)*, p. 67, quoted by L. Tandit, "Bol'shevistskaia vnutri-partiinaia demokratiia" (Bolshevik Intra-Party Democracy), *Part. Stroit.*, 1938, No. 9, p. 40.

degree to which the Soviet theoretic emphasis on mass participation was followed in practice during the 1934-41 period. As the reader might expect, the same difficulties in evaluation have to be faced here as were encountered in the investigation of the mass role of the Communist Party in the firm.

In the first place, it should be pointed out that participation from the ranks is not a concept which has been emphasized primarily in good times and allowed to slide in periods of difficulties. In fact, it was in 1937—at the beginning of the heavy Purge Period in industry—that participation and "democracy" were given their greatest stress.

As we have seen in the previous chapter, it was at the February-March, 1937, Plenum of the Central Committee of the Communist Party that frequent elections, the secret ballot, and voting for individual candidates rather than for lists were instituted within the Party.[9] It was at this Plenum that Stalin made the statement, quoted above, on the need for "learning from the masses." In implementation of this statement, the Party Plenum called for the institution of regular monthly gatherings of the "actives" of every plant.[10] When the Commissariat of Heavy Industry got off to a bad start in production work in early 1937, the Commissariat's daily newspaper *Za Industrializatsiiu* responded by laying stress on the need for greater criticism of industrial executives by the plant employees and demanded that their remarks be closely heeded.[11] As a result of the impetus given by this Plenum, the trade unions began to take steps toward more formal democracy, and, in particular, they held the first general elections in many years. It was also in 1937 that the first national elections under the new Soviet constitution took place. In November, 1936, after the first major Purge trials had already occurred, the Communist Party rolls were opened to new members for the first time in over two years.[12]

Thus it can be seen that political difficulties were met by a vast

[9] Resolution of the Plenum of the TsK VKP(b), of February 27, 1937, in *Z.I.*, March 6, 1937, p. 1.

[10] *Z.I.*, April 24, 1937, p. 1, and May 23, 1937, p. 1.

[11] Cf. *Z.I.*, February and March, 1937.

[12] Post. of the TsK VKP(b) of September 29, 1936, in *Part. Stroit.*, 1936, No. 19, pp. 3-5.

increase of emphasis on the importance of participation and "democracy"—in the Soviet sense of the word, as explained above. Whatever the extent to which true participation was actually realized, it is clear that Soviet leaders considered it to be of great importance and a significant weapon in their struggle to overcome political and economic difficulties.

DIRECT PARTICIPATION BY WORKERS IN ADMINISTRATION: This is one of the forms of participation first stressed by Soviet leaders. Its virtual renunciation in the thirties is indicative of the demands placed upon all forms of participation, and of Soviet willingness to renounce those forms which offer no promise of raising efficiency.

In 1934, the XVIIth Party Congress put forth a demand for socialist combination-of-work in factory production with work in State administrative bodies.[13] This activity was considered as a major step along the lines of Lenin's desire for each worker to fulfill unremunerated State duties after his regular workday.[14] By bringing volunteer production workers into administrative organizations, these bodies were to be infused with new life and were to be brought closer to the working population.

However, this type of participation died stillborn. It had been begun by a few leading firms of Moscow and then of Leningrad. But in early 1935, at what seems to have been the height of the movement, there were only 11,839 production workers also fulfilling tasks in State administration. By the end of 1936, there were no more than 7,000 to 8,000 such people.[15] Little attention had been given to the movement by the trade unions.[16] I have not seen the movement mentioned again after 1936.

The death of this form of participation could only have been due to its failure to improve the work of the administrative bodies. Part-time, volunteer, untrained personnel appear to have been

[13] *XVII s"ezd VKP(b)*, pp. 671-73.
[14] G. Zelenko and E. Khvishchevskii, "Bol'she vnimaniia shefstvu i sotssovmestitel'-stvu" (More Attention to Patronage and Socialist Combination-of-Work), *Vopr. Profdvizh.*, 1935, No. 5-6, p. 21.
[15] *Ibid.*, p. 22. Also, S. Kotliar, "O shefstve predpriiatii nad gosudarstvennym apparatom i o sotsialisticheskom sovmestitel'stve" (On the Patronage by the Firms over the State Apparatus and on Socialist Combination-of-Work), *Vopr. Profdvizh.*, 1936, No. 12, pp. 70-71.
[16] Kotliar, *op. cit.*, pp. 71-74.

more of a nuisance than a useful adjunct to the professional staff. The renunciation of the movement meant giving up the development of an idea which Lenin had warmly espoused, a development which the last Party Congress—the highest body in the land—had endorsed.

ADVANCEMENT OF THE RANK AND FILE TO LEADERSHIP POSTS: It must be said that Soviet leaders have been highly successful in developing mobility throughout industry. We have seen what large-scale advancement there was to industrial and Party leadership at all lower and intermediate levels. The same situation existed within the trade unions.[17] If we go along with Soviet thinkers in considering such advancement a form of mass participation in the running of the country, we must say that this form has been very fully developed.

EMPLOYEE SUGGESTIONS AND CRITICISM: The broadest form taken by mass participation in production is the supervision over management and the suggestion of new ideas to it. Unfortunately, it is precisely in this area that we are on weak ground in judging the reality of the participation.

Criticism and suggestions are expected to be given by employees mainly through conferences.[18] The meetings enlisting the widest attendance are the "production conferences."

The production conferences have been greatly emphasized.[19] Sometimes all the employees of the whole plant will be welcome, but more frequently the conferences are composed of the workers in a single department or even a shop or brigade. Normally, there is no selection of those allowed to attend. Since a conference is usually held in order to discuss the problems of a relatively small

[17] "K itogam vyborov profsoiuznykh organov" (On the Results of the Elections of the Trade-Union Organs), *Profsoiuzy SSSR*, 1938, No. 1, pp. 76-77. M. Stepanov, head of the Organizational Sector of the Central Council of the Trade Unions, "Nekotorye itogi otchëtov i vyborov fabzavmestkomov" (Some Results of the Reportings and Elections of the Plant and Local Union Committees), *Profsoiuzy SSSR*, 1939, No. 8-9, pp. 49 and 56.

[18] Cf. Arakelian, *Upravlenie sotsialisticheskoi promyshlennost'iu*, p. 217. Here it is stated that the trade unions participate in the administration and organization of industry primarily through their activity in organizing production conferences.

[19] Cf. Shvernik, Report to the XIth Plenum of the Central Council of the Trade Unions (hereafter cited as the VTsSPS), *op. cit.*, p. 14.

unit, full attendance of the workers of the unit should not be prohibitively unwieldy. The conferences are expected to hear reports from the plant director or head of the department or shop, discuss the reports and criticize the work of management, and make concrete suggestions for improving the work of the production unit.[20] One director describes how, on taking office, he called a production conference of all the workers in an assembly department which was lagging behind in plan fulfillment. Only after the conference, and on the basis of the discussion there, did the plant administration work out a concrete program of organizational and technical measures designed to secure increases in production.[21]

In addition to the functions described above, the conferences have the task of "mobilizing wide masses"—this latter being more a propaganda than a participation function.

On the plant level, another type of conference which has been pushed heavily is that of the plant's "production actives."[22] These conferences are viewed as of major importance in giving management better use of the experience of the participating employees, and are stressed as part of the program of "learning from the masses."[23] On the other hand, they are not intended to discuss minor departmental problems as do the production conferences.[24] Like the production conferences, they are considered vital in that they provide an audience for efforts to mobilize worker support for managerial efforts.[25] The February-March, 1937, Plenum of the Central Committee of the Communist Party called for regular monthly meetings of plants' "actives."[26]

Conferences of a plant's "production actives" are expected to last for one or two evenings.[27] Often, however, they last for five or six.[28] Normally, they are carried on by means of reports, discussion

[20] Arakelian, *Upravlenie sotsialisticheskoi promyshlennost'iu*, p. 217.
[21] Director P. Taranichev, writing in *Mash.*, December 31, 1938, p. 3.
[22] Cf. lead editorial, *Mash.*, July 17, 1939, p. 1. Also, Malenkov's Report to the XVIIIth Party Conference, *Ch.M.*, February 16, 1941, p. 4.
[23] *Ibid.*
[24] Director S. Birman, *Z.I.*, May 24, 1937, p. 2.
[25] Malenkov, Report to the XVIIIth Party Conference, *Ch.M.*, February 16, 1941, p. 4.
[26] *Z.I.*, April 24, 1937, p. 1, and May 23, 1937, p. 1.
[27] *Z.I.*, May 26, 1937, p. 2.
[28] *Ibid. Z.I.*, May 9, 1937, p. 2.

of the reports, and, in individual cases, by resolutions of the meetings as to proposed action.[29]

The fact that the national leadership has desired the organization of real work conferences, and not solely of mass meetings to stir up enthusiasm, is indicated by the heavy stress that has been placed on the need for criticism of management at these conferences. Conferences have been criticized because management personnel did not point out their own errors, and because the discussion of the "actives" was not concrete and pointed, failing to name specific executives as at fault for deficiencies in the plant's work.[30] Directors and department superintendents have been reprimanded for acting as though their obligation to the conference was only to make reports and was not also to take heed of the concrete criticism made there.[31] When the work of "production actives" was weak and conferences were not called in many plants, Central Committee member Malenkov declared that this was to a large extent due to the fear on the part of managerial personnel of developing mass criticism of themselves.[32]

How extensive and successful have these production and "actives'" conferences been? The evidence is conflicting. There are no over-all statistics for "actives'" conferences, but there are figures for production conferences which are extremely impressive. A study of 1,852 firms from all industries in the fourth quarter of 1933 showed that brigade and group conferences had taken place in 83.4 percent of the firms. There had been an average of 105 conferences per firm during the quarter, and each employee had taken part in an average of 2.4 conferences.[33] During 1943 and 1944, armament firms alone held 93,000 department, shop, and brigade conferences.[34]

On the other hand, top Soviet leaders have denounced the work of both production conferences and conferences of "production

[29] Director S. Birman, *Z.I.*, May 24, 1937, p. 2.
[30] Cf. *Z.I.*, April 3, 1937, p. 3, and the lead editorial in *Mash.*, July 17, 1939, p. 1.
[31] Cf. *Z.I.*, March 27, 1937, p. 3.
[32] Malenkov, Report to the XVIIIth Party Conference, *Ch.M.*, February 16, 1941, p. 4.
[33] A. Deviakovich, "Sotssorevnovanie i udarnichestvo" (Socialist Competition and Shock-Work), *Vopr. Profdvizh.*, 1934, No. 5, p. 83. The 1,852 firms studied employed 2,654,000 workers.
[34] A. Arakelian, *Rezervy predpriiatii na sluzhby piatiletke* (The Reserves of the Firms in the Service of the Five-Year Plan), (Moscow: 1948), p. 85.

actives" as highly unsatisfactory. In 1941, the Central Council of the Trade Unions stated that production conferences were being convoked irregularly and that concrete production problems were not being discussed.[35] The Council's chief secretary declared that the conferences' decisions were usually standardized and repeated from month to month in precisely the same language.[36] In 1941, Malenkov declared that in many commissariats the "actives" were no longer even meeting and that the importance of "actives" had to be reestablished.[37]

The same sort of conflicting materials exists regarding the significance of production suggestions by employees. In the second quarter of 1933, seven suggestions per hundred workers were received.[38] During 1943 and 1944, 130,750 suggestions were offered at the production conferences of the armament industry.[39] In 1946, there were 473,000 inventions and suggestions for rationalization and technical modernization brought forth in all firms of the country; 253,000 suggestions were introduced into production in the same year.[40] In 1949, and solely in industrial firms, 450,000 inventions and rationalization suggestions were introduced into production.[41] In the Moscow Stalin Automobile Plant alone, there were 11,514 suggestions received—of which 9,520 were accepted—during a period in 1938 and 1939 which could not have exceeded a couple of months.[42]

On the other hand, the number of authors' certificates and patents given out have been relatively few. (These two forms taken together are comparable to the patents issued by other countries.) In the 29 months from August, 1936, to January, 1939, only 3,902

[35] Post. of the XIth Plenum of the VTsSPS of April 4, 1941, in *O zarabotnoi plate sluzhashchikh; sbornik ukazov, postenovlenii i polozhenii* (On the Wages of White-Collar Workers; A Collection of Laws, Decrees, and Statutes), (Moscow: 1941), p. 8.

[36] Shvernik, Report to the XIth Plenum of the VTsSPS, *op. cit.*, p. 14.

[37] Malenkov, Report to the XVIIIth Party Conference, *Ch.M.*, February 16, 1941, p. 4.

[38] "Profsoiuzy pered XVII s"ezdom partii" (The Trade Unions before the XVIIth Congress of the Party), *Vopr. Profdvizh.*, 1934, No. 1, p. 5.

[39] Arakelian, *Rezervy predpriiatii na sluzhby piatiletke*, p. 85.

[40] *Ibid.*, p. 39.

[41] N. Sokolov, "Tekhnicheskii progress v narodnom khoziaistve SSSR" (Technical Progress in the National Economy of the USSR), *Planovoe Khoziaistvo*, 1950, No. 3, p. 5.

[42] Vlasov, chairman of the plant's union committee, as reported in *Mash.*, April 24, 1939, p. 1.

were issued for the whole country. The writer who presented this figure compared it with 17,800 patents given out in England in 1936 alone, and over 40,000 issued in the United States in the same year.[43] Such a figure for the USSR of formulated inventions actually patented may well be compatible both with the above figures of total suggestions and with the proportion of these which Soviet writers have indicated are accepted. But if so, then it is quite likely a significant indication of the very minor importance of most of the accepted suggestions taken individually.[44]

PARTICIPATION BY THE "BEST": Where employee participation is successfully aroused, it is still not the participation of all which is considered as of prime importance. Soviet leaders are mainly interested in the activity of those whose knowledge and ability enable them to make real contributions.

Clearly this is true of the form of participation which is embodied in the advancement of rank-and-file workers. But it holds almost equally with regard to the choice of participants in conferences. The heavy emphasis on the mass work of Party members in the plant, meeting in closed session, is one proof of this.[45] Another proof is the importance given to the highly select group called "production actives."

The production conferences include all employees. But it is the "actives" who are relied on for important discussions. For example, when in January, 1937, the Commissar of Heavy Industry ordered the organization of competitions in metallurgical plants,[46] the Bureau of the Moscow Regional Committee and the Moscow City Committee of the Communist Party issued a joint implementing decree. They called for departmental and plant meetings of all employees to discuss the questions involved in organizing such competitions. But it was the "actives" who were to meet separately with

[43] Engineer P. Nikitin, chief of the Bureau for Following the Registration of Patents of the State Planning Commission attached to the SNK SSSR, writing in *Ind.*, April 1, 1939, p. 2.

[44] Alternatively, of course, it may simply reflect the inefficiency of the Soviet patent office.

[45] See Chapter XII.

[46] *Z.I.*, January 3, 1937, p. 1.

managerial, Party, and trade-union leaders to work out the concrete measures for organizing the competitions.[47]

Who are included in "actives' " conferences? It has been emphasized that the conferences cannot be useful unless their individual members are well chosen.[48] Malenkov has described "actives" as composed of junior management personnel, engineers, technicians, and Stakhanovite workers.[49] There are no over-all figures on the proportion of "production actives" to the total work force of heavy industry, but I do have data for some individual firms.

In the Gor'kii Molotov Automobile Plant, with a force of 34,700 employees, about one thousand took part in the meetings of "actives" in the first half of 1937 and 100 spoke in the discussions. This compares with the Party meetings of the firm, where over 1,350 Communists spoke.[50] In the Red Proletariat Machine-Construction Plant, with over 4,000 employees, only 300 took part in the first "active" in 1937.[51] In the Red Triangle Rubber Goods Firm, with probably over 33,000 employees, only 40 people spoke at the "actives' " conference in early 1937.[52]

Thus it would appear that the "production actives" make up a group in the plant no larger than the Party unit and probably smaller. Undoubtedly, there is considerable overlapping. But the functions of each group are quite different. It is those who are technically most proficient who compose the "production active."

MANAGERIAL GUIDANCE OF CONFERENCES AND MASS SUPERVISION: A serious problem in the exercise of mass supervision over management is that the firm's administration itself is expected to play a major role in guiding the participation of employees.

It is management which has been given the prime responsibility for calling meetings of "production actives," and it also appears that it has had a vital role in choosing the personnel to be re-

[47] Z.I., January 5, 1937, p. 1.
[48] Lead editorial in Z.I., May 23, 1937, p. 1 .
[49] Malenkov, Report to the XVIIIth Party Conference, Ch.M., February 16, 1941, p. 4.
[50] Z.I., May 14, 1937, p. 2, and June 22, 1937, p. 3.
[51] Z.I., July 23, 1935, p. 3, and June 4, 1937, p. 2. Mash., April 29, 1939, p. 2.
[52] Z.I., August 16, 1935, p. 3, and May 9, 1937, p. 2.

cruited to these "actives."[53] Since the "actives' " conferences should be composed of personnel with enough technical know-how to be able to analyze their plant's problems and offer useful suggestions, it is the managerial staff which is felt to be in the best position to indicate the participants. Production conferences have been the joint responsibility of the union and management, but in many cases the task was entirely turned over to the plant administrations.[54] When commissions of plant employees have been organized to inspect the condition of tools, jigs, and fixtures, the plant directors have been given a major role in choosing the commissions' members and in seeing that they are active and effective.[55]

This managerial responsibility and authority seem to have been considered essential for the proper functioning of participation.[56] But often enough, the plant administrations have cut themselves off from the rank and file of the employees and have tried to function without their supervision.[57] As we have seen above, "actives" were often not developed because the plant managements saw no reason to encourage criticism of themselves. During the war and with the existence of wartime labor discipline, industrial executives generally seem to have made use of the opportunity for further playing down mass participation.[58]

PARTICIPATION MAY BE DISCOURAGED BY THE EXISTENCE OF MASS ORGANIZATIONS

The existence of organizations designed to enlist worker participation in the life of the plant does not always accomplish this end. In fact, in individual cases it may have the reverse effect.

Until 1938, Groups for Workers' Inventions existed in plants. These were composed of inventors and rationalizers among the plant personnel, and their function was to encourage the develop-

[53] Cf. lead editorial in Z.I., May 23, 1937, p. 1.

[54] N. M. Shvernik, Report to the VIth Plenum of the VTsSPS, Vopr. Profdvizh., 1937, No. 9-10, p. 27.

[55] Cf. Prikaz of V. L'vov, Commissar of the Machine-Construction Commissariat, of January 2, 1939, in Mash., January 3, 1939, p. 1.

[56] The justification for this will be more fully explored in the discussion of the Stakhanovite movement below.

[57] Lead editorial in Pravda, April 7, 1937, reprinted in Za Prom. Kadry, 1937, No. 5, p. 26.

[58] Arakelian, Upravlenie sotsialisticheskoi promyshlennost'iu, p. 215.

ment of new ideas and to approve premiums for rationalizers among the employees. However, in April, 1938, the Commissar of Machine Construction sharply criticized the work of these groups in handling rationalization proposals. He said that they only formed an additional bottleneck to the acceptance of ideas, since their approval was required as well as that of management.[59] Apparently as a result of this and like criticism, the groups were abolished.[60] It was felt that more rationalization schemes would be developed if the workers and management had direct contact, without an organization serving as intermediary.

THE STAKHANOVITE MOVEMENT

The Stakhanovite movement has been highly publicized both within and outside the Soviet Union as a tremendous expression of worker participation. The importance of the movement makes it well worth examining as a study in how participation has been combined with other factors making for efficiency.

The movement began when on August 30, 1935, Stakhanov, a coal-mine foreman, dug 102 tons of coal with his crew instead of the standard norm of seven tons.[61] By the middle of September, the Stakhanovite movement had taken over the newspapers and its extension throughout the economy was being pressed.

The Soviet description of this movement to raise production by more efficient work, and through technical and work reorganization, is that it began among the workers themselves. Stalin has described the Stakhanovite movement as having started "almost spontaneously from below, without any pressure by the managements of our firms. More than this, the movement was born and became widespread to a large degree in spite of the desire of our firms' managements, and even in conflict with them."[62] Ordzhonikidze, Commissar of Heavy Industry, said that when he had first asked industrial executives what they were doing to apply the

[59] Commissar A. D. Bruskin, writing in *Pravda,* April 19, 1938, p. 3.
[60] *Pravda,* December 4, 1940, p. 2.
[61] Commissar G. K. Ordzhonikidze, Speech of November 14, 1935, Z.I., November 15, 1935, p. 1.
[62] I. Stalin, Speech to the First All-Union Stakhanovite Conference on November 17, 1935, Z.I., November 22, 1935, p. 1.

Stakhanovite methods, some answered that the movement did not concern them, that it was the affair of the coal miners. "One comrade even said that, in his opinion, it was the affair of the trade unions and that they ought to propagandize him."[63]

Soviet speakers and writers have recorded opposition to Stakhanovism. However, they have found it not among the workers, but rather among managerial personnel. A vivid expression of this phenomenon is given in a cartoon by A. Bazhenov, in which an industrial executive glares out from his office window at a group of Stakhanovites walking by. "After this, they'll raise my plan!" he mutters to the sympathetic stooge standing beside him.[64]

Indeed, plant managements have been hard pressed by their Stakhanovite movements. A director of a machine-construction plant said that all managements of machine-building firms with Stakhanovite movements were being tormented by the contradiction between the need for more raw materials in view of their workers' increased production capabilities and their own inability to procure these materials.[65] Other managements have been subjected to heavy pressure to provide more efficient working conditions, to improve the flow of unfinished goods through the plant, to reorganize the shops so that workers on machines would be relieved of auxiliary work during which time their machines stand idle.

The Stakhanovite organizations within the plants have put pressure on management for reorganizations which would speed up production and permit greater earnings under the prevailing piece-rate system. Higher authorities have reproached managers and engineers for lagging behind the Stakhanovites, for sticking to memorized formulae instead of innovating, for having learned nothing since they were graduated from school while their workmen are able to see new production possibilities.[66] Cartoonist Bazhenov depicted a typical manager as jumping up from his desk and

[63] G. K. Ordzhonikidze, Speech to the First All-Union Stakhanovite Conference on November 16, 1935, Z.I., November 18, 1935, p. 2.

[64] Z.I., October 14, 1935, p. 2.

[65] Director B. Gutnov, writing in Z.I., October 30, 1935, p. 2.

[66] G. K. Ordzhonikidze, Report to the Plenum of the TsK VKP(b) on December 21, 1935, in Org. Uprav., 1935, No. 6, p. 14. A. Andreev, Speech to the Plenum of the TsK VKP(b) on December 24, 1935, in Part. Stroit., 1936, No. 1, pp. 12-13.

running after a group of Stakhanovites, calling out as he runs: "Wait up! I'll lead you!"[67]

Managers unable to satisfy the demands made upon them have often given spurious "aid to the Stakhanovite movement." They have created ideal conditions for one or a few Stakhanovites, who thus have been enabled to set records, and have ignored the work conditions and supply problems of the other workers.[68]

Soviet reporting almost certainly gives a distorted picture of the reactions aroused by the Stakhanovite movement. Managers unable to satisfy all the demands of their workers for more favorable work conditions have been denounced as "blocking the Stakhanovite movement." In reality, they most probably favored it as an aid to plan fulfillment. The Soviet propaganda approach of depicting the movement as one which received its impetus essentially from the workers naturally caused lack of publicity for adverse worker reaction. But there must have been many workers who resented the Stakhanovite movement because of the higher work norms which came with it and because of the extra skill and effort demanded.

Without attempting to give any quantitative picture of worker reactions to Stakhanovism, it should be pointed out that there are, however, good reasons to think that at least a substantial part of the rank and file may well favor it. Patriotism and the desire to "build Socialism" play their part as motivational factors. There is the sort of mass enthusiasm which is engendered by discussions, speeches, and resolutions. Then too, the multitude of competitions between firms, departments, shops, and even individuals appeal to the competitive drive which seems to be strong among most people in many societies, including the Soviet.[69] In addition, financial reward also exercises a major influence.

With regard to this last, the birth of the Stakhanovite movement saw a tremendous expansion in the use of progressive piece rates. The absence of Stakhanovism among certain groups of workers has

[67] *Z.I.*, October 12, 1935, p. 2.
[68] Cf. *Z.I.*, March 10, 1937, p. 3. "Ocherednye zadachi organizatsii proizvodstva v 1938 g.," p. 16.
[69] Soviet writers consider these competitions to be of fundamental importance. Cf. K. Ia. Kornitskii, "Stakhanovskie metody raboty v mashinostroenii" (Stakhanovite Methods of Work in Machine Construction), *Org. Uprav.*, 1937, No. 1, p. 17.

frequently been explained by their being paid under poorly designed wage systems which do not sufficiently encourage high productivity.[70] It is scarcely an accident that the Stakhanovite movement flowered in precisely the period when rationing of consumers' goods was ended and when, therefore, workers had considerably more to gain from high money earnings. It would seem that throughout the prewar period, work norms were set at levels which most workers exceeded and at which a large proportion could take home heavy extra earnings.[71] Workers have had an important personal stake in improvements in work organization, technical conditions, and materials flow. This is particularly true in that, as we saw in Chapter VI, work norms have generally been changed only in accord with national campaigns and not with altered production conditions in an individual plant or department.

STAKHANOVITES AS PARTICIPATORS: Soviet writers have described Stakhanovism as arising from the rank-and-file workers and as being

[70] Cf. Director A. D. Bruskin, Speech at the 1936 Council of the NKTP, in *Z.I.*, June 28, 1936, p. 4.

[71] In December, 1935, before norm revisions, about 40 percent of heavy industry's workers overfulfilled their norms by 20 to 40 percent, and 50 percent overfulfilled them by 50 percent or more. (G. K. Ordzhonikidze's remarks at the December, 1935, Plenum of the TsK VKP[b], cited by R. Besher in "Stakhanovskoe dvizhenie i proizvoditel'nost' truda" [The Stakhanovite Movement and Labor Productivity], *Problemy Ekonomiki*, 1936, No. 2, p. 56.) In July, 1936, shortly after the first general norm revisions, the percentages of those overfulfilling their norms were 70.9 percent in ferrous metallurgy, 77.2 percent in machine construction and metal fabrication, and 77.0 percent in the manufacture of principal chemicals; the proportion of those exceeding their norms by 50 percent or more was 15.6 percent, 18.5 percent, and 15.0 percent respectively. By December, 1936, when norm fulfillment had leveled off, the figures for overfulfillment were 87.9 percent, 84.6 percent, and 83.3 percent; those for 50 percent overfulfillment were 26.4 percent, 28.5 percent, and 20.1 percent. (A. Vinnikov, "K peresmotru norm vyrabotki v promyshlennosti" (Toward the Revision of the Work Norms in Industry), *Plan*, 1937, No. 8, p. 38. The figures are based upon a sample study made by TsUNKhU.) In December, 1936, over 24 percent of all the workers of heavy industry are reported to have exceeded their work norms by at least 50 percent. (*Z.I.*, March 18, 1937, p. 1.) The year 1938, with no norm increases, seems to have seen an increase in those fulfilling over 150 percent of their norms. (Cf. A. Grigor'ev, "Uporiadochit' zarplatu, ukrepit' tekhnicheskoe normirovanie" [For Bringing Order into Wages and Strengthening Technical Norm-Making], *Planovoe Khoziaistvo*, 1938, No. 10, p. 78. I. Iunovich, "Voprosy truda i zarabotnoi platy v mashinostroenii" (Questions of Labor and Wages in Machine Construction), *Planovoe Khoziaistvo*, 1939, No. 6, p. 74. V. K. L'vov, Commissar of Machine Construction, writing in *Mash.*, January 16, 1939, p. 3.) Although higher work norms were introduced into the aviation industry at the end of 1938, yet in January, 1939, 88.7 percent of the aviation workers were fulfilling their norms and 31.2 percent were exceeding them by 50 percent or more. (*Mash.*, January 14, 1939, p. 1.)

an expression of their participation in the improvement of production. In what does this participation consist? In trying to answer this question, I shall treat as "participation" any efforts on the part of plant workers which go beyond those required for the performance of their minimum duties.

One obvious form is that of innovations developed by the workers on the job and perhaps introduced directly by them. Stakhanov achieved his production increase primarily through a change in work organization. As operator of his mining crew's automatic cutting tool, he was relieved of all auxiliary work and thus was able to use his tool continuously instead of by starts and stops.[72] The machine operator Busygin, who brought the Stakhanovite movement into the vehicle-construction industry, almost doubled his output of forgings through a technological change: he increased the speed of operation of his cutting tool considerably beyond that formerly used.[73]

Busygin began the tradition of Stakhanovites themselves introducing their own innovations. Only twenty days after Stakhanov set his first production record, Busygin raised his machine's cutting speed on his own responsibility, and was at first fired for his "novelty."[74] In 1937, the Stakhanovite grinder, Kotova, was applauded for refusing to set up her own single machine, insisting instead on operating two to eight different machines with the elimination of all auxiliary work.[75] In the Soviet literature on Stakhanovism, references are constantly being made to the introduction of innovations by the foremen or skilled workers themselves.

But most Stakhanovites are not innovators. This fact can best be seen from an examination of the criteria used for determining which workers are Stakhanovites, and by the statistics showing the enormous proportion of workers who are entitled to this designation.

Stakhanovites are defined as highly efficient workers and employees. Stalin has depicted them as "people who fully possess the

[72] Kornitskii, *op. cit.*, pp. 19 and 21.
[73] G. K. Ordzhonikidze, Speech of November 14, 1935, in *Z.I.*, November 15, 1935, p. 1. Kornitskii, *op. cit.*, pp. 23-24.
[74] Cf. I. Stalin, Speech to the First All-Union Stakhanovite Congress of November 17, 1935, in *Z.I.*, November 22, 1935.
[75] Kornitskii, *op. cit.*, p. 23.

technique of their trade and who draw the utmost results from this technique."[76]

Since it has been held to be a significant honor for a worker to be listed as a Stakhanovite, the problem has arisen as to how to determine those worthy of being classified as such. The Leningrad Kirovskii Machine-Construction Plant decided in 1936 to consider as Stakhanovites only those "who bring forth rationalization suggestions [and] changes in technological processes of production." But this approach was rejected.[77] Instead, all those who achieved specified production results have been considered Stakhanovites.[78] For example, in the Moscow Red Proletariat Machine-Construction Plant it was decided to list as a Stakhanovite anyone who fulfilled 130 to 150 percent of his work norm and at least one third of whose production was judged to be of "excellent" quality.[79]

Those workers who cannot meet the qualifications of a Stakhanovite, but are still above the efficiency standards set as "normal," are listed as shock workers. In the Red Proletariat Plant, shock workers were those who fulfilled 105 to 120 percent of their work norms and whose production was generally "good" and some of it "excellent" in quality.[80]

Stakhanovites are viewed by Soviet writers as "advanced" workers in the sense that they are efficient. But that may be their only quality which is deemed progressive. A questionnaire directed to the Stakhanovites in the Moscow Hammer and Sickle Metallurgical Firm who were not Party members revealed that most Stakhanovites of that particular plant rarely read more than the plant newspaper, that the educational level of many was very low, and that some were not even sufficiently literate to fill out the questionnaire and thus had to answer the questions orally.[81]

A huge proportion of industrial workers have been listed as

[76] I. Stalin, Speech to the First All-Union Stakhanovite Conference of November 17, 1935, Z.I., November 22, 1935, p. 1.

[77] Z.I., November 20, 1936, p. 3. Post. of the Leningrad City Committee of the Communist Party of December 21, 1936, in Z.I., December 23, 1936, p. 3.

[78] G. K. Ordzhonikidze, Speech at the Session of June 29, 1936, of the Council of the NKTP, in Org. Uprav., 1936, No. 4, pp. 12-13.

[79] Z.I., August 1, 1936, p. 3.

[80] Ibid.

[81] Z.I., March 18, 1936, p. 3. There were 1,563 Stakhanovites, including those who were Party members, in the firm at that time.

Stakhanovites and shock workers. Official trade-union statistics for union members in industry show that on July 1, 1938, Stakhanovites composed 29.1 percent of the work force and that shock workers made up an additional 18.4 percent. On July 1, 1939, the figures were respectively 33.8 percent and 18.7 percent.[82] In ferrous metallurgy, 6.6 percent of all workers were Stakhanovites as of November 1, 1935, 25.2 percent as of July 1, 1936, and 40 percent by 1939.[83]

With the existence of this proportion of Stakhanovites to the total industrial work force, we see that Soviet leaders carried into practice their theoretic rejection of restricting to innovators the application of the term Stakhanovite. Only a very few Stakhanovites could have been innovators in the tradition of Stakhanov and Busygin.

A second type of "participation," other than that of innovation, consists in supervision by a worker of his group's work area, care for cleanliness, checking on plant equipment, insistence on the provision of satisfactory work conditions by management. This form of participation in improving production involves no innovations, but it does require extra work outside the regular job. A Stakhanovite may or may not be a participator in this sense; he may be highly efficient without having any interest in taking on extra duties.

"Participation" also consists in self-education and improvement of one's skill, in greater attention to eliminating waste motions and idle time, in a readiness to accept and adapt to new work methods. On the average, one might say that the Stakhanovite participates at least to this extent, for this is the road to greater efficiency and self-improvement. A most difficult type of participation to measure, it may often be expressed mainly in a psychological attitude. But

[82] Otdel statistiki VTsSPS (Statistical Sector of the Central Council of the Trade Unions), *Statisticheskii spravochnik* (Statistical Handbook), (Moscow: 1939), Issue III, pp. 4 and 16. The study was based on samples for each year of over six million union members out of a total union membership in industry of nine and one-third million. The percentages of Stakhanovites and shock-workers for the total work force were probably lower, but as 80 to 82 percent of all workers were union members, the percentages given present a sufficiently accurate picture for our purposes.

[83] "Slavnaia godovshchina" (The Glorious Anniversary), *Org. Uprav.*, 1937, No. 5, p. 8. Merkulov, Commissar of Ferrous Metallurgy, Speech at the XVIIIth Party Congress, in *Ind.*, March 22, 1939, p. 4.

as industrial managers in the Soviet Union or in capitalist countries could equally testify, enlisting such participation is often crucial to managerial success in improving production.

A considerable feeling seems to have developed in Soviet industry that Stakhanovites should also be participators in a fourth sense: as leaders in all forms of mass participation. The higher the proportion of Stakhanovites in plant and department trade-union committees, the more praiseworthy the condition has been held to be.[84] One Stakhanovite, objecting to this situation, said that in his plant the notion had developed that all Stakhanovites were *ipso facto* public-spirited men. The result of this was that he, as a Stakhanovite, was obliged to be a representative at all sorts of meetings.[85]

On the other hand, data published for 104 trade unions in 1938, and for 161 in 1939 (each figure being considerably over one half of the total number of unions in existence), show that Stakhanovites did not occupy a share of the elected union posts in plants which was out of proportion to the percentage of Stakhanovites in the national industrial work force. Thus, after the 1938 elections, only 26 percent of the members of the plant union committees were Stakhanovites, and the 1939 elections merely raised the percentage to 29 percent.[86] These figures should make us extremely hesitant about assuming that workers who have participated in elements of the life of the plant not directly tied to production have been most likely to be Stakhanovites.

MANAGEMENT'S ROLE IN THE STAKHANOVITE MOVEMENT: While the Soviet leadership has held that Stakhanovism must be a mass movement, it has insisted equally strongly that is must be led by managerial and engineering personnel.[87] Moreover, national leadership is required. For, "if individual parts of our economy are backward while others move forward, there may be a disruption in

---

[84] Cf. Remizov, chairman of the Central Committee of the Union of Workers of Heavy Machine Construction, Speech to the VIIth Plenum of the VTsSPS on September 3, 1938, referred to in *Mash.*, September 4, 1938, p. 1.

[85] Letter from a Stakhanovite in the Moscow Caliber-Tool Plant, *Z.I.*, April 9, 1937, p. 1.

[86] "K itogam vyborov profsoiuznykh organov," p. 77. M. Stepanov, *op. cit.*, p. 55.

[87] Cf. G. K. Ordzhonikidze, Speech at the Session of June 29, 1936 of the Council of the NKTP, *Org. Uprav.*, 1936, No. 4, p. 13.

the flow of production. . . ."[88] The December, 1935, Plenum of the Central Committee of the Communist Party insisted that the Stakhanovite movement had different tasks in different industrial branches, and it set forth the lines to be pursued in each.[89]

Where managerial direction of the Stakhanovite movement has been unsuccessful, production has suffered. K. M. Ots, director of an assembly plant, complained that his production was halted because larger plants, which customarily shipped him parts, had developed their Stakhanovite movements in assembly work but not in parts' production. Thus they no longer had work for his auxiliary assembly plant.[90] Within plants, unfinished production has accumulated.[91] Managerial failure to properly coordinate production has caused the utter collapse of the Stakhanovite movements of some plants.[92]

CONCLUDING REMARKS: The Stakhanovite movement has been directed toward the increase of efficiency in production. "Stakhanovite methods of work" is the Soviet phrase synonymous with the American phrase, "methods used in progressive plants."[93]

Many factors are considered necessary for the development of a proper Stakhanovite movement in a plant. Managerial and engineering leadership is essential. Guidance and propaganda by the Party and trade-union organizations are needed.[94] Worker "participation," in all the forms described above, is held to be vital.

Thus it would appear true that the Stakhanovite movement is an expression of worker efforts toward improving production

[88] A. A. Andreev's Speech at the December, 1935, Plenum of the Central Committee of the Communist Party, quoted by A. Il'in, "Partiinaia rabota na zavodakh metallurgii" (Party Work in Metallurgical Plants), *Part. Stroit.*, 1936, No. 24, pp. 56-57.

[89] Resolution of the TsK VKP(b) of December 25, 1935, in *Z.I.*, December 26, 1935, p. 1.

[90] *Z.I.*, December 5, 1935, p. 4.

[91] Petrovskii, head of the Glavk of Intermediate Machine Construction, quoted in *Z.I.*, February 17, 1936, p. 3.

[92] In the case of the Moscow Stalin Automobile Plant, it reduced the number of Stakhanovites by three fifths within a few months. (*Z.I.*, October 12, 1936, p. 3.)

[93] Cf. Kornitskii, *op. cit.* In this article, proper Stakhanovite methods under different sorts of production conditions are described. With very few changes, the article could have appeared in an American management magazine or industrial-engineering textbook.

[94] Cf. Malenkov, Report to the XVIIIth Party Conference, in *Ch.M.*, February 16, 1941, p. 4.

which go beyond the requirements of the individual worker's own job. But Stakhanovism is equally an expression of managerial leadership and of Party guidance. Worker "participation" is only one of several elements necessary for a successful movement. The number of Stakhanovites in a plant, and equally their success in production, is by itself no indication of the extent of worker participation—in any of the four enumerated senses—in the plant's production life.

THE TRADE UNIONS

The Soviet trade unions are held to be the most important organizations of employees. They are responsible for caring for workers' needs from their earliest childhood to the end of their life.[95] They are esteemed as the strongest "transmission belt" existing between the Party and the masses of workers.[96] Lenin declared in an often repeated phrase that they should be "the school for Communism," and thus that they "should in particular be the school . . . for all the masses of workers . . . for administering socialist industry. . . ."[97] From this, the conclusion has been drawn that "the work of the trade-union apparatus should be built on the maximum participation of the working masses. It must be remembered that the union leaders and employees are not officials but rather organizers of the masses."[98]

UNION MEMBERSHIP SIZE AND FUNCTIONS: Roughly 80 percent of Soviet industrial workers have belonged to trade unions.[99] In membership, therefore, they are broad employee organizations.

Functions given to unions cover an extremely wide range. The

[95] I. Stalin, Speech of May, 1935, to trade-union leaders, paraphrased by V. Polonskii, "Stakhanovskoe dvizhenie i profsoiuzy" (The Stakhanovite Movement and the Trade Unions), *Vopr. Profdvizh.*, 1934, No. 11-12, p. 21.

[96] Lead editorial in *Ind.*, August 28, 1940, p. 1.

[97] Lenin, *Sochineniia*, Volume XXVII, p. 152. This was quoted in 1937 by Kl. Nikolaeva in "Partorganizatsii i perestroika raboty profsoiuzov" (The Party Organizations and the Reconstruction of the Work of the Trade Unions), *Part. Stroit.*, 1937, No. 11, p. 7. Nikolaeva, a secretary of the VTsSPS, quoted Lenin's statement as still applying to union work.

[98] N. M. Shvernik, Speech to the Concluding Session of the Vth Plenum of the VTsSPS on December 31, 1934, *Vopr. Profdvizh.*, 1934, No. 12, pp. 17-18.

[99] Cf. F. Rudnitskaia, "Okhvat rabataiushchikh profsoiuznym chlenstvom" (The Extent to which Workers are Trade-Union Members), *Vopr. Profdvizh.*, 1934, No. 6, p. 101. Otdel statistiki VTsSPS, *Statisticheskii spravochnik*, Issue III, p. 4.

unions have major legal rights in the wage field. Changes in work norms and piece rates are to be made only with the approval of higher union officials,[100] and union permission is required for any overtime work.[101] Unions form plant commissions with management representatives to settle individual labor disputes which may arise. The main channel of appeal is to higher union bodies, which have the right to make decisions which management must obey unless it wishes to appeal to the courts.[102]

Unions bear major responsibility for safety conditions, and have under their administration thousands of safety inspectors.[103] They are expected to supervise the fulfillment of firms' plans for the construction of housing and nurseries, and for the operation of dining rooms, commercial stores, etc.[104]

The unions operate the social insurance system of the country directly. They own and manage sanitariums, vacation spots, clubs, and libraries.[105] They organize tourist excursions, athletics, art activities.

Finally, they engage in a great deal of agitation and education among the rank-and-file workers. Before elections to the Supreme Soviet, they have organized study circles reaching millions of workers. Lectures are given constantly. Antireligious propaganda has been expected of them; so, too, has the conducting of classes for illiterates.[106] They are supposed to help organize production conferences, work in developing the Stakhanovite movements, and strive for greater labor discipline by the workers.

However, union organizations on the plant level do not fulfill

[100] Post. No. 48 of the SNK SSSR of January 14, 1939, *BFKhZ*, 1939, No. 4/5.

[101] "Konsultatsiia o sverkhurochnykh rabotakh" (Consultation on Overtime Work), *Vopr. Profdvizh.*, 1937, No. 16, p. 58.

[102] D. Dubovskii, "Izmenit' poriadok rassmotreniia trudovykh konfliktov" (For a Change in the System of Reviewing Labor Conflicts), *Profsoiuzy SSSR*, 1940, No. 2-3, p. 84.

[103] V. Polonskii, a secretary of the VTsSPS, writing in *Z.I.*, January 8, 1936, p. 2. Arakelian, *Upravlenie sotsialisticheskoi promyshlennost'iu*, p. 221.

[104] Post. of the VIIth Plenum of the VTsSPS of September, 1938, in *Postanovleniia plenumov VTsSPS* (Decrees of the Plenums of the Central Council of the Trade Unions), 9th edition (Moscow: 1949), p. 139.

[105] For the extent of such properties, cf. Post. of the VIIIth Plenum of the VTsSPS of April 28, 1939, *Part. Stroit.*, 1939, No. 10, p. 63. Also, Arakelian, *Upravlenie sotsialisticheskoi promyshlennost'iu*, pp. 220-21.

[106] N. M. Shvernik, Report to the VIIth Plenum of the VTsSPS on September 2, 1938, *Profsoiuzy SSSR*, 1938, No. 13, pp. 28-30.

the most important functions of trade unions in most capitalist countries. They have no voice in setting basic wage rates or the general level of work norms. Nor are they in a position to press management for serious "fringe benefits" other than those already included in the plan approved by the State.[107]

PARTICIPATION IN UNION WORK: Our interest in the trade unions is in their role as organizations mustering mass participation. Statistics presented in this regard are most impressive. It is claimed that in 1934 there were three million active participators in the trade-union movement (16 percent of the total membership), and that there were five million in 1939 (21 percent of the membership).[108] A breakdown of the "participators" into specific categories shows that, for 147 of the 163 unions, there were in March-May, 1935:

Members of factory and local union committees (of these, full-time union employees numbered 41,800)	538,500
Members of department committees and department organizers	202,300
Group organizers	424,300
Collectors of membership dues	495,700
Safety inspectors	219,400
Social-insurance delegates and collectors of social-insurance fees	358,900
Participants in mass supervisory work	861,600
Total	3,111,600[109]

Of these trade-union workers, only about 76,500 were union employees.[110]

However, when the statistics are evaluated in terms of other So-

---

[107] As mentioned above, national union organs do play a formal role in determining questions of wages and norms. But, as we shall see below, these organs do not seem to have been particularly responsive to the desires of the union membership.

[108] N. M. Shvernik, Speech at the XVIIIth Party Congress, in *Profsoiuzy SSSR*, 1939, No. 2-3, pp. 41-48.

[109] TsUNKhU, Gosplana SSSR, *SSSR strana sotsializma* (The USSR, the Country of Socialism), (Moscow: 1936), p. 97. The total given in the table is 10,900 greater than the sum of the figures given. See also F. Rudnitskaia, "Profsoiuznyi aktiv v nizovykh proforganizatsiiakh" (The Trade-Union "Active" in the Lower Union Organizations), *Vopr. Profdvizh.*, 1936, No. 2, p. 91.

[110] N. Evreinov, a secretary of the VTsSPS, "O sokrashchenii platnogo profapparata" (On Reducing the Paid Trade-Union Staff), *Vopr. Profdvizh.*, 1937, No. 1, p. 5.

viet materials, the reality of the participation of the "activists" listed appears highly dubious.

Throughout the period studied, the Central Council of the Trade Unions continued to demand reductions in paid staff, but the demands were greeted only by further increases. In September, 1934, a 36 percent cut in the staff of all union organs above the plant level was demanded.[111] In December, 1936, a large cut was again ordered.[112] The same was true for September, 1938,[113] but by 1939, trade-union employees had risen to 194,000 in 179 unions.[114] This compared with 76,500 in all the unions in 1936, not counting those employed in cultural institutions.[115] The year 1940 saw still another rise in the number of paid employees, and once more a reduction was insisted upon by the Central Council.[116]

The secretary and Plenum of the Central Council of the Trade Unions declared in 1937 that the unions had failed to bring workers as voluntary participators into either the administration of social insurance or safety inspection. The entire work of the trade unions, from top to bottom, was founded primarily upon the operations of a paid staff.[117] In 1940 the union secretary voiced the same complaint about the lack of mass participation, particularly in regard to work above the plant level.[118] The explanation for this condition, he said, was that union officials considered it far easier to perform trade-union tasks with a large force of employees than through volunteer part-time participation of the membership.[119]

This continued reliance on officials rather than on a volunteer "active" makes one suspect that the statistics on participation cover hundreds of thousands or even millions of people whose activity

[111] Post. of the IVth Plenum of the VTsSPS, *Postanovleniia plenumov VTsSPS*, p. 73.

[112] N. Evreinov, *op. cit.*, p. 5.

[113] N. M. Shvernik, Report to the VIIth Plenum of the VTsSPS, *Profsoiuzy SSSR*, 1938, No. 13, p. 22.

[114] *Ind.*, August 28, 1940, p. 1.

[115] N. Evreinov, *op. cit.*, p. 5.

[116] *Ind.*, August 28, 1940, p. 1.

[117] Post. of the VIth Plenum of the VTsSPS, *Postanovleniia plenumov VTsSPS*, pp. 120-21. N. M. Shvernik, Conversation with the chairmen of the department union committees of the Moscow Stalin Automobile Plant, in *Vopr. Profdvizh.*, 1937, No. 18, pp. 4-5.

[118] N. M. Shvernik, Reworked Stenographic Report to the Xth Plenum of the VTsSPS, in *Part. Stroit.*, 1940, No. 15-16, pp. 8-11.

[119] *Ibid.*, p. 8.

has been virtually nil. In any case, the unions have certainly not been based upon "maximum participation." Union officials have not been primarily "organizers of the masses." The desires of Soviet leaders in this field have been far from fulfilled.

DEMOCRACY WITHIN THE UNIONS: At least through 1936, democracy within the unions was a negligible factor. The absence of proper elections was frequently commented on by top Soviet leaders,[120] but nothing was done until 1937. At this point, in line with what was happening in the Communist Party at the same time, conditions were exposed with considerable publicity. There had been no general elections for a long period; the union organs had grown independent of the membership and rarely even called meetings; union officials had come to ignore worker complaints and suggestions.[121] In 1937, new elections were called, voting by lists instead of for individuals was forbidden, and the secret ballot was instituted.[122]

In the 1937 elections, there was a turnover of 70 to 80 percent of the membership of plant committees of the unions, and a 65 percent turnover of the plant union chairmen.[123] In at least several recorded cases, there were more candidates put up for secret voting than there were elective posts.[124] The September, 1938, Plenum of the Central Council of the Trade Unions declared that democracy had been considerably strengthened.[125]

General elections took place again in both 1939 and 1940. The overwhelming majority of those elected on the plant level were not Party members.[126] But by 1939, the "problem" of voters having

[120] Cf. N. M. Shvernik, Report to a gathering of trade-union leaders and others on November 18-19, 1935, in *Vopr. Profdvizh.*, 1935, No. 10, pp. 21-23.
[121] Post. of the VIth Plenum of the VTsSPS, *Postanovleniia plenumov VTsSPS*, p. 120.
[122] *Ibid.*, p. 124.
[123] N. M. Shvernik, Report to the VIIth Plenum of the VTsSPS of September 2, 1938, *Profsoiuzy SSSR*, 1938, No. 13, p. 21.
[124] M. Stepanov, *op. cit.*, pp. 54-55. In the Karl Marx Plant of Leningrad, 37 candidates were listed for 25 posts. M. Gorbunov, secretary of the Party committee of the Leningrad Karl Marx Plant, "Rukovodstvo vyborami proforganov" (Guidance of the Trade-Union Elections), *Part. Stroit.*, 1937, No. 13, p. 56.
[125] Post. of the VIIth Plenum of the VTsSPS, *Postanovleniia plenumov VTsSPS*, pp. 137-38.
[126] In 1939, 75 percent of the members of the plant union committees were not Party members or candidates. (M. Stepanov, *op. cit.*, p. 55.)

to choose between a number of candidates greater than the number of elective positions had been eliminated.[127] According to the head of the Organizational Sector of the Central Council of the Trade Unions, this was the case because the possible candidates had now worked for a long time in the given plant, were well known to the workers, and thus there was no difficulty in selecting the proper candidates.[128] Whatever one might have thought of this argument if union work had been conducted on a high level, the actual fact is that the unions were in poor shape. This makes the above rationalization particularly dubious.

This absence of contested elections combined with the material to be presented in the following section would seem to indicate that the union officialdom and the Communist Party were in actual control of the union movement far more than was the membership.

THE PROBLEM OF ISOLATION FROM THE MEMBERSHIP: It would appear that the absence of control by the membership has had highly dysfunctional effects from the Soviet viewpoint on the work of the unions. It has seriously weakened the degree of member participation in their activities.

In May, 1935, Stalin pointed out to the leaders of the Central Council of the Trade Unions that the whole union movement was passing through a most serious crisis. The rank-and-file membership are dissatisfied with the unions, he said, and see no prospect of change. The average worker is even beginning to wonder, he declared, whether trade unions are necessary at all in the Soviet Union.[129]

All this, Stalin declared, was a result of the lack of democracy within the trade unions and of the rigidity of the union leadership in not altering their program with the times. They were continuing the policy of the First Five-Year Plan of bending all efforts towards rapid industrialization, and did not realize that a situation making possible higher living standards had been achieved. In the

[127] *Ibid.*, pp. 54-55.
[128] *Ibid.*
[129] Stalin's remarks as described by V. Polonskii, a secretary of the VTsSPS, at a meeting on November 18, 1935. (Polonskii, *op. cit.*, pp. 20-21.) See also, N. Evreinov, "O svoeobraznom krizise professional'nykh soiuzov" (On the Singular Crisis of the Trade Unions), *Vopr. Profdvizh.*, 1935, No. 11-12, pp. 7-11.

new circumstances, Stalin noted, the basis of union activity should be the working out of questions of improving cultural life and material well-being.[130]

It would seem that we would be justified in blaming this crisis on the absence of membership control over the union organs. Clearly the rank and file were not unwilling to have more stress placed on clubs, social insurance benefits, sanitariums, etc. In fact, it was precisely their demands for these benefits, and the union leaders' lack of response, which created the threat to the union and Party movement.

In June, 1938, the unions took an important step favoring their members' interests. The chief secretary of the Central Council of the Trade Unions announced that the unions were beginning to take part in the setting of work norms and piece rates. In the absence of union supervision, management had often set piece rates arbitrarily and too low. But, the union secretary admitted, the trade unions had done nothing to protect their members until now, when the Economic Council attached to the Council of Commissars had demanded that they engage in such activity.[131] In June, 1938, following the lead of higher authorities, the Central Council of the Trade Unions ordered the establishment of workers' commissions in the plants to supervise norm-setting by management and to make suggestions to management.[132] The union leadership, unresponsive to their members' wishes, could apparently be moved into new actions only by pressure from top Party and Government leaders.

THE WEAK CONDITION OF THE UNIONS: While it is extremely difficult to evaluate the success achieved by the Soviet trade unions in carrying out their functions, it would appear that their accomplishments were not impressive. This conclusion is based on the material presented above and on official reports of top union leaders and decrees of top union bodies.[133]

[130] *Ibid.*
[131] N. M. Shvernik, Reworked Stenographic Report of June 1, 1938, to a conference of officials and employees of trade-union central committees, in *Profsoiuzy SSSR,* 1938, No. 12, pp. 13-16.
[132] Statute approved by the Presidium of the VTsSPS on June 23, 1938, *BFKhZ,* 1938, No. 25.
[133] Cf. Post. of the VIth Plenum of the VTsSPS, *Postanovleniia plenumov VTsSPS,*

The weakness of the unions caused them to face great difficulties in obtaining and retaining able leadership personnel. The existence of poor leadership, in turn, acted to prevent improvement of union work. During the prewar period, the Soviet unions seem to have been unable to break out of this vicious circle.

In May, 1935, Stalin declared that many people objected to going into trade-union work, considering it of second- and third-rate importance.[134] The head of the Organizational Sector of the Central Council of the Trade Unions, in explaining why there had been a 70 percent turnover of the members of factory and local union committees in the 1939 elections, declared that it was mainly because the former committee members had grown in personal stature and had advanced into Government and economic work.[135] From this, it would appear that mainly those unfit for more "important" work remained in the union leadership, and that the more capable personnel went on to other jobs.

All this causes me to believe that the unions have not exerted major influence upon the policies of plant management. While the plant union committees may have played an important role in protecting workers from illegal and unusual practices on the part of individual managements, they do not seem to have interfered with the one-man-authority-and-responsibility of management in anything like the fashion of the Party plant committees.

CONCLUDING STATEMENT ON THE TRADE UNIONS: The difficulties which have plagued the Soviet trade-union movement appear to me to point up a basic problem implicit in the Soviet desire to employ widespread worker participation for carrying out policies determined by the Party leadership.

Enlisting mass participation is a difficult task under any circum-

pp. 117-23. Shvernik, Report to the VIth Plenum of the VTsSPS, *Vopr. Profdvizh.*, 1937, No. 9-10, pp. 27-28. Shvernik, Report to the VIIth Plenum of the VTsSPS, *Profsoiuzy SSSR*, 1938, No. 13, pp. 26-34. Shvernik, Report to the VIIIth Plenum of the VTsSPS, *Profsoiuzy SSSR*, 1939, No. 5, pp. 23-24. Shvernik, Reworked Stenographic Report to the Xth Plenum of the VTsSPS, *Part. Stroit.*, 1940, No. 15-16, pp. 8-14. Post. of the XIth Plenum of the VTsSPS of April 4, 1941, in *O zarabotnoi plate sluzhashchikh*, p. 8. The cited reports appear to me to go far beyond the usual limits of the Soviet "self-criticism" which is used to improve an organization that is still working in what is considered to be a generally healthy fashion.

[134] Polonskii, *op. cit.*, p. 21.
[135] M. Stepanov, *op. cit.*, p. 56.

stances. The automatic response of "let George do it" seems to be as typically Russian as it is American. But the Soviet leaders have created for themselves an additional major obstacle.

All mass organizations are expected to be guided by the Party units existing within them and by the Party programs. If the membership pushes for another policy, it is the duty of the leadership of their mass organization to educate them to the "wisdom" of the Party program.

But the Party cannot fulfill its role as coordinator of all elements in Soviet society without opposing the special interests of individual groups. In the case of the trade unions specifically, the Party policy has given primary stress to their servicing worker needs only during the period of the New Economic Policy before 1928 and in the relatively crisis-free years of 1935-38.

The trade-union dilemma arises from this fact. For while the trade unions represent the special interests of the industrial workers of their industries, they are guided by a policy which is oriented around national considerations as determined by top national leadership. Yet it is the special interests of industrial workers which can most easily be made into a major impetus for arousing mass worker participation. The separation between these special interests and national policies would seem to have been sharply accentuated by the extremely ambitious over-all Soviet program for investment and military preparedness.

CONCLUDING REMARKS

The strong emphasis placed upon mass participation by Soviet leaders stems essentially from their conception of administrative problems as being primarily political rather than technical.

The stress on mass participation and supervision is designed to maintain worker influence over plant management. The basic argument in favor of this influence rests, of course, on a conception of the function of management—that it does not perform a purely technical role. There is also a subsidiary postulate behind this policy—that management should react to each problem which confronts it by making an evaluation based on all the peculiar details of the local situation, rather than by classifying the situation under one or more general rules given to it by higher authorities. From this postulate, Soviet thinkers have drawn the conclusion that worker suggestions and supervision are bound to keep management closer to concrete reality than it would otherwise be, and thus immeasurably help it to formulate and execute correct decisions.

The Soviet leaders further lay great stress on the recruitment of leadership personnel from the rank-and-file workers and treat the advancement of workers as a major form of participation. Aside from the political and moral reasons for this policy, it is founded upon the belief that such a source of recruitment helps to keep administrators close to concrete industrial problems and to the psychology of their workers.

However, participation offers two difficulties. It may degenerate into unproductive and time-consuming conferences which are insufficiently fruitful to warrant the necessary effort. Secondly, worker participation may get out of hand and be directed towards goals not in line with those of the top national leadership.

The dysfunctional elements of participation, like those of Communist Party influence, have been combated at the expense of weakening the functional characteristics.

Thus the type of participation most developed has been that of the outstanding "actives." It has been hoped that in this way fruitless discussion would be reduced to a minimum. Even such participation, however, seems often to have been slighted by management when it thought it politically feasible to do so.

To meet the problem of participation pushing forward goals undesirable to the national leadership, the doctrine of Party guidance has been employed. It would appear, however, that this "solution" sharply reduced the degree of participation which could be mustered.

All in all, it can be said that the Soviet emphasis on mass participation has met certain problems of administration, but in turn has created new ones. A rather middle-of-the-road policy has been followed, one which does not sacrifice overmuch for the sake of developing worker participation. Such a policy has not succeeded in making participation into the powerful tool which Soviet leaders would like it to be.

XIV: Conclusion

STRENGTHS AND WEAKNESSES OF SOVIET ADMINISTRATION

NON-SOVIET WRITERS have frequently described Soviet industry as being operated in a highly bureaucratic fashion. They have declared that a major weakness of the Soviet economy is its vast increase in bureaucracy over that prevailing in capitalist countries.

Western sociologists have widely used the term bureaucracy to mean the "formal, organized social structure" idealized in Max Weber's model of bureaucratic structure.[1] If we adopt this usage of the term, then it appears an open question whether Soviet industry is not, to the contrary, less bureaucratic than are most giant firms in capitalist society.[2] Sociologists write of "the trend towards increasing bureaucratization in Western Society, which Weber had

---

[1] R. K. Merton, *Social Theory and Social Structure* (Chicago: 1949), p. 151. (This model will be described below.)

[2] Usually, of course, bureaucracy as applied to the Soviet Union refers solely to the dysfunctional features. While these exist in considerable plenitude in Soviet industrial administration, we are concerned here with a system of operation in which these elements are inevitably contained along with functional elements. Sometimes the Soviet Union appears to be described as highly bureaucratic solely because of the immense proportion of the population which works in establishments owned by the Government. The term "bureaucracy" is used synonymously with planned and centralized control over the economy as opposed to the regulation of production and distribution through the market and the pricing system. Such a use of the concept of "bureaucracy," however, seems to lead to confusion. This is best indicated by the fact that some of the disadvantages of Soviet administration which arise from their very rejection of the bureaucratic pattern as it is described by Western sociologists are nevertheless ascribed to "Soviet bureaucracy." For such a description of bureaucracy, cf. Barrington Moore, Jr., *Soviet Politics—The Dilemma of Power* (Cambridge, Mass.: 1950), Chapter XII and especially pp. 295-97. The question of planning versus market control over allocation of resources is a most important one and certainly deserves attention. But to discuss it under the subject-heading of "bureaucracy" leads to the befuddlement of the issues traditionally handled under this term.

long since foreseen. . . ."[3] In the light of the material presented throughout this study, it does not seem that we can definitely point to a like trend as existing in Soviet industry.[4]

In fact, it is precisely in its antibureaucratic development that major strengths and weaknesses of Soviet industrial administration can be found. A comparison with the functional and dysfunctional elements of the Weberian model of bureaucracy may be most helpful in bringing forth the linked advantages and disadvantages of the Soviet administrative system. For Soviet administrators, like those in other countries, have striven for the virtues of bureaucracy without its evils. Where Soviet administration has sharply deviated from the behavior patterns idealized by Weber, the costs and gains of this approach can be understood most clearly in terms of Weber's model.

WEBERIAN MODEL OF BUREAUCRACY:[5] Bureaucratic structure is conceived as designed for "rationality" and efficient administration. The ideal toward which it tends is one of policy making at the top with the rapid and accurate implementation of policies by all lower strata of officialdom. The bureaucrat is represented as a technician and organizer. He is an "expert"—prepared to carry out any program presented to him.

The bureaucracy is organized hierarchically and in a highly formalized fashion, each member having carefully delineated functions which go with his post. An official's actions are governed by general but clearly defined rules; his task is to break down each case coming before him into elements which fall under the appro-

---

[3] Merton, *op. cit.*, p. 159.

[4] Bienstock, however, finds the Soviet system of promotion and demotion "reminiscent of civil-service rules and customs in other countries or, better, of an army." (G. Bienstock, S. M. Schwarz, and A. Yugow, *Management in Russian Industry and Agriculture* [London, New York, Toronto: 1944], p. 92.)

[5] Its first basic presentation was worked out by Max Weber. See *From Max Weber: Essays in Sociology*, translated and edited by H. H. Gerth and C. Wright Mills (New York: 1946), Chapter VIII. A sharper treatment with a working out of the dysfunctions of bureaucracy is in Merton, *op. cit.*, Chapter V.

In order to bring forth most sharply the differences between Weber's concept of bureaucracy and Soviet administrative practice, I somewhat exaggerate Weber's analysis of the features of bureaucracy. I employ sharper blacks and whites than he did so that in this way there may be set up a more clear-cut model against which to examine Soviet administration. This action seems to me to be in line with Weber's own purpose in developing his picture of the "ideal" bureaucratic type.

priate regulations. He does not look at a question roundly and consider how in his view it should best be treated; rather, he picks out the salient features of the question, categorizes them according to the rules, and acts accordingly.

Bureaucracy is geared to efficiency; its virtues are those making for smooth and speedy functioning of the administrative machine along the lines determined by its heads. The relevant functional aspects of the model are as follows.

1. Actions of all officials are predictable. So long as he is technically competent, it does not matter which individual holds a given post and makes a particular decision; any other person in the same office would resolve the question similarly. For no decision is "arbitrary" in the sense of being given on the basis of the judge's personal evaluation; it is made on the basis of rules.

2. Since lower officials are not policy makers, they do not make independent decisions. Centrally determined policy is carried out, rather than being pondered by executives with power to ignore or alter it.

3. Duties in the bureaucracy are shared among different people so that the greatest advantage can be taken of division of labor. Each official can employ his own special knowledge in applying rules, since he is not required to consider all the aspects of cases presented to him. It is only those officials who draw up the general rules who must make evaluative decisions; personnel with the broadest ability can be concentrated at this level.

4. Decisions are made rapidly since they are only a matter of applying rules. Similarly, supervision by higher officials is relatively easy; they need not evaluate the quality of decisions, but only the degree to which they conform to regulations.

5. The effect of personalized relationships between officials is eliminated as a major factor in their work. Duties and authority reside in the office—not in the man who temporarily fills it.

6. Similarly, appointment and advancement are determined by objective criteria rather than by personal influence. Objective examinations and rating systems are used; these essentially test for "expertism."

However, the very features which make for the efficiency of the bureaucratic model have their reverse, dysfunctional side. The weaknesses which they create are as follows.

1. Questions are not studied individually in all their ramifications. Rather, they are treated as combinations of major features, the treatment of each of which is prescribed in specific regulations. The result is that cases are handled according to "rule," although the result may be quite contrary to common sense and to the needs of the given situation. The public's complaints of "bureaucracy" revolve to a considerable extent around this aspect.

2. It is only by going through channels—often a slow and laborious process—that ideas of lower officials can be put into practice. Since these officials are in touch with the concrete problems, they are in a position to work out new approaches which would be helpful. But they cannot use these concepts on their own authority; they can only make suggestions to their superiors, hoping that at some higher level of the bureaucracy their ideas will be incorporated into the general rules. Thus initiative is stifled. Adoption of new major ideas is, at best, delayed for long periods; minor changes are lost because they are not worth the effort required to push them through to the upper levels of the bureaucracy.

3. The result of these two weaknesses is that the bureaucratic system can neither rapidly adjust to changes in the tasks confronting it, nor quickly improve methods of handling old tasks. It is conservative, bound by precedent and rule.

4. The masses outside of the bureaucracy cannot directly influence the work of lower officials. They may help determine the general rules—for even in a dictatorship, regulations will normally be designed with an eye to popularity if this does not cause them to conflict with the goals of the top leaders. But the populace cannot have a direct effect upon the actions and decisions of lower bureaucrats. Since these bureaucrats are technicians whose task it is to apply rules, clearly, there is no place for "outsiders" to influence specific decisions. Thus the bureaucracy becomes divorced from the population and may unwittingly use highly unpopular methods; in addition, the creative ideas of those outside the bureaucracy are totally inaccessible to officialdom.

5. In order to protect officials from being dismissed or kept from

advancement by superiors because of personal animosity, their tenure is secured and promotion tends to be made according to seniority. But this freezes inefficient bureaucrats in their posts and even leads to their rising automatically in the hierarchy as they grow older. Talent is thereby held down; the higher officials are all older men. The enthusiasm and fresh conceptions of youth are prevented from exerting much influence upon policy.

The value of this model of bureaucratic structure may be interpreted as not depending upon the accuracy with which it depicts any specific administrative system, but rather as lying in its usefulness as a pattern within which to organize data, as a "searchlight" for guiding the study of concrete situations. The model presents an extreme of theoretic behavior unrealizable in the real world. It is not a normative model, for its dysfunctional aspects are considered to be of great importance. It contains highly functional elements, valuable for the efficient operation of an administrative apparatus, combined with extremely harmful and dysfunctional characteristics. Its weaknesses and strengths are presented as reverse sides of the same coin—and as equally inseparable.

AN EXAMINATION OF SOVIET ADMINISTRATIVE PRINCIPLES IN THE LIGHT OF THE WEBERIAN MODEL OF BUREAUCRACY: If we think of Soviet administrative principles as embodied in an idealized model, its advantages over the Weberian model would be the following. Problems are studied concretely and handled in terms of all their individual features rather than according to the rules under which they fall. Changes in existing methods can be made rapidly, with executives at all levels introducing new ideas on their own responsibility. The administrative system is not conservative, but rather is able to reflect rapidly changing conditions and new and better conceptions of how to handle old problems. A high proportion of the executives are youthful, and it is most difficult for an inefficient or hidebound official to retain his post and rise through seniority. The workers outside the administration are encouraged to criticize and make suggestions, efforts are made to insure that their reactions directly affect the work of those firm executives with whom they are in contact, and the type of *esprit de corps* which is intended to protect functionaries from the criticism of nonofficials is strongly condemned.

But these advantages are bought by serious lapses from the standards of Weber's model. Since no fixed rules govern their decisions, officials at all levels become policy makers. Their actions cease to be predictable, and are "arbitrary" in the sense that another individual would act differently in the same job. There are no clear-cut criteria for judging the success of executives, even after the results of their decisions have become known. The abandonment of functional organization of administration, and of decision making through the application of rules, sacrifices division of labor. Likewise, since a new decision is required for each case, speed of decision making is sharply reduced. Particularly with the overlapping of functions, authority is divided and resides in the man rather than solely in the post he holds. Thus, personal relations become of major importance in determining the scope of an executive's authority. Moreover, with the elimination of fixed criteria and examinations for promotion, advancement by personal influence becomes a serious problem. The encouragement of worker participation presents the danger of its running out of hand and of striving for goals contrary to those of the national leadership. Participation may also prove extremely wasteful of the time and efforts of all involved.

The Soviet leaders have made strenuous efforts to overcome the dysfunctional implications of their methods of administering industry.

Their stress upon initiative, and on over-all evaluation of problems by executives on all levels, has been accompanied by the absence of any single criterion of success. The resulting difficulties have been countered by placing emphasis upon "business accounting," thus setting up the composite criterion of monetary success, although never allowing it to replace or even dominate the other criteria (such as quantity of production) which are contained within it.

While "over-all success" has been the usual test for a manager, relatively minor rules have on occasion been strictly enforced. Selective enforcement of the formal rules under which management operates has served to keep them alive and in the consciousness of executives. Thus, while most rules could generally be broken with impunity by a "successful" management, on occasion swift punishment would follow even a minor transgression.

The strains involved in the "arbitrariness" of decisions by lower officials have been eased through labeling all policy decisions as "political" and giving the Communist Party bodies the right to supervise and influence the making of such decisions. By doing this, it has been hoped to develop a common policy throughout the economy. But in practice, this approach has led to division of authority over industrial operations between plant executives and Party units. As a result of the problems arising from this division, Party control has been restrained and tempered with respect for the industrial executives' own authority.

Finally, the time-wasting aspects of mass participation are countered by concentrating on the active participation of only the "best" employees. The risk of mass participation moving into unwanted channels has been combated by organizing all participation around Party leadership. This last, however, seems to have had the effect of reducing the participation which can be mustered.

Thus it can be seen that in their need for retaining, so far as is possible, functional elements contained in Weberian bureaucracy, the Soviet leaders have had to compromise in their attempts to root out the dysfunctional elements. The practical results demanded of officials have often compelled them to rely on methods of Weberian "bureaucratic efficiency" and to ignore the administrative standards established in Party theory. It is to this practical need for compromise with bureaucracy that I ascribe the continuous presence of bureaucratic malpractices in Soviet industry, despite their incessant condemnation from all sides.[6]

SOVIET THEORETIC TREATMENT OF BUREAUCRACY: It is interesting

[6] An example is the treatment of disputes between firms of the same glavk. Such disputes are supposed to be resolved by the head of the glavk personally. However, in most cases the glavki heads have given the task to arbitrators whom they appoint. This delegation of authority has been roundly condemned by the commissariats, which have demanded its cessation. Nevertheless, it has continued unabated. The reason would appear to be that the glavki heads have to allocate authority if they are to function at all. See *Mash.*, October 18, 1937, p. 1. M. El'evich, "Razreshenie sporov khozorganov, vkhodiashchikh v odin glavk" (Deciding Disputes Between Economic Organs within the Same Glavk), *Arbitrazh*, 1939, No. 5, pp. 20-21.

to note that Soviet thinkers, to the best of my knowledge, have not analyzed in books or articles published after the twenties the reasons for the continuance of bureaucratic malpractices in Soviet society. There has been no development of the thought that dysfunctional aspects of administration are related to functional characteristics.

Instead, bureaucracy has been painted in relatively simple terms. To the Soviet writer, it is purely a negative feature of administration. Its essential characteristics have been seen as the isolation of officials from the thinking of their employees and from the concrete problems of the organizations they head, and as resulting in their lack of initiative and their satisfaction with "tried and trusted" methods. The obstacles to the destruction of bureaucracy are considered great, but they are viewed as lying in individual personality failures and in the apathy which holds back efficient "control from below" as well as "control from above."

I have come across only two cases where bureaucratic malpractices were explained as inevitable accompaniments of measures required at the time. It is exceedingly interesting that in both these cases the conditions which had necessitated bureaucratic behavior were considered by the speakers to have already disappeared.

At the Party Congress of 1934 which ordered the elimination of functional administration in industry (a form attacked as highly bureaucratic), a member of the Central Committee of the Communist Party who was also a high official in the Commissariat of Heavy Industry explained that functional organization had been previously necessary due to "the lack of people, the low cultural level of the existing cadre, the absence among them of experience in directing a complex economic structure. . . ."[7] Here the speaker clearly thought of functional and dysfunctional aspects as being inseparably linked, and considered it possible to eliminate the dysfunctional elements only when the functional characteristics were no longer required.

At the 1939 Party Congress, Politbureau candidate Zhdanov pointed to the method of mass purges within the Communist Party (the investigation of each Communist to determine his

[7] M. M. Kaganovich, Speech to the XVIIth Party Congress, in *Org. Uprav.,* 1934, No. 3, p. 5.

worthiness to remain a member) as encouraging bureaucracy. This encouragement consisted of the campaign nature of the purges (a great number of people had to be examined in a relatively short period), which required the establishment of a definite single standard by which to measure everyone. The pressure of the campaigns, he said, caused the violation of the principle of individual and differentiated judgment of people. Thus Zhdanov stated that no more mass purges of the Party should take place; yet he defended earlier purges as necessary at the time they occurred. It was only because the "cleansing" of the Party had been so thorough, he stated, that such campaigns could be avoided in the future.[8]

The failure to develop generally the concept of linked functional and dysfunctional aspects is particularly curious in that the exposure of "contradictions" throughout society is a basic dialectic method of Marxists. It has been authoritatively stated that contradictions exist in Soviet society as well as in all others.[9] It has been demanded of Soviet economists that they discover such theoretic contradictions through study of the practical experience of the Soviet economy. New generalizations, rather than illustrations of theoretic concepts already stated by Soviet leaders, have been insisted upon. But the demands have not been met.[10]

How can we explain this failure of Soviet economists to demonstrate the contradictions inherent in their industrial administration? My own guess is that it is primarily due to the Soviet feeling that one should not present officials with ready-made excuses for "bureaucratic" behavior. They should not be permitted to say: "Oh, that's not my fault! It's a result of the contradictions!"

It is in accord with this conception that only contradictions relating to the past history of Soviet administration have been exposed, and that only high-ranking Soviet leaders have assumed even this responsibility.

The apparent policy of presenting bureaucracy solely as an evil may in the short run be useful to the Soviet Union. But it seems a good example of the type of obstacle which has prevented Soviet

[8] A. Zhdanov, Report to the XVIIIth Party Congress, *Ind.*, March 21, 1939, p. 5.

[9] K. V. Ostrovitianov, "O zadachakh nauchno-issledovatel'skoi raboty v oblasti ekonomiki," p. 28.

[10] For a recent statement of this type from an authoritative Soviet source, cf. *ibid.*, pp. 27-28.

theoretic economists from doing work which is considered fruitful even by the Soviet leaders, and from developing theory which can be a guide to improved Soviet practice.[11]

SINGLE VS. MULTICRITERIA OF SUCCESS

We have seen that Soviet industry employs a complex system of multicriteria both for decision making and for evaluating the success of past actions. The problems of "arbitrariness" in decision making, and of wasted effort due to the need for separate solution of basically similar questions, have been expounded. We have studied the Soviet efforts to develop the common-denominator criterion of financial success, and their reluctance to lean on it too heavily to the disadvantage of its component criteria.

But we have still to face the question of why no satisfactory single criterion for decision making has been developed. This problem is of major consequence for our study not only for its own sake, but also because the independence of firm management has rested to a considerable extent upon the fact that higher authorities have been forced to leave management considerable leeway in interpreting the plans and relative priorities sent down from above. This has been the case because of the impossibility of developing any single unambiguous standard for management to use in making decisions.

In this section we shall examine the problem of why no single criterion has been set up. As we have seen earlier, firm managements have virtually no control over investment.[12] Thus decisions regarding this vital matter will be disregarded.[13] Our interest is in those decisions in which firm managements are directly involved as

[11] For a recent statement of such work deficiencies from an authoritative Soviet source, cf. *ibid.*, pp. 27-28.

[12] One might ask if directors do not play a large role in determining investment through their use of the director's fund and other sources of moneys which they can manipulate both legally and illegally. It is this writer's opinion that the sum total of deviations from planned investment which arise from such manipulations are of very minor importance.

[13] Since we are not concerned with investment, there is no need for entering into the controversy as to whether the Soviet use of the labor theory of value rather than the marginal utility theory of value leads to wrong decisions from the viewpoint of obtaining the maximum production from the minimum use of resources. (It has been suggested that, in any case, there is little basis for supposing that Soviet planners generally apply the labor theory of value in their investment decisions.) The issue of

participants, that is, questions of the proper amount and types of products to produce, the specific production methods to employ, and the proper choice between alternative inputs of labor, materials, and fuels.

If Soviet administrators could incorporate all economic operations into their plans, with such accuracy that success could be defined as 100 percent fulfillment of an organization's plan, then no further criterion for decision making would be necessary. However, it seems inherent in the very nature of planning that only the roughest approximations to this situation should be realizable. The reasons for this can be briefly summarized as follows.

1. The original plans are incomplete and imperfect expressions of the period's program as perceived by top authorities. Partially, this is because the details of the top leadership's goals have not been fully worked out. Partially, it is because the plans for the different elements of the economy are not fully consistent with one another.

2. There is imperfect execution of the plans. It seems inevitable that many individual firms should find either that they cannot fulfill all aspects of their plans or that they can fulfill all planned indices and, in addition, overfulfill some. Both types of cases would force changes in the plans of all the many organizations affected by the resultant alterations in conditions of supply, transportation, available labor, and demand for their own products. Even if there were over-all balance between under- and overfulfillment of plans, individual variations would compel that there be changes in regional planning.

3. In addition to imperfections in the planning process and in the execution of the plans, there is the factor of uncertainty in prognostications about future events. But assumptions regarding

whether the possible use of the labor theory of value leads to faulty investment decisions is essentially that of whether capital is overly concentrated in methods of production requiring heavy investments for long periods due to the fact that no interest is charged for the use of this capital. In the limited area where Soviet firm managements do decide on capital use, investment by them is only permissible if it is to be liquidated quickly and before interest, even if it were required, could become a serious factor. Cf. M. Zil'bershtein, "Kontrol' za vneplanovymi kapitalovlozheniiami" (Control over Nonplanned Capital Investment), *Kredit i Khorzraschët*, 1937, No. 19, p. 26. Circular No. 5398 of the State Bank of the USSR of May 22, 1939, *BFKhZ*, 1939, No. 17/18.

these events are needed both for determining the plan's objectives and for plotting its details. (Examples of such uncertain events are the value and specific importance of inventions which are implemented during the period, crop conditions, and international conditions causing reorientations of planning priorities.)

From this presentation of the difficulties involved in exact planning, I would conclude that plan fulfillment is not in itself a sufficient operational criterion of success. If a unitary criterion is to be used at all, it must be one of a different character.

A NON-SOVIET SOLUTION.[14] Oskar Lange has attempted to develop a theoretic scheme in which all factors involved in the evaluation of alternative measures for a socialist society are reduced to monetary terms.[15] In Lange's model of a socialist economy, plant management need only compare money costs with revenue to determine appropriate action.

In this model, accounting prices (which need not be identical with the prices paid by consumers) are set for all products by a Central Planning Board whose function is restricted to price fixing.[16] Each firm management is supposed to make its decisions regarding current production by applying the criterion of maximizing profit while paying for its factors of production and selling its products at the current centrally established prices.[17] If production of a given item turns out to be too low to meet the demand at that price, the Central Planning Board raises the price. This normally would simultaneously cut demand and increase the supply, thus making for an equilibrium between them. If the demand is below the supply, the price is cut.

Under Lange's Rules for managerial behavior, concrete deci-

[14]Cf. A. Bergson, "Socialist Economics," in *A Survey of Contemporary Economics,* edited by H. S. Ellis (Philadelphia-Toronto: 1948), pp. 412-48, for a rounded treatment of non-Soviet theory on the problems of evaluating alternatives in a socialist economy.

[15] O. Lange, "On the Economic Theory of Socialism," in *On the Economic Theory of Socialism,* edited by B. E. Lippincott (Minneapolis: 1938).

[16] Since we are not concerned with investment problems, Lange's proposals regarding their solution are not being considered here.

[17] More precisely, the two guiding principles are that the amount of production is to be determined by operating at the point where the marginal value of product equals its marginal cost, and that the amount of each factor of production to be used is decided in the same fashion.

sions as to current production are decentralized to the plant level. Yet the Central Planning Board keeps full control over the net effects of these decisions through its price-fixing and monetary powers. Prices, of course, are set in such a way as to realize the Central Planning Board's policies.[18] Thus the Central Planning Board sets policy and the plant managements execute it, and the managements are presented with a single criterion of success so long as they obey the Rules stated above. This criterion is: Will a given policy yield the greatest possible profit?[19]

WHY SOVIET LEADERS REJECT FINANCIAL RESULTS AS THE UNITARY CRITERION OF SUCCESS: We have seen that Soviet leaders seem to agree with Lange as to the importance of the problem of setting up criteria for evaluating alternative measures. They accept a considerable proportion of the decentralization of specific production decisions which his system allows. By stressing business accounting, they clearly have gone some distance along the path of having the national leadership guide current production policy by means of price-setting. But they have not gone very far along this last path, for they have retained all the physical indices of plan fulfillment and have refused to lay too great emphasis on financial criteria.

D. Chernomordik, dealing with problems of how to determine proper investment, seems to have expressed the prevailing Soviet attitude towards all economic decisions when he wrote "that even the best constructed coefficient cannot be the sole nor even one of the main criteria of effectiveness in a planned socialist economy, nor can it make possible the answering of the complex problems brought forth by reality. . . ."[20] Kozlov, expounding the lessons of Soviet experience, has stressed the dangers of overemphasizing busi-

[18] This policy may, but need not, be that production should follow consumer dictates.

[19] This statement of Lange's criterion is not entirely accurate. Lange recognizes that there will be firms and perhaps whole industries which, when they produce at the point where marginal cost equals marginal value of product, will have an average cost higher than the price at which they sell their product. But these are considered exceptional cases, and even for them any proposed measure can be evaluated by a unitary money test.

[20] D. Chernomordik, "Effektivnost' kapital'nykh vlozhenii i teoriia vosproizvodstva" (Effectiveness of Capital Investments and the Theory of Reproduction), *Voprosy Ekonomiki,* 1949, No. 6, p. 80.

ness accounting and thus bringing about neglect of quality, poor assortment of goods produced, etc.[21] *"The correct unity of business accounting and of the socialist plan is not self-created, does not arise automatically."*[22]

Let us examine critically the Lange model in order to develop some of the difficulties which would be involved in putting into practice in the Soviet economy any such scheme for determining appropriate action by financial considerations alone.[23] But first we must be clear as to the essential demand which any unifying criterion would have to meet. It would have to be an efficient expression of the planning priorities of the top authorities rather than of individual consumers or of firms purchasing industrial equipment and materials. Thus prices could not be set freely on the market, but would have to be determined by price-setting boards.[24]

There are, of course, numerous specific questions as to the practicality of Lange's model, just as there would be for any purely theoretic construction.[25] But far more important, there are serious objections to the entire concept of expressing central policies solely in price relationships.

One major objection lies in the fact that considerations of a multitude of Soviet policies enter into all specific decisions. To quote Chernomordik, Soviet theorists demand that questions should be decided "from principled political, class and national economic considerations rather than from narrowly one-sided economic conclusions."[26] The difficulties involved in reducing all pol-

[21] G. Kozlov, *Khoziaistvennyi raschët v sotsialisticheskom obshchestve* (Business Accounting in a Socialist Society), (Moscow-Leningrad: 1945), p. 14.

[22] *Ibid.* Italics in original.

[23] Soviet writers themselves have not dealt with the Lange model.

[24] The basic assumption here and in the following discussion is that the Lange model would be used within the framework of the Soviet conception of the direct function of a planned integration of the economy—the fulfillment of the detailed goals of top authorities.

[25] E.g., the difficulty in preventing plant managers from speculating as to price changes, and so producing goods and purchasing supplies at levels corresponding to the prices they expect to be announced soon rather than at levels determined by current prices. The problem of keeping managers of those plants which are in a monopolistic position from acting as do monopolists in capitalist society. The danger that when slopes of supply and demand functions for important products have low elasticities or are even negative, the price mechanism will achieve desired ends in a most slow and uncertain fashion.

[26] Chernomordik, *op. cit.,* p. 80.

icy questions into price terms can be seen from the following imaginary example.

A small machine-building plant is located in a relatively undeveloped national-minority area in the eastern interior of the USSR. The problem with which we are concerned is: What should be the plant's total production for the year and how should the quantitative relationship between the various machines produced be determined? In Lange's model, the plant management would decide these questions on the basis of prices set by the Central Planning Board. Many different factors would be weighed by the Planning Board when it sets these prices, and it would have to give each a valuation in price terms.[27] Some of the factors most difficult to handle in this fashion would be the following.

1. Since the factory is located in the interior, it would be well situated for production of machinery needed directly for defense. Its being small would be an advantage from the point of view of industrial dispersion for protection against air attack.

2. On the other hand, as the plant is in an undeveloped area, it would be fitting to use it for producing machinery needed in developing the region. Such production—as opposed to that of machinery for defense—would reduce cross-shipment of equipment by railroad in and out of the district.

3. Because the area is populated by a national minority, it would be in line with Soviet nationality policy to produce both as much machinery as possible and types requiring for their production the highest skills. The local inhabitants would be raised to a higher "cultural" level through learning complex skills in the plant.

4. However, the lack of existing skills among the local population might force the plant management to bring in people from other areas of the country to perform the most skilled jobs. Such a consequence of immediate increase in the amount and complexity of machinery produced would be harmful for at least two reasons. It would require the movement of a labor force with the resultant problems of housing, readjustment, etc. In addition, the use of outsiders for the most skilled work might prevent local peo-

[27] O. Lange, *op cit.*, pp. 103-8.

ple from moving up into these positions, as they might otherwise do in a few years after they had received the necessary training.

5. Transport facilities for the area are likely to be deficient. If metals must be shipped in from other districts, high machine production here would place a strain on existing transportation. Even if the machinery produced were to be used in the area, it would ease transportation difficulties if the plant produced at less than capacity and if machinery from other plants nearer to metal fabricators was shipped in. This might be allowed to continue while railroad construction was under way or until measures had been taken to reduce other transportation needs of the district.

6. Even if present requirements for machinery would dictate a given assortment and level of production, either or both might be considered inappropriate because of anticipated future needs. It might be expected that in the following year the plant would switch much of its production to another type of equipment which would then be required in the area. Because of this expectation, it might be held desirable for the plant to engage now in limited production of such machinery in order to solve the production problems involved and to be ready to produce efficiently and without breakdowns the following year.

At least theoretically, all of these policy considerations could be reduced into price terms by a Central Planning Board and its regional subdivisions.[28] But only a pricing system which accurately reflected the Central Planning Board's evaluation of the relative weights to be given to conflicting policy aims could serve as the sole guide to production. Yet such a system would require a price-setting apparatus of immense size. It would be this apparatus which would have to analyze the problems of each plant in order to set appropriate money figures for all the "social costs" and "social gains" of alternative decisions. If these policy matters were given serious consideration with regard to each plant's problems, the local price-setting boards would be taking over many of the present functions of the glavki and the commissariats. But their task would

[28] "Social costs" and "social gains" could be set up as accounting devices which all plant managements would be instructed to consider in determining both their marginal production costs and the revenues received for their products.

be far more difficult. Like the glavki and commissariats, they would have to determine the desirable policies for all plant managements to follow in their many fields of activity. But after they had completed this work, they would then have to begin to formulate a price policy for each plant which would motivate its management to act in the desired fashion.

In addition to this tremendous price-setting operation to be performed at the beginning of each planning period, a constant process of making revisions would be necessary. This would seem essential because of the inevitable imperfections of the original prices as an expression of the planners' objectives, and because of the probable need for the constant revision of the objectives themselves during at least the latter part of the periods.[29]

Even if "proper" prices could be set, it would be necessary for firm managements to be motivated to change production decisions promptly in "rational" accord with price changes. But there are considerable doubts as to the speed and effectiveness of any pricing system's influence upon production decisions by plant management. During the Second World War, for example, the governments of none of the major powers cared to risk doing without such direct controls as those of rationing and of priorities on materials for production. After the wartime experience, even such a confirmed prewar laissez-faire economist as Lionel Robbins[30] expressed the belief that a free pricing system could not have been a successful substitute for the British wartime direct economic controls.[31]

EVALUATION OF THE SOVIET MULTICRITERIA SYSTEM: In view of the above objections to applying a Lange-type scheme of decision by financial results to the Soviet economy, what can we say about the Soviet method of using many different criteria?

The English economist Maurice Dobb denies the existence of any serious difficulty in this practice. He maintains that a socialist economy—through the centralization of fundamental decisions af-

[29] Cf. the discussion on pp. 272-73.
[30] L. Robbins, *The Economic Problem in Peace and War* (London: 1947), p. 30 ff.
[31] Cf. Bergson, *op. cit.*, pp. 434-40, for a further treatment of difficulties involved in Lange's model.

fecting the whole country—establishes a rationality which is missing in capitalist society. Dobb sees no need for reducing problems requiring central decisions into terms of the common denominator of money; the elements can be analyzed individually and a decision made directly without first transposing them into a common value-form.[32] The ease of solution seems to rest, in his opinion, on the supposed fact that wide groups of choices are linked together, and that at any point of decision only a few sets of choices are possible.[33]

As to our problem of decentralized decisions made by firm managements, he implies that no difficulty in rational calculation exists. All factors can be expressed in price terms, and managements will make their decisions according to expected results as measured by the common denominator of money. Dobb gives the impression that he believes that in the Soviet Union the financial criterion is the basis for management decisions.[34] He does not, however, delve explicitly into the problem of how management makes its decisions when evaluation according to financial results would determine different actions than would evaluation by some other standard of plan fulfillment (e.g., product quality).

From this statement of Dobb's position, the reader will see that his analysis is of no aid in dealing with our problem. For we are concerned only with decision making on the plant management level. But Dobb, essentially interested in central planning, is ambiguous on this point. If he believes that both "plan fulfillment" and financial success are relevant standards to use, then he offers no help in showing how management should deal with the multiplicity of resulting criteria. His analysis of how various considerations can be handled without translation into the common denominator of money applies only to the problems confronting central authorities. If, on the other hand, he believes that management should use the unitary criterion of financial success, his position with regard to our problem is essentially the same as Lange's. The fact that he may erroneously believe that this is also the Soviet position is irrelevant.

Ludwig von Mises and Frederick A. von Hayek have taken an

[32] M. Dobb, *Political Economy and Capitalism* (New York: 1937), pp. 304-7.

[33] Dobb, *Soviet Economic Development Since 1917* (London: 1948), pp. 4-6.

[34] Dobb, *Political Economy*, pp. 307-8, and *Soviet Economic Development*, pp. 32-33.

opposite position, arguing that no socialist state can in practice solve the problem of rationally evaluating alternatives. Since there are no private businessmen competing with each other for the factors of production (labor, materials, and fuels in the cases we are considering), they declare that these factors cannot be evaluated with respect to each other. They cannot be reduced to a common money price, and so "in a socialist commonwealth . . . money can play no role in economic calculation."[35] A "decision [between alternatives] would depend at best upon vague estimates; it would never be based upon the foundation of an exact calculation of value."[36] "Thus in the socialist commonwealth every economic change becomes an undertaking whose success can be neither appraised in advance nor later retrospectively determined. . . . Socialism is the abolition of rational economy."[37]

If we interpret Hayek's and Mises' statements in the narrowly economic sense, and without the implications which they themselves attach, I would say that Soviet experience bears out their views. This is the case when we define "rational calculation" as meaning only a system of exact numerical balancing of gains and losses involved in alternative decisions, and a balancing process which is conducted scientifically in the sense that rules can be established for it.

The Soviet use of multicriteria in judging success implies a priority system. If management is to use its own discretion in determining which criteria have the greatest relative importance for it at the moment, then it must be guided by priorities set forth by higher bodies. This, indeed, is what happens in Soviet industry; the priority method of decision making fills a major niche in the evaluation of the success of management. Where analysis through the method of "plan fulfillment" ends, analysis according to the rule of "achievement of priorities" comes in to round out the picture. In present Soviet methodology, the two are inseparable.

But as we have seen throughout this study, decision making according to priorities leaves a considerable element of "arbitrari-

[35] L. von Mises, "Economic Calculation in the Socialist Commonwealth," *Collectivist Economic Planning*, edited by F. A. von Hayek (London: 1935), pp. 107-8.
[36] *Ibid.*, p. 109.
[37] *Ibid.*, p. 110.

ness" in managerial decisions. Different managers in the same position would interpret the priorities differently. No firm's production is completely geared to a balanced economic plan for the entire country.

This system of making decisions according to priorities seems analogous to the "storming" methods which at one time were accepted within Soviet plants. These methods involved meeting quarterly and annual production quotas by the concentration of work into the last weeks and days of the period. Plan fulfillment was achieved through extensive overtime work, exhaustion of stocks of materials and semifabricates, and general disruption of production scheduling. In 1931 "storming" was still sufficiently accepted in the Soviet Union so that a plant representative at an all-Union conference could proudly describe the work of his plant in 1930 as having contained a "storming quarter."[38] But by 1936 this pride in "storming" was considered as a queer reflection of the primitive methods of the past.[39]

Just as "storming" was the precursor of "scheduling" within a plant, it may be that Soviet decision making through evaluation of a problem in terms of many criteria should be considered as a primitive form of the Soviet interfirm planning of the future. On the other hand, it seems quite possible that no satisfactory method will be devised for eliminating the element of "arbitrariness" in managerial decisions.

It is my view that only future events can show which conception of Soviet planning is more correct. It would be rash indeed to predict that advances in planning methodology will never be so great as to permit the Soviet planning system to shift over to the exclusive use of the single criterion of profitability. Furthermore, it is quite likely that with time the rapidity of the changes in the structure of the Soviet economy and society will lessen. Such an occurrence would tend to reduce the difficulty of the task to be performed by the pricing system, and thus might make complete reliance upon it more practicable.

[38] Proshin, representative of the Kol'chuginskii Plant, at the First All-Union Conference of Employees of Socialist Industry held from January 30 through February 5, 1931. (*Z.I.*, February 4, 1936, p. 4.)
[39] *Z.I.*, February 4, 1936, p. 4.

At the same time, it should be recognized that no economy has ever developed a pricing system designed to meet the requirements which would be demanded of the type of single-criterion system we are discussing.

In a freely functioning capitalist economy, the pricing system has an important but still a limited function. Its task is that of giving force to the principle of "consumers' sovereignty," expressed against the backdrop of relative supply schedules for the various goods. The supply and demand elements of the market express themselves in relative prices in such a way that production represents the relative strengths of consumers' desires[40] for the different individual products.[41]

But a pricing system which expresses only "consumers' sovereignty" in this narrow sense has grave limitations. It has no place for the consideration of external economies and diseconomies which affect consumers as a group rather than as individuals. Nor is it capable of expressing the preferences of society acting as a whole, for it is limited to the expression of individual desires.

Soviet administration has failed to make prices express the national leadership's criteria of decision making. In capitalist countries, too, the system of free prices has generally been abandoned when national goals have been given priority over those of individuals; price control, rationing, and materials allocations have taken over. More normally, under capitalism, the pricing system has been eliminated in those sectors of the economy over which the government has control and whose products it has then distributed free of charge (e.g., the school system and police protection).

It may indeed be that the price system is not a sufficiently powerful tool for the expression of all the conflicting goals of any national administration, that no administration could in practice determine relative prices so that they could be a satisfactory representation of the relative weights it placed upon the importance of

[40] The preferences of different consumers do not have equal weight. They are, of course, weighted in proportion to the amount of money which each has to spend.

[41] This conception is highly idealized. For example, it ignores the very major extent to which consumers' desires are created through advertising, copying of neighbors, etc., after the products have already been manufactured.

different products. When a pricing system is given a more complex task than the unitary one of epitomizing "consumers' sovereignty," any form of government might well find it inadequate for use alone.[42]

As shown in this discussion, there appears to me to be a strong likelihood that the present Soviet "priority" concept will never be replaced by any single-criterion supplement to the "plan-fulfillment" test. Irrespective of future developments, however, it should be pointed out that one cannot correctly draw the conclusion from Soviet inability to "calculate rationally" (in the sense of calculating in terms of a single criterion), that capitalism is a more efficient type of economy than is that of the Soviet Union.[43] It is true that private businessmen seem to have, in a freely operating capitalist economy, a single criterion for their decisions—the expected rate of return.[44] But rational calculation should mean more than the ability to decide questions by a unitary criterion; it should also mean that the criterion is an appropriate one. Socialists, of course, would argue that the profit criterion is totally inappropriate from a social standpoint. "Welfare economists" would also reject the idea that it is completely appropriate. Monopolistic features and the existence of external economies and diseconomies mar its perfection. So do social gains and losses which do not affect individual profits.[45] So does the need for uncoordinated guesses by businessmen as to the future in cases where their actions will collectively determine that same future about which they are individually making forecasts.

Thus the absence of "rational calculation" in the Soviet economy can only be taken as one factor in the argument as to the greater efficiency of the socialist or the capitalist economic system. It may well be that no economic system can realize a procedure of "rational calculation" in terms of national interest comparable to a plant management's calculations in terms of the "efficient operation" of its plant.

[42] For this idea I am indebted to a suggestion of Professor Arthur R. Burns.
[43] Cf. F. A. von Hayek, "The Nature and History of the Problem," *Collectivist Economic Planning*, pp. 36-37, for such a conclusion.
[44] For a discussion of this point, cf. Chapter IX, footnote 1.
[45] Pigou's factory smoke case.

THE POLITICAL NATURE OF DECISIONS MADE BY INDUSTRIAL EXECUTIVES

We have not yet examined the validity of the Soviet position that in their system all important economic decisions are basically political, and that therefore all industrial executives must orient their professional thinking on the job in political terms.

This conception is of fundamental importance to an understanding of the Soviet economy. Clearly it runs directly counter to the traditional view in capitalist countries that plant managers are essentially technicians who should be able to carry out efficiently any program given them. It is of basic significance to the position of those socialists who wish to employ Soviet economic methods without adopting a one-party political system and without placing any party in a position to guide all developments in the society.

In my opinion, there are two arguments which might tend to support the Soviet conception that their plant executives must be politically oriented if they are to function in the way desired by the national leadership.

The first argument rests on the absence of any unitary criterion for decision making. Executives on all levels must solve problems in terms of a number of standards which are often in conflict. There are no fixed rules by which they can give appropriate weights to the different standards. Thus their problem is not simply that of deciding on the best way to realize a given objective, but it is rather that of weighing the relative importance of conflicting goals of action.

It seems to me that a manager who does not inwardly accept the Party position as to the needs of the moment could not successfully carry out such an evaluation task. For he could not simply take the Party goals as "given" factors, and apply them to his specific problem. His understanding of their relative significance and of the orientation lying behind them would have to be as close as possible to that of the top national leadership which has set forth these goals. Only in this fashion could his application of the many criteria to his specific problem be similar to the type of application intended by the top leadership.

The second argument regards the need for what Soviet writers call "Bolshevik tempering." A Soviet plant executive is in a difficult position with relation to the employees under him. On the one hand, he is supposed to be an organizer of mass participation, a leader who orients his own work around the creative initiative of his workers and who actively brings forth this initiative. On the other hand, he represents and must enforce "Soviet discipline." There is no place for the executive who curries favor with "undisciplined" employees when he should be punishing them. It is the executive who must raise work norms and cut piece rates. It is he who must enforce laws making punishable lateness for work or unjustifiable absences.

Clearly the industrial executive who can come "close to the masses" and yet enforce "Soviet discipline" on these same masses, requires a high degree of "Bolshevik tempering." It seems reasonable to suppose that the executive who wholeheartedly accepts the ideas of the national leadership that both practices are necessary—and in the forms in which they are laid down—will be far more successful in carrying out his tasks than will the executive who simply accepts them as "given" factors in his problem of personally succeeding in his post.

THE SOVIET DIRECTOR AS ENTREPRENEUR

Throughout this study, we have seen the great powers granted to directors and the considerable autonomy left to them. From the point of view of practical independence in making concrete decisions, the Soviet director may be conceived of as an entrepreneur.

But the director's entrepreneurial activity is restricted to one field—that of developing better methods for carrying out the existing Party line. The successful director must look at his work with the eyes of the Politbureau, so far as possible interpreting his problems in the same way that Stalin would. The guide to his entrepreneurial activity must still be, in Commissar Ordzhonikidze's words, "Party activity and belief—above all and before all!"

Appendices

Appendix A: Significance of the Reorganization of the Administrative Structure of Industry

IN CHAPTER II we described the reorganization of glavki and commissariats and the creation of the Economic Council which took place during the thirties. However, we did not try to analyze this entire reorganizational process in terms of what was actually changed thereby.

Soviet leaders declare that the advantage of the reorganization was that it created more specialized glavki and commissariats able to get closer to the problems of individual production units.[1] But might we not consider that the former trusts graduated to the status of glavki, the glavki to that of commissariats, and the commissariats to that of the Economic Council attached to the Council of Commissars? Overall promotion by itself does not indicate genuine change.

I think our question should be answered in two ways. In so far as the new system brought general promotion, it involved a certain increase in the powers of the different intermediary organs. For the head of a glavk can exert more influence than the leader of a trust.[2]

A second and more important result of the reorganization was greatly to extend the collegium (group) system of administration and decision making.

As was seen above in the text of Chapter II, Stalin himself has pointed out the great advantages inherent in decision making by collegia. But despite this high evaluation of collegia, their use in Soviet industry has been very limited. It has been felt that they prevent clear

[1] Cf. V. Molotov's concluding remarks of March 17, 1939, to the XVIIIth Party Congress, *Problemy Ekonomiki*, 1939, No. 3, p. 78.

[2] Soviet observance of this principle can be seen in the 1940 elimination of some glavki rather than of trusts, and in the placing of the trusts themselves directly under the commissariats. This was done where the trusts were composed of many small firms. (Venediktov, *Gosudarstvennaia sotsialisticheskaia sobstvennost'*, p. 729.) In this way, one intermediate link was removed without giving the remaining one higher status than it was felt to deserve.

allocation of responsibility and authority, and thus that efficiency in the day-to-day leadership of an organization is lost beneath the feet of its many leaders. It is for this reason, that economic bodies through the rank of commissariat have been headed by a single individual.

The Economic Council, formed as a result of the reorganization of the commissariats, has been considered as in a different position. Since it supervises the whole economy, and not just a single sector of industry, its work has been judged as too multisided for any single man to master and direct. Thus it has been organized on the collegium system and its decisions have been those of the group. The nearest approach to this within the commissariats has been a system of one-man-decision based on group advice.[3] The influence and advantage of a "commission of equals" such as the Economic Council, is strikingly illustrated by the fact that the All-Union Central Council of the Trade Unions gave much more attention to wage questions after its representative had found that wages were being discussed at virtually every session of the Economic Council.[4]

Appendix B: Sources for Chapter III and Discussion of the Sampling Procedure and Results

FOR THE 1934-36 STATISTICS presented in Chapter III, the following sources were used.

1. All material on foremen was taken from a study made by the Central Statistical Agency (TsUNKhU) for the entire economy as of November 1, 1933. The study covered 120,997 foremen ("mastery" and "desiatniki"), with 68,386 of them in the Commissariat of Heavy Industry. In most commissariats and other organizations, at least 90 percent of all foremen were included in the sample. A. E. Beilin, *Kadry spetsialistov SSSR, ikh formirovanie i rost (The Cadre of Specialists of the USSR, Its Formation and Growth)*, (Moscow: 1935), pp. 5-7, 224-25.

[3] I. I. Evtikhiev and V. A. Vlasov, *Administrativnoe pravo SSSR* (Administrative Law of the USSR), (Moscow: 1946), p. 16. Text for law institutes and faculties.

[4] N. M. Shvernik, secretary of the Central Committee of the All-Union Council of the Trade Unions, reworked stenographic report of June 1, 1938, to a Conference of Officials and Employees of Trade-Union Central Committees, *Profsoiuzy SSSR*, 1938, No. 12, pp. 14-15.

2. A sample study of the Commissariat of Heavy Industry taken in 1934. Sektor obshchikh izdanii ONTI NKTP (Sector of General Publications of the Organization of Scientific-Technical Publication of the Commissariat of Heavy Industry), *Kadry tiazhëloi promyshlennosti v tsifrakh (Cadre of Heavy Industry in Figures)*, (Moscow: 1936), pp. 166-81.

3. A sample study of the Commissariat of Heavy Industry taken as of April 10, 1936. TsUNKhU, *Trud v SSSR*, pp. 307-12 and 375.

4. A sample study of the Commissariat of Heavy Industry taken in 1936. *Kadry tiazhëloi promyshlennosti*, pp. 166-81.

5. A study as of October 1, 1934, of 543 directors and heads of "constructions" (units which were not entirely built up or equipped, and whose production in proportion to their planned capacity was considered as still too low to bring them into the category of "firm"). While this study was presented as a treatment of all such personnel in the Commissariat of Heavy Industry, it was in reality clearly only a sample. *Ibid.*, pp. 162-63.

6. A similar study as of October 1, 1936, of 944 directors and heads of constructions. *Ibid.*, pp. 162-63.

In studies No. 2 to No. 4 (in the above numbering), the following size samples were used for each of the groups of executives.

	No. 2	No. 3	No. 4
Directors	457	608	779
Chief engineers (technical directors)	240	468	670
Heads of departments	343		267
Heads of glavki	34	32	39

The studies (again in the above numbering) used as a basis for the percentage figures given in the text of Chapter III (pp. 50-56) were the following.

	Party Membership	Period of Joining the Party	Age	Education	Period in the Industrial Branch
Directors	2, 3, 4, 5, 6	2, 3, 4	2, 3, 4, 6	2, 3, 4	3
Chief engineers	2, 3, 4	2, 3, 4	2, 3, 4	2, 3, 4	3
Department superintendents	2, 4		2, 4	2, 4	
Glavki heads	2, 3, 4	2, 3, 4	2, 3, 4	2, 3, 4	3
Foremen	1			1	

	Social Position	Social Origin	Period at the Same Post
Directors	3	2, 4	2, 3, 4, 6
Chief engineers	3	2, 4	2, 3, 4
Department superintendents		2, 4	2, 4
Glavki heads	3	2, 4	2, 3, 4
Foremen	1		

My own sample is composed of directors mentioned in the newspapers or magazines of the period. The overwhelming majority of directors were reported on in the industrial newspapers *Z.I.*, *Ind.*, and *Mash.*

The first approximation to the sample finally used was reached by the process of selection now to be described. All directors about whom I read any personal biographical material were included. Also included were directors who wrote articles which held anything sufficiently pertinent to this study to be worth noting. Furthermore, I included directors of all firms concerning which I had information as to the number of employees, or the number of Communist Party members, or any noteworthy piece of data. The inclusion of a director in the sample automatically meant the inclusion of his firm, and all previous or future directors of that same plant were wherever possible also included. If a director in the sample was transferred to head another firm, this new firm and all its directors automatically became part of the sample.

The vast majority of the firms in the sample entered it early as judged both by the chronological coverage of my study and by the time spent by me in collecting information. Most firms were included as of 1934 and 1935. Firms brought in after 1936 were all either new firms created when old ones, formerly in the sample, were split up, or were firms entered because directors already in the sample had been transferred to them.

To what extent does this sample present a reliable picture of the firms of Heavy Industry, and so of their directors? First, it is a sizable proportion of the total number of firms. The number of firms in the Commissariat of Heavy Industry before they were distributed among newly formed commissariats is not given accurately in Soviet statistics, but roughly one tenth of those firms which were within the Commissariat in 1936 are included in my sample of 224. It is true that this is a far from random selection, being heavily weighted in favor of the larger plants which naturally received most newspaper attention. At the same time, smaller firms have not been ignored. Secondly, while I do not know just how heavily my sample of firms is weighted toward size, this weighting is in the same direction as the firms' importance in the economy and so is not altogether harmful to the representativeness of such a rough sample as this one. Finally, there is nothing to indicate that this bias affects those frequency distributions drawn from the sample.

Aside from its bias toward size, my sample appears to be fairly random. Thus I consider the sample to be a fairly good one.

After all my notes on directors had been taken, the sample included 224 firms and 505 directors. At this point, the sample of directors was further reduced to include only those for whom I had a definite record of appointment, a record of removal, or evidence showing that they were directors of a given firm for over one year. This further selection was made in order to eliminate those who were mentioned casually, and who might in reality have been only acting directors or temporary appointees.[1] In this fashion, the final sample of individual directors, irrespective of how many different firms each headed during his career, was reduced to 321.

These 321 directors were now sorted according to the period in which they headed their firms. In this way, a list was compiled of the total number of directors in each period. If a director headed one firm in two different periods, he was counted in each. If he headed two firms successively within a single period, he was counted twice in its listing.

The period division corresponds to the pre-Purge, Purge, and post-Purge years.

Period I.	January, 1934, through March, 1937
	189 directors listed
Period II.	April, 1937, through June, 1938
	203 directors listed
Period III.	July, 1938, through June, 1941
	136 directors listed

The final sample was manipulated to yield the following data.

1. The homogeneity of the three periods. They were tested for their homogeneity with regard to appointments and removals of directors, recorded as a percentage of the total number of directors listed.

	Period I	*Period II*	*Period III*
Total listed	189	203	136
Appointments	74	106	43
Removals	65	84	48

Using the formula $\sigma_{D_p}^2 = p_0 q_0 \left(\dfrac{1}{N_1} + \dfrac{1}{N_2} \right)^2$ homogeneity was indicated between Periods I and III. (If the two were homogeneous, the difference in percentage of appointments to listings would occur 16 times out of 100 due to chance, and that of removals to listings 87 times out of 100.) On the other hand, homogeneity between Period II and either I or III was shown to be highly unlikely. (The difference in percentage of appointments between I and II would occur only 0.94 times out of 100 due to chance, and that between II and III still less often. The difference in percentage of removals between I and II would occur

---

[1] In view of the large proportion of directors who remained at the head of a firm for less than one year, this reduction of my sample introduces another source of bias. The significance and even direction of this bias is unknown.

[2] $\sigma_{D_p}^2$ is the standard deviation squared of the difference between two proportions. p_0 is the weighted mean proportion, q_0 is $1 - p_0$, and N_1 and N_2 are the total number of cases in the two samples to which the proportions relate.

0.8 times out of 100 due to chance. The only case of no significance between the percentage differences was for II and III, where the difference in removals would occur 26 times out of 100 due to chance.)[3]

2. The immediately previous posts held by directors. The following distribution resulted.

| | PERIOD I | | PERIOD II | | PERIOD III | |
	No.	Percent	No.	Percent	No.	Percent
Firm posts below director	17	33.3	14	38.9	10	38.5
Chief engineer	10	19.6	6	16.7	6	23.1
Department superintendent	2	3.9	5	13.9	2	7.7
Other firm posts	5	9.8	3	8.3	2	7.7
Director elsewhere	16	31.4	15	41.7	12	46.2
Posts in organs above the firm	18	35.3	7	19.4	4	15.4
Total	51	100.0	36	100.0	26	100.1

Using the chi-square test, homogeneity was indicated between Periods II and III. (If the two were homogeneous, the differences in percentages

[3]The above computations disregard completely the effect of the time factor, in that the three periods are of uneven length. One would expect that a long period would show a higher rate of turnover by the above method than would a short one; for, as more months are added, the total of appointments and dismissals changes more sharply in percentage terms than does the total of directors listed. However, I am unable to treat the time factor accurately.

If it were possible to employ the usual method of comparing average rates of turnover for each period, with the denominator of each fraction consisting of the average number of directors at any one time, then no problem would exist. Unfortunately, this cannot be done because I have only a very incomplete coverage of each of the firms whose directors enter into my sample. A proper use of the "average-turnover" method would require that if one director of a given plant enters the sample for any of the three periods, all other directors of that plant during the 1934-41 years must also enter it.

One might think that I need only compare the turnover rate of the longer period with the turnover rate of the shorter one multiplied by the ratio of the relative lengths of the periods. But such a procedure would exaggerate the relative turnover rate for the shorter period. It disregards the increase in the figure of total directors listed which is caused by the extra turnover itself, for it operates with the ratio

$$\frac{\text{directors removed or appointed}}{\text{total directors listed}} \times \frac{\text{length of the longer period}}{\text{length of the shorter period}}$$

which assumes that only the numerator of "directors removed or appointed" is understated by the brevity of the period, while the denominator of "total directors listed" is stated accurately and needs no correction for time.

Thus it is evident that the method used in the text for comparing the rates of turnover in the different periods gives figures for the two shorter periods which are too low for accurate comparison with the longer period, while the method of multiplying the original ratios by the ratios of the relative lengths of the periods provides figures

would occur more than 10 times out of 100 due to chance.) Homogeneity between Period I and the combined percentages of II and III was shown as doubtful (the differences would occur 5 to 10 times out of 100 due to chance), and it is clear from information mentioned in Chapter III that Period I was extraordinary in its proportion of directors who had earlier been in higher organs.

The total sample for Period I was 27.0 percent of all directors listed in this period, for Period II it was 17.7 percent of all those listed, and for Period III, 19.1 percent.

3. The next step in directors' careers after their removal from their firm. The distribution was as follows.

	PERIOD I		PERIOD II		PERIOD III	
	No.	Percent	No.	Percent	No.	Percent
Dismissal or transfer to a post in a firm lower than director	19	38.8	17	45.9	11	37.9
Transfer to another post as director	17	34.7	10	27.0	7	24.1
Transfer to an organ above the firm level	9	18.4	8	21.6	9	31.0
Other	4	8.2	2	5.4	2	6.9
Total	49	100.1	37	99.9	29	99.9

The chi-square test indicates homogeneity of all three periods. (If I and III were homogeneous, the differences in percentages would occur between 10 and 50 times—and closer to 50—out of 100 due to chance. The differences between II and the combined percentages of I and III would occur more than 50 times out of 100 due to chance.)

The total sample for Period I was 74.4 percent of all directors listed in this period, for Period II 44.0 percent of all those listed, and for Period III 60.4 percent.

4. Directors who became commissars or assistant commissars of industrial commissariats or heads of glavki before July, 1941. A director is

which are too high. The correct figures for purposes of comparison would lie between those gotten by these two alternative methods.

Fortunately, both methods give the same results in our case. The method used in the text understates the difference between Period II and Periods I and III, yet it still indicates that the turnover was significantly higher in Period II. This conclusion would only be strengthened if we used the alternative method described in this footnote. Furthermore, neither method shows a significant difference between Periods I and III. The method of this footnote reduces the difference in proportions of appointments to total directors during the two periods, and does not increase to a significant level the difference between the proportions of removals. (The difference between the adjusted percentage of removals in periods I and III would occur 48 times out of 100.)

Thus we are left with our original conclusion—that homogeneity is indicated between Periods I and III, and that the rate of turnover in Period II was significantly higher than that found in the other two periods.

counted in each period in which he was a director, and twice in the same period if he headed two plants then.

	PERIOD I		PERIOD II		PERIOD III	
	No.	Percent	No.	Percent	No.	Percent
Directors reaching high position	12	6.3	23	11.3	16	11.8
Total directors listed	189	100.0	203	100.0	136	100.0

5. Process by which director reached his post. The sample for this distribution is so small that it is only worth recording because of the sharp drop after Period I in the proportion of the third category to the total. This drop is in line with expectations.

	PERIOD I		PERIOD II		PERIOD III	
	No.	Percent	No.	Percent	No.	Percent
Advanced from worker ranks, getting an engineering education along the way after much industrial experience	2	20.0	6	50.0	3	37.5
Received an engineering education early and then advanced in industry	0	0.0	2	16.7	2	25.0
Advanced after success in nonindustrial work served as a base for the industrial career	8	80.0	4	33.3	3	37.5
Total	10	100.0	12	100.0	8	100.0

Appendix C: Procurement and Marketing Apparatus above the Firm Level

MARKETING ORGANS above the firm level have the function of helping to compose the marketing plans for their branch and of supervising their proper execution. They are expected to study the needs of the entire economy for the products of their industry in order properly to orient production planning; they draw up "general conditions" according to which specific contracts are to be made; they supervise the quality and assortment of their industry's products in order to insure that they have been manufactured according to specifications; they compose price lists (subject to higher approval) and enforce them.[1] They also inspect consuming plants to check that their stocks on hand and consumption per product unit do not exceed the norms laid down

[1] Shein, *Snabzhenie zavodov*, p. 16.

for them.[2] In many branches, they purchase the entire production of their industry (thus vastly simplifying the marketing problem of the firms), and handle its sale to the consuming firms.[3] Finally, in order to fulfill such a middleman function, these organs have possession of networks of warehouses from which to supply the needs of those plants whose purchases are not great enough to warrant direct shipment from the producing firms.[4]

The procurement organs play an equally comprehensive role. They are held responsible for planning the composite needs of their branches for centrally allocated goods and for defending these plans before higher bodies; for distributing allotments of these items among the firms of their industry and for helping them actually to buy the allotted supplies; for making purchases for the firms of their industry of goods decentrally distributed; for helping to establish and supervise norms for the firms of stocks on hand and of consumption of materials per product unit; and finally, for redistributing the surplus stocks of the plants.[5] To help them in supplying their firms, they—like the marketing organs—operate warehouse systems.

All firms of heavy industry are serviced by procurement organs of their own branch.[6] Marketing organs have provided almost as complete a coverage except in the machine-construction industry. (Here, due both to the specialized character of the products, many of which are built to specifications, and to the limited circle of clients of each firm, there have frequently been no branch marketing organs.)[7] Both

---

[2] Post. No. 712 of the SNK SSSR of June 3, 1938 *BFKhZ*, 1938, No. 19/20, p. 22.

[3] In 1935, marketing was handled in this fashion in the coke-chemical and nonferrous metals industries among others. Cf. E. Lange, "Kredit i denezhnoe obrashchenie v 1935 g." (Credit and Monetary Circulation in 1935), *Planovoe Khoziaistvo*, 1936, No. 4, pp. 134-35. In 1940, chemicals, metal, rubber, and construction materials were among the products thus sold. See M. Gomberg and N. Itskhok, "Organizatsiia bankom raschëtov po tranzitnym otgruzkam tovarov" (Organization of Accounts by the Bank for Transit Shipment of Goods), *Den'gi i Kredit*, 1940, No. 1, p. 32. On January 1, 1936, one third of the total credits outstanding on bills of lading, for goods purchased by firms of heavy industry and then in transit, had been granted to marketing organs. See Lange, *op. cit.*, p. 135.

[4] Cf. Korostin and Cherniakhovskii, "Zadachi skladskogo metallosnabzheniia i rabota skladov Stal'sbyta i snabsbytov" (Tasks of Warehousing in Metal Procurement and the Work of the Warehouses of the Steel Marketing Organ and of the Procurement-Marketing Agencies), *Snab. i Sklad.*, 1935, No. 2, p. 27. Shein, *Snabzhenie zavodov*, p. 16.

[5] Shein, *Snabzhenie zavodov*, pp. 17 and 21-22.

[6] F. P. Kashchenko, "Meropriiatiia po uporiadocheniiu raboty otraslevykh snabov i sbytov" (Measures for Bringing Order into the Work of the Branch Procurement and Marketing Organs), *Snab. i Sklad.*, 1936, No. 6, p. 21.

[7] E. Mitel'man, "Sistema otpusknykh tsen i pereraspredelenie oborotnykh sredstv v tiazhëloi promyshlennosti" (The System of Prices and the Redistribution of Working Capital in Heavy Industry), *Plan*, 1936, No. 9, p. 11. Some, however, were scheduled to operate in 1940 in the Commissariat of Heavy Machine Construction. (Cf. Post. No. 463 of the SNK SSSR of April 5, 1940, *SPR*, 1940, article 287.)

procurement and marketing organs have normally serviced only those nificant role in affecting the work of the Communist Party and of the ing bodies have also handled sales for other firms which manufactured types of goods that were primarily produced within the marketing organ's commissariat.[8]

While firms have received their supplies and marketed their goods primarily through these procurement and marketing organs, there are three different methods by which these organs service their firms. Producing firms may ship their goods to warehouses of the marketing or procurement organs, from which they are redirected to consumer plants. Producer firms may be attached to consumer plants and be instructed to make contracts with them for regular shipments. Finally, all arrangements between consumer and producer firms may be conducted through the marketing and procurement organs, with producers receiving periodic instructions to ship specified quantities to particular consumers.

Of these three methods, supply from warehouses has played a very minor role in the handling of metals,[9] and probably in the work of marketing organs in general. It has, however, accounted for about half the total turnover of procurement organs.[10]

The second method, that of direct attachment of the producer to consumer firms, seems to have been used in many branches of heavy industry, particularly among the larger firms.[11] It has regularly accounted for over half of the turnover of ferrous metals.[12] This elimination, except for purposes of planning, of the marketing and procurement organs offers the two great advantages of eliminating excess work and of bringing the buyer and supplier into direct contact in working out terms of supply. It also lends greater stability throughout the planning year to all firms, since alteration of the quantities to be shipped is made more difficult than when a marketing or procurement organ takes part

[8] Cf. Post. No. 712 of the SNK SSSR of June 3, 1938, *BFKhZ*, 1938, No. 19/20.

[9] Cf. Korostin and Cherniakhovskii, *op. cit.*, p. 28.

[10] Forty-seven percent for those of 26 national commissariats during 1939. See A. Nesterovskii and R. Tsetlin, "Uporiadochit' material'no-tekhnicheskoe snabzhenie promyshlennosti" (In Order to Bring Order into the Materials-Technical Procurement for Industry), *Planovoe Khoziaistvo*, 1940, No. 4, p. 50.

[11] Cf. Rubinshtein, assistant head of the Machinery and Tool-Marketing Agency, in "Dogovory 1936 goda" (1936 Contracts), *Arbitrazh*, 1936, No. 4, p. 9. B. Edel'shtein, head of the Organizational-Planning Sector of the Glavk for Marketing Electrical Equipment, writing in Ind., December 18, 1939, p. 3.

[12] "Kak razvertyvaetsia zakliuchenie dogovorov" (How to Extend the Conclusion of Contracts), *Biulleten' Gosarbitrazha*, 1935, No. 2, p. 20. G. Privorotskii, "Dogovory po vnutripromyshlennomu snabzheniiu" (Contracts Regarding Intra-Industry Procurement), *Arbitrazh*, 1936, No. 8, p. 6. *Khoziaistvennye dogovory v tiazhëloi promyshlennosti* (Economic Contracts in Heavy Industry), collected by Khr. Bakhchisaraitsev and S. Drabkin, 5th edition (Moscow: 1937), p. 55.

in all transactions as an intermediary.[13] However, flexibility in shifting supplies to other plants is clearly weakened. A second disadvantage of the system of direct attachment is that the producer firm must negotiate separately with a host of different purchasers instead of with a single middleman.

At least through 1937,[14] the predominant position was held by the third method—that of handling goods and materials through "transit" supply direct from producer to consumer and without warehousing en route, but with the necessary paper work being done by an intermediary marketing or procurement organ.[15] It was primarily these bodies which made direct contracts with firms.[16] Thus, with the exception of machine-construction and metallurgical firms, it would seem probable that most plants have had direct relations with procurement and marketing organs rather than with other firms.[17]

Branch marketing and procurement organs for heavy industry were developed during the three years of 1933-35, increasing in number from three to forty-six.[18] During this period, they carried on most of the industry's procurement and marketing work, although there also existed a procurement-marketing organ of the Commissariat of Heavy Industry. But as the procurement organs were not closely tied to the glavki, they were unable to allot to the firms centrally distributed goods or to supervise their activities closely. Their role was essentially that of purchasing and sales representative of the firms of their branch.[19] This situation was altered in 1936, when procurement and marketing was taken over by the glavki themselves.[20] The move strengthened the control functions of the reorganized procurement and marketing organs, as they were now incorporated into the main administrative structure of the commissariat-glavk-firm hierarchy.

The double pattern of glavk and commissariat procurement organs has meant a considerable duplication of work. While this was tolerable as long as there was only one or even a few commissariats in heavy industry, the same structure was continued mechanically as the commissariats and glavki multiplied.[21] Only in April, 1940, was the duplica-

[13] Cf. Prikaz No. 759 of the NKTP of June 2, 1934, *Prikazy i rasporiazheniia NTKP.* Also, Prikaz No. 1267 of the NKTP of December 4, 1935, *Z.I.,* December 10, 1935, p. 1.

[14] I have not been able to find out about the later period, but there are no indications that it saw a change.

[15] Iakobson, "Problemy organizatsii . . . ," p. 4.

[16] Privorotskii, "Dogovory po . . . ," p. 6. The exception for large heavy industry plants cited in this reference can be primarily accounted for by the firms of ferrous metallurgy and of machine construction.

[17] This conclusion is not a certain one. But in any case, a very great number of firms have had such ties.

[18] Kashchenko, *op. cit.,* pp. 21-22.

[19] Iakobson, "O zadachakh . . . ," pp. 19-20.

[20] Post. of the TsIK and SNK SSSR of July 15, 1936, *BFKhZ,* 1936, No. 21, p. 31.

[21] *Ind.,* February 11, 1940, p. 3.

tion eliminated by abolishing all local offices of the glavk procurement organs.[22] With this, the function of the glavk procurement organs was essentially limited to that of preparing supply plans for the glavk, of distributing allotments of centrally distributed supply among the firms, and of supervising the consumption of materials and the stocks on hand of their firms.[23]

This highly complex structure of both branch and commissariat marketing and procurement organs presents a bewildering picture. Indeed, since much of the system simply grew planlessly with the years, there has been much overlapping. It was asserted in 1937 that there existed no clear demarcation between the functions of the different systems,[24] and this confusion seems to have continued in the later period. All organs had their own warehouses through which they serviced consuming firms; all also served as middlemen in making arrangements for shipments direct from producer to consumer plants. The different procurement organs acquired materials where they could, a great deal of them illegally and in violation of every formal division of function.[25] All competed on the market for decentralized supply.[26] The location in some cities of duplicating warehouses of different procurement and marketing organs was accompanied by a complete absence of warehouses in other areas. In such districts, shipments had to be made direct from plant to plant although the quantities involved often were so small as to make such direct shipment almost prohibitively expensive and wasteful of railroad facilities.[27]

None the less, although frequently it seemed to have been lost in the confusion, there was an underlying principle behind the existence of each of these overlapping systems. The marketing organs were oriented

[22] Post. No. 460 of the SNK SSSR of April 5, 1940, SPR, 1940, article 255.

[23] Cf. Shein, Snabzhenie zavodov, pp. 21-22. Long before this 1940 decree, however, the procurement organs of the glavki had lost much of their importance. In 1935-36, these procurement-marketing bodies had had 76 percent of the total procurement and marketing employees of the Commissariat of Heavy Industry and of its glavki. See N. A. Vorob'ev-Nabatov, "Sistema snabsbytov v 1935 g." (The System of Procurement-Marketing Organs in 1935), Snab. i Sklad., 1936, No. 5, p. 18, and Z.I., June 23, 1936, p. 3. According to the 1934 plan, they were to carry out 84 percent of the total marketing operations. See G. Sakharov, "K voprosu o perestroike organizatsii snabzheniia i sbyta v tiazhëloi promyshlennosti" (On the Question of Reorganizing Procurement and Marketing in Heavy Industry), Snab. i. Sklad., 1934, No. 6, pp. 21-22. But by 1939, glavki of 26 All-Union Commissariats handled only 25 percent of the purchases of their commissariats. See Nesterovskii and Tsetlin, op. cit., p. 50. In 1940 they had only 22 percent of the total employees engaged in procurement organs above the firm level. See Post. No. 460 of the SNK SSSR of April 5, 1940, SPR, 1940, article 255.

[24] B. Iakobson, writing in Z.I., April 22, 1937, p. 3.

[25] Cf. the statistical study described by S. Volikov, head of the Administration for Marketing Metals, in Ind., December 31, 1938, p. 2.

[26] Ind., February 11, 1940, p. 3.

[27] Ibid.

primarily toward a few large firms which consumed heavy quantities of their products. They serviced these firms either through arrangements for direct shipments by producer firms or from their own warehouses, and due to their specialization were able to give better service than could the procurement organs which handled many types of materials. The procurement organs, on the other hand, dealt in a multitude of products, and were much like country general stores in that firm managements trading with them could fill all their varied needs for materials at one place rather than having to shop around.[28]

Likewise, there was a division of function between the procurement organs of the glavki and those of the commissariats, at least through 1936. The glavki procurement organs dealt almost entirely in centrally distributed goods,[29] while the commissariat procurement unit had a relative weight of decentralized supply in its annual turnover which fluctuated downwards from 71 percent to 66 percent from 1934 through 1936.[30] This difference reflected the fact that the commissariat procurement organ was mainly oriented toward the receipt of supplies from local sources.[31]

But it was the need for assuring supplies for the firms of their branch which seems to have been basic to the continued growth of the procurement organs. Each has attempted to protect "its" firms from the ever-present danger of supply shortages. Thus both commissariat and glavk procurement organs expanded their work at the expense of the marketing organs' direct relationship with firms, and glavk procurement organs continued to develop their own network of offices and bases even when commissariat supply would have been more efficient.[32]

One aspect of the procurement and marketing picture which we have not yet considered is the disposal of surplus equipment and materials belonging to firms. "Surplus" is defined as the amount above the norm allowed for stocks on hand. The materials involved have to

[28] Sakharov, "K voprosu o perestroike snab i sbyt," pp. 22-24. Korostin and Cherniakhovskii, op. cit., pp. 27-28.

[29] G. A. Dlugach, "Snabzhenie tiazhëloi promyshlennosti cherez otraslevye snaby" (Procurement for Heavy Industry Through Branch Procurement Organs), Snab. i Sklad., 1936, No. 1, p. 23.

[30] Vorob'ev-Nabatov, op. cit., pp. 15-16. I. S. Person, "O tovarooborote sistemy Soiuzsnabsbyta za 1936 g." (On the Trade Turnover of the System of All-Union Procurement-Marketing Agencies during 1936), Snab. i Sklad., 1937, No. 4, p. 22.

[31] Article by I. Saltanov, head of the All-Union Procurement-Marketing Agency, Z.I., June 23, 1936, p. 3.

[32] Cf. Ind., July 8, 1938, p. 2. All of these organs had the right to handle the allotments of centralized supply for the firms, and thus it was possible for a number of different systems to try to service the same plants. Cf. A. Freshkon, "Ispolnenie dogovorov na realizatsiiu fondov i kontingentov" (Fulfillment of Contracts for the Realization of Funded and Contingent Goods), Snab. i Sklad., 1936, No. 8-9, p. 26. Also, V. Aizin, "O nekotorykh preddogovornykh sporakh" (On Some Precontract Disputes), Arbitrazh, 1938, No. 7, pp. 15-16.

a large extent been in plentiful supply relative to demand and thus rather difficult to sell to other firms.[33]

Until 1941, a dual system operated for the collection and marketing of these surpluses. On the one hand, organizations were established with powers to requisition with payment all surpluses; on the other hand, firms were allowed to sell on their own all but a selected group of products. In addition, the procurement and marketing organ of the Commissariat of Heavy Industry was allowed to buy surpluses offered to it by firms and to resell them,[34] and this organ issued a bulletin six times a month listing goods offered for sale or requested for purchase by firms. But in the latter thirties, firms' rights of independent disposal of surpluses became increasingly circumscribed.[35] While the degree of centralized planning of supply was thus increased, the problem was created of the freezing of stocks which the centralized organs could not handle or of which they were not informed.[36] Finally in 1941, a culmination was reached with the abolition of the right of firms to sell or exchange any materials or equipment without orders from above.[37] Thus the procurement and marketing of surpluses came increasingly— and finally completely—under the sway of central planning. While firms were still paid for their surpluses, they had lost all legal right to free disposal of them.

Appendix D: The Commissariat of Internal Affairs and Supervision over Plant Managements

THROUGHOUT THE PERIOD STUDIED, this commissariat exercised, among other functions, that of the political police of the country. Our interest here is in the possible significance of this function for the en-

[33] L. V. Karpova, "Soiuzpredspros v 1935 godu" (The All-Union Organization for Requests and Offers in 1935), *Snab. i Sklad.*, 1935, No. 3, p. 20.

[34] Post. No. 2482 of the SNK SSSR of November 15, 1933, *BFKhZ*, 1934, No. 1, p. 15. Karpova, *op. cit.*, p. 20.

[35] Prikaz No. 7612 of the NKTP of December 2, 1938, approved by the Economic Council on November 29, 1938, *Arbitrazh v sovetskom khoziaistve*, pp. 448-49. Post. No. 262 of the SNK SSSR and the TsK VKP(b) of February 21, 1940, *SPR*, 1940, article 124. V. Sitnin, "Krupnyi rezerv material'nykh resursov," pp. 46-47.

[36] Sitnin, "Krupnyi rezerv material'nykh resursov," pp. 46-47.

[37] Ukaz (Pronouncement) of the Presidium of the Supreme Soviet of the USSR of February 10, 1941, *Ch.M.*, February 11, 1941, p. 1. Venediktov, *Gosudarstvennaia sotsialisticheskaia sobstvennost'*, pp. 427-28.

forcement of controls over management. Thus this Appendix should be read together with the material in Chapter XI relating to organs concerned with enforcement of controls over management.

Basing his report upon postwar interviews with Soviet nonreturnees and defectors from the Soviet Army and Military Government, Merle Fainsod writes that each factory of any size in the Soviet Union has its "Special Section," a branch of the political police. This Special Section has been directly responsible to higher authorities within the Commissariat of Internal Affairs, rather than to the plant manager or the administration of the industrial glavk or commissariat. The Special Section ". . . maintains a dossier on every employee, and has its network of informers scattered throughout the factory."[1]

The Special Section in a plant would seem to direct its attention primarily to the safeguarding of State security and to the prevention and discovery of political offenses. Thus Fainsod writes that "its major task is to discover and root out disaffection wherever it finds it."[2] The question naturally arises, however, of how broad the definition of State security has been.

As stated in Chapter I, an independent investigation of the role of the political police lies beyond the scope of this book. Nevertheless, assuming the accuracy of the above information about the Special Sections—which comes originally from people who had fled the Soviet Union or who had refused to return to it after the war—let us explore the possible controls over firm management which may have resulted from the existence of these Special Sections.

In the first place, the exercise of initiative and autonomy vis-à-vis higher authorities may have been sharply lessened by management's knowledge that all actions were being taken under the very nose of the Commissariat of Internal Affairs which might interpret them as subversive. While such a reduction in initiative may of course have occurred, it seems to me that this argument should be considered in the light of the evidence as to the considerable initiative and autonomy which has existed in Soviet heavy industry. Equally important, an industrial management which could not achieve planned results might have found its failure interpreted as deliberate sabotage.[3] Thus if a management felt that exercise of initiative or even violation of instructions from superiors would improve its plan fulfillment, the presence and activity of the Special Section might give added impetus to the urge for showing this sort of initiative. I would conclude that there is no necessity for believ-

[1] M. Fainsod, "Controls and Tensions in the Soviet System," *The American Political Science Review*, Vol. XLIV, No. 2 (June, 1950), p. 280.

[2] *Ibid.*

[3] This would have been particularly likely during the Purge Period of 1937-38, which is precisely when managements would have been most uneasy regarding the Special Sections in their plants.

ing that management's fear of the Special Section in its plant would have affected the exercise of initiative by the firm. Indeed, if the exercise of initiative was affected, it seems impossible to be sure whether it would have been increased or reduced.[4]

Secondly, the head of the Special Section in a firm may have been an important figure in the running of the plant. In view of his partial authority over determining what actions were subversive,[5] he may have seriously interfered with the director's one-man-authority-and-responsibility.[6] The head of the Special Section may also have played a significant role in affecting the work of the Communist Party and of the mass organizations within the firm.

If it were actually the case that the head of the Special Section played this important role in the work of the firm's administration and of the firm's Party and mass organizations, it would mean that there was a serious extension of divided responsibility within the firm beyond that described elsewhere in this book. But the nature of this division of authority would appear to be the same as took place when the firm's Communist Party organization usurped some of the powers of management.[7] Thus while one-man-authority-and-responsibility might have been further weakened in degree, its exercise would not have been changed in kind.[8]

Certainly the presence of the Special Sections in the firms of heavy industry, to the extent that they were active in the fashion described by Fainsod, must have added considerable pressure upon management, Communist Party and trade-union officials, and all rank-and-file workers to act "properly" according to Soviet norms. But there seems no a priori reason to believe that they would have been important in helping to define these norms for all industry, and no way of knowing in which direction their influence would have been felt.

[4] For a parallel discussion of the effect on managerial initiative of the 1937-38 Purge, cf. Chapter VII.

[5] Fainsod seems to imply that there was general agreement among the nonreturnees and defectors interviewed in 1949 that the Special Sections appeared to operate with a greater degree of independence than did the local representatives of either the Party or the industrial administration. (Fainsod, *op. cit.*, p. 281.)

[6] For such a view, see F. Beck and W. Godin (pseudonyms), *Russian Purge and the Extraction of Confession,* translated from the German original by Eric Mosbacher and David Porter (London: 1951), p. 134.

[7] Cf. Chapter XII.

[8] Ernest V. Hollis, Jr., who has done considerable research in the United States on the subject of the political police, has in a letter of May 21, 1952, to the writer given as his opinion that the head of the Special Section does not play the role described above. Mr. Hollis writes: "I have come across no evidence that in the 1934-1941 period police representatives in the plants and factories tried to share the administrative initiative with the managers in any such sense as the Party and trade-union groups attempted to do. The role of the political police in the USSR during the 1934-41 period does not fit in with such a procedure."

Bibliography

Abbreviations

BFKhZ	Biulleten' finansovogo i khoziaistvennogo zakonodatel'stva
Ch.M.	Chërnaia Metallurgiia
Gosbank	State Bank
Gosplan	State Planning Commission
Ind.	Industriia
Mash.	Mashinostroenie
NKTP	National Commissariat of Heavy Industry
Org. Uprav.	Organizatsiia Upravleniia
Part. Stroit.	Partiinoe Stroitel'stvo
Post.	Decree
SNK SSSR	Council of Commissars of the USSR
Snab. i Sklad.	Snabzhenie i Skladskoe Khoziaistvo Prompredpriiatii
SPR	Sobranie postanovlenii i rasporiazhenii pravitel'stva SSSR
SSSR	USSR
SZ	Sobranie zakonov i rasporiazhenii raboche-krest'ianskogo pravitel'-stva SSSR
TsIK SSSR	Central Executive Committee of the USSR
TsK	Central Committee
TsUNKhU	Central Administration of National Economic Accounting
VKP(b)	All-Union Communist Party (Bolshevik)
VKP(b) v rez.	Vsesoiuznaia Kommunisticheskaia Partiia (b) v rezoliutsiiakh i resheniiakh s"ezdov, konferentsii i plenumov TsK
Vopr. Profdvizh.	Voprosy Profdvizheniia
VTsSPS	All-Union Council of the Trade Unions
Za Prom. Kadry	Za Promyshlennye Kadry
Z.I.	Za Industrializatsiiu

Bibliography of Works Cited

THIS BIBLIOGRAPHY is divided into six sections: Books and Monographs, Legal Sources, Newspapers, Magazines, Articles, and Speeches and Reports. It is hoped that this detailed division of materials will be useful to readers who know Russian, particularly in view of the difficulties in quickly compiling a list of the publications dealing with heavy industry. These bibliographical difficulties apply particularly to newspapers, magazines, and legal sources. Speeches and reports usually have a more official character than do books and articles and thus are separated from them in this bibliography. Articles and books have been placed in different categories so that the reader can most easily glance over the list of books which, unlike the articles, make up a reference source supplementary to that of the magazines.

BOOKS AND MONOGRAPHS

Arakelian, A. Rezervy predpriiatii na sluzhby piatiletke (The Reserves of the Firms in the Service of the Five-Year Plan). Moscow, 1938.
——— Upravlenie sotsialisticheskoi promyshlennost'iu (Administration of Socialist Industry). Moscow, 1947.
Arbitrazh v sovetskom khoziaistve (Arbitration in the Soviet Economy). Collected by V. N. Mozheiko and Z. I. Shkundin, 4th edition. Moscow, 1948.
Beck, F., and W. Godin (pseudonyms). Russian Purge and the Extraction of Confession. Translated from the German original by Eric Mosbacher and David Porter. London, 1951.
Beilin, A. E. Kadry spetsialistov SSSR, ikh formirovanie i rost (The Cadre of Specialists of the USSR, Its Formation and Growth). Moscow, 1935.
Berman, Harold J. Justice in Russia. Cambridge, Mass., 1950.
Bienstock, G., S. M. Schwarz, and A. Yugow. Management in Russian Industry and Agriculture. London, New York, Toronto, 1944.
Bol'shaia Sovetskaia Entsiklopediia (The Large Soviet Encyclopedia). Moscow, 1947.

But, A. I.   Planirovanie v tsvetnoi metallurgii (Planning in Nonferrous Metallurgy).   Moscow, 1946.

Chakovsky, A.   It is Morning Here.   Translated from the Russian by B. Isaaks.   In *Soviet Literature,* 1950, No. 9.

Dobb, Maurice.   Political Economy and Capitalism.   New York, 1937.

——— Soviet Economic Development since 1917.   London, 1948.

Evtikhiev, I. I., and V. A. Vlasov.   Administrativnoe pravo SSSR (Administrative Law of the USSR).   Moscow, 1946.   Text for law institutes and faculties.

Finansirovanie i kreditovanie kapital'nykh vlozhenii (Financing and Crediting of Capital Investments).   Edited by V. M. Buzyrev.   Moscow-Leningrad, 1941.   Issued as a study-aid for the financial-economic institutes.

From Max Weber: Essays in Sociology.   Translated and edited by H. H. Gerth and C. Wright Mills.   New York, 1946.

Grazhdanskoe pravo (Civil Law).   Volume I.   Edited by Professors M. M. Agarkov and D. M. Genkin.   Moscow, 1944.

Hubbard, Leonard E.   Soviet Labour and Industry.   London, 1942.

Inkeles, A.   Public Opinion in Soviet Russia.   Cambridge, Mass., 1950.

Iotkovskii, A. A.   Material'noe snabzhenie i sbyt produktsii promyshlennogo predpriiatiia (Materials Procurement and the Marketing of the Products of the Industrial Firm).   Leningrad, 1941.

Istochniki sovetskogo grazhdanskogo prava (Sources of Soviet Civil Law).   Volume I.   Moscow, 1938.   Study-aid for colleges.

Khoziaistvennye dogovory v tiazhëloi promyshlennosti (Economic Contracts in Heavy Industry).   Collected by Khr. Bakhchisaraitsev and S. Drabkin.   5th edition.   Moscow, 1937.

Kontorovich, V.   Tekhpromfinplan promyshlennogo predpriiatiia (The Technical-Industrial-Financial Plan of the Industrial Firm).   Moscow, 1948.

——— Voprosy planirovaniia predpriiatiia (Questions of Planning for a Firm).   Moscow, 1941.

Kozlov, G.   Khoziaistvennyi raschët v sotsialisticheskom obshchestve (Business Accounting in a Socialist Society).   Moscow, 1945.

Kreditnyi slovar' dlia bankovskikh i finansovykh rabotnikov (Credit Dictionary for Banking and Financial Personnel).   Moscow-Leningrad, 1935.

Kurskii, A.   Sotsialisticheskoe planirovanie narodnogo khoziaistva SSSR (Socialist Planning of the National Economy of the USSR).   Moscow, 1945.

Lenin, V.   Sochineniia (Collected Works).   2d edition.   Volumes XXII and XXVII.   Moscow-Leningrad, 1929.

Lenin i Stalin: Sbornik proizvedenii k izucheniiu istorii VKP(b) (Lenin and Stalin: Collection of Works for the Study of the History of the

All-Union Communist Party [Bolshevik]). Volumes II and III. Moscow, 1936.

Littlepage, John D., and Demaree Bess. In Search of Soviet Gold. New York, 1937.

Luganin, Ia. "Administration and Planning of Industry in the U.S.S.R." Manuscript translation from the original Russian of the Soviet author, no Russian copy being available. (The manuscript was seen at the now defunct American Russian Institute in New York City.)

Mashinostroitel'naia promyshlennost' SSSR: spravochnik zavodov, stroitel'stv, trestov i glavnykh upravlenii soiuznoi, respublikanskoi i mestnoi mashinostroitel'noi i metalloobrabatyvaiushchei promyshlennosti (The Machine-Construction Industry of the USSR: Reference Book on Plants, Constructions, Trusts, and Chief Administrations of All-Union, Republic, and Local Machine-Construction and Metal-Fabricating Industry). Volume I. Moscow, 1933.

Merton, R. K. Social Theory and Social Structure. Chicago, 1949.

Moore, Barrington, Jr. Soviet Politics—The Dilemma of Power. Cambridge, Mass., 1950.

Narodnokhoziaistvennyi plan na 1936 god (The National Economic Plan for 1936). 2d edition. Moscow, 1936.

NKTP, otchëtno-ekonomicheskii sektor (The Commissariat of Heavy Industry, the Accounting-Economic Sector), Tiazhëlaia promyshlennost' SSSR za 1931-1934 gg. (Heavy Industry of the USSR during 1931-1934). Moscow, 1935. Materials for the report of the Commissar of Heavy Industry, S. Ordzhonikidze, to the VIIth Congress of Soviets of the USSR.

NKTP, sektor obshchikh izdanii ONTI (The Commissariat of Heavy Industry, the Sector of General Publications of the Organization of Scientific-Technical Publication). Kadry tiazhëloi promyshlennosti v tsifrakh (Cadre of Heavy Industry in Figures). Moscow, 1936.

Notkin, A. I. Ocherki teorii sotsialisticheskogo vosproizvodstva (Outline of the Theory of Socialist Reproduction). Moscow, 1948.

Ordzhonikidze, G. K. Izbrannye stat'i i rechi 1911-1937 (Selected Articles and Speeches 1911-1937). Edited by A. I. Mikoian, L. Z. Mekhlis, L. P. Beriia, and Z. G. Ordzhonikidze. Moscow, 1939.

O zarabotnoi plate sluzhashchikh; sbornik ukazov, postanovlenii i polozhenii (On the Wages of White-Collar Workers; a Collection of Laws, Decrees, and Statutes). Moscow, 1941.

Partiinoe khoziaistvo; sbornik dokumentov i materialov (Party Housekeeping; a Collection of Documents and Materials). Moscow, 1945.

Postanovleniia plenumov VTsSPS (Decrees of the Plenums of the All-Union Central Council of the Trade Unions). 10th edition. Moscow, 1949.

Rezoliutsii XVIII s"ezda VKP(b) 10-21 marta 1939 g. (Resolutions of the XVIIIth Congress of the All-Union Communist Party [Bolshevik] of March 10-21, 1939). Moscow, 1939.

Robbins, Lionel. The Economic Problem in Peace and War. London, 1947.

Roethlisberger, F. J., and W. J. Dickson. Management and the Worker. Cambridge, Mass., 1939.

Schwartz, H. Russia's Soviet Economy. New York, 1950.

Scott, John. Behind the Urals. Cambridge, Mass., 1942.

Selznick, Philip. TVA and the Grass Roots. Berkeley and Los Angeles, 1949.

Shein, P. A. Material'no tekhnicheskoe snabzhenie machinostroitel'-nykh zavodov (Materials-Technical Procurement of Machine-Construction Plants). Moscow-Leningrad, 1947.

———— Organizatsiia material'nogo snabzheniia sotsialisticheskogo prompredpriiatiia (Organization of Materials Procurement for a Socialist Industrial Firm). Moscow, 1939.

Smith, Bruce. Police Systems in the United States. New York and London, 1940.

Soveshchanie khoziaistvennikov, inzhenerov, tekhnikov, partiinykh i profsoiuznykh rabotnikov tiazhëloi promyshlennosti 20-22 sentiabria 1934 g. (Conference of Executives, Engineers, Technicians, Party and Trade-Union Workers of Heavy Industry of September 20-22, 1934). Stenographic report. Moscow-Leningrad, 1935.

Sovetskoe gosudarstvennoe pravo (Soviet State Law). Moscow, 1948. Issued by the Ministry of Higher Education of the USSR as a text-book for law schools and law faculties.

Stalin, I. Voprosy Leninizma (Problems of Leninism). 10th edition. Moscow, 1938. 11th edition. Moscow, 1947.

TsUNKhU Gosplana SSSR (The Central Administration of National Economic Accounting of the State Planning Commission of the USSR). SSSR strana sotsializma (The USSR, the Country of Socialism). Moscow, 1936.

TsUNKhU Gosplana SSSR. Trud v SSSR (Labor in the USSR). Edited by A. S. Popov. Moscow, 1936.

TsUNKhU Gosplana SSSR. Zarabotnaia plata inzhenerno-tekhnicheskikh rabotnikov i sluzhashchikh v sentiabre-oktiabre 1934 g. (Salaries of Engineering-Technical Workers and White-Collar Workers in September-October, 1934). Moscow, 1936.

TsUNKhU Gosplana SSSR, Otdel uchëta truda (Sector for Calculating Labor). Sostav rukovodiashchikh rabotnikov i spetsialistov Soiuza SSSR (The Composition of Administrative Personnel and of Specialists of the USSR). Moscow, 1936.

Turetskii, Sh. Ia. Vnutripromyshlennoe nakoplenie v SSSR (Intra-Industry Accumulation in the USSR). Moscow, 1948.

Usoskin, M. M. Kratkosrochnyi kredit v narodnom khoziaistve SSSR

(Short-Term Credit in the National Economy of the USSR). Leningrad, 1948.

Veitsman, N. Analiz khoziaistvennykh pokazatelei predpriiatiia (Analysis of Economic Indices of the Firm). Moscow, 1943.

Venediktov, A. V. Dogovornaia distsiplina v promyshlennosti (Contract Discipline in Industry). Leningrad, 1935.

———— Gosudarstvennaia sotsialisticheskaia sobstvennost' (State Socialist Property). Moscow-Leningrad, 1948.

Voprosy partiino-organizatsionnoi raboty (Questions of Organizational Party Work). Moscow, 1948.

Vsesoiuznaia kommunisticheskaia partiia (b) v rezoliutsiiakh i resheniiakh s"ezdov, konferentsii i plenumov TsK (The All-Union Communist Party [Bolshevik] in Resolutions and Decisions of Congresses, Conferences and Plenums of the Central Committee). Part II: 1925-35. 5th edition. Moscow, 1936. 6th edition. Moscow, 1941.

Vtoroi piatiletnii plan razvitiia narodnogo khoziaistva SSSR (The Second Five-Year Plan for the Development of the National Economy of the USSR). Volume I. Moscow, 1934.

VTsSPS, Otdel statistiki (The All-Union Central Council of the Trade Unions, Statistical Sector). Statisticheskii Spravochnik (Statistical Handbook). Issue III. Moscow, 1939.

XVII s"ezd vsesoiuznoi kommunisticheskoi partii (b), 26 ianvaria—10 fevralia 1934 g. (XVIIth Congress of the All-Union Communist Party [Bolshevik], January 26–February 10, 1934). Stenographic report. Moscow, 1934.

XVIII s"ezd vsesoiuznoi kommunisticheskoi partii (b) (XVIIIth Congress of the All-Union Communist Party [Bolshevik]). Stenographic report. Moscow, 1939.

LEGAL SOURCES

Biulleten' finansovogo i khoziaistvennogo zakonodatel'stva (Bulletin of Financial and Economic Laws and Regulations). Cited as *BFKhZ*.

Prikazy i rasporiazheniia NKTP (Orders and Instructions of the Commissariat of Heavy Industry).

Sobranie postanovlenii i rasporiazhenii pravitel'stva SSSR (Collection of Decrees and Orders of the Government of the USSR). Cited as *SPR*. (Its first issue appeared in March, 1938.)

Sobranie zakonov i rasporiazhenii raboche-krest'ianskogo pravitel'stva SSSR (Collection of the Laws and Orders of the Worker-Peasant Government of the USSR). Cited as *SZ*. (Its last issue was 1938, No. 1, being superseded by *SPR*.)

Vedomosti verkhovnogo soveta SSSR (Journal of the Supreme Soviet of the USSR).

NEWSPAPERS

Chërnaia Metallurgiia (Ferrous Metallurgy). Organ of the Commissariat of Ferrous Metallurgy of the USSR. Cited as *Ch.M.* (Its first issue appeared October 1, 1940.)

Industriia (Industry). Organ of a changing number of heavy industry commissariats. Cited as *Ind.* (It appeared from September 5, 1937, through September 29, 1940.)

Mashinostroenie (Machine Construction). Organ of the Commissariat of Machine Construction and of the Commissariat of Defense Industry. Cited as *Mash.* (It appeared from September, 1937, to October, 1939.)

Pravda (Truth). Organ of the Central Committee and the Moscow Committee of the Communist Party.

Trud (Labor). Organ of the All-Union Central Council of the Trade Unions.

Za Industrializatsiiu (For Industrialization). Organ of the Commissariat of Heavy Industry. Cited as *Z.I.* (Its last issue appeared on September 4, 1937, when it was superseded by *Ind.* and *Mash.*)

MAGAZINES

American Political Science Review.

American Sociological Review.

Arbitrazh (Arbitration). Organ of the State Arbitration Tribunal attached to the Council of Commissars of the USSR. (Its first issue was in October, 1935, when it superseded *Biulleten' Gosarbitrazha.*)

Biulleten' Gosarbitrazha (Bulletin of the State Arbitration System). Organ of the State Arbitration Tribunal attached to the Council of Commissars of the U.S.S.R.) (Its last issue was in September, 1935.)

Bol'shevik (Bolshevik). Organ of the Central Committee of the Communist Party.

Den'gi i Kredit (Money and Credit). Organ of the State Bank of the USSR. (Its first issue was in May, 1938, when it superseded *Kredit i Khozraschet.*)

Izvestiia Akademii Nauk SSSR, otdelenie ekonomiki i prava (Bulletin of the Academy of Sciences of the USSR, Division of Economics and Law).

Kredit i Khozraschët (Credit and Business Accounting). Organ of the Administration of the State Bank of the USSR. (It last appeared in early 1938, and was superseded by *Den'gi i Kredit.*)

Organizatsiia Upravleniia (Organization of Administration). Organ of the Central Scientific-Investigatory Institute of the Organization of Production and the Administration of Industry of the Commissariat of Heavy Industry. Cited as *Org. Uprav.*

Partiinoe Stroitel'stvo (Party Organization). Organ of the Central Committee of the Communist Party. Cited as *Part. Stroit.*

Partiinyi Organizator (Party Organizer). Magazine of the Leningrad Regional and City Party Committees.

Plan (Plan). Organ of the State Planning Commission and of the Central Administration of National Economic Accounting of the USSR. (The last issue appeared about August, 1937.)

Planovoe Khoziaistvo (Planned Economy). Magazine of the State Planning Commission and of the Central Administration of National Economic Accounting of the USSR.

Predpriiatie (The Firm). An economic-technical journal, organ of the F. E. Dzerzhinskii Club RNKh.

Problemy Ekonomiki (Problems of Economics). Organ of the Institute of Economics of the Communist Academy, and then of the Academy of Sciences of the USSR.

Profsoiuzy SSSR (Trade Unions of the USSR.). Organ of the All-Union Central Committee of the Trade Unions. (The first issue appeared in January, 1938.)

Snabzhenie i Skladskoe Khoziaistvo Prompredpriiatii (The Procurement and Warehouse Economy of the Industrial Firms). Journal of the All-Union Procurement-Warehousing-Packaging-Organ and of the All-Union Procurement-Marketing-Agency of the Commissariat of Heavy Industry. Cited as *Snab. i Sklad.*

Soviet Literature. (This is a postwar publication.)

Voprosy Ekonomiki (Problems of Economics). (This is a postwar magazine, published by *Pravda* and successor to *Mirovoe khoziaistvo i mirovaia politika.*)

Voprosy Profdvizheniia (Questions of Trade Unionism). Organ of the All-Union Central Committee of the Trade Unions. Cited as *Vopr. Profdvizh.* (Its last issue appeared in late 1937, and it was succeeded by *Profsoiuzy SSSR.*)

Za Promyshlennye Kadry (For Industrial Cadre). Published by the Commissariat of Heavy Industry. Cited as *Za Prom. Kadry.*

ARTICLES

A., V. "Zametki o signalizatsiiakh" (Notes on Reporting), *Arbitrazh,* 1937, No. 7.

Aberbakh, I. "Oborotnye sredstva i kreditovanie promyshlennosti" (Working Capital and Crediting of Industry), *Den'gi i Kredit,* 1940, No. 4-5.

Abramov, I. "Zavod im. Kominterna v bor'be za rentabel'nost' " (The Comintern Plant in the Fight for Profitability), *Plan,* 1935, No. 13.

"Aktiv pravleniia gosudarstvennogo banka" (The "Active" of the Administration of the State Bank), *Kredit i Khozraschet,* 1937, No. 7.

Aizin, V. "O nekotorykh preddogovornykh sporakh" (On Some Pre-Contract Disputes), *Arbitrazh,* 1938, No. 7.

—— "Pravovoe znachenie zaiavok" (The Legal Significance of Statements), *Arbitrazh,* 1937, No. 20.

Aleksandrovskaia, K. "Signalizatsii mestnykh organov Gosarbitrazha" (The Reporting by Local Organs of the State Arbitration System), *Arbitrazh,* 1939, No. 8.

"Arbitrazhnaia praktika" (Arbitration Practice), *Arbitrazh,* 1938, No. 2.

Aristov, N. "Organizovannyi nabor rabochei sily" (Organized Recruitment of Labor Force), *Planovoe Khoziaistvo,* 1939, No. 11.

Baikova, L. M. "O dispetcherizatsii na zavode 'Sharikopodshipnik'" (On Dispatching in the Plant Ball-Bearing Works), *Org. Uprav.,* 1937, No. 3.

Barvinskii, E. "Izuchenie khoziaistva—osnova ulusheniia kreditnoi raboty" (The Study of the Economy Is the Basis for Improving Credit Work), *Kredit i Khozraschët,* 1936, No. 9.

Bergson, A. "Socialist Economics," in *A Survey of Contemporary Economics,* edited by H. S. Ellis, Philadelphia-Toronto, 1948.

Berkovskii, B. "Kreditovanie promyshlennosti i kontrol' rublem" (The Crediting of Industry and the Control by the Ruble), *Kredit i Khozraschët,* 1937, No. 5.

—— "Otvetstvennoe khranenie tovarov i kreditovanie na summy v puti" (The Storage of Goods with Responsibility for Them and the Crediting of Goods en Route), *Kredit i Khozraschët,* 1937, No. 6.

Besher, R. "Stakhanovskoe dvizhenie i proizvoditel'nost' truda" (The Stakhanovite Movement and Labor Productivity), *Problemy Ekonomiki,* 1936, No. 2.

Birman, A. "Nekotorye voprosy ukrepleniia khoziaistvennogo raschëta v promyshlennosti" (Some Questions of Strengthening Business Accounting in Industry), *Problemy Ekonomiki,* 1941, No. 1.

Bogolepov, M. "K peresmotru tsen na oborudovanie" (Toward a Revision of Prices for Equipment), *Plan,* 1937, No. 7.

Bratus', S., and M. El'evich. "Sbyti i otvetstvennost' po dogovoram" (Marketing Organs and Responsibility for Contracts), *Biulleten' Gosarbitrazha,* 1935, No. 18.

Braude, A., and R. Dorogov. "K itogam otraslevykh konferentsii mashinostroeniia" (On the Results of the Branch Conferences of Machine Construction), *Plan,* 1936, No. 11.

Bregel', E. and A. Tsagolov. "Naznachenie i funktsii deneg v sotsialisticheskoi ekonomike" (The Assignment and Functions of Money in a Socialist Economy), *Planovoe Khoziaistvo,* 1940, No. 12.

Brigada TsIO (Brigade of the Central Scientific-Research Institute for the Organization of Production). "Spetsializatsiia i kooperirovanie v glavsredmashe" (Specialization and Cooperation in the Glavk of Medium Machine Construction), *Org. Uprav.,* 1937, No. 6.

Burmistenko, M. "O podbore i vydvizhenii kadrov" (On the Selection and Promotion of Personnel), *Part. Stroit.,* 1939, No. 15.

—— "Smelee vydvigat' kadry" (For a Bolder Promotion of Personnel), *Part. Stroit.,* 1939, No. 5.

Chernomordik, D. "Effektivnost' kapital'nykh vlozhenii i teoriia vosproizvodstva" (Effectiveness of Capital Investments and the Theory of Reproduction), *Voprosy Ekonomiki,* 1949, No. 6.

Dedikov, N. "Bol'shevistskii pod"ëm partiinoi raboty" (Bolshevik Improvement of Party Work), *Part. Stroit.,* 1938, No. 11.

Deviakovich, A. "Sotssorevnovanie i udarnichestvo" (Socialist Competition and Shock Work), *Vopr. Profdvizh.,* 1934, No. 5.

Dlugach, G. A. "Snabzhenie tiazhëloi promyshlennosti cherez otraslevye snaby" (Procurement for Heavy Industry Through Branch Procurement Organs), *Snab. i Sklad.,* 1936, No. 1.

"Dnevnik soveshchaniia: Glavnoe—rabota s kazhdym otdelnym kommunistom" (The Minutes of a Conference: The Main Item is Work with Each Individual Communist), *Part. Stroit.,* 1935, No. 16.

Dobrovenskii, G. "Kooperirovanie promyshlennosti" (Cooperation of Industry), *Problemy Ekonomiki,* 1938, No. 3.

"Dogovory 1936 goda" (1936 Contracts), *Arbitrazh,* 1936, No. 4.

"Do kontsa likvidirovat' posledstviia vreditel'stva v planovykh organakh" (Toward Completely Eliminating the Remnants of Wrecking in the Planning Organs), *Planovoe Khoziaistvo,* 1937, No. 5-6.

Dubnov, I. "Rabota vslepuiu" (Working Blindfold), *Kredit i Khozraschët,* 1935, No. 9-10.

Dubnov, I., and E. Mitel'man. "Kontrol' rublem v tiazhëloi promyshlennosti" (Control by the Ruble in Heavy Industry), *Kredit i Khozraschet,* 1934, No. 22.

Dubovskii, D. "Izmenit' poriadok rassmotreniia trudovykh konfliktov" (For a Change in the System of Reviewing Labor Conflicts), *Profsoiuzy SSSR,* 1940, No. 2-3.

"Edinonachalie i pravo kontroliia" (One-Man-Authority-and-Responsibility and the Right of Supervision), *Part. Stroit.,* 1940, No. 18.

Egorov, V. "Za stalinskoe vydvizhenie partkadrov" (For the Stalinist Advancement of Party Cadre), *Part. Stroit.,* 1937, No. 13.

El'evich, M. "Razreshenie sporov khozorganov, vkhodiashchikh v odin glavk" (Deciding Disputes Between Economic Organs Within the Same Glavk), *Arbitrazh,* 1939, No. 5.

Emel'ianov, A. "O metodakh opredeleniia ekonomicheskoi effektivnosti primeniia mashin v sovetskom khoziaistve" ("On Methods of Defining the Economic Effectiveness of the Application of Machines in the Soviet Economy), *Voprosy Ekonomiki,* 1949, No. 11.

Eventov, L. "K itogam bor'by dvukh sistem za 20 let" (On the Results of the Fight Between the Two Systems Over 20 Years), *Planovoe Khoziaistvo,* 1937, No. 8.

Evreinov, N. "O sokrashchenii platnogo profapparata" (On the Re-
duction of the Paid Trade-Union Staff) *Vopr. Profdvizh.*, 1937, No. 1.
———— "O svoeobraznom krizise professional'nykh soiuzov" (On the
Singular Crisis of the Trade Unions), *Vopr. Profdvizh.*, 1935, No.
11-12.
Fainsod, M. "Controls and Tensions in the Soviet System," *The
American Political Science Review,* Vol. XLIV, No. 2 (June, 1950).
Fedulov, P. "Partiinyi komitet odnogo tsekha" (The Party Commit-
tee of One Department), *Part. Stroit.*, 1938, No. 14.
Firin, M. "Organizatsiia zarabotnoi platy v tiazhëloi promyshlen-
nosti" (The Organization of Wages in Heavy Industry), *Planovoe
Khoziaistvo,* 1937, No. 1.
———— "O sovmeshchenii rabot" (On Combining Trades), *Vopr. Profdvizh.*, 1935, No. 5-6.
Fishkis, Ia. "Ustranit' nedostatki v vydache ssud na vremennye
nuzhdy" (For the Elimination of Deficiencies in the Giving of Loans
for Temporary Needs), *Kredit i Khozraschët,* 1937, No. 18.
Freshkon, A. "Ispolnenie dogovorov na realizatsiiu fondov i kon-
tingentov" (Fulfillment of Contracts for the Realization of Funded
and Contingent Goods), *Snab. i Sklad.*, 1936, No. 8-9.
Gaisinovich, I. "Sistema pokazatelei narodnokhoziaistvennogo plana
rainonov na 1937 g." (The System of Indices for the National Economic Plan of Districts for 1937), *Plan,* 1937, No. 2.
Gal'perin, Ts. "Iz opyta sostavleniia vtorogo piatiletnego plana"
(From the Experience of Establishing the Second Five-Year Plan),
Planovoe Khoziaistvo, 1936, No. 3.
Gamburg. "O praktike shtrafov v organakh arbitrazha" (On the Prac-
tice of Fines in the Arbitration Organs), *Biulleten' Gosarbitrazha,*
1935, No. 2.
———— "Rabota organov arbitrazha" (Work of the Arbitration Or-
gans), *Biulleten' Gosarbitrazha,* 1935, No. 9/10.
Gol'dberg, S., and Ia. Fishkes. "Upravlenie ne znaet finansov zavodov"
(The Administration Doesn't know the Finances of the Plants),
Kredit i Khozraschët, 1936. No. 12.
Goloshchekin, F. I. "O rabote Gosudarstvennogo arbitrazha v 1937
g." (On the Work of the State Arbitration System in 1937), *Arbi-
trazh,* 1938, No. 7.
———— "Piat' let Gosarbitrazha" (Five Years of State Arbitration),
Arbitrazh, 1936, No. 10.
Gomberg, M., and N. Itskhok. "Organizatsiia bankom raschetov po
tranzitnym otgruzkam tovarov" (Organization of Accounts by the
Bank for Transit Shipment of Goods), *Den'gi i Kredit,* 1940, No. 1.
Gomberg, M., and I. Naumov. "Kreditno-raschëtnaia rabota" (Credit-
Accounting Work), *Den'gi i Kredit,* 1940, No. 4-5.

Gorbunov, M. "Rukovodstvo vyborami proforganov" (Guidance of the Trade-Union Elections), *Part. Stroit.*, 1937, No. 13.

Gorelik, I. "Pervye itogi vnedreniia novykh norm v chërnoi metallurgii" (First Results of the Introduction of New Norms in Ferrous Metallurgy), *Plan,* 1936, No. 10.

"Gosbank v period zaversheniia stroitel'stva sotsializma" (The State Bank in the Period of Completing the Building of Socialism), *Den'gi i Kredit,* 1939, No. 4.

Greidenberg, M. "Problema oborotnykh sredstv promyshlennosti" (The Problem of Working Capital of Industry), *Plan,* 1935, No. 24.

Grigor'ev, A. "Novye formy sotsialisticheskogo truda" (New Forms of Socialist Labor), *Planovoe Khoziaistvo,* 1939, No. 9.

―――― "Uporiadochit' zarplatu, ukrepit' tekhnicheskoe normirovanie" (For Bringing Order into Wages and Strengthening Technical Norm Making), *Planovoe Khoziaistvo,* 1938, No. 10.

Gruev, N. "Neskol'ko zamechanii ob uproshchenii sistemy planirovaniia" (Some Remarks on the Simplification of the Planning System), *Predpriiatie,* 1935, No. 15.

Gur'ev, S. "Usilit' kontrol' nad otkazom ot adtsepta" (In Order to Strengthen Control over Acceptance-Refusals), *Kredit i Khozraschët,* 1937, No. 23.

Gurov, S. "O lovkosti ruk i o 'znakomom parne' " (About Sleight of Hand and "Clever Fellows"), *Predpriiatie,* 1934, No. 5-6.

Hayek, F. A. von. "The Nature and History of the Problem," in *Collectivist Economic Planning,* edited by F. A. von Hayek, London, 1935.

Iakobson, B. N. "O zadachakh snabzhenchesko-sbytovykh sistem v sviazi s reorganizatsiei otraslevykh snabov i sbytov" (On the Tasks of the Procurement-Marketing Systems in Connection with the Reorganization of the Branch Procurement and Marketing Organs), *Snab. i Sklad.,* 1937, No. 2.

―――― "Problemy organizatsii i planirovanie promsnabzheniia v tret'ei piatiletke" (Problems of Organization and the Planning of Industrial Supply in the Third Five-Year Plan), *Snab. i Sklad.,* 1937, No. 9.

Iakobson, B. N., and L. M. Rozenberg. "Eshchë ob organizatsii i praktike metallosnabzheniia" (More on the Organization and Practice of Metal Procurement), *Snab. i Sklad.,* 1937, No. 6.

Il'in, A. "Partiinaia rabota na zavodakh metallurgii" (Party Work in Metallurgical Plants), *Part. Stroit.,* 1936, No. 24.

Iunovich, I. "Voprosy truda i zarabotnoi platy v mashinostroenii" (Questions of Labor and Wages in Machine Construction), *Planovoe Khoziaistvo,* 1939, No. 6.

"Kadry-arbitrazham" (Arbitration Cadre), *Biulleten' Gosarbitrazha,* 1934, No. 6.

Kaganovich, Iu. "Smelee vydvigat' bespartiinykh na rukovodia-shchuiu rabotu" (For the Bolder Advancement of Non-Party People to Administrative Work), *Part. Stroit.*, 1938, No. 11.

Kaganovich, M. M. "Perestroika upravleniia predpriiatiem—boevaia zadacha tiazhëloi promyshlennosti" (The Reconstruction of the Administration of the Firm Is an Emergency Task of Heavy Industry), *Org. Uprav.*, 1934, No. 3.

"Kak razvërtyvaetsia zakliuchenie dogovorov" (How to Extend the Conclusion of Contracts), *Biulleten' Gosarbitrazha*, 1935, No. 2.

Karpova, L. V. "Soiuzpredspros v 1935 godu" (The All-Union Organization for Requests and Offers in 1935), *Snab. i Sklad.*, 1935, No. 3.

Kashchenko, F. P. "Meropriiatiia po uporiadocheniiu raboty otraslevykh snabov i sbytov" (Measures for Bringing Order into the Work of the Branch Procurement and Marketing Organs), *Snab. i Sklad.*, 1936, No. 6.

Kasimovskii, E. "O kreditovanii gotovykh izdelii" (On the Crediting of Finished Goods), *Den'gi i Kredit*, 1940, No. 6-7.

Katsenbogen, B. Reply to the book review of P. Vasil'ev. In *Org. Uprav.*, 1938, No. 1.

Kheifets, N. "Zhaloby na resheniia" (Complaints about Decisions), *Arbitrazh*, 1936, No. 8.

Kheinman, S. "Ob izlishkakh rabochei sily i o proizvoditel'nosti truda" (On Excess Labor Force and on Labor Productivity), *Problemy Ekonomiki*, 1940, No. 11/12.

Kholodnyi, R. "Planirovanie tovarnoi produktsii" (Planning Marketable Production), *Planovoe Khoziaistvo*, 1940, No. 4.

Khromov, P. "K voprosu ob oborotnykh fondakh promyshlennosti" (On the Question of the Working Capital of Industry), *Problemy Ekonomiki*, 1937, No. 1.

"Khronika: V Gosplane SSSR" (Chronicle: In the State Planning Commission of the USSR), *Planovoe Khoziaistvo*, 1938, No. 3 and No. 5.

"K itogam vyborov profsoiuznykh organov" (On the Results of the Elections of the Trade-Union Organs), *Profsoiuzy SSSR*, 1938, No. 1.

Koltunov, N. "Svoevremenno dovodit' plan do predpriiatiia" (For the Working Out on Time of the Plan for the Firm), *Plan*, 1935, No. 6.

"Konsul'tatsiia" (Consultation), *Plan*, 1937, No. 2.

"Konsultatsiia o sverkhurochnykh rabotakh" (Consultation on Overtime Work), *Vopr. Profdvizh.*, 1937, No. 16.

Kontorin, D. "O sekretare raionnogo komiteta partii" (On the Secretary of the District Committee of the Party), *Part. Stroit.*, 1936, No. 19.

Kornitskii, K. Ia. "Stakhanovskie metody raboty v mashinostroenii"

(Stakhanovite Methods of Work in Machine Construction), *Org. Uprav.*, 1937, No. 1.

Korostin and Cherniakhovskii. "Zadachi skladskogo metallosnabzheniia i rabota skladov Stal'sbyta i snabsbytov" (Tasks of Warehousing in Metal Procurement and the Work of the Warehouses of the Steel Marketing Organ and of the Procurement-Marketing Agencies), *Snab. i Sklad.*, 1935, No. 2.

Koshelev, F. "O bol'shevistskikh metodakh upravleniia sotsialisticheskim khoziaistvom" (On the Bolshevik Methods of Administering the Socialist Economy), *Den'gi i Kredit,* 1940, No. 6-7.

Kotliar, S. "O shefstve predpriiatii nad gosudarstvennym apparatom i o sotsialisticheskom sovmestitel'stve" (On the Patronage by the Firms over the State Apparatus and on Socialist Combination-of-Work), *Vopr. Profdvizh.*, 1936, No. 12.

Krupskaia, N. "Lenin i Stalin o bor'be s biurokratizmon" (Lenin and Stalin on the Fight Against Bureaucracy), *Part. Stroit.*, 1937, No. 2.

Kuznetsov, A. A. "Ob itogakh XVIII Vsesoiuznoi konferentsii VKP (b)" (On the Results of the XVIIIth All-Union Conference of the All-Union Communist Party [Bolshevik]), *Partiinyi Organizator,* 1941, No. 5-6.

Lange, E. "Kredit i denezhnoe obrashchenie v 1935 g." (Credit and Monetary Circulation in 1935), *Planovoe Khoziaistvo,* 1935, No. 4.

Lange, Oskar. "On the Economic Theory of Socialism," in *On the Economic Theory of Socialism,* edited by B. E. Lippincott, Minneapolis, 1938.

——— "The Working Principles of the Soviet Economy," in *U.S.S.R. Economy and the War,* New York, 1943.

Lifshits, I., and S. Abramov. "Za kul'turnuiu eksploatatsiiu zhilishchnogo fonda v tiazhëloi promyshlennosti" (For a Cultured Use of the Housing Fund in Heavy Industry), *Vopr. Profdvizh.*, 1935, No. 5-6.

Lobanov, F., and P. Mitropol'skii. "Likvidatsiia neplatezhei—odna iz tsentral'nykh zadach Gosbanka" (The Liquidation of Nonpayments is One of the Central Tasks of the State Bank), *Kredit i Khozraschët,* 1937, No. 22.

Lokshin, E. "Organizatsionnye problemy promyshlennosti SSSR" (Organizational Problems of the Industry of the USSR), *Problemy Ekonomiki,* 1939, No. 4.

M., M. "Zadachi promsnabzheniia" (Tasks of Industrial Procurement), *Snab. i Sklad.*, 1937, No. 11.

Maizenberg, L. "O khoziaistvennom plane" (On the Economic Plan), *Planovoe Khoziaistvo,* 1949, No. 10.

Martynov, I. "Zabotlivo vyrashchivat' partaktiv" (For Solicitously Nurturing the Party Active), *Part. Stroit.*, 1937, No. 13.

Masterov, S. "Kontrol' pervichnykh partorganizatsii v deistvii" (Supervision over the Primary Party Organizations in Action), *Part. Stroit.,* 1939, No. 11.

Mises, Ludwig von. "Economic Calculation in the Socialist Commonwealth," in *Collectivist Economic Planning,* edited by F. A. von Hayek, London, 1935.

Mitel'man, E. "Nado li detsentralizovat' planirovanie kreditov?" (Must the Planning of Credit Be Decentralized?), *Kredit i Khozraschët,* 1936, No. 14.

—— "Sistema otpusknykh tsen i pereraspredelenie oborotnykh sredstv v tiazhëloi promyshlennosti" (The System of Prices and the Redistribution of Working Capital in Heavy Industry), *Plan,* 1936, No. 9.

—— "Tovarnaia rabota banka" (The Goods Work of the Bank), *Kredit i Khozraschët,* 1934, No. 18.

Mozheiko, V. "Metody sutiazhinchestva" (Methods of Going to Law about Nothing), *Arbitrazh,* 1937, No. 12.

"Nekotorye itogi vyborov partiinykh organov" (Some Results of the Elections of Party Organs), *Part. Stroit.,* 1937, No. 10.

"Nekotorye vyvody k itogam raboty Gosarbitrazha za 1 kvartal 1936 g." (Some Conclusions on the Results of the Work of the State Arbitration System during the First Quarter of 1936), *Arbitrazh,* 1936, No. 13.

Nemzer, L. "The Kremlin's Professional Staff: the 'Apparatus' of the Central Committee, Communist Party of the Soviet Union," *American Political Science Review,* Vol. XLIV, No. 1 (March, 1950).

Nesterovskii, A., and Tsetlin, R. "Uporiadochit' material'no-tekhnicheskoe snabzhenie promyshlennosti" (In Order to Bring Order into the Materials-Technical Procurement for Industry), *Planovoe Khoziaistvo,* 1940, No. 4.

Nikolaeva, Kl. "Partorganizatsii i perestroika raboty profsoiuzov" (The Party Organizations and the Reconstruction of the Work of the Trade Unions), *Part. Stroit.,* 1937, No. 11.

"Novoe polozhenie o raionnykh planovykh komissiiakh" (The New Statute on the District Planning Commissions), *Planovoe Khoziaistvo,* 1938, No. 1.

"Ocherednye zadachi organizatsii proizvodstva v 1938 g." (The Next Tasks in the Organization of Production in 1938), *Org. Uprav.,* 1938, No. 1.

"Ofitsial'nyi otdel" (Official Sector), *Biulleten' Gosarbitrazha,* 1934, No. 18.

"Organizatsiia proizvodstva v tretei piatiletke i zadachi TsIO" (The Organization of Production in the Third Five-Year Plan and the Tasks of the Central Scientific-Research Institute for the Organization of Production), *Org. Uprav.,* 1937, No. 4.

"Organizatsionno-partiinuiu rabotu—na uroven' politicheskikh zadach"

(Toward Raising Organizational Party Work to the Level of the Political Tasks), *Part. Stroit.*, 1934, No. 5-6.

"Organy arbitrazha v 1933 g." (Arbitration Organs in 1933), *Biulleten' Gosarbitrazha,* 1934, No. 6.

Orlov, S. "Eshchë o kreditovanii tranzitnykh otgruzok" (More on Crediting of Shipments en Route), *Kredit i Khozraschët,* 1937, No. 12.

Orlova. "Bank v bor'be za ekonomiiu zarabotnoi platy" (The Bank in the Fight for Wage Economies), *Den'gi i Kredit,* 1940, No. 2-3.

"O rukovodstve partiinoi pechat'iu" (On Guidance of the Party Press), *Part. Stroit.,* 1940, No. 9.

Ostrovitianov, K. V. "O zadachakh nauchno-issledovatel'skoi raboty v oblasti ekonomiki" (On the Tasks of Scientific-Investigatory Work in the Field of Economics), *Izvestiia Akademii Nauk SSSR, otdelenie ekonomiki i prava,* 1950, No. 1.

———— "Politika i ekonomika v sotsialisticheskom obshchestve" (Politics and Economics in Socialist Society), *Problemy Ekonomiki,* 1939, No. 6.

———— "Sotsialisticheskoe planirovanie i zakon stoimosti" (Socialist Planning and the Law of Value), *Voprosy Ekonomiki,* 1948, No. 1.

"Otchët otdela kadrov na plenume raikome" (A Report of the Personnel Branch to the Plenum of the District Committee), *Part. Stroit.,* 1940, No. 21.

Otdel organizatsii proizvodstva NKTI and TsIO NKTP (Sector of the Organization of Production of the NKTI and the Central Scientific-Research Institute for the Organization of Production of the Commissariat of Heavy Industry). "Osnovnye polozheniia po organizatsii dispetcherskoi sistemy upravleniia na mashinostroitel'nykh predpriiatiiakh" (The Main Conditions for the Organization of a Dispatching System of Direction in Machine-Construction Firms), *Org. Uprav.,* 1934, No. 4. The NKTI may be a misprint for NKTP, or may stand for the Nauchnyi komitet tekhnicheskoi informatsii (Scientific Committee for Technical Information).

Otdel rukovodiashchikh partiinykh organov TsK VKP(b) (Sector of Guiding Party Organs of the Central Committee of the All-Union Communist Party [Bolshevik]). "Instruktsiia k zapolneniiu partiinykh dokumentov novogo obraztsa" (Instructions for Filling Out the New Party Documents), *Part. Stroit.,* 1936, No. 5.

"Ovladet' bol'shevistskim stilem organizatsionno-prakticheskogo rukovodstva" (For Mastering the Bolshevik Style of Organizational-Practical Leadership), *Part. Stroit.,* 1934, No. 8.

"O zadachakh partiinykh organizatsii v oblasti promyshlennosti i transporta" (On the Tasks of Party Organizations in the Field of Industry and Transportation), *Partiinyi Organizator,* 1941, No. 4, p. 29.

Patolichev, N. "O sochetanii partiino-politicheskoi i khoziaistvennoi raboty" (On the Uniting of Party Political and Economic Work), *Part. Stroit.*, 1939, No. 14.

"Peredovaia" (Lead), *Kredit i Khozraschët*, 1937, No. 4.

Person, I. S. "O tovarooborote sistemy Soiuzsnabsbyta za 1936 g." (On the Trade Turnover of the System of All-Union Procurement-Marketing Agencies during 1936), *Snab. i Sklad.*, 1937, No. 4.

Piastunovich, S. "Za deistvennost' signalizatsii" (For Real Reporting), *Arbitrazh*, 1939, No. 2.

Pikus. "V tekhnicheskoi li gramatnosti snabzhentsev reshenie voprosa?" (Is the Solution of the Question Contained in the Technical Understanding of the Procurement Agents?), *Predpriiatie*, 1934, No. 8.

"Pis'mo glavarbitra NKTP t. Zangvilia" (Letter from Comrade Zangvil', Chief Arbitrator of the Commissariat of Heavy Industry), *Arbitrazh*, 1935, No. 14.

"Planirovanie v poslevoennyi period i novaia struktura Gosplana" (Planning in the Postwar Period and the New Structure of the State Planning Commission), *Planovoe Khoziaistvo*, 1946, No. 5.

"Podniat' delo podbora kadrov na nauchno bol'shevistskuiu vysotu" (In Order to Raise the Selection of Personnel to a Scientific and Bolshevik Height), *Part. Stroit.*, 1939, No. 13.

Poliak, G. "O fonde direktora promyshlennogo predpriiatiia" (On the Director's Fund of an Industrial Firm), *Planovoe Khoziaistvo*, 1938, No. 4.

Polonskii, V. "Stakhanovskoe dvizhenie i profsoiuzy" (The Stakhanovite Movement and the Trade Unions), *Vopr. Profdvizh.*, 1934, No. 11-12.

Privorotskii, G. "Dogovory po vnutripromyshlennomu snabzheniiu" (Contracts Regarding Intra-Industry Procurement), *Arbitrazh*, 1936, No. 8.

———— "Nekotorye voprosy razresheniia sporov po promyshlennomu snabzheniiu" (Some Questions in Deciding Disputes Regarding Industrial Procurement), *Arbitrazh*, 1937, No. 5.

"Profsoiuzy pered XVII s"ezdom partii" (The Trade Unions Before the XVIIth Congress of the Party), *Vopr. Profdvizh.*, 1934, No. 1.

Proselkov, A. "Kontrol' za raskhodovaniem fondov zarabotnoi platy" (Control over the Overexpenditure of Wage Funds), *Den'gi i Kredit*, 1939, No. 8.

Protsenko, P. "Usileniem partraboty obespechit' dal'neishii rost proizvodstva" (Secure the Further Growth of Production by Strengthening Party Work), *Part. Stroit.*, 1934, No. 15.

"Rabota organov Gosarbitrazha v pervom polugodii 1935 g." (The Work of the Organs of State Arbitration in the First Half of 1935), *Biulleten' Gosarbitrazha*, 1935, No. 18.

"Rabotu Gosplana—na uroven' novykh zadach" (The Work of the

State Planning Commission—on the Level of the New Tasks), *Planovoe Khoziaistvo*, 1938, No. 2.

Raskin, L. "Pobeda metallurgii—pobeda kadrov" (The Victory of Metallurgy is the Victory of Cadre), *Za Prom. Kadry*, 1935, No. 3.

Rozhkov, A. "Promyshlennyi otdel obkoma" (The Industrial Branch of the Regional Committee), *Part. Stroit.*, 1940, No. 21.

Rudnitskaia, F. "Okhvat rabotaiushchikh profsoiuznym chlenstvom" (The Extent to which Workers are Trade-Union Members), *Vopr. Profdvizh.*, 1934, No. 6.

———— "Profsoiuznyi aktiv v nizovykh proforganizatsiiakh" (The Trade-Union "Active" in the Lower Union Organizations), *Vopr. Profdvizh.*, 1936, No. 2.

Sakharov, G. "K voprosu o perestroike organizatsii snabzheniia i sbyta v tiazhëloi promyshlennosti" (On the Question of Reorganizing Procurement and Marketing in Heavy Industry), *Snab. i Sklad.*, 1934, No. 6.

———— "Snabzhenie i sbyt v tiazhëloi promyshlennosti" (Procurement and Marketing in Heavy Industry), *Biulleten' Gosarbitrazha*, 1934, No. 14.

Samulenko, A. G. "Stakhanovskoe dvizhenie i otraslevye konferentsii v khimicheskoi promyshlennosti" (The Stakhanovite Movement and the Branch Conferences in the Chemical Industry), *Org. Uprav.*, 1936, No. 3.

Shabanov, G. "Aktiv'no borot'sia s pereraskhodom fondov zarplaty" (In Order to Actively Fight Against Overexpenditure of Wage Funds), *Kredit i Khozraschët*, 1937, No. 23.

Shamberg, M. "Protiv volikity pri priëme novykh chlenov v VKP(b)" (Against Red Tape in Admitting New Members into the All-Union Communist Party [Bolshevik]), *Part. Stroit.*, 1938, No. 7.

Shefer, F. F. "Zadacha rentabel'nosti predpriiatii i rol' uchëta" (The Task of Firm Profitability and the Role of Accounting), *Org. Uprav.*, 1935, No. 4.

Shenger, Iu. "O denezhnykh rezervakh sotsialisticheskogo khoziaistva i ikh roli v kreditnom planirovanii" (On the Monetary Reserves of the Socialist Economy and Their Role in Credit Planning), *Planovoe Khoziaistvo*, 1937, No. 11-12.

———— "Organizovat' bor'bu s debitorsko-kreditorskoi zadolzhennost'iu" (In Order to Organize the Fight Against Non-Bank Debts), *Kredit i Khozraschët*, 1937, No. 19.

———— "Protiv mekhanicheskogo kreditovaniia" (Against Mechanical Crediting), *Den'gi i Kredit*, 1940, No. 10.

———— "Zadachi Gosbanka v bor'be s pereraskhodovaniem fondov zarplaty" (The Tasks of the State Bank in the Fight Against the Overexpenditure of Wage Funds), *Kredit i Khozraschët*, 1937, No. 23.

Shneerov, A. "Ustanovlenie tsen i spory o tsenakh v praktike Gosarbitrazha" (The Setting of Prices and Price Disputes in the Practice of the State Arbitration System), *Arbitrazh, 1938,* No. 20.

Shokhin, A. "Vrednaia podmena khoziaistvennykh organov" (Harmful Substitution for Economic Organs), *Part. Stroit.,* 1937, No. 6.

Shvarts, G. "Voprosy ukrepleniia platëzhnoi distsipliny" (Questions in the Strengthening of Payment Discipline), *Den'gi i Kredit,* 1939, No. 7.

Sibiriachka, Z. "Opyt organizatsii grupp sochuvstvuiushchikh na predpriiatii" (The Experience of the Organization of Groups of Sympathizers in the Firm), *Part. Stroit.,* 1934, No. 11.

Siptits, B. "Voprosy, trebuiushchie ofitsial'nogo raz"iasneniia" (Questions Requiring Official Determination), *Arbitrazh,* 1936, No. 19.

"Sistema Gosudarstvennogo arbitrazha v 1934 g." (The System of State Arbitration in 1934), *Biulleten' Gosarbitrazha,* 1935, No. 9/10.

Sitnin, V. "Gosbank i mashinostroenie" (The State Bank and Machine Construction), *Den'gi i Kredit,* 1940, No. 1.

———— "Krupnyi rezerv material'nykh resursov" (The Large Reserve of Materials Resources), *Planovoe Khoziaistvo,* 1940, No. 12.

Sitnin, V., and Z. Simkin. "Usilit' kontrol' rublem v tiazhëloi promyshlennosti" (In Order to Strengthen Control by the Ruble in Heavy Industry), *Planovoe Khoziaistvo,* 1940, No. 2.

"Slavnaia godovshchina" (Glorious Anniversary), *Org. Uprav.,* 1937, No. 5.

Smekhov, B. "Planirovanie remonta osnovnykh fondov" (Planning Repair of Fixed Capital), *Planovoe Khoziaistvo,* 1940, No. 10.

Smirnov, G. "K itogam pervogo polugodiia 1937 goda" (On the Results of the First Half of 1937), *Plan,* 1937, No. 13.

Sobol', V. "Ob oborotnykh sredstvakh" (On Working Capital), *Problem Ekonomiki,* 1937, No. 3-4.

Sokolov, A. "Uzlovye voprosy partraboty na predpriiatiiakh" (Crucial Questions of Party Work in the Firms), *Part. Stroit.,* 1934, No. 20.

Sokolov, N. "Tekhnicheskii progress v narodnom khoziaistve SSSR" (Technical Progress in the National Economy of the USSR), *Planovoe khoziaistvo,* 1950, No. 3.

"Soveshchanie glavnogo arbitra pri SNK SSSR s glavnymi arbitrami soiuznykh respublik" (Conference of the Chief Arbitrator Attached to the Council of Commissars of the USSR with the Chief Arbitrators of the Union Republics), *Arbitrazh,* 1938, No. 9-10.

Stalin, I. Letter of July 28, 1950, to A. Kholopov. In *Soviet Literature,* 1950, No. 9.

Stepanov, M. "Nekotorye itogi otchëtov i vyborov fabzavmestkomov" (Some Results of the Reportings and Elections of the Plant and Local Union Committees), *Profsoiuzy SSSR,* 1939, No. 8-9.

———— "Polnost'iu vypolnit' direktivu TsK o pishchevykh predpriiatiiakh" (For the Complete Fulfillment of the Instructions of the

Central Committee regarding the Food-Processing Firms), *Part. Stroit.*, 1934, No. 12.

Sukharevskii, B. "Material'nye balansy promyshlennoi produktsii v narodnokhoziaistvennom plane" (Materials Schedules of Industrial Production in the National Economic Plan), *Planovoe Khoziaistvo*, 1937, No. 11-12.

Tandit, L. "Bol'shevistskaia vnutripartiinaia demokratiia" (Bolshevik Intra-Party Democracy), *Part. Stroit.*, 1938, No. 9.

T-ov, L. "O rabote predpriiatiia po materialam arbitrazha" (On the Work of the Firm According to Materials of Arbitration), *Arbitrazh*, 1938, No. 6.

Tochinskii, A., and V. Rikman. "Novye tekhnicheskie normy v chërnoi metallurgii" (New Technical Norms in Ferrous Metallurgy), *Planovoe Khoziaistvo*, 1936, No. 6.

Tokarev, V. "O metodakh otsenki vypolneniia plana po assortimentu" (On Methods of Evaluating the Fulfillment of the Plan According to Assortment), *Planovoe Khoziaistvo*, 1938, No. 8.

Tsvetkov, V. "Kazhdyi chlen partkoma—organizator, agitator, propagandist" (Each Member of the Party Committee is an Organizer, an Agitator, and a Propagandist), *Part. Stroit.*, 1937, No. 13.

Turetskii, Sh.Ia. "Ekonomika proizvodstva i kachestvennye pokazateli plana" (Economy of Production and the Qualitative Indices of the Plan), *Planovoe Khoziaistvo*, 1940, No. 8.

——— "Nekotorye voprosy narodnokhoziaistvennogo planirovaniia" (Some Questions of National Economic Planning), *Problemy Ekonomiki*, 1940, No. 7.

——— "O khoziaistvennom raschëte" (On Business Accounting), *Planovoe Khoziaistvo*, 1939, No. 1.

——— "Usilit' vnimanie k kachestvennym pokazateliam" (In Order to Concentrate Attention on Qualitative Indices), *Planovoe Khoziaistvo*, 1938, No. 9.

——— "Voprosy tsenoobrazavaniia" (Questions of Price Formation), *Planovoe Khoziaistvo*, 1938, No. 6.

Ugarov, A. "Vybory partorganov v moskovskoi organizatsii" (Elections of the Party Organs in the Moscow Organization), *Part. Stroit.*, 1938, No. 9.

"Usilit' kontrol' za ispolneniem reshenii partii" (For Strengthening Control Over the Execution of Party Decisions), *Part. Stroit.*, 1939, No. 12.

Usoskin, M. "Voprosy kreditovaniia i raschëtov v sviazi s neplatëzhami" (Questions of Crediting and of Accounts in Connection with Nonpaying Bodies), *Den'gi i Kredit*, 1940, No. 4-5.

Vasil'ev, E. "Sotsialisticheskaia distsiplina truda" (Socialist Discipline of Work), *Planovoe Khoziaistvo*, 1940, No. 9.

Vasil'ev, P. Review of *Organizatsiia proizvodstva v mashinostroenii*

(Organization of Production in Machine Construction), in *Org. Uprav.*, 1938, No. 1.

Vidgor, M. "Voprosy finansirovaniia i kontrolia kapital'nogo remonta" (Questions of Financing and Supervising Capital Repair), *Den'gi i Kredit*, 1940, No. 8-9.

Vilenskii, L. "Finansovye voprosy promyshlennosti" (Financial Questions of Industry), *Planovoe Khoziaistvo*, 1938, No. 10.

Vinnikov, A. "K peresmotru norm vyrabotki v promyshlennosti" (Toward the Revision of the Work Norms in Industry), *Plan*, 1937, No. 8.

Volchenkov, V. "Partiinyi kontrol' deiatel'nosti administratsii" (Party Supervision over the Activity of the Administration), in *Partiinaia rabota na transporte* (Party Work in Transport), edited by V. E. Tsaregorodtsev, Moscow, 1948.

Vorob'ev-Nabatov, N. A. "Sistema snabsbytov v 1935 g." (The System of Procurement-Marketing Organs in 1935), *Snab. i Sklad.*, 1936, No. 5.

"V tsentral'nom komitete VKP(b)" (In the Central Committee of the All-Union Communist Party [Bolshevik]), *Part. Stroit.*, 1939 No. 21. 1939, No. 19. 1934, No. 2.

"Vybory partiinykh organov v pervichnykh partorganizatsiiakh" (Elections of Party Organs in Primary Party Organizations), *Bol'shevik*, 1941, No. 6.

Zabozlaev, N. "Bol'she operativnosti v bor'be s pereraskhodami fondov zarabotnoi platy" (More of an Operational Character to the Fight Against Overexpenditure of Wage Funds), *Kredit i Khozraschët*, 1938, No. 4.

————— "Fondy zarplaty—pod bditel'nyi bankovskii kontrol' " (Wage Funds under Vigilant Bank Control), *Den'gi i Kredit*, 1938, No. 5.

————— "Novoe v kontrole za fondami zarplaty" (What is New in Control over Wage Funds), *Den'gi i Kredit*, 1939, No. 1.

"Za povyshenie kachestva raboty promyshlennosti" (For Raising the Quality of the Work of Industry), *Planovoe Khoziaistvo*, 1937, No. 1.

"Za reshitel'nuiu perestroiku bankovskoi rabotu" (For the Determined Reconstruction of Bank Work), *Den'gi i Kredit*, 1940, No. 6-7.

Zelenko, K., and E. Khvishchevskii. "Bol'she vnimaniia shefstvu i sotssovmestitel'stvu" (More Attention to Patronage and Socialist Combination-of-Work), *Vopr. Profdvizh.*, 1935, No. 5-6.

Zhdanov, V. "Iskorenit' avtomatism v kreditovanii raschetnykh dokumentov v puti" (For the Elimination of Automatism in Crediting Bills of Lading), *Den'gi i Kredit*, 1939, No. 6.

Zil'bershtein, M. "Kontrol' za vneplanovymi kapitalovlozheniiami" (Supervision over Nonplanned Capital Investment), *Kredit i Khozraschët*, 1937, No. 19.

Zodionchenko, S. "Rabota chlenov raikoma partii" (Work of the Members of the District Committee of the Party), *Part. Stroit.*, 1937, No. 17.

Zverov, A. "Sovetskii finansy i Otechestvennaia voina" (Soviet Finances and the Patriotic War), *Planovoe Khoziaistvo*, 1944, No. 2.

SPEECHES AND REPORTS

Andreev, A. Report of December 24, 1935, to the Plenum of the Central Committee of the Communist Party. *Org. Uprav.*, 1936, No. 1.

Birman, S. Speech at the 1936 Council of the Commissariat of Heavy Industry. *Z.I.*, July 3, 1936.

Kaganovich, L. M. Report to the XVIIth Congress of the Communist Party. *XVII s"ezd VKP(b)*.

―――― Speech of June 28, 1934, to the Plenum of the Party Control Commission attached to the Central Committee of the Communist Party. *Part. Stroit.*, 1934, No. 13.

Kaganovich, M. M. Speech to the XVIIIth Party Congress. *Ind.*, March 23, 1939.

Malenkov, G. M. Report to the XVIIIth Party Conference. *Ch.M.*, February 16, 1941.

Malyshev, V. A. Speech of May 28, 1939, to the Supreme Soviet of the USSR. *Mash.*, May 30, 1939.

Merkulov, F. A. Speech to the XVIIIth Party Congress. *Ind.*, March 22, 1939.

Mikoian, A. Speech of March 13, 1939, to the XVIIIth Party Congress. *XVIII s"ezd VKP(b)*.

Molotov, V. M. Report of March 28, 1937, to the Plenum of the Central Committee of the Communist Party. *Z.I.*, April 20-21, 1937.

―――― Report of March 14, 1939, to the XVIIIth Party Congress on the Third Five-Year Plan. *XVIII s"ezd VKP(b)*.

―――― Concluding remarks of March 17, 1939, to the XVIIIth Party Congress. *Problemy Ekonomiki*, 1939, No. 3.

Ordzhonikidze, G. K. (Sergo). Speech of September 20, 1934, to the Conference of Workers of Heavy Industry. *Z.I.*, September 22, 1934.

―――― Speech of May 12, 1935, to the Council attached to the Commissariat of Heavy Industry. *Org. Uprav.*, 1935, No. 3.

―――― Speech of November 14, 1935. *Z.I.*, November 15, 1935.

―――― Speech of November 16, 1935, to the First All-Union Stakhanovite Conference. *Z.I.*, November 18, 1935.

―――― Report of December 21, 1935, to the Plenum of the Central Committee of the Communist Party. *Org. Uprav.*, 1935, No. 6.

―――― Speech of June 29, 1936, to the Council attached to the Commissariat of Heavy Industry. *Org. Uprav.*, 1936, No. 4.

Pichugina, P. N.   Speech to the Second Session of the Supreme Soviet of the USSR.   *Mash.*, August 14, 1938.

Piterskii.   Speech to the First Plenum of the Council attached to the Commissariat of Heavy Industry.   *Z.I.*, May 12, 1935.

Shvernik, N. M.   Speech of December 31, 1934, to the Concluding Session of the Vth Plenum of the Central Council of the Trade Unions.   *Vopr. Profdvizh.*, 1934, No. 12.

—— Report to a gathering of trade-union leaders and others meeting on November 18-19, 1935.   *Vopr. Profdvizh.*, 1935, No. 10.

—— Report to the VIth Plenum of the Central Council of the Trade Unions.   *Vopr. Profdvizh.*, 1937, No. 9-10.

—— Conversation with the chairmen of the department union committees of the Moscow Stalin Automobile Plant.   *Vopr. Profdvizh.*, 1937, No. 18.

—— Reworked stenographic report of June 1, 1938, to a conference of officials and employees of trade-union central committees.   *Profsoiuzy SSSR*, 1938, No. 12.

—— Report of September 2, 1938, to the VIIth Plenum of the Central Council of the Trade Unions.   *Profsoiuzy SSSR*, 1938, No. 13.

—— Speech to the XVIIIth Party Congress.   *Profsoiuzy SSSR*, 1939, No. 2-3.

—— Report to the VIIIth Plenum of the Central Council of the Trade Unions.   *Profsoiuzy SSSR*, 1939, No. 5.

—— Reworked stenographic report to the Xth Plenum of the Central Council of the Trade Unions.   *Part. Stroit.*, 1940, No. 15-16.

—— Report to the XIth Plenum of the Central Council of the Trade Unions.   *Profsoiuzy SSSR*, 1941, No. 4.

Stalin, I.   Speech of November 17, 1935, to the First All-Union Stakhanovite Conference.   *Z.I.*, November 22, 1935.

—— Speech of March 3, 1937, to the February-March Plenum of the Central Committee of the Communist Party.   *Z.I.*, March 29, 1937.

—— Concluding Words of March 5, 1937, to the February-March Plenum of the Central Committee of the Communist Party.   *Z.I.*, April 1, 1937.

Zhdanov, A.   Report of February 26, 1937, to the Plenum of the Central Committee of the Communist Party.   *Z.I.*, March 11, 1937.

—— Report to the XVIIIth Party Congress.   *Ind.*, March 21, 1939.

Index

Index

Studies of the Russian Institute

COLUMBIA UNIVERSITY

SOVIET NATIONAL INCOME AND PRODUCT IN 1937
  By Abram Bergson

THROUGH THE GLASS OF SOVIET LITERATURE: VIEWS
OF RUSSIAN SOCIETY
  Edited by Ernest J. Simmons

THE PROLETARIAN EPISODE IN RUSSIAN LITERATURE,
1928-1932
  By Edward J. Brown

MANAGEMENT OF THE INDUSTRIAL FIRM IN THE USSR:
A STUDY IN SOVIET ECONOMIC PLANNING
  By David Granick